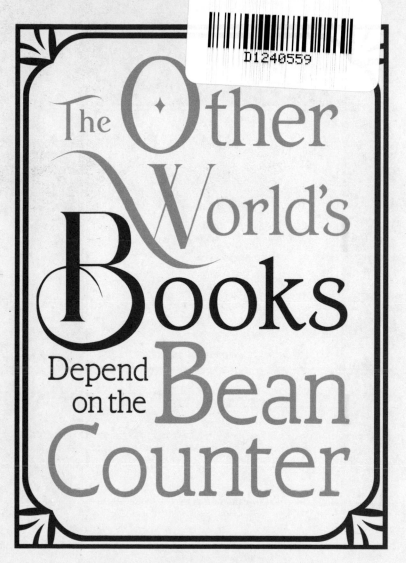

The Other World's Books Depend on the Bean Counter

2

Kazuki Irodori

ORIGINAL STORY
Yatsuki Wakatsu

CHARACTER DESIGN
Kikka Ohashi

CONTENTS

✳

**THE OTHER WORLD'S BOOKS
DEPEND ON THE BEAN COUNTER**

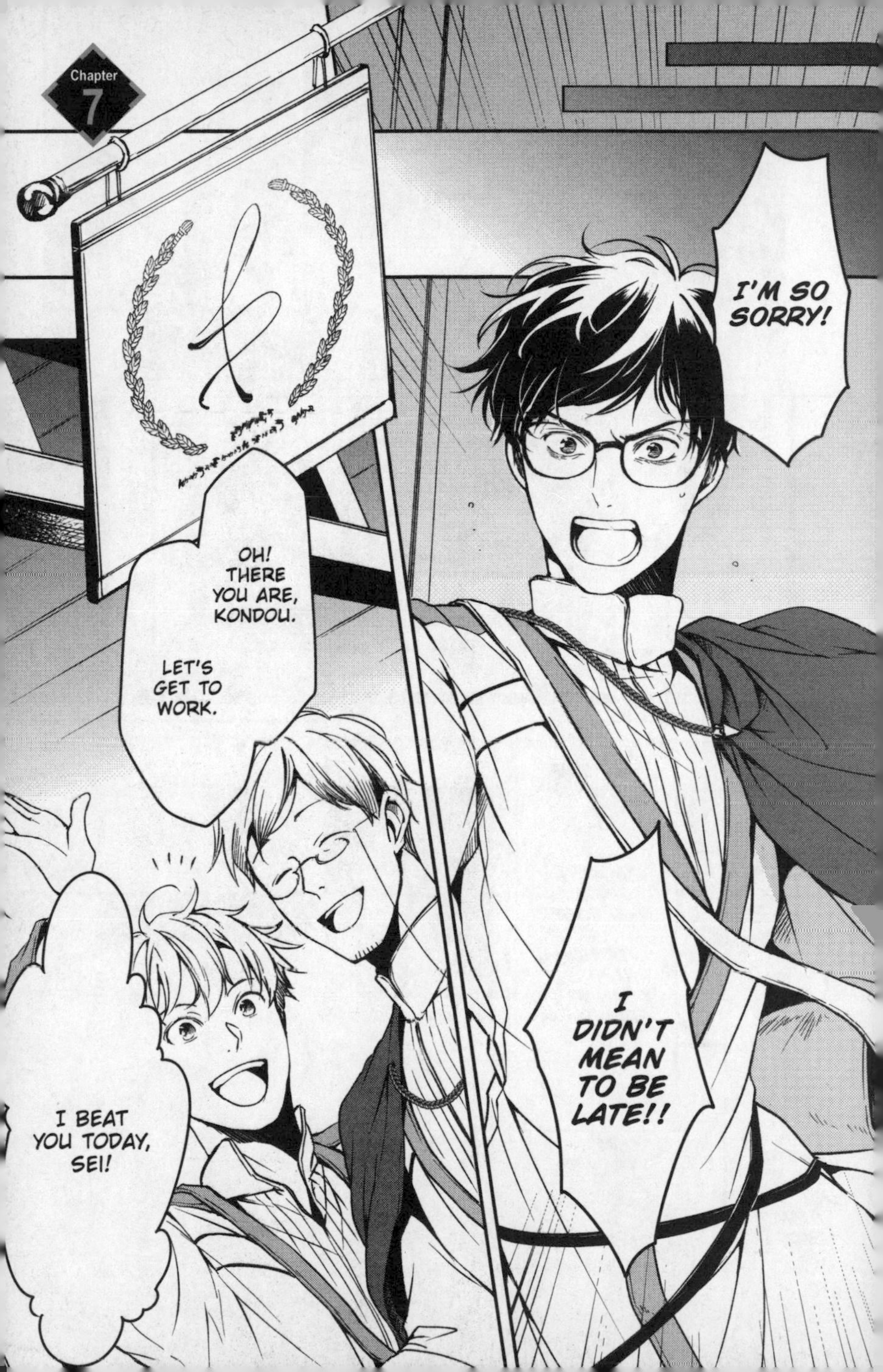
Chapter 7
I'M SO SORRY!
OH! THERE YOU ARE, KONDOU.
LET'S GET TO WORK.
I DIDN'T MEAN TO BE LATE!!
I BEAT YOU TODAY, SEI!

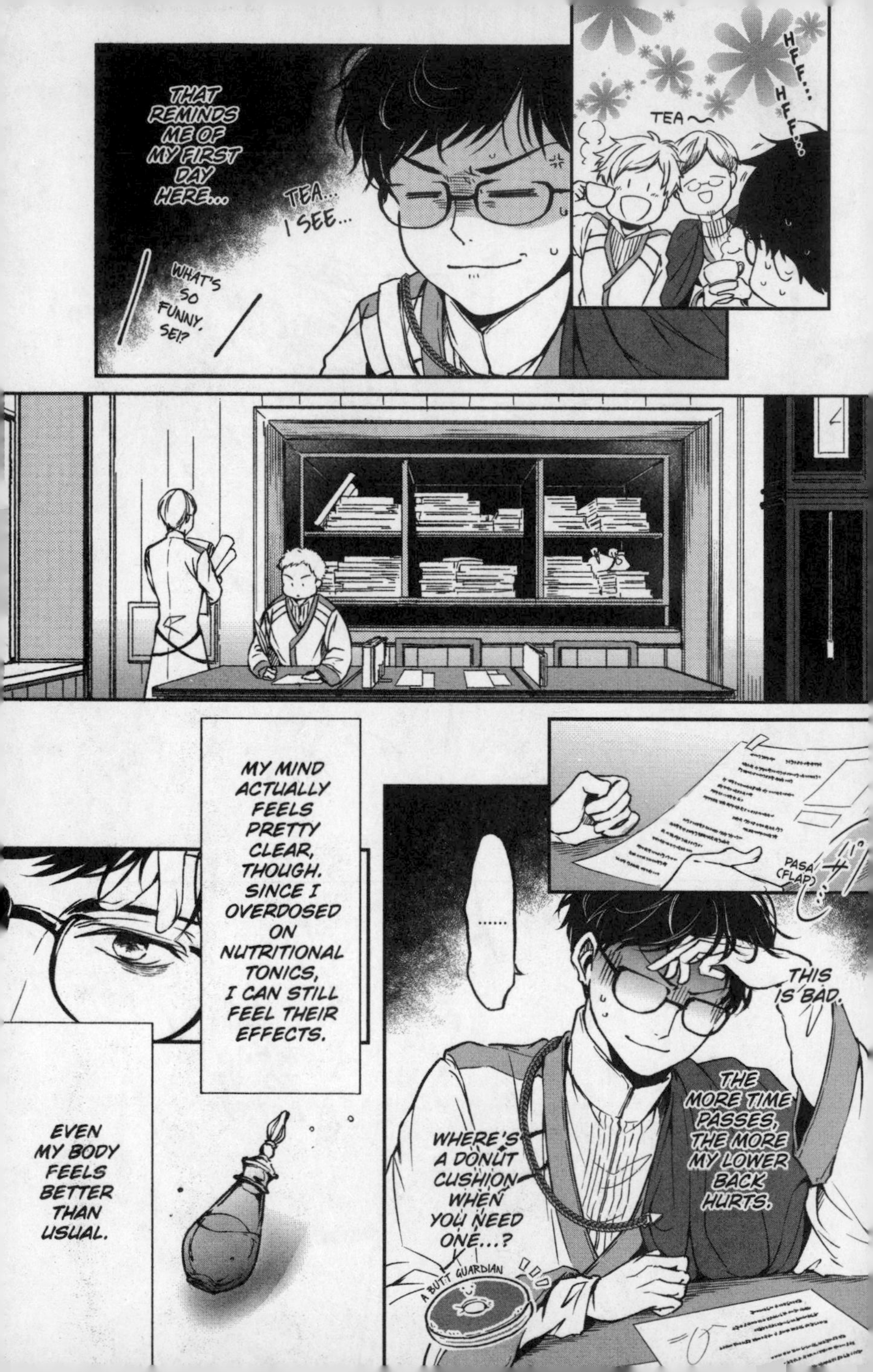
HFF... HFF...
TEA~
TEA... I SEE...
THAT REMINDS ME OF MY FIRST DAY HERE...
WHAT'S SO FUNNY, SEI!?
PASA (FLAP)
......
THIS IS BAD.
THE MORE TIME PASSES, THE MORE MY LOWER BACK HURTS.
WHERE'S A DONUT CUSHION WHEN YOU NEED ONE...?
A BUTT GUARDIAN
MY MIND ACTUALLY FEELS PRETTY CLEAR, THOUGH. SINCE I OVERDOSED ON NUTRITIONAL TONICS, I CAN STILL FEEL THEIR EFFECTS.
EVEN MY BODY FEELS BETTER THAN USUAL.

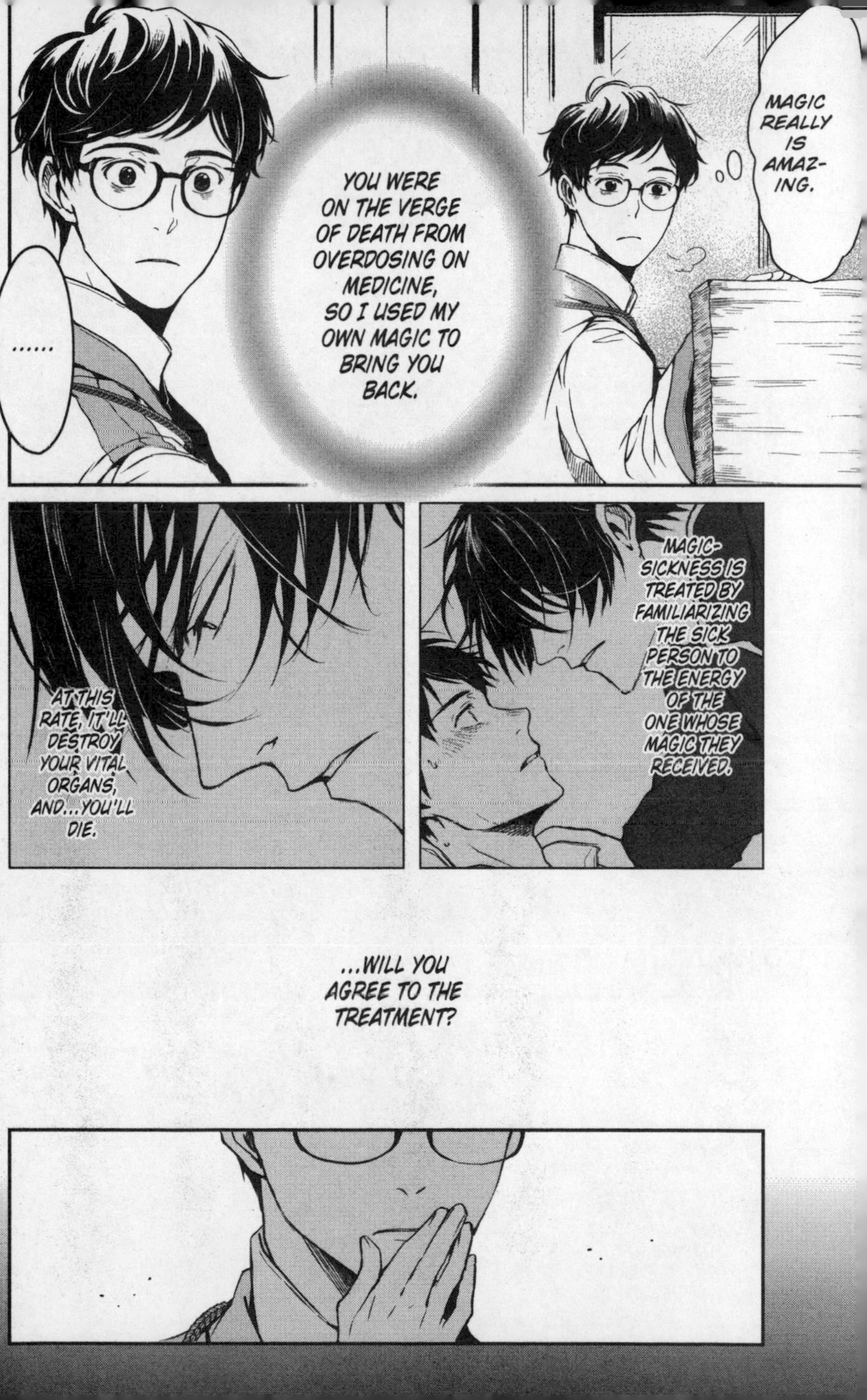
MAGIC REALLY IS AMAZ-ING.
YOU WERE ON THE VERGE OF DEATH FROM OVERDOSING ON MEDICINE, SO I USED MY OWN MAGIC TO BRING YOU BACK.
......
MAGIC-SICKNESS IS TREATED BY FAMILIARIZING THE SICK PERSON TO THE ENERGY OF THE ONE WHOSE MAGIC THEY RECEIVED.
AT THIS RATE, IT'LL DESTROY YOUR VITAL ORGANS, AND...YOU'LL DIE.
...WILL YOU AGREE TO THE TREATMENT?

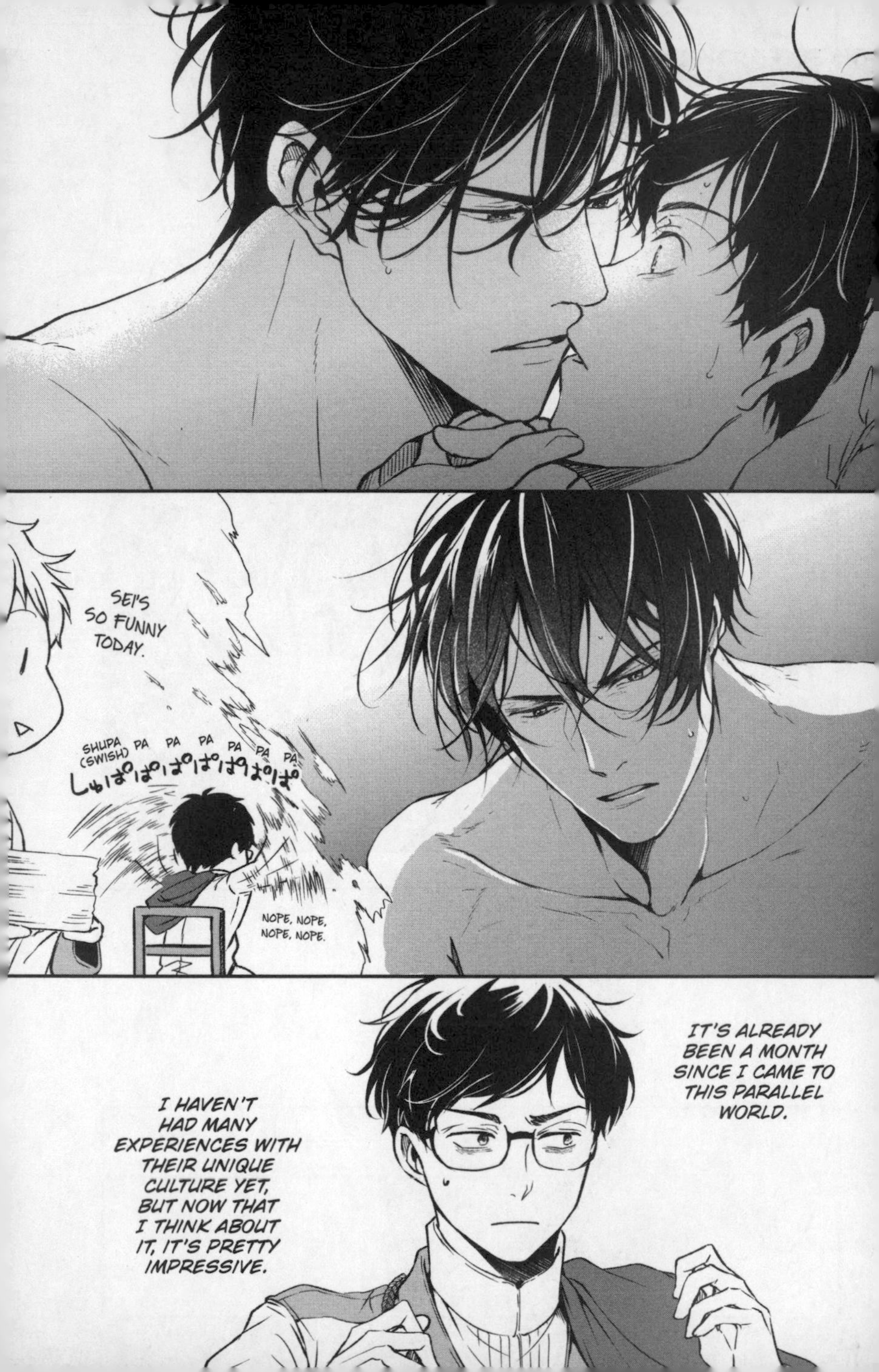
SEI'S SO FUNNY TODAY.
SHUPA (SWISH) PA PA PA PA PA PA
しゅぱぱぱぱぱぱぱ
NOPE, NOPE, NOPE, NOPE.
IT'S ALREADY BEEN A MONTH SINCE I CAME TO THIS PARALLEL WORLD.
I HAVEN'T HAD MANY EXPERIENCES WITH THEIR UNIQUE CULTURE YET, BUT NOW THAT I THINK ABOUT IT, IT'S PRETTY IMPRESSIVE.

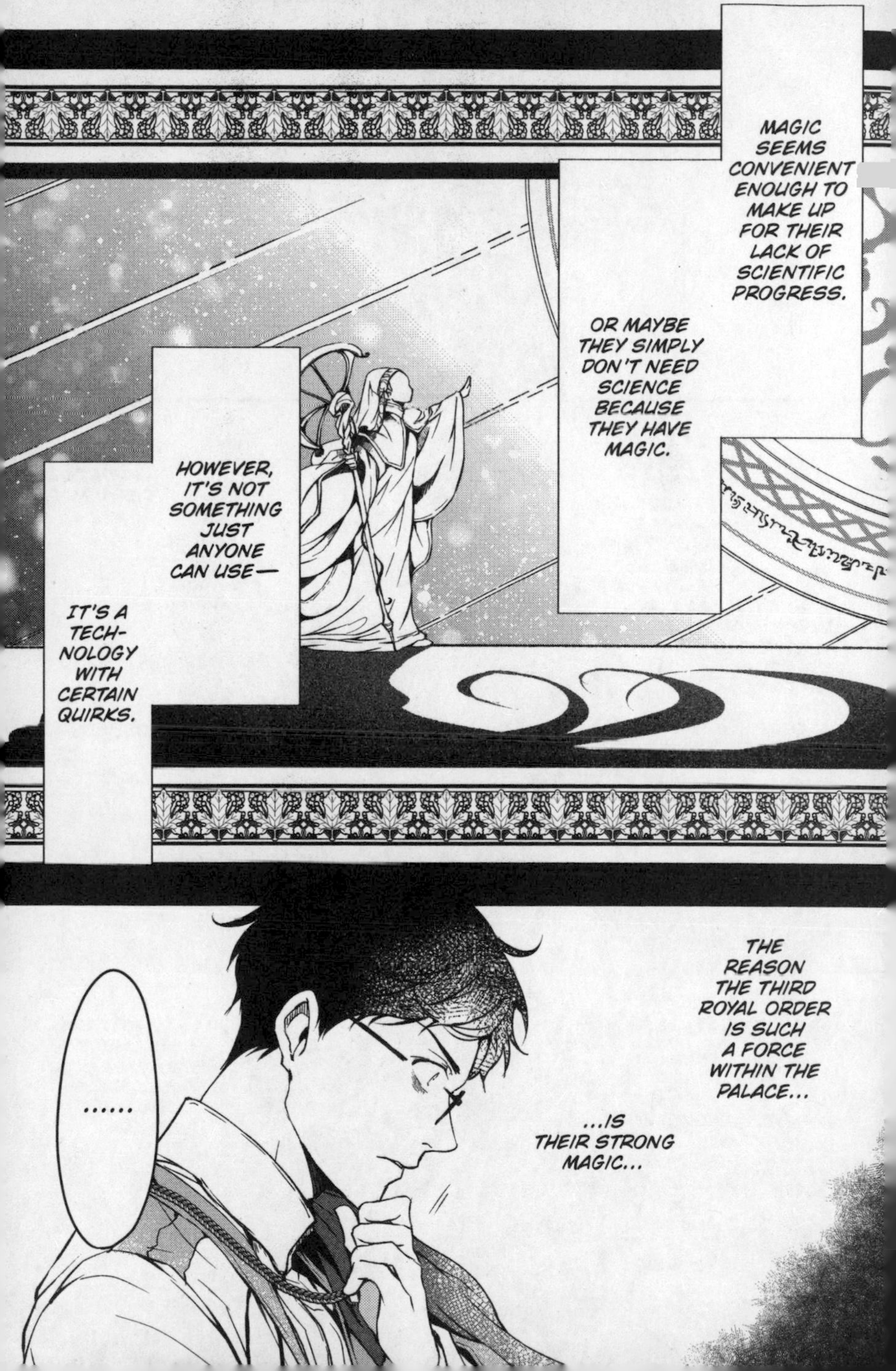
MAGIC SEEMS CONVENIENT ENOUGH TO MAKE UP FOR THEIR LACK OF SCIENTIFIC PROGRESS.
OR MAYBE THEY SIMPLY DON'T NEED SCIENCE BECAUSE THEY HAVE MAGIC.
HOWEVER, IT'S NOT SOMETHING JUST ANYONE CAN USE—
IT'S A TECH-NOLOGY WITH CERTAIN QUIRKS.
THE REASON THE THIRD ROYAL ORDER IS SUCH A FORCE WITHIN THE PALACE...
...IS THEIR STRONG MAGIC...
......

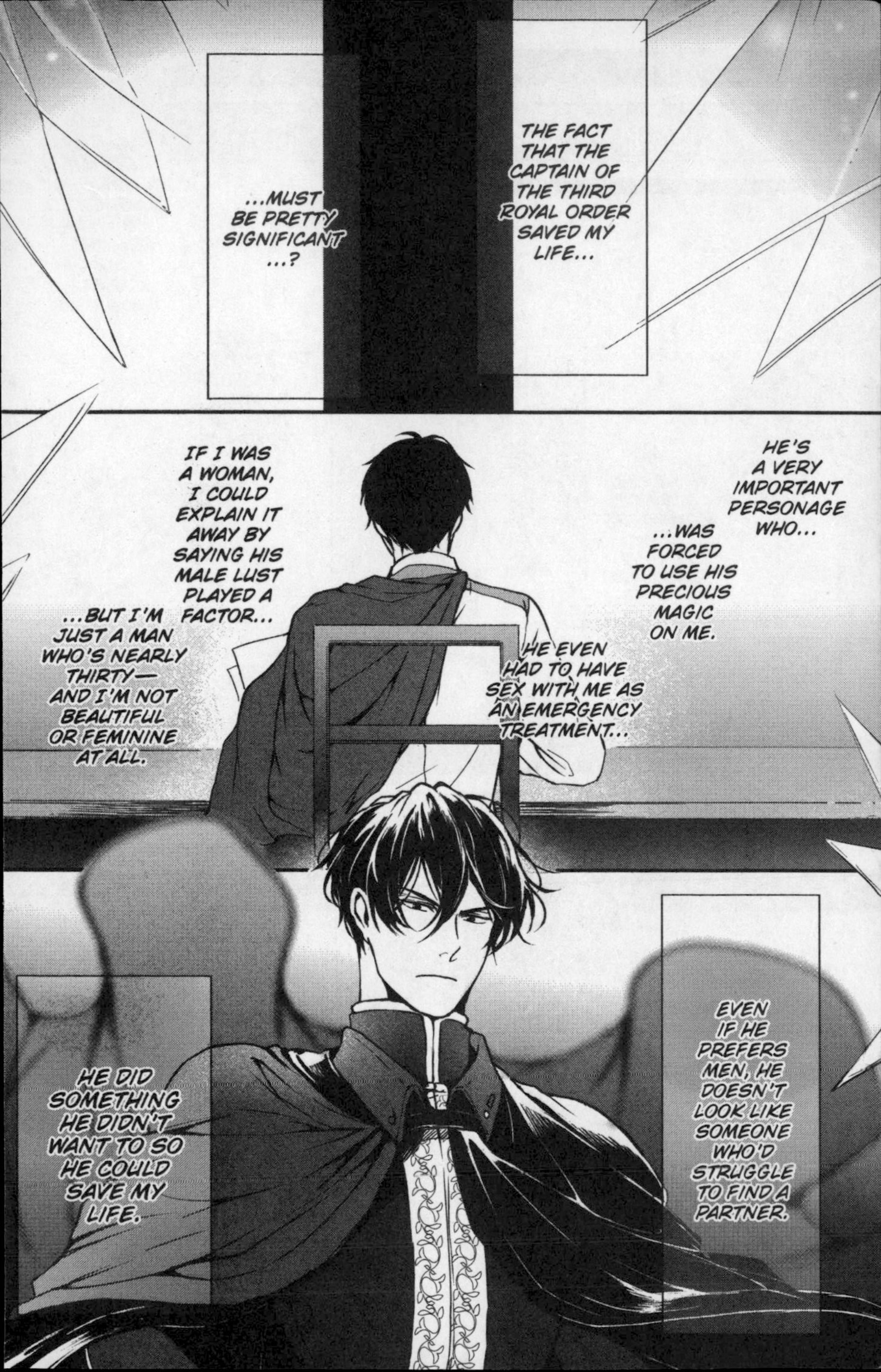
THE FACT THAT THE CAPTAIN OF THE THIRD ROYAL ORDER SAVED MY LIFE...
...MUST BE PRETTY SIGNIFICANT ...?
HE'S A VERY IMPORTANT PERSONAGE WHO...
...WAS FORCED TO USE HIS PRECIOUS MAGIC ON ME.
HE EVEN HAD TO HAVE SEX WITH ME AS AN EMERGENCY TREATMENT...
IF I WAS A WOMAN, I COULD EXPLAIN IT AWAY BY SAYING HIS MALE LUST PLAYED A FACTOR...
...BUT I'M JUST A MAN WHO'S NEARLY THIRTY— AND I'M NOT BEAUTIFUL OR FEMININE AT ALL.
EVEN IF HE PREFERS MEN, HE DOESN'T LOOK LIKE SOMEONE WHO'D STRUGGLE TO FIND A PARTNER.
HE DID SOMETHING HE DIDN'T WANT TO SO HE COULD SAVE MY LIFE.

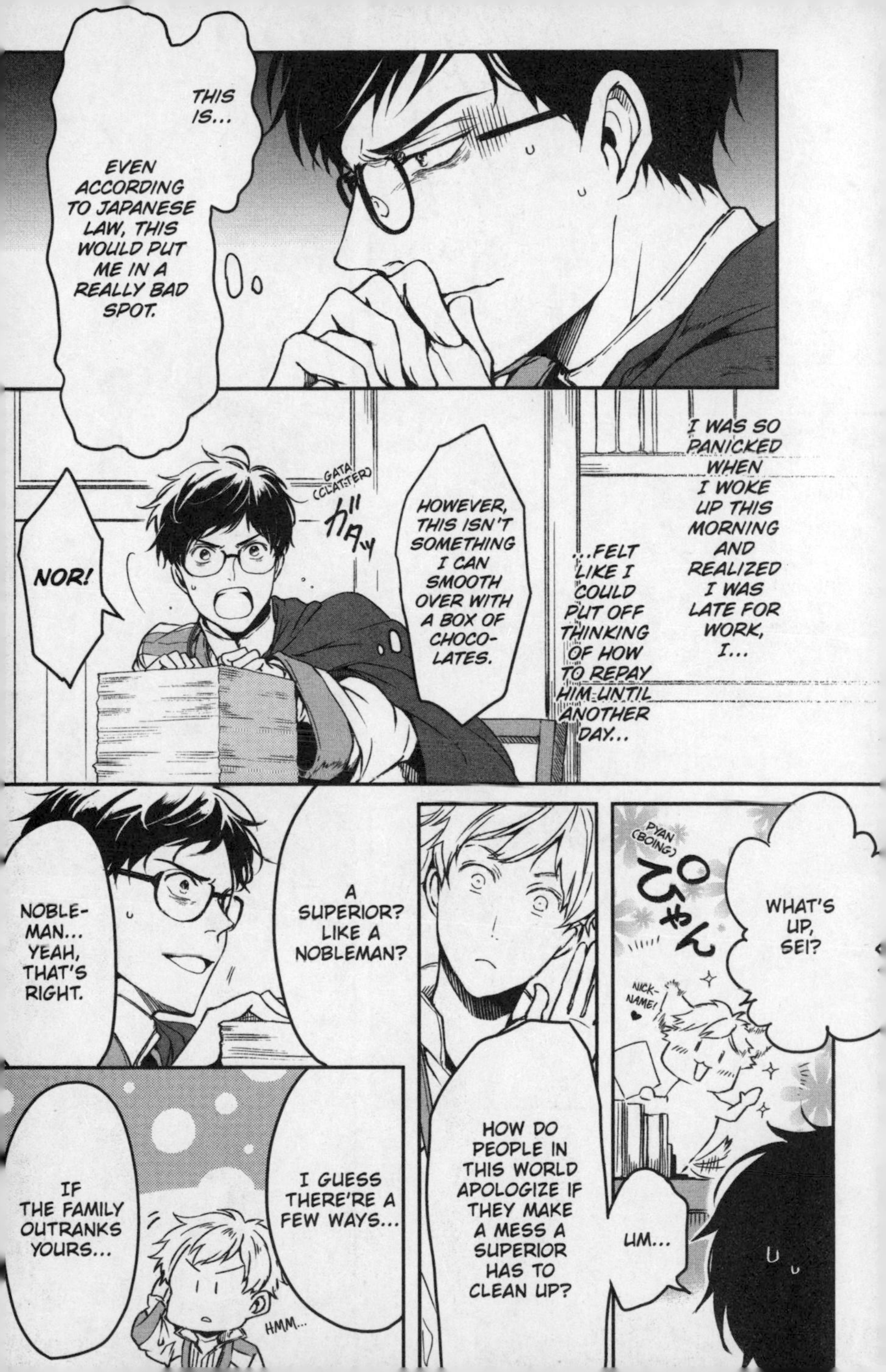
THIS IS...
EVEN ACCORDING TO JAPANESE LAW, THIS WOULD PUT ME IN A REALLY BAD SPOT.
I WAS SO PANICKED WHEN I WOKE UP THIS MORNING AND REALIZED I WAS LATE FOR WORK, I...
...FELT LIKE I COULD PUT OFF THINKING OF HOW TO REPAY HIM UNTIL ANOTHER DAY...
HOWEVER, THIS ISN'T SOMETHING I CAN SMOOTH OVER WITH A BOX OF CHOCOLATES.
GATA (CLATTER)
NOR!
PYAN (BOING)
WHAT'S UP, SEI?
NICKNAME!
UM...
HOW DO PEOPLE IN THIS WORLD APOLOGIZE IF THEY MAKE A MESS A SUPERIOR HAS TO CLEAN UP?
A SUPERIOR? LIKE A NOBLEMAN?
NOBLEMAN... YEAH, THAT'S RIGHT.
I GUESS THERE'RE A FEW WAYS...
IF THE FAMILY OUTRANKS YOURS...
HMM...

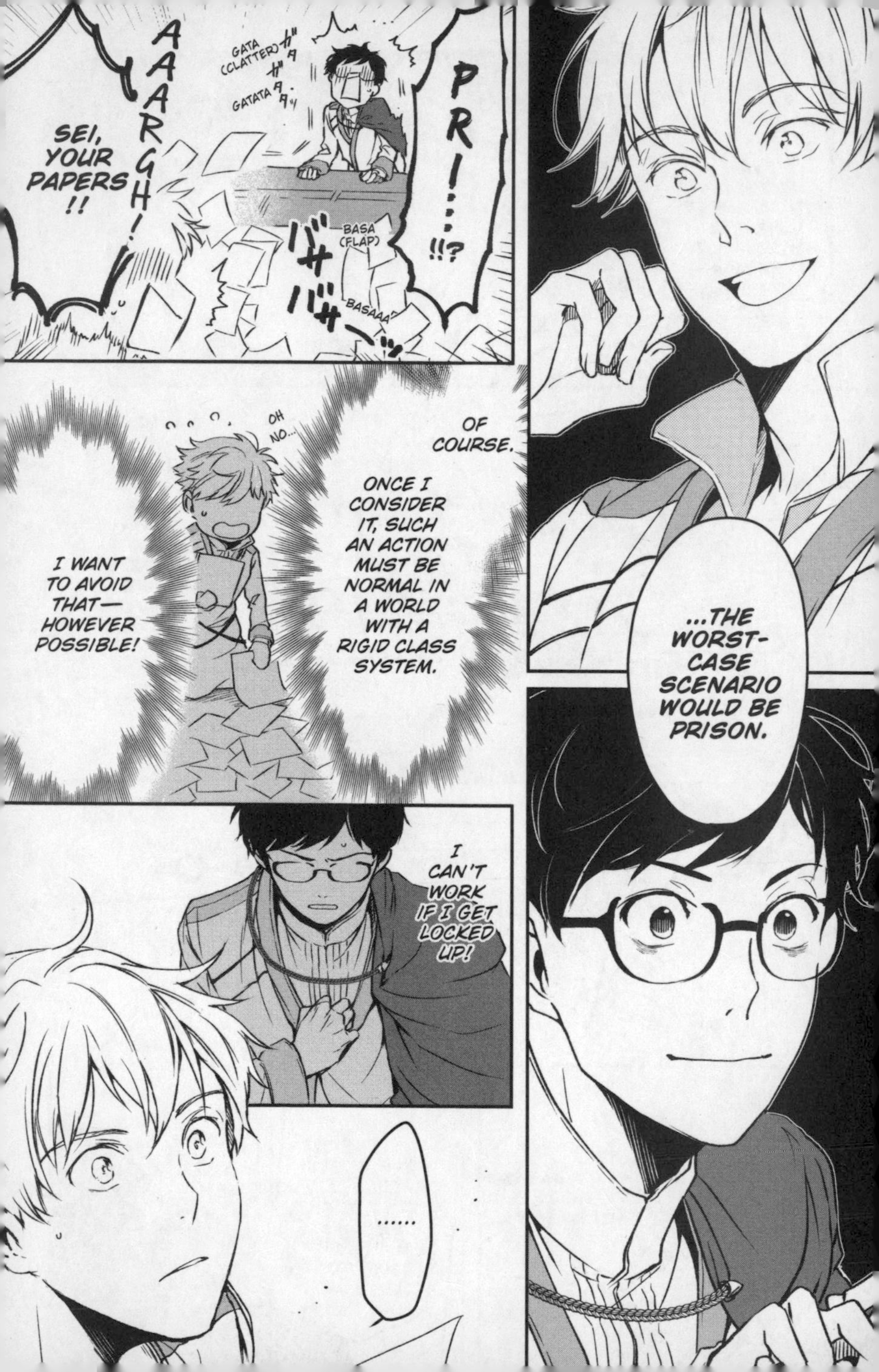
...THE WORST-CASE SCENARIO WOULD BE PRISON.
PRI...!!?
AAAARGH!
SEI, YOUR PAPERS!!
GATA (CLATTER)
GATATA
BASA (FLAP)
BASAAA
OF COURSE.
ONCE I CONSIDER IT, SUCH AN ACTION MUST BE NORMAL IN A WORLD WITH A RIGID CLASS SYSTEM.
OH NO...
I WANT TO AVOID THAT—HOWEVER POSSIBLE!
I CAN'T WORK IF I GET LOCKED UP!
......

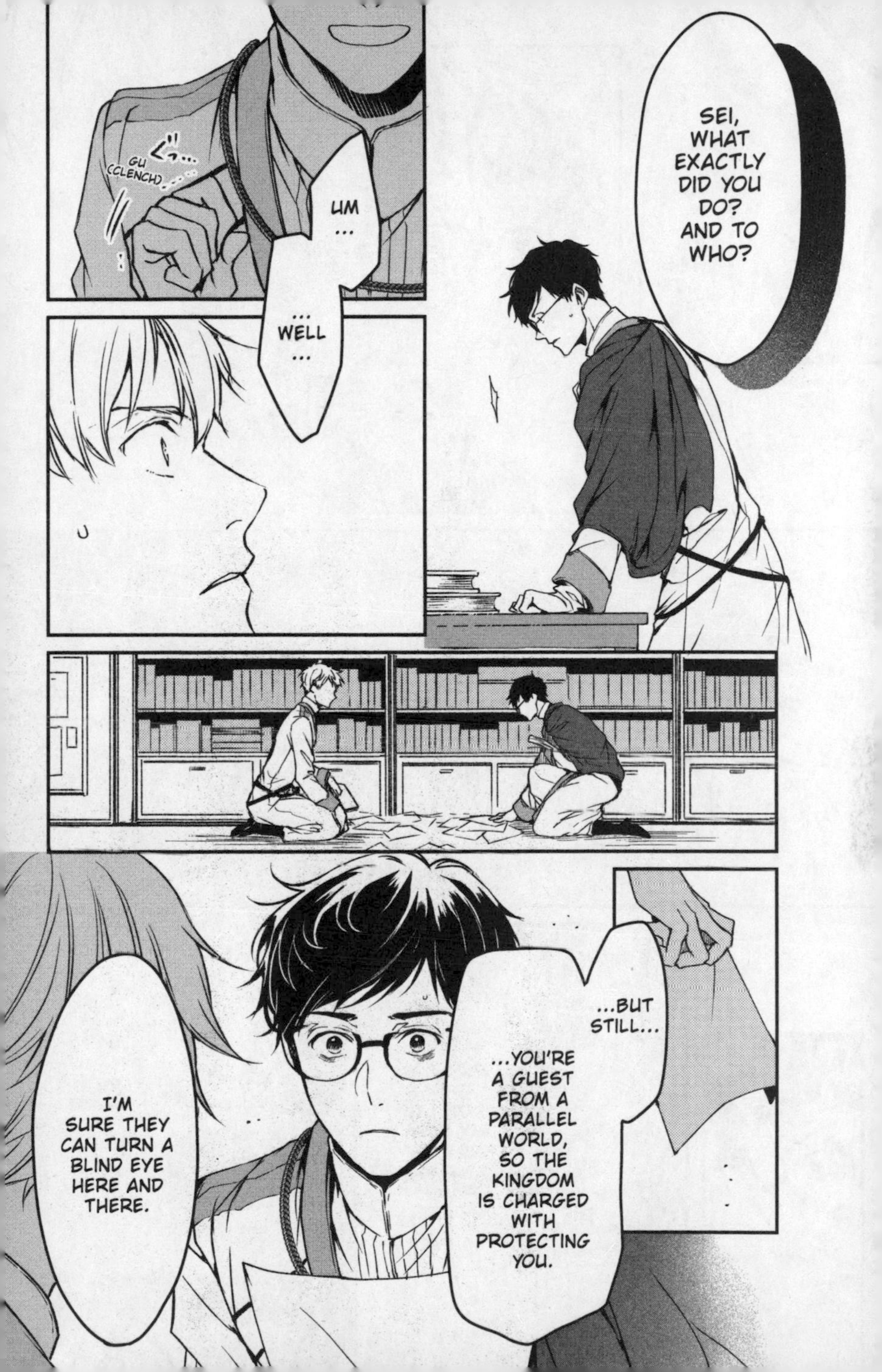

SEI, WHAT EXACTLY DID YOU DO? AND TO WHO?
ぐっ…
GU (CLENCH)
UM …
… WELL …
…BUT STILL…
…YOU'RE A GUEST FROM A PARALLEL WORLD, SO THE KINGDOM IS CHARGED WITH PROTECTING YOU.
I'M SURE THEY CAN TURN A BLIND EYE HERE AND THERE.

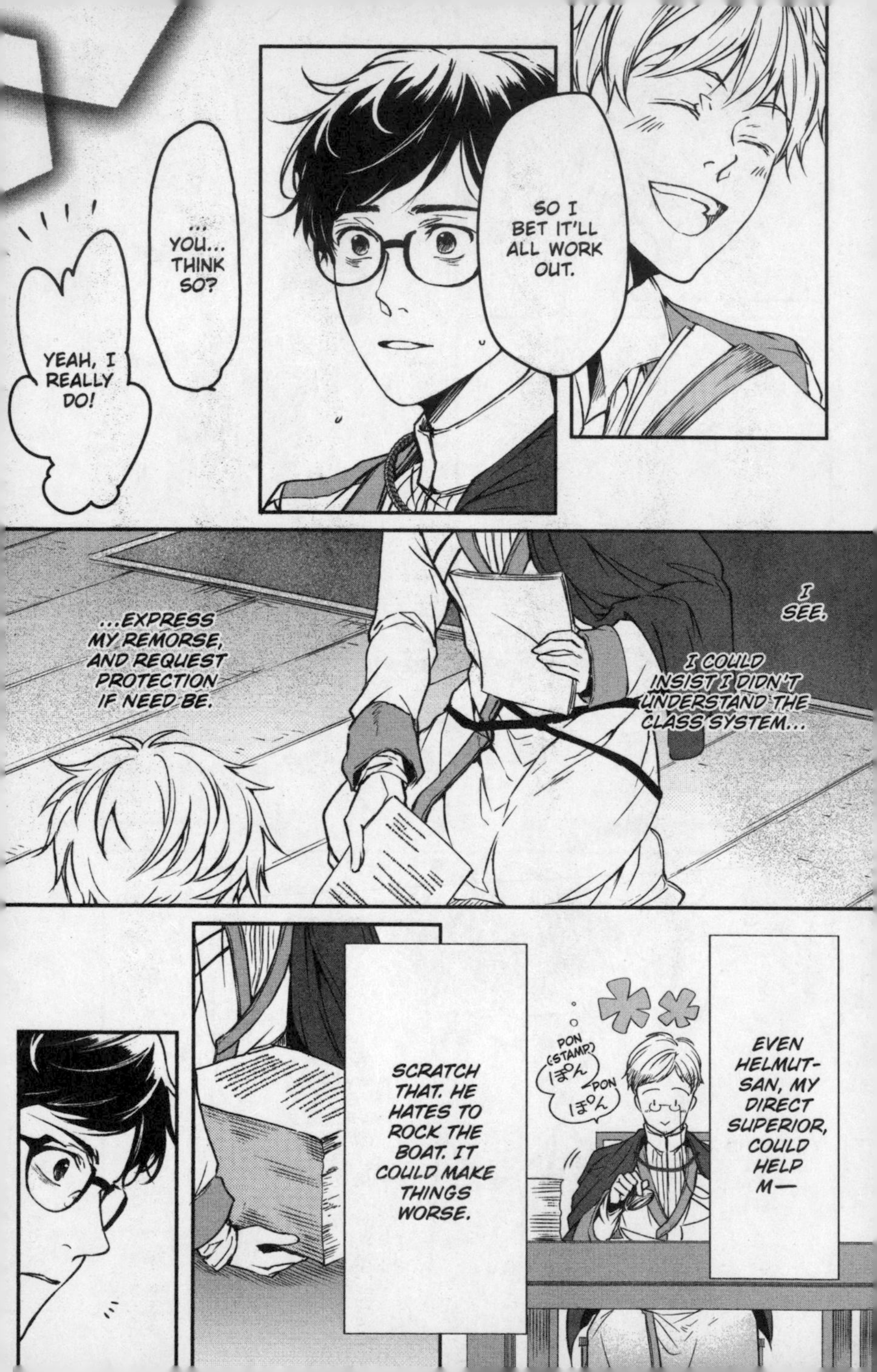
SO I BET IT'LL ALL WORK OUT.
... YOU... THINK SO?
YEAH, I REALLY DO!
I SEE.
I COULD INSIST I DIDN'T UNDERSTAND THE CLASS SYSTEM...
...EXPRESS MY REMORSE, AND REQUEST PROTECTION IF NEED BE.
EVEN HELMUT-SAN, MY DIRECT SUPERIOR, COULD HELP M—
PON (STAMP) ぽん
PON ぽん
SCRATCH THAT. HE HATES TO ROCK THE BOAT. IT COULD MAKE THINGS WORSE.

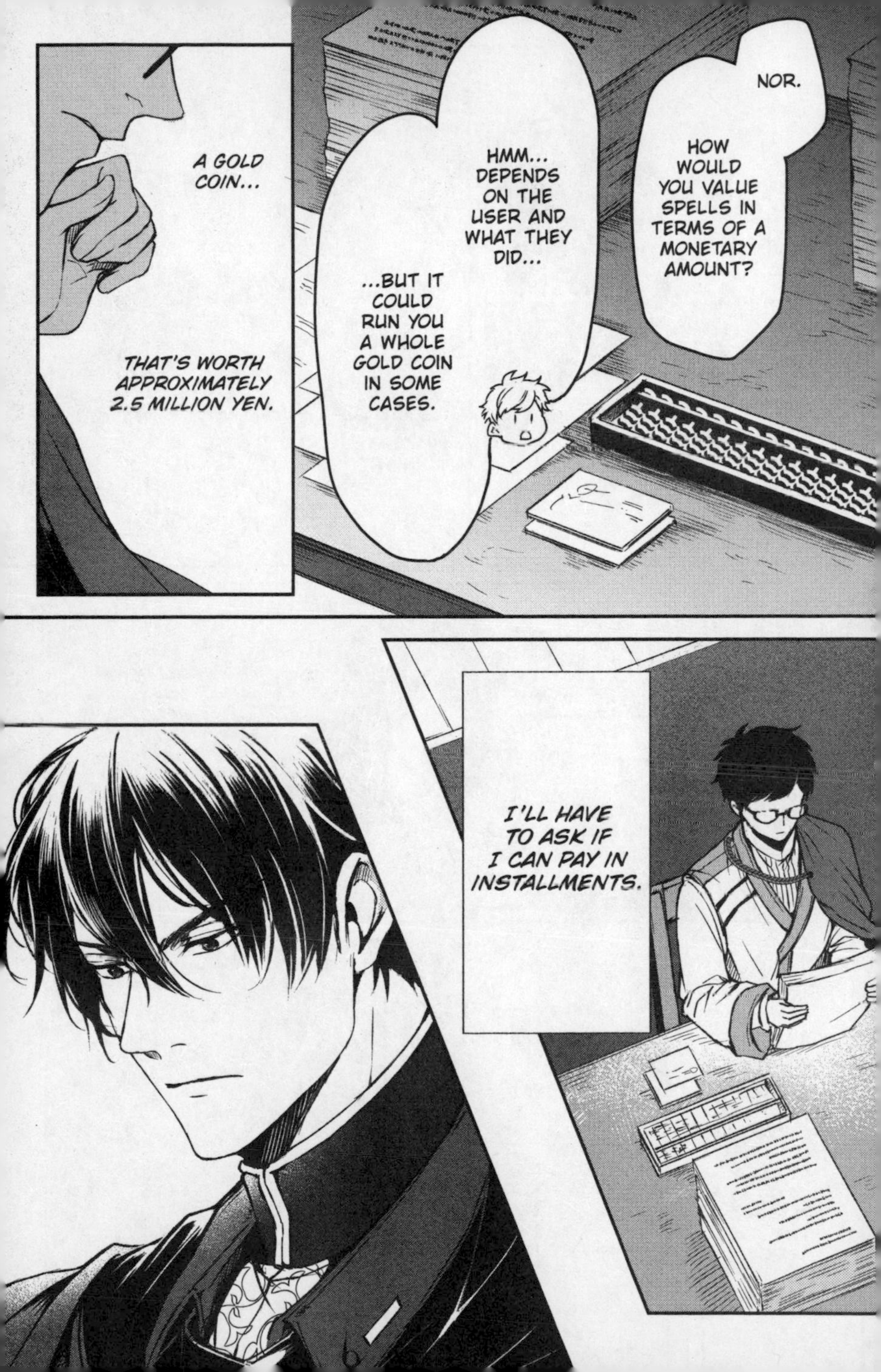
NOR.
HOW WOULD YOU VALUE SPELLS IN TERMS OF A MONETARY AMOUNT?
HMM... DEPENDS ON THE USER AND WHAT THEY DID...
...BUT IT COULD RUN YOU A WHOLE GOLD COIN IN SOME CASES.
A GOLD COIN...
THAT'S WORTH APPROXIMATELY 2.5 MILLION YEN.
I'LL HAVE TO ASK IF I CAN PAY IN INSTALLMENTS.

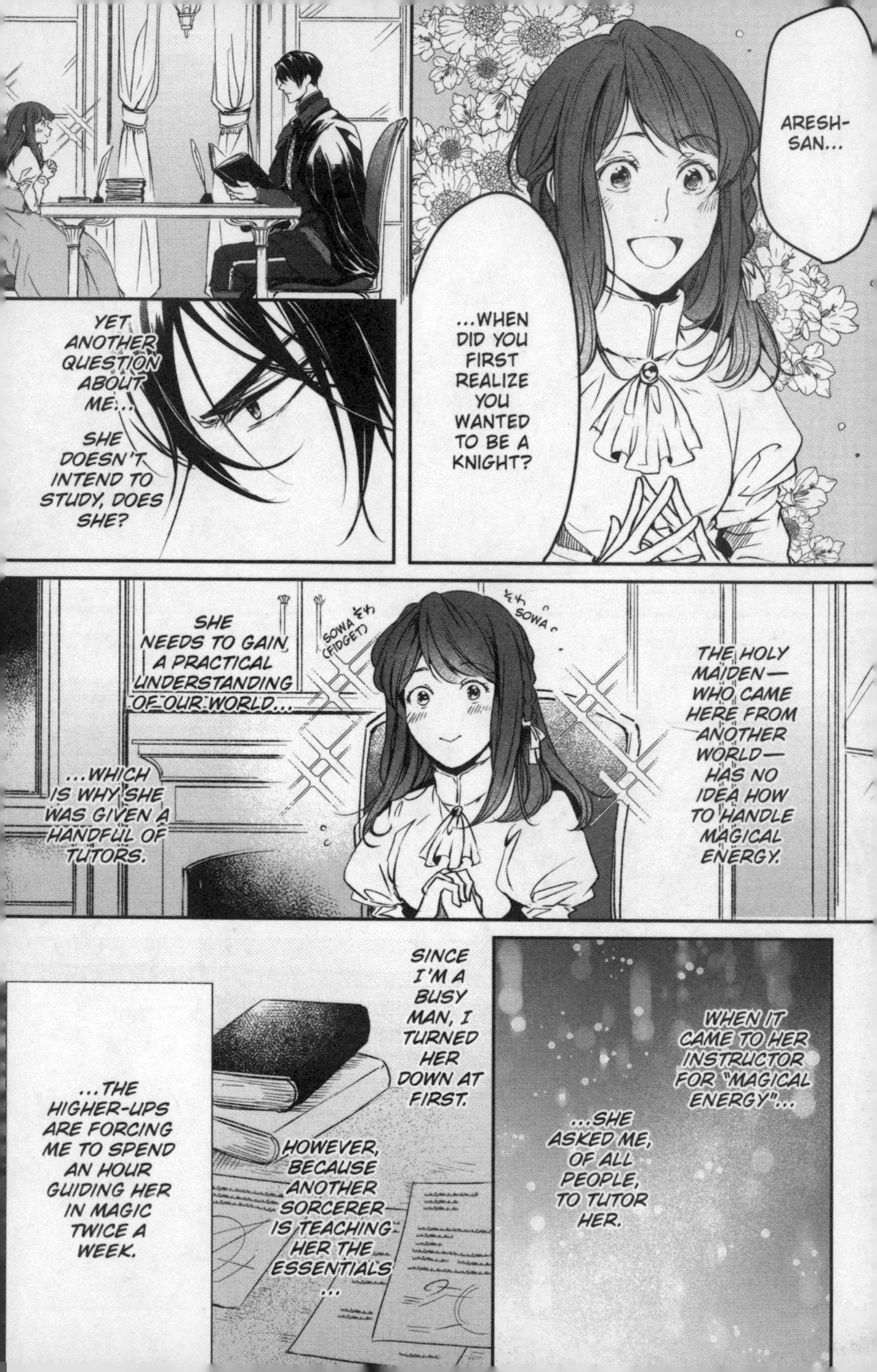
ARESH-SAN...
...WHEN DID YOU FIRST REALIZE YOU WANTED TO BE A KNIGHT?
YET ANOTHER QUESTION ABOUT ME...
SHE DOESN'T INTEND TO STUDY, DOES SHE?
THE HOLY MAIDEN—WHO CAME HERE FROM ANOTHER WORLD—HAS NO IDEA HOW TO HANDLE MAGICAL ENERGY.
そわ SOWA
SOWA そわ (FIDGET)
SHE NEEDS TO GAIN A PRACTICAL UNDERSTANDING OF OUR WORLD...
...WHICH IS WHY SHE WAS GIVEN A HANDFUL OF TUTORS.
WHEN IT CAME TO HER INSTRUCTOR FOR "MAGICAL ENERGY"...
...SHE ASKED ME, OF ALL PEOPLE, TO TUTOR HER.
SINCE I'M A BUSY MAN, I TURNED HER DOWN AT FIRST.
HOWEVER, BECAUSE ANOTHER SORCERER IS TEACHING HER THE ESSENTIALS...
...THE HIGHER-UPS ARE FORCING ME TO SPEND AN HOUR GUIDING HER IN MAGIC TWICE A WEEK.

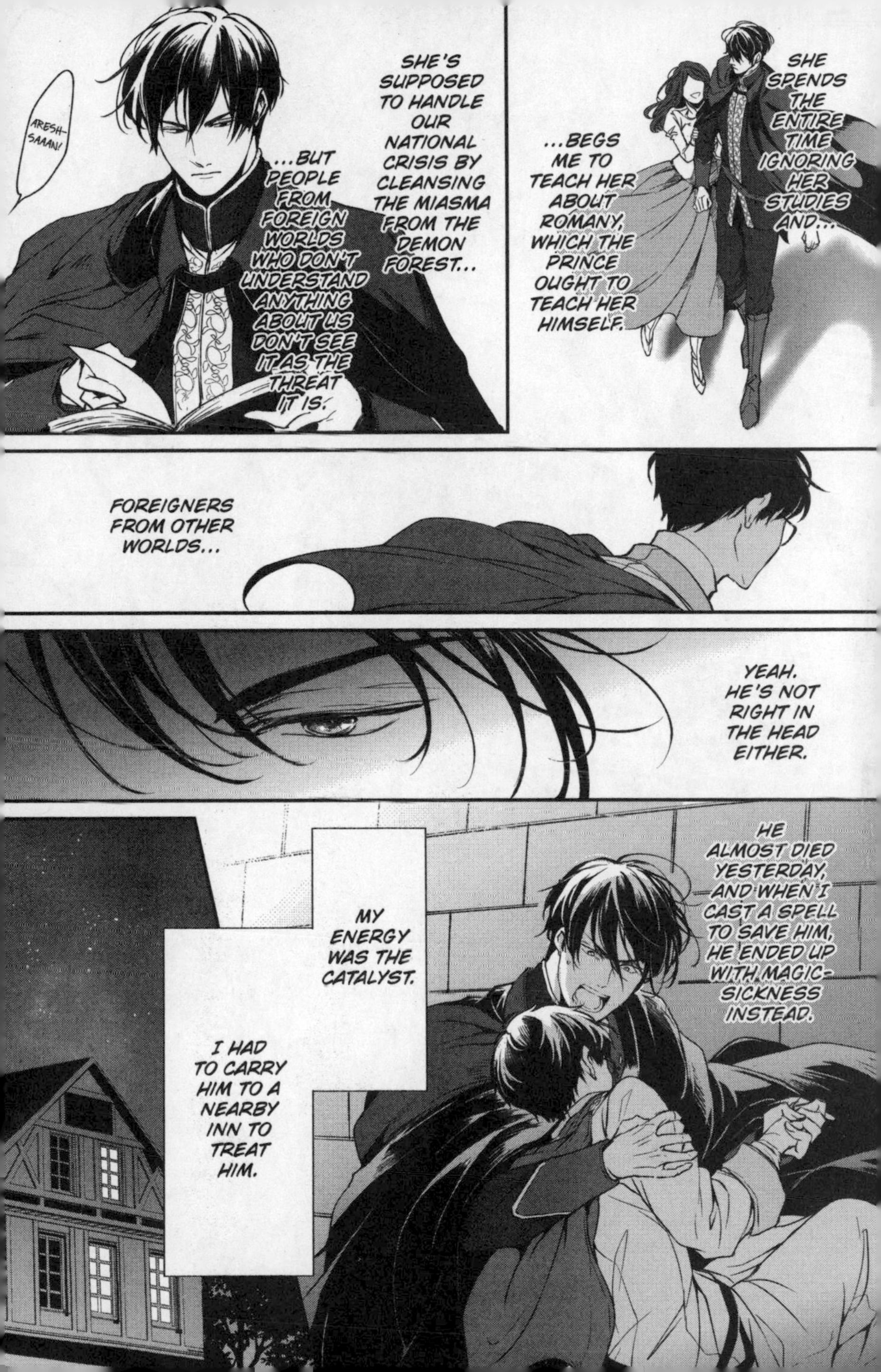
SHE SPENDS THE ENTIRE TIME IGNORING HER STUDIES AND...
...BEGS ME TO TEACH HER ABOUT ROMANY, WHICH THE PRINCE OUGHT TO TEACH HER HIMSELF.
SHE'S SUPPOSED TO HANDLE OUR NATIONAL CRISIS BY CLEANSING THE MIASMA FROM THE DEMON FOREST...
...BUT PEOPLE FROM FOREIGN WORLDS WHO DON'T UNDERSTAND ANYTHING ABOUT US DON'T SEE IT AS THE THREAT IT IS.
ARESH-SAAAN!
FOREIGNERS FROM OTHER WORLDS...
YEAH. HE'S NOT RIGHT IN THE HEAD EITHER.
HE ALMOST DIED YESTERDAY, AND WHEN I CAST A SPELL TO SAVE HIM, HE ENDED UP WITH MAGIC-SICKNESS INSTEAD.
MY ENERGY WAS THE CATALYST.
I HAD TO CARRY HIM TO A NEARBY INN TO TREAT HIM.

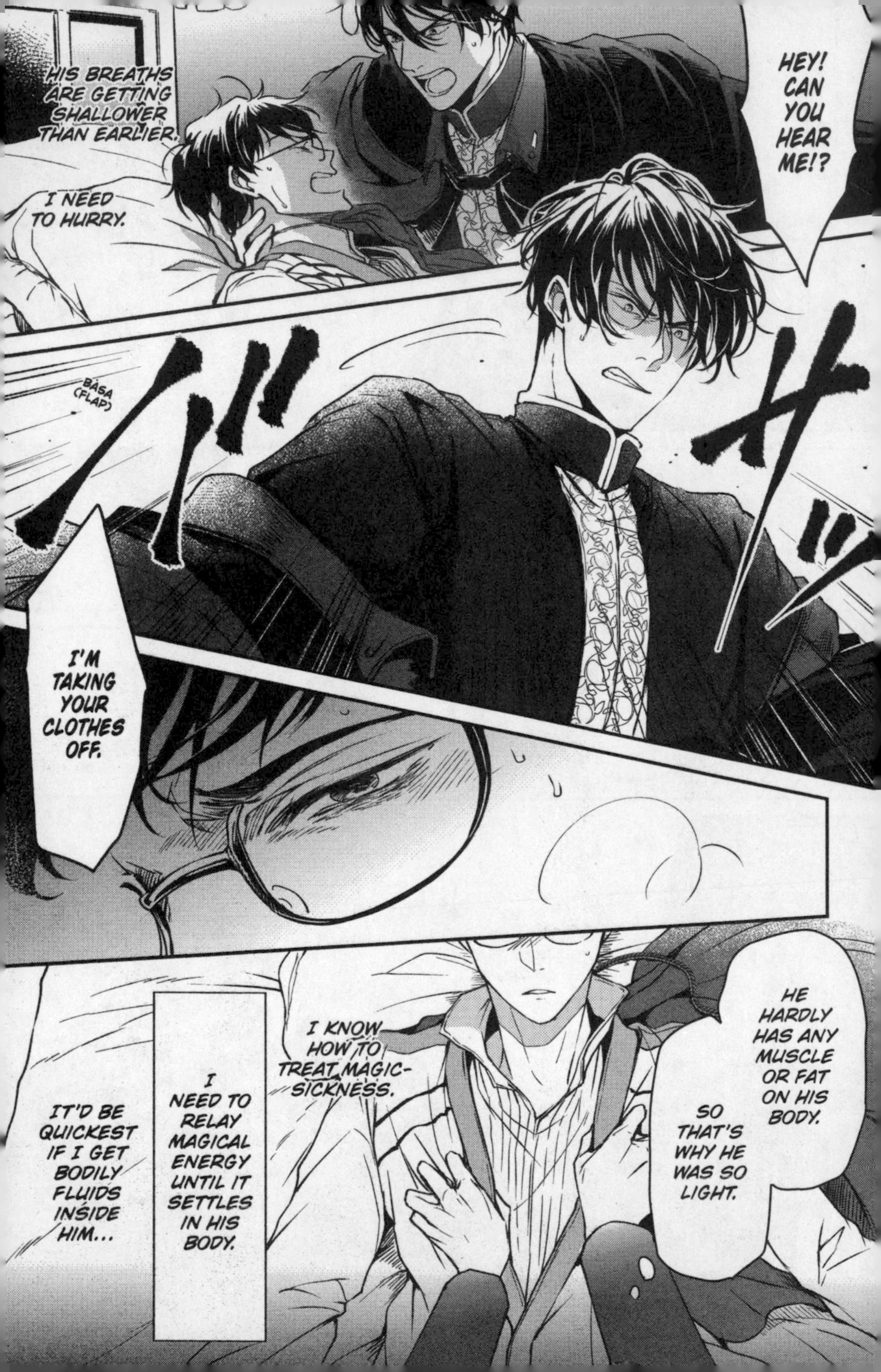
HEY! CAN YOU HEAR ME!?
HIS BREATHS ARE GETTING SHALLOWER THAN EARLIER.
I NEED TO HURRY.
BASA (FLAP)
I'M TAKING YOUR CLOTHES OFF.
HE HARDLY HAS ANY MUSCLE OR FAT ON HIS BODY.
SO THAT'S WHY HE WAS SO LIGHT.
I KNOW HOW TO TREAT MAGIC-SICKNESS.
I NEED TO RELAY MAGICAL ENERGY UNTIL IT SETTLES IN HIS BODY.
IT'D BE QUICKEST IF I GET BODILY FLUIDS INSIDE HIM...

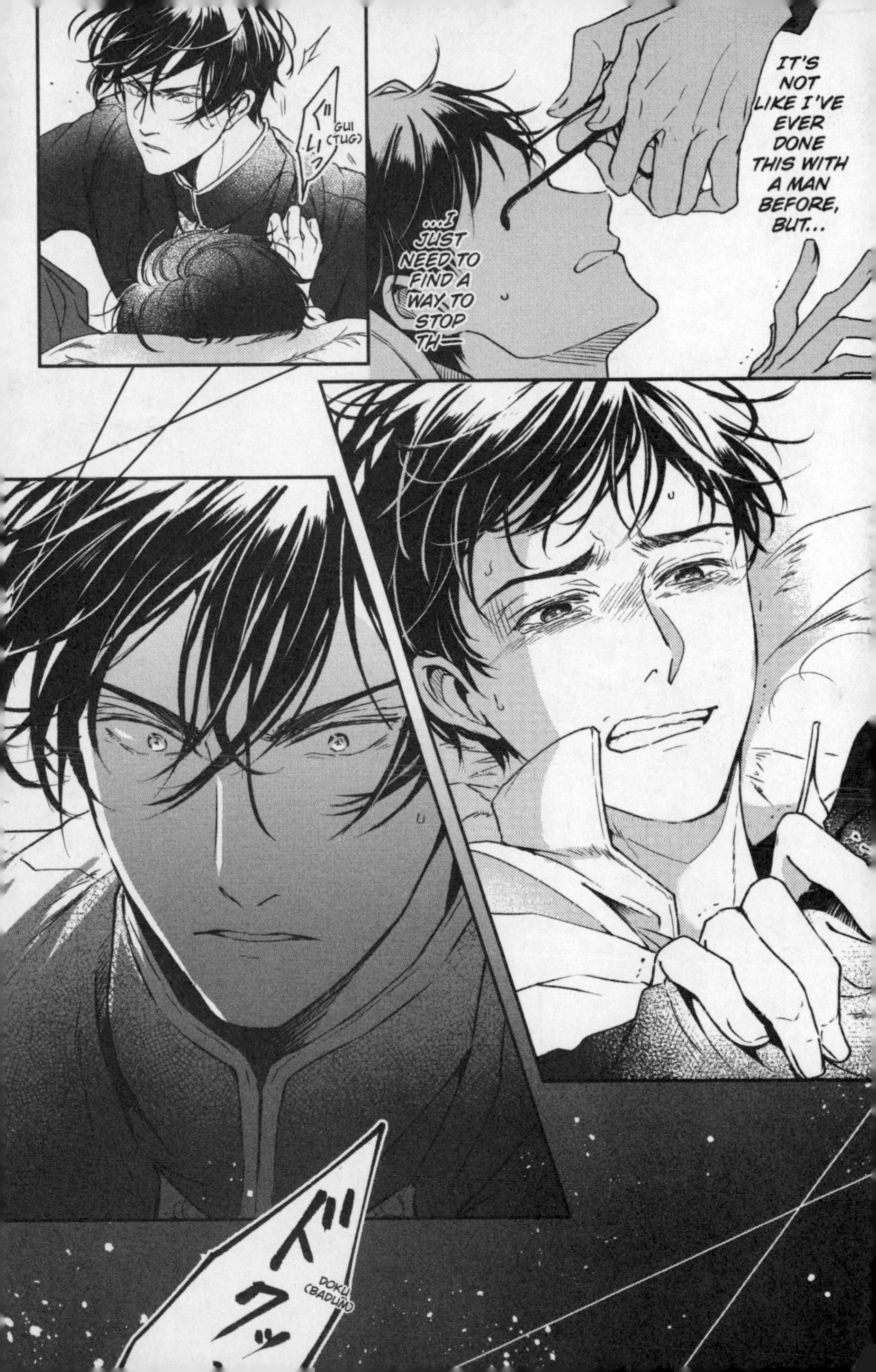
IT'S NOT LIKE I'VE EVER DONE THIS WITH A MAN BEFORE, BUT...
...I JUST NEED TO FIND A WAY TO STOP TH—
ぐいっ
GUI (TUG)
ドクッ
DOKU (BADUM)

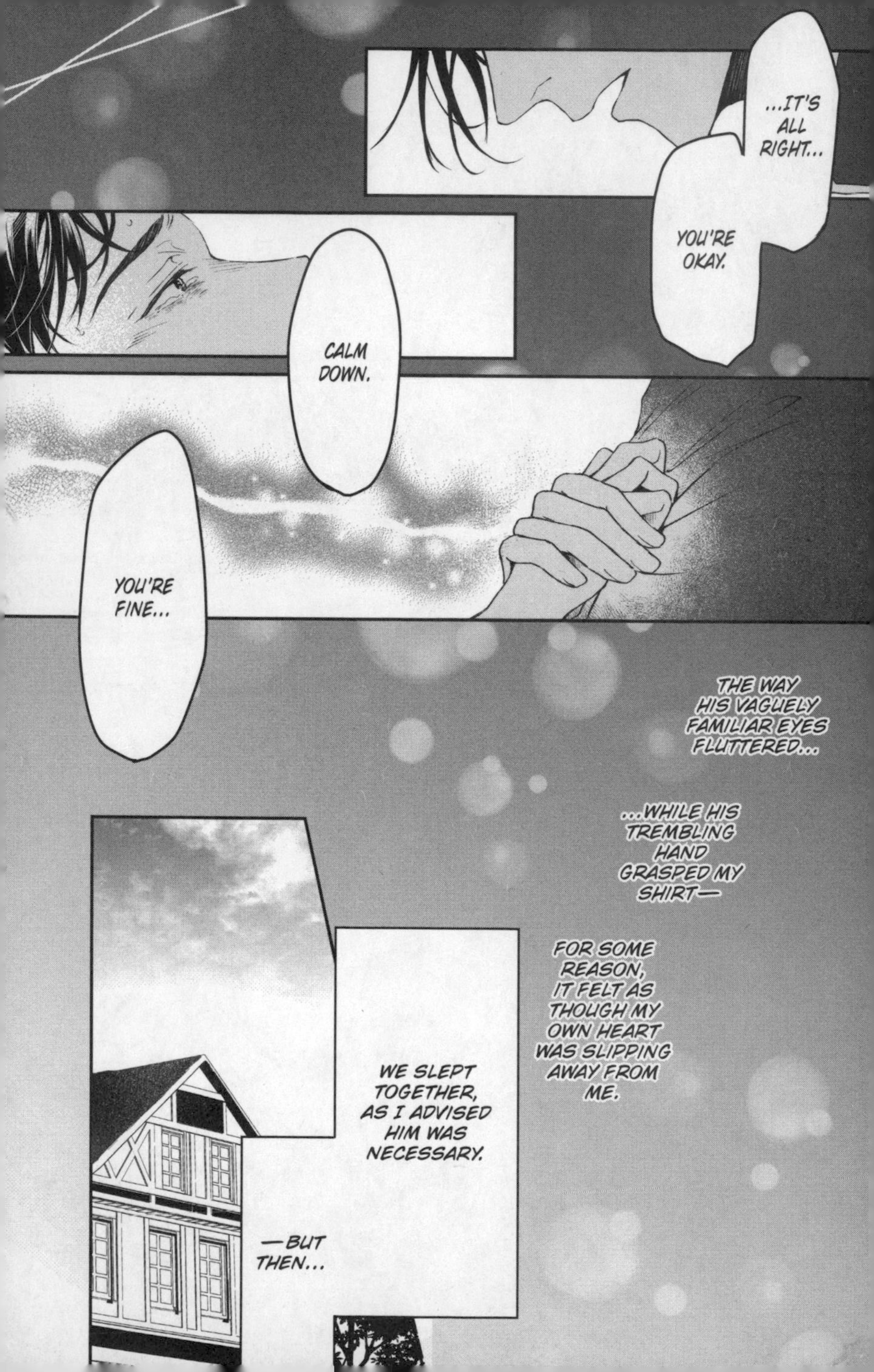
...IT'S ALL RIGHT...
YOU'RE OKAY.
CALM DOWN.
YOU'RE FINE...
THE WAY HIS VAGUELY FAMILIAR EYES FLUTTERED...
...WHILE HIS TREMBLING HAND GRASPED MY SHIRT—
FOR SOME REASON, IT FELT AS THOUGH MY OWN HEART WAS SLIPPING AWAY FROM ME.
WE SLEPT TOGETHER, AS I ADVISED HIM WAS NECESSARY.
—BUT THEN...

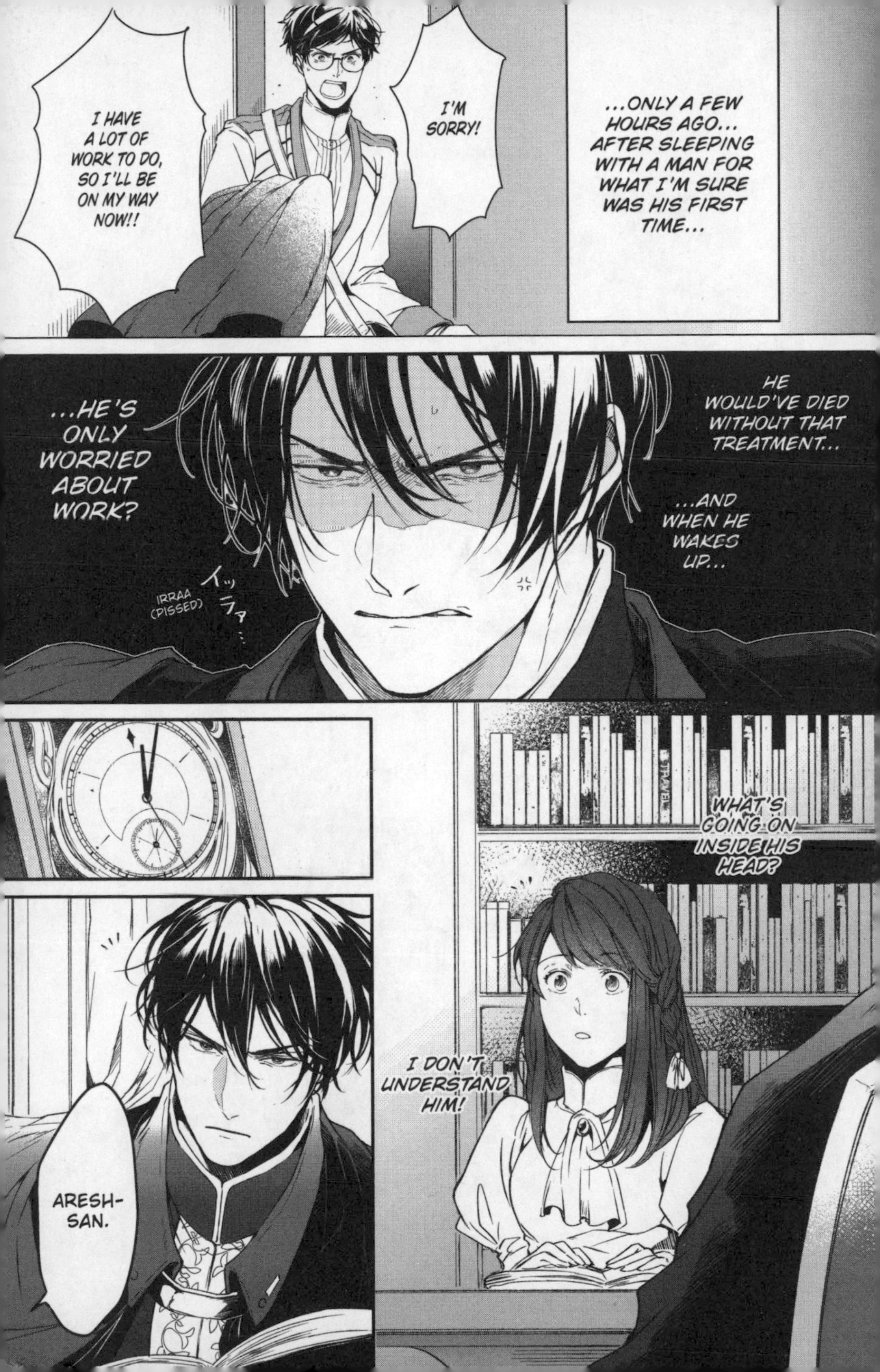
...ONLY A FEW HOURS AGO... AFTER SLEEPING WITH A MAN FOR WHAT I'M SURE WAS HIS FIRST TIME...
I'M SORRY!
I HAVE A LOT OF WORK TO DO, SO I'LL BE ON MY WAY NOW!!
HE WOULD'VE DIED WITHOUT THAT TREATMENT...
...AND WHEN HE WAKES UP...
...HE'S ONLY WORRIED ABOUT WORK?
イッラァ…
IRRAA (PISSED)
WHAT'S GOING ON INSIDE HIS HEAD?
I DON'T UNDERSTAND HIM!
ARESH-SAN.

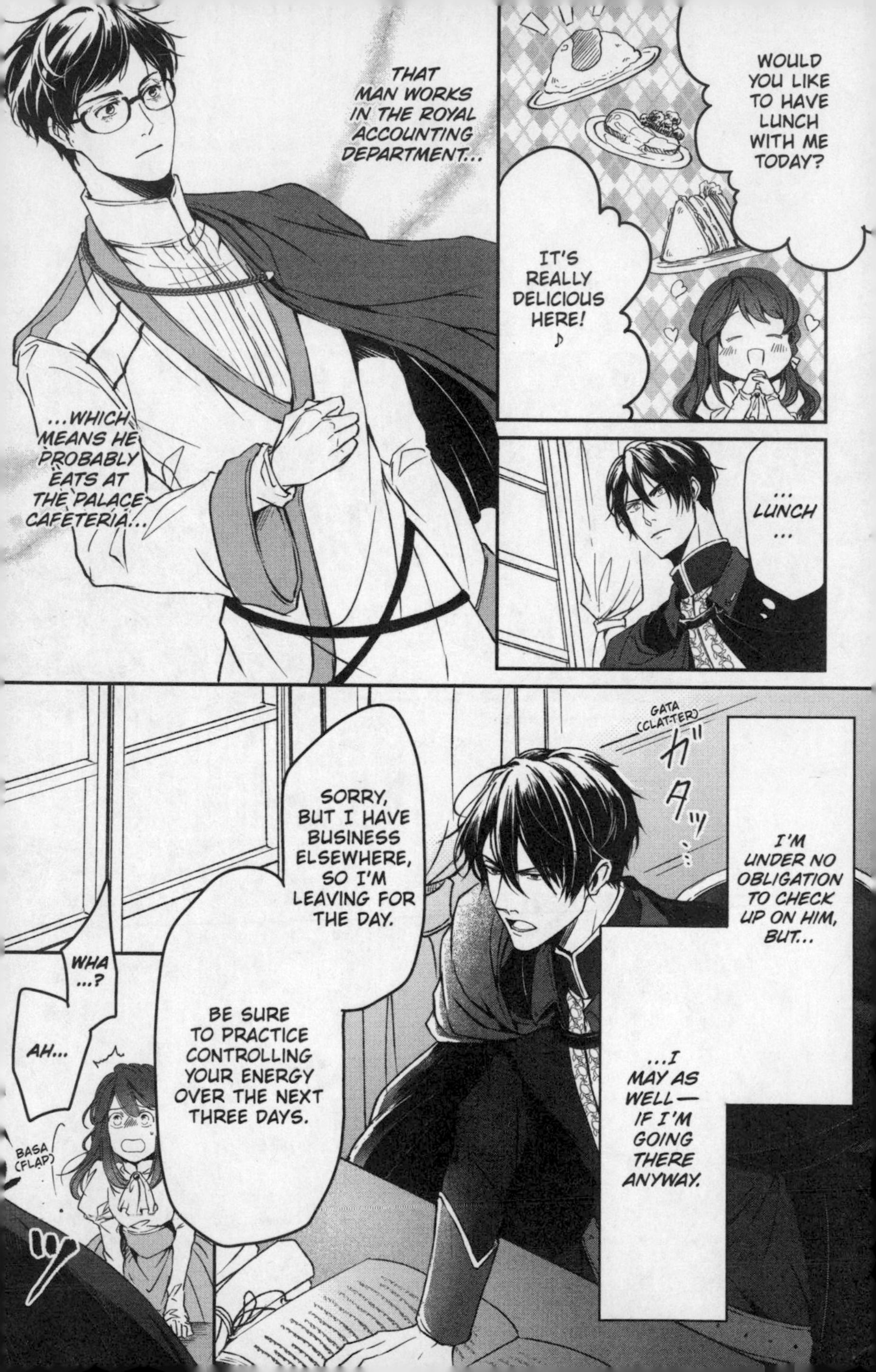
WOULD YOU LIKE TO HAVE LUNCH WITH ME TODAY?
IT'S REALLY DELICIOUS HERE! ♪
... LUNCH ...
THAT MAN WORKS IN THE ROYAL ACCOUNTING DEPARTMENT...
...WHICH MEANS HE PROBABLY EATS AT THE PALACE CAFETERIA...
GATA (CLAT-TER)
ガタッ
I'M UNDER NO OBLIGATION TO CHECK UP ON HIM, BUT...
...I MAY AS WELL— IF I'M GOING THERE ANYWAY.
SORRY, BUT I HAVE BUSINESS ELSEWHERE, SO I'M LEAVING FOR THE DAY.
BE SURE TO PRACTICE CONTROLLING YOUR ENERGY OVER THE NEXT THREE DAYS.
WHA ...?
AH...
BASA (FLAP)

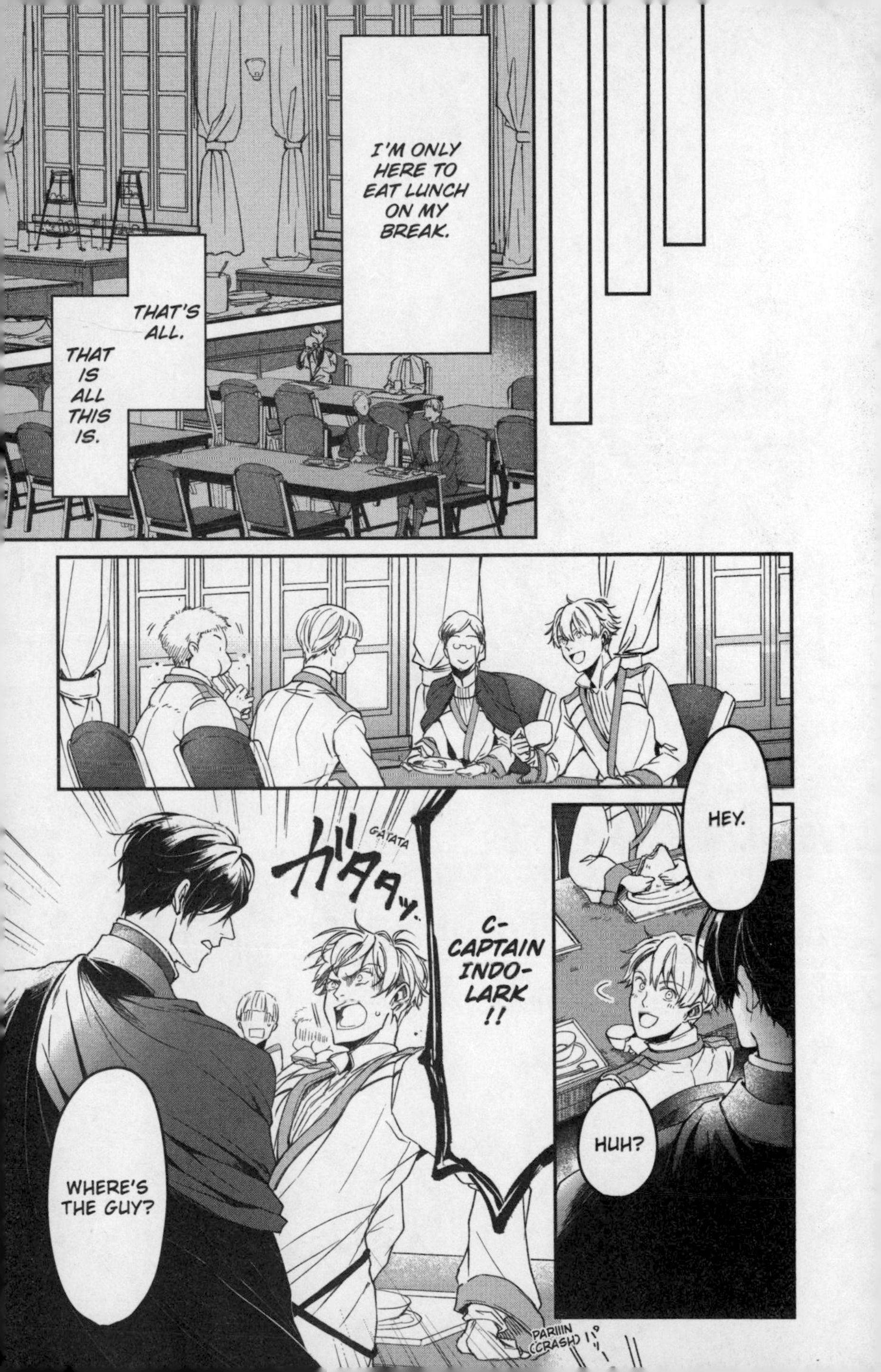
I'M ONLY HERE TO EAT LUNCH ON MY BREAK.
THAT'S ALL.
THAT IS ALL THIS IS.
HEY.
HUH?
ガタタッ GATATA
C-CAPTAIN INDO-LARK!!
WHERE'S THE GUY?
PARIIIN (CRASH)

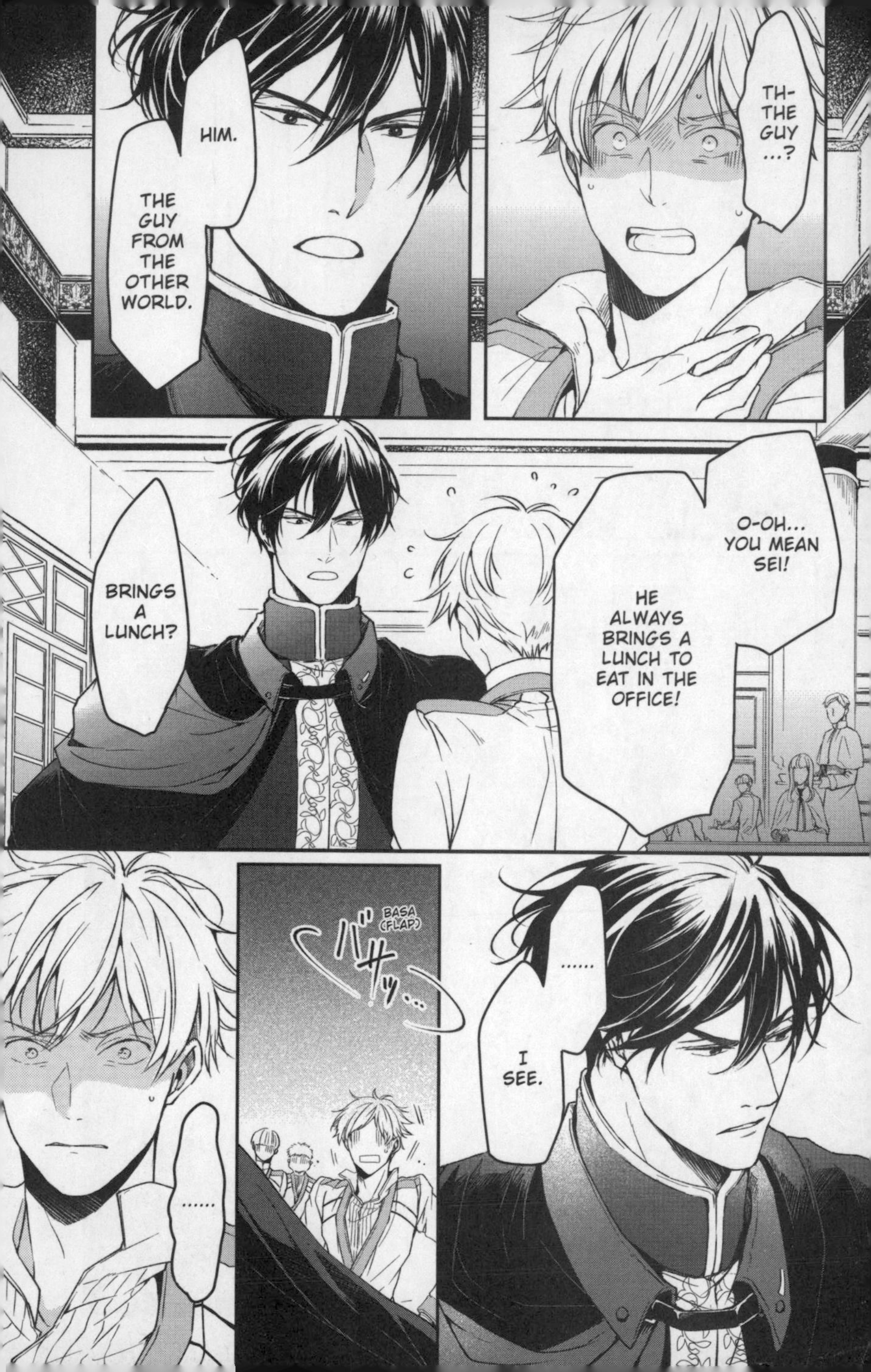
TH- THE GUY ...?
HIM.
THE GUY FROM THE OTHER WORLD.
O-OH... YOU MEAN SEI!
HE ALWAYS BRINGS A LUNCH TO EAT IN THE OFFICE!
BRINGS A LUNCH?
......
I SEE.
BASA (FLAP)
バサッ...
......

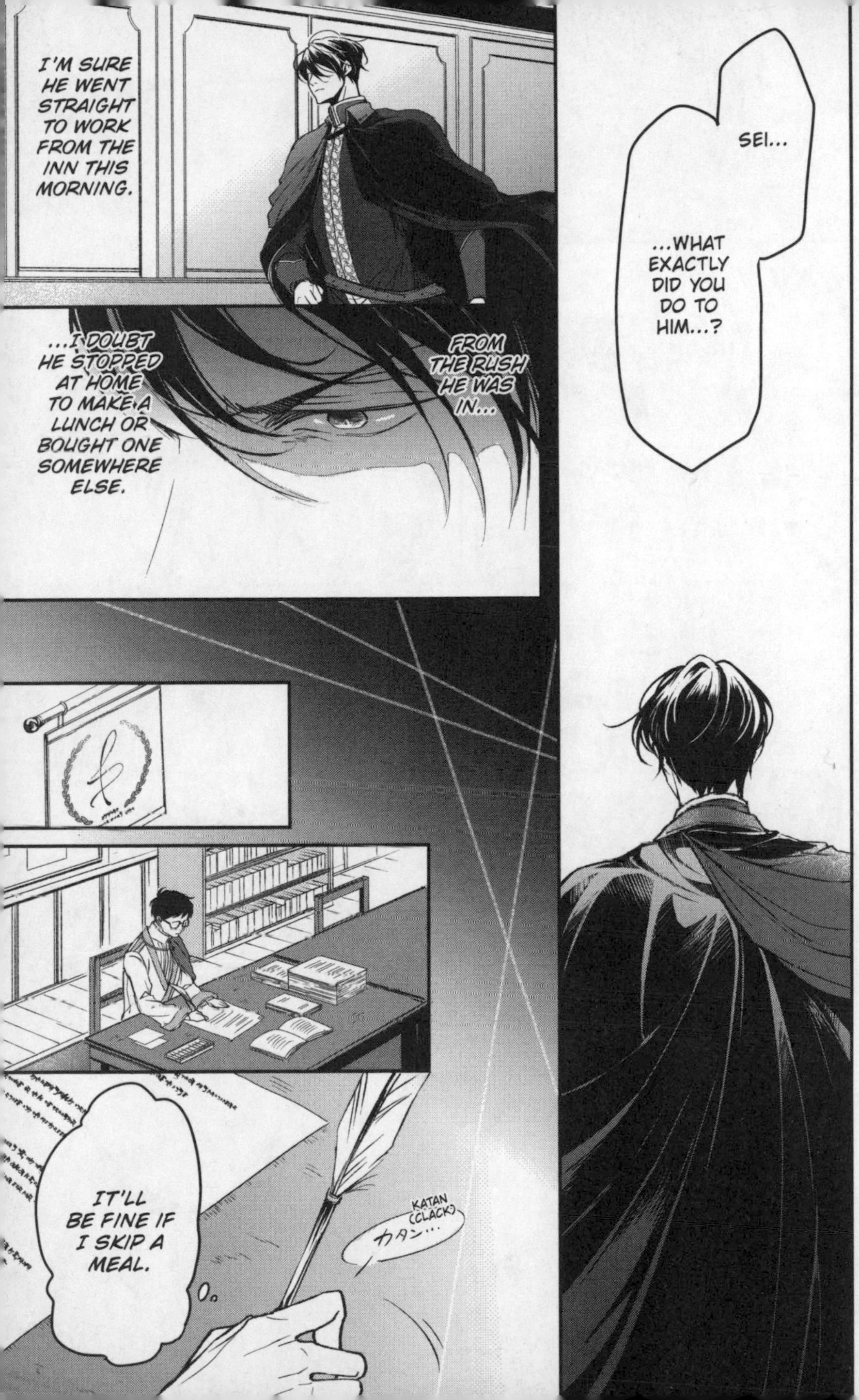
SEI...
...WHAT EXACTLY DID YOU DO TO HIM...?
I'M SURE HE WENT STRAIGHT TO WORK FROM THE INN THIS MORNING.
FROM THE RUSH HE WAS IN...
...I DOUBT HE STOPPED AT HOME TO MAKE A LUNCH OR BOUGHT ONE SOMEWHERE ELSE.
KATAN (CLACK)
カタン…
IT'LL BE FINE IF I SKIP A MEAL.

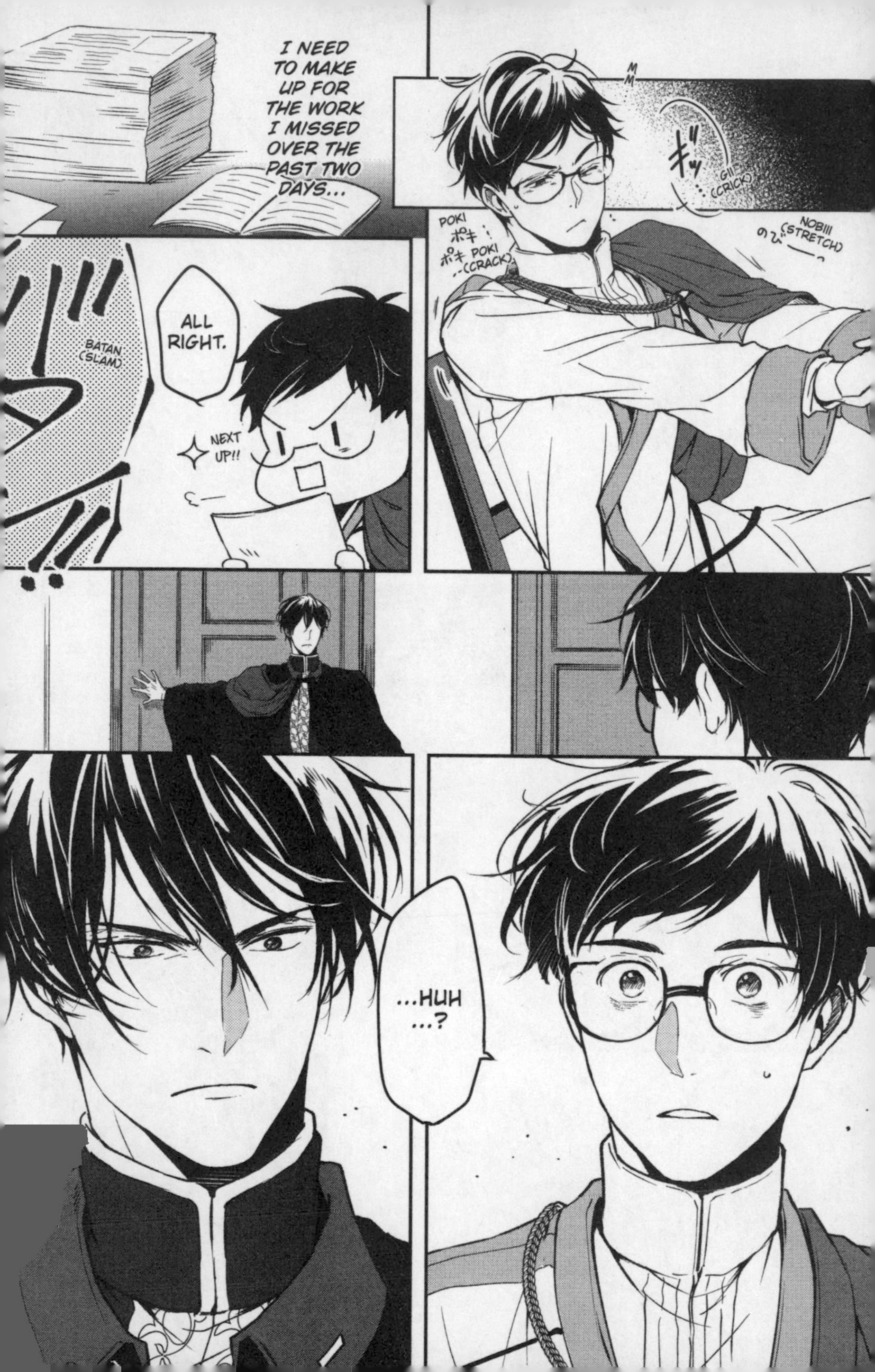
MM
ギッ
GII (CRICK)
POKI
ポキ
ポキ
POKI (CRACK)
のび
NOBIII (STRETCH)
I NEED TO MAKE UP FOR THE WORK I MISSED OVER THE PAST TWO DAYS...
ALL RIGHT.
BATAN (SLAM)
NEXT UP!!
...HUH ...?

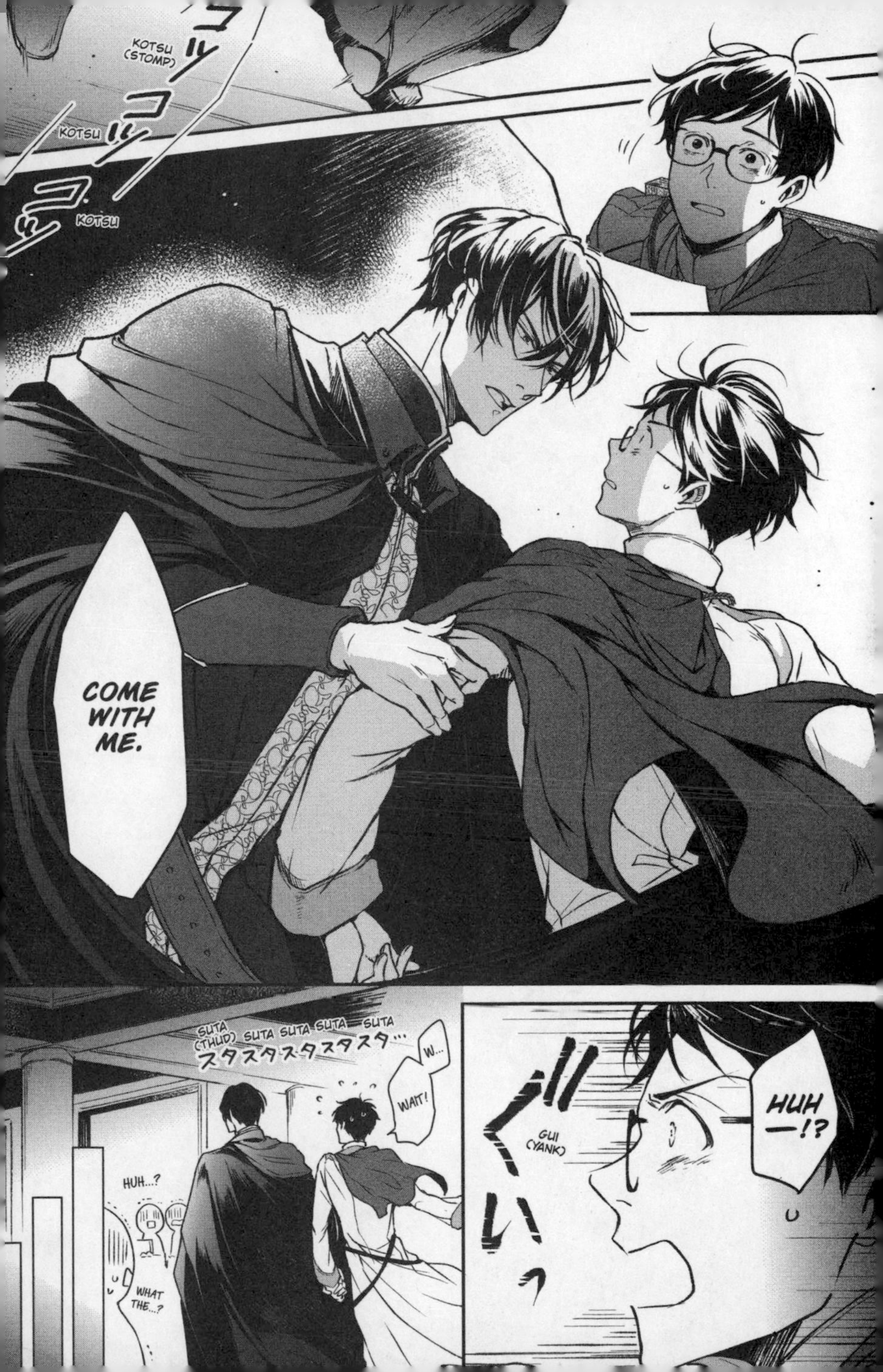
コツ
KOTSU (STOMP)
コツ
KOTSU
コツ
KOTSU
COME WITH ME.
HUH —!?
ぐいっ
GUI (YANK)
SUTA (THUD) SUTA SUTA SUTA SUTA
スタスタスタスタ…
W...
WAIT!
HUH...?
WHAT THE...?

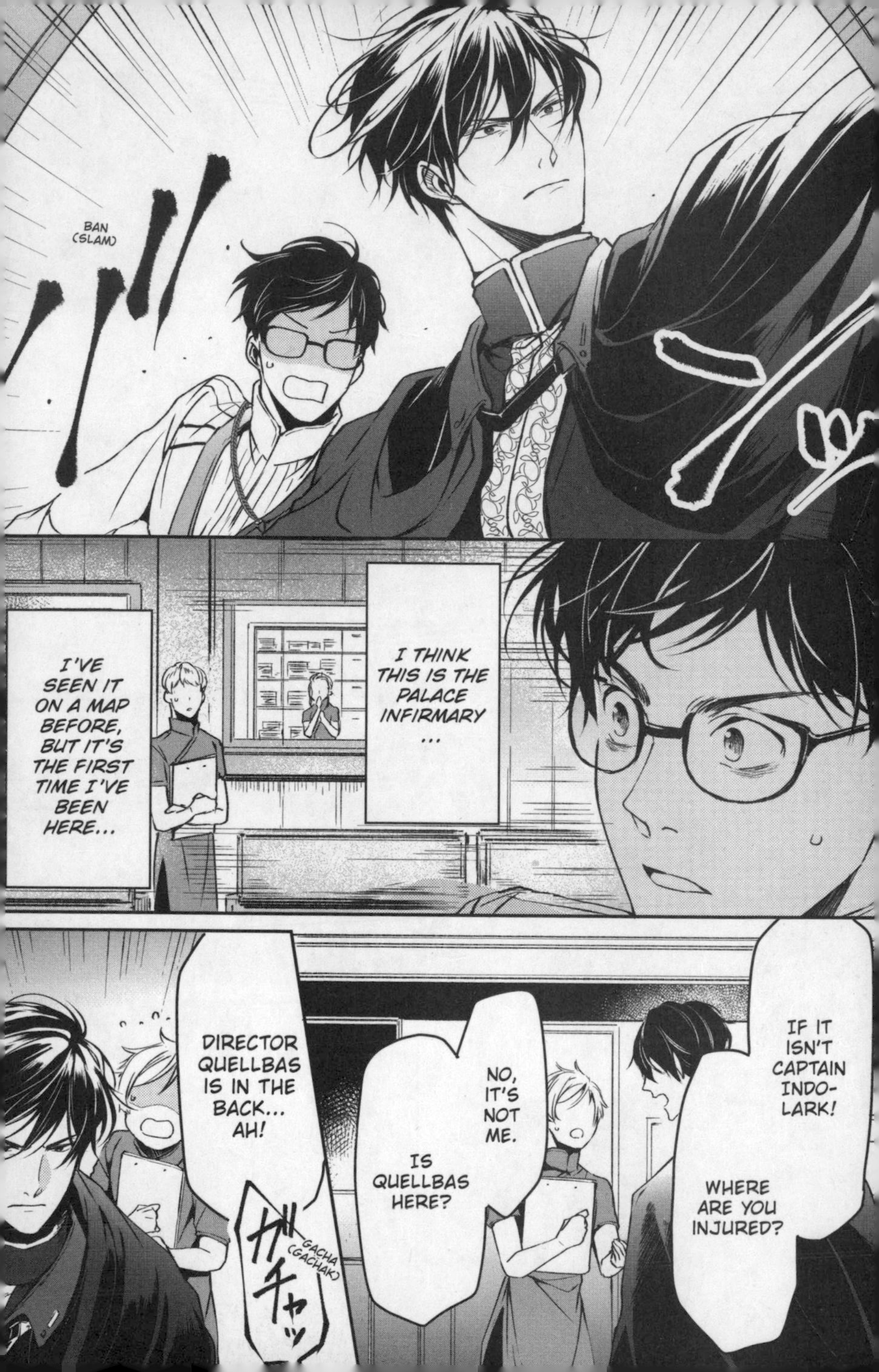
BAN (SLAM)
I THINK THIS IS THE PALACE INFIRMARY...
I'VE SEEN IT ON A MAP BEFORE, BUT IT'S THE FIRST TIME I'VE BEEN HERE...
IF IT ISN'T CAPTAIN INDO-LARK!
WHERE ARE YOU INJURED?
NO, IT'S NOT ME.
IS QUELLBAS HERE?
DIRECTOR QUELLBAS IS IN THE BACK... AH!
GACHA (GACHAK)

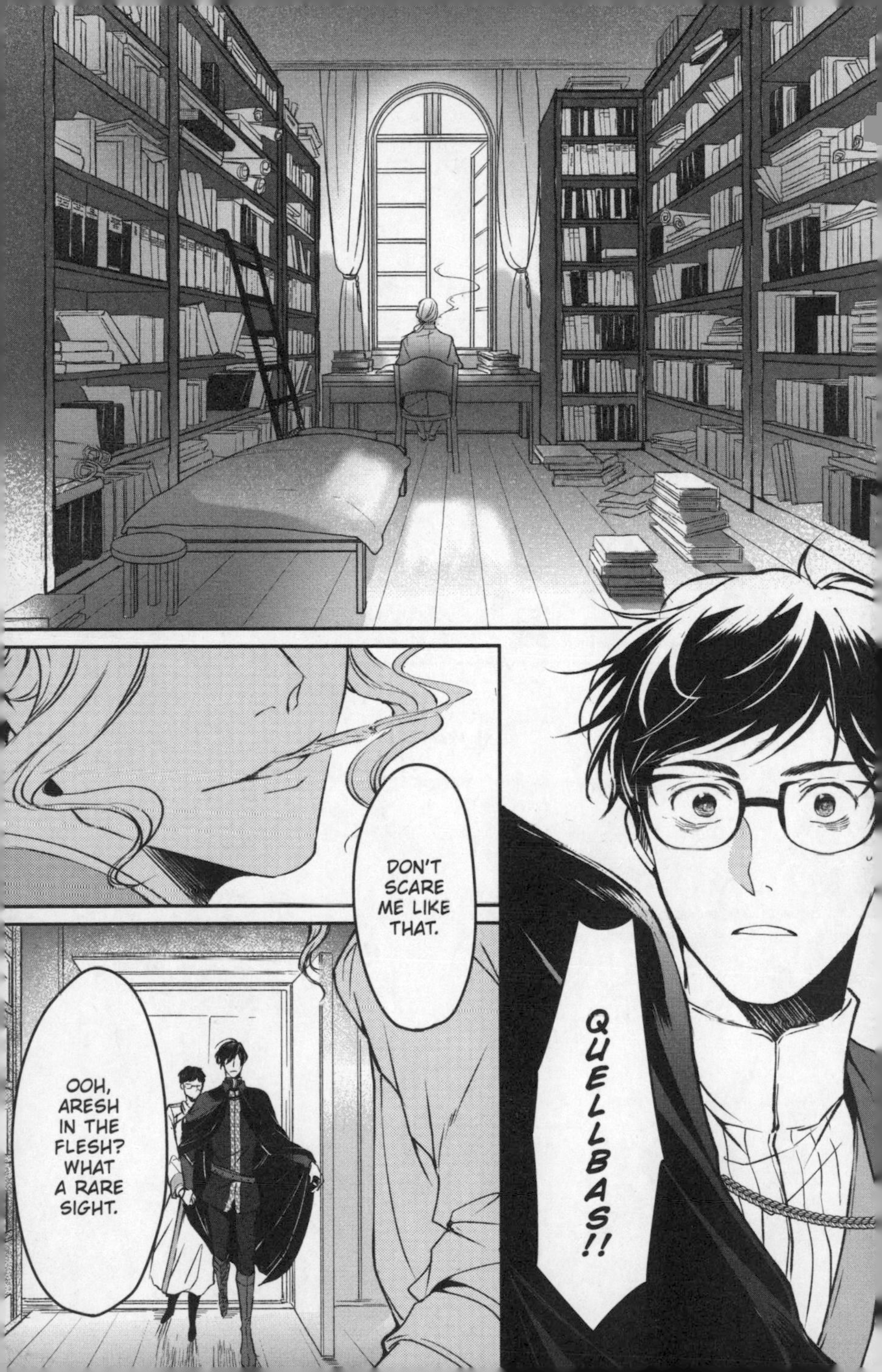
QUELLBAS!!
DON'T SCARE ME LIKE THAT.
OOH, ARESH IN THE FLESH? WHAT A RARE SIGHT.

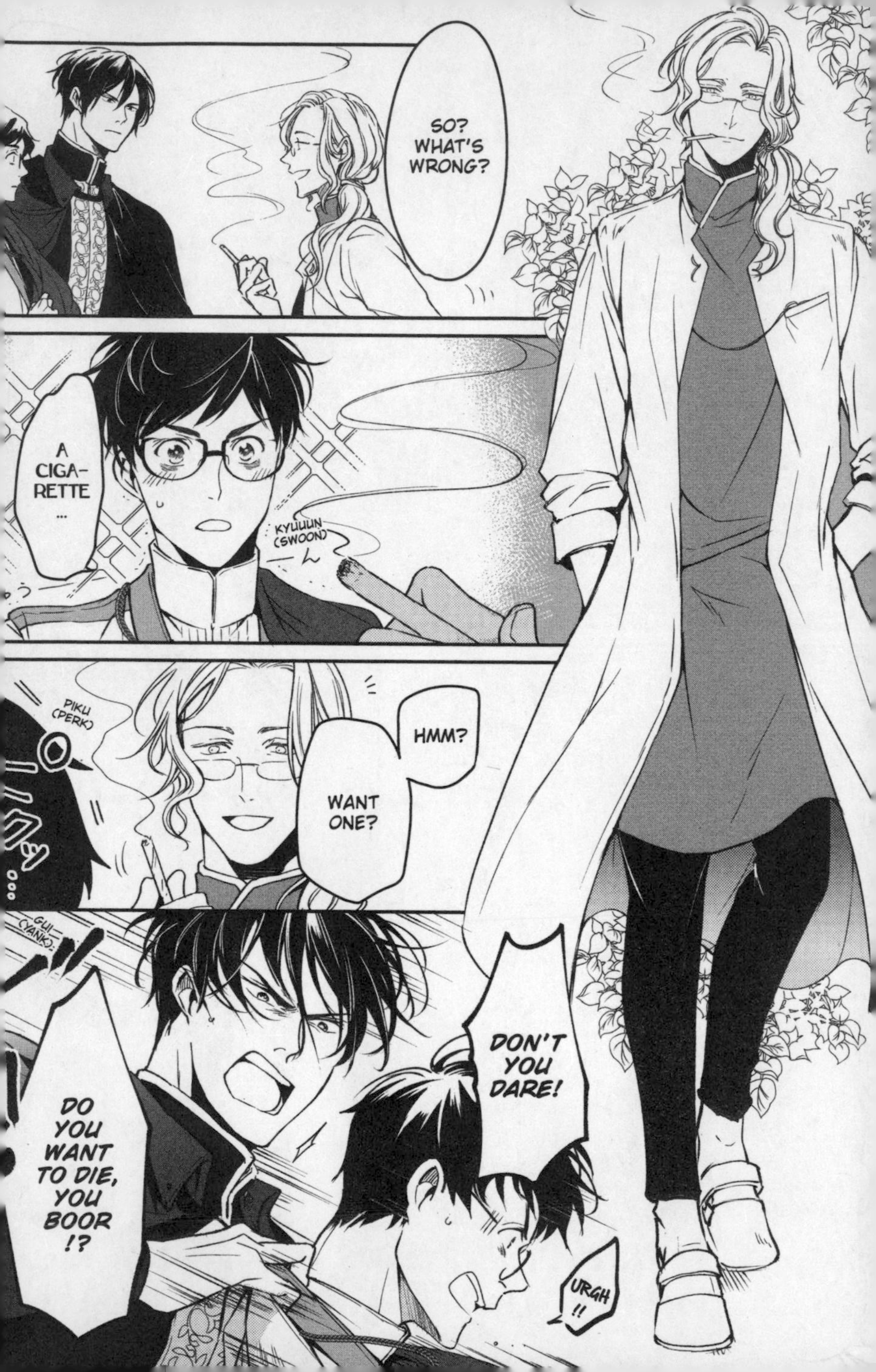
SO? WHAT'S WRONG?
A CIGARETTE...
KYUUUN (SWOON)
HMM?
WANT ONE?
PIKU (PERK)
GUI (YANK)
DON'T YOU DARE!
DO YOU WANT TO DIE, YOU BOOR!?
URGH!!

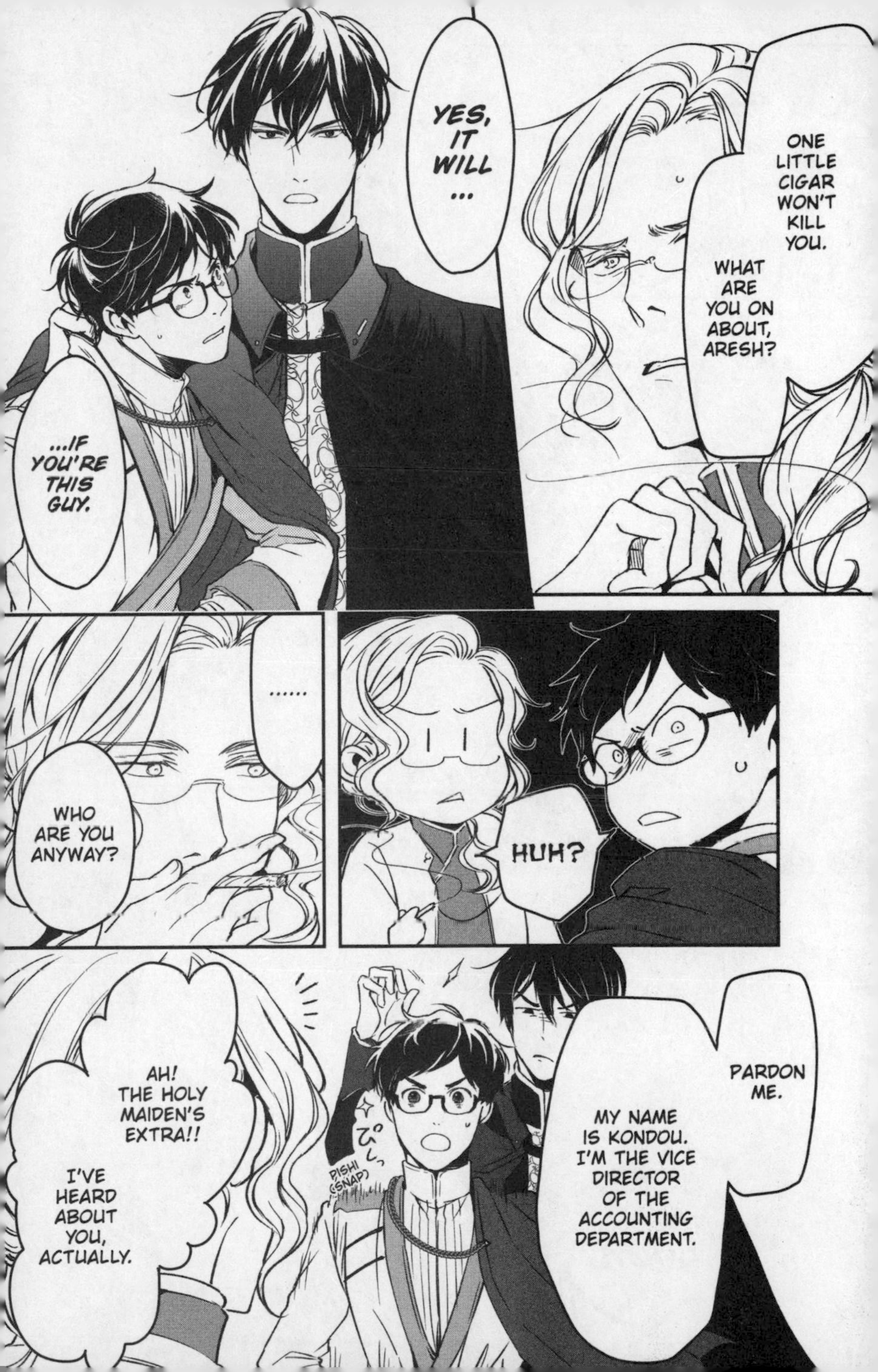
ONE LITTLE CIGAR WON'T KILL YOU.
WHAT ARE YOU ON ABOUT, ARESH?
YES, IT WILL...
...IF YOU'RE THIS GUY.
HUH?
......
WHO ARE YOU ANYWAY?
PARDON ME.
MY NAME IS KONDOU. I'M THE VICE DIRECTOR OF THE ACCOUNTING DEPARTMENT.
PISHI (SNAP)
AH! THE HOLY MAIDEN'S EXTRA!!
I'VE HEARD ABOUT YOU, ACTUALLY.

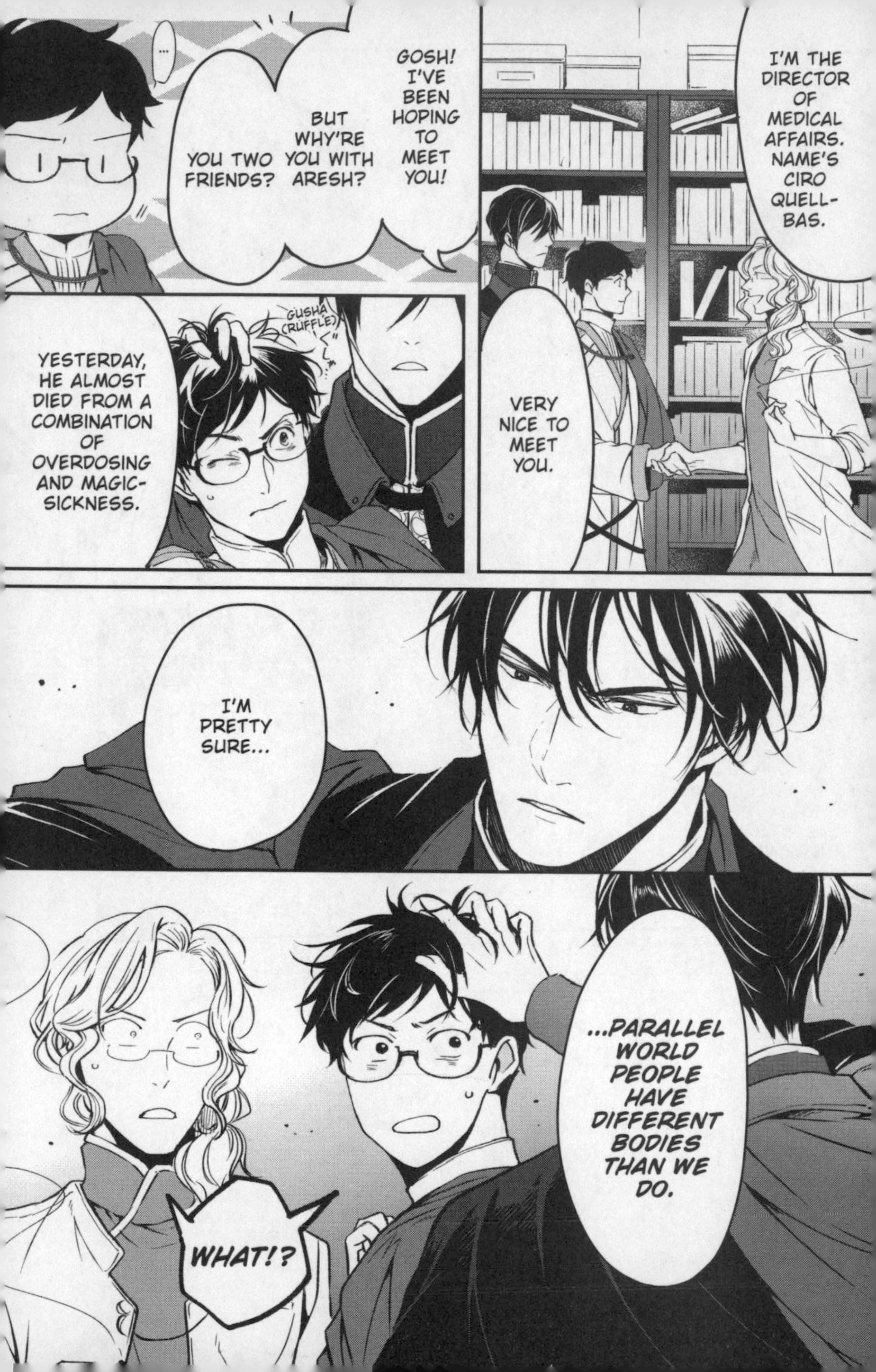
I'M THE DIRECTOR OF MEDICAL AFFAIRS. NAME'S CIRO QUELL-BAS.
VERY NICE TO MEET YOU.
GOSH! I'VE BEEN HOPING TO MEET YOU!
BUT WHY'RE YOU WITH ARESH?
YOU TWO FRIENDS?
...
GUSHA (RUFFLE)
YESTERDAY, HE ALMOST DIED FROM A COMBINATION OF OVERDOSING AND MAGIC-SICKNESS.
I'M PRETTY SURE...
...PARALLEL WORLD PEOPLE HAVE DIFFERENT BODIES THAN WE DO.
WHAT!?

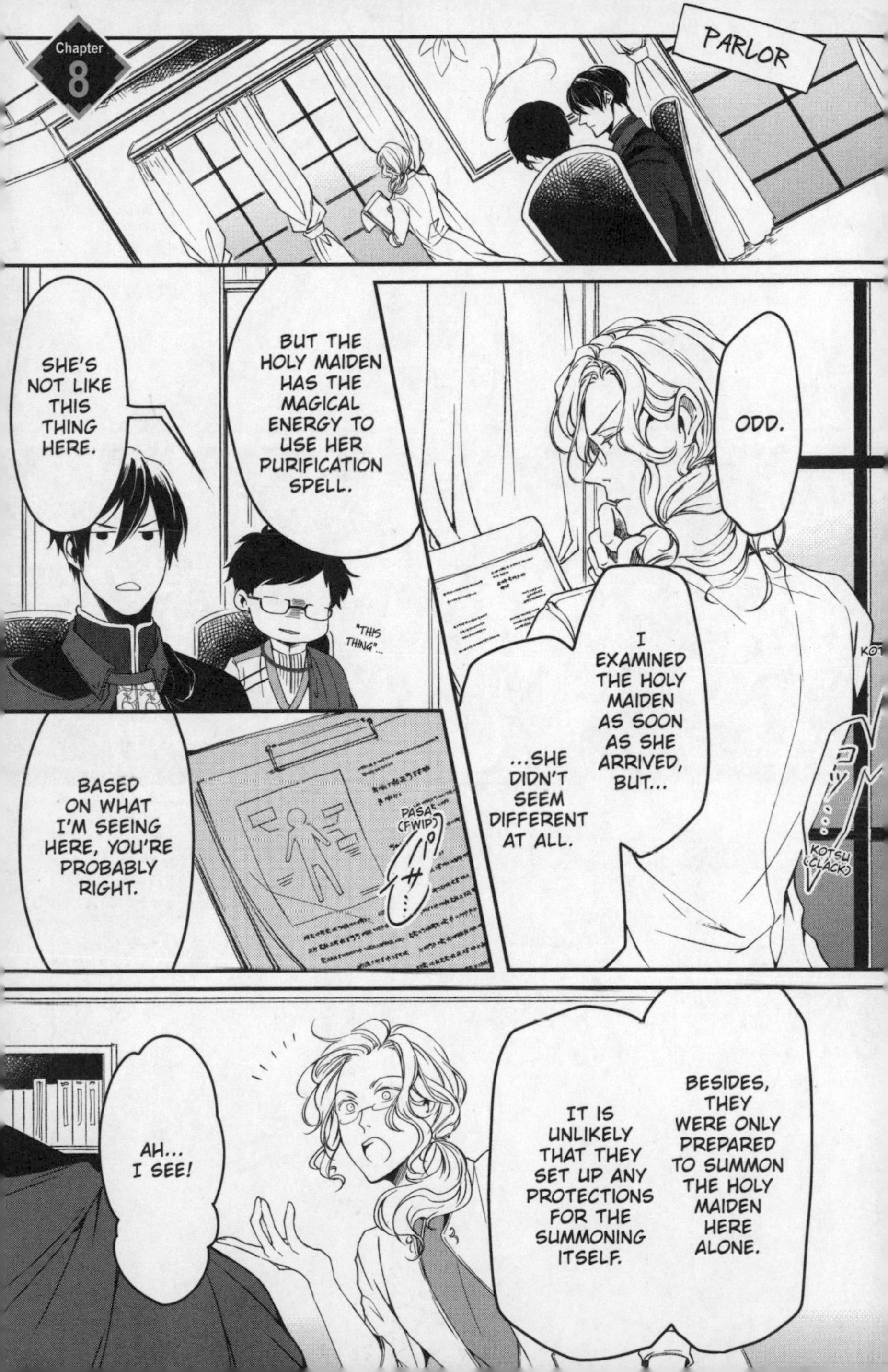
Chapter 8
PARLOR
ODD.
I EXAMINED THE HOLY MAIDEN AS SOON AS SHE ARRIVED, BUT...
...SHE DIDN'T SEEM DIFFERENT AT ALL.
KOTSU (CLACK)
BUT THE HOLY MAIDEN HAS THE MAGICAL ENERGY TO USE HER PURIFICATION SPELL.
SHE'S NOT LIKE THIS THING HERE.
"THIS THING"...
PASA (FWIP)
BASED ON WHAT I'M SEEING HERE, YOU'RE PROBABLY RIGHT.
BESIDES, THEY WERE ONLY PREPARED TO SUMMON THE HOLY MAIDEN HERE ALONE.
IT IS UNLIKELY THAT THEY SET UP ANY PROTECTIONS FOR THE SUMMONING ITSELF.
AH... I SEE!

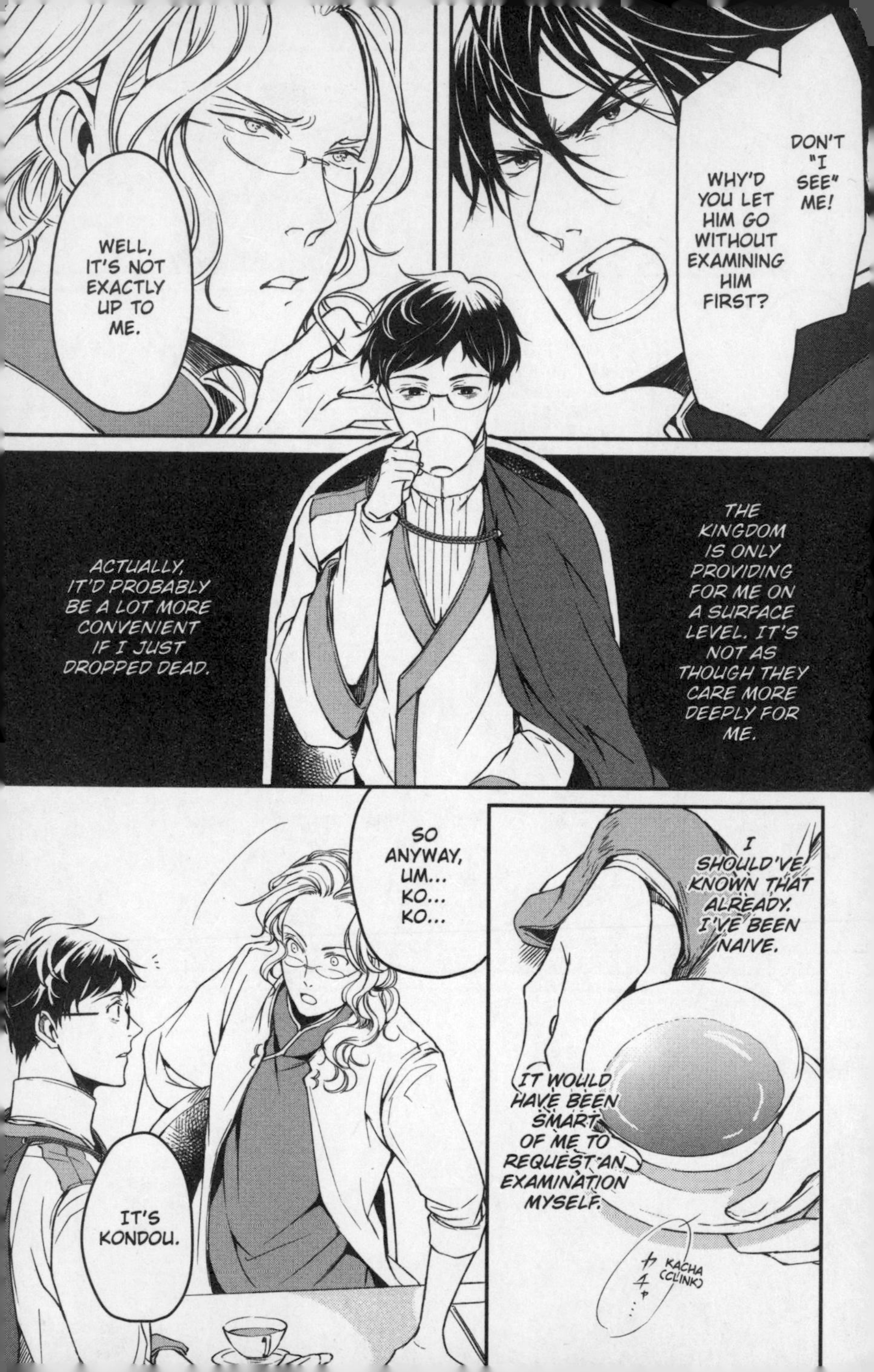
DON'T "I SEE" ME!
WHY'D YOU LET HIM GO WITHOUT EXAMINING HIM FIRST?
WELL, IT'S NOT EXACTLY UP TO ME.
THE KINGDOM IS ONLY PROVIDING FOR ME ON A SURFACE LEVEL. IT'S NOT AS THOUGH THEY CARE MORE DEEPLY FOR ME.
ACTUALLY, IT'D PROBABLY BE A LOT MORE CONVENIENT IF I JUST DROPPED DEAD.
I SHOULD'VE KNOWN THAT ALREADY. I'VE BEEN NAIVE.
IT WOULD HAVE BEEN SMART OF ME TO REQUEST AN EXAMINATION MYSELF.
カチャ…
KACHA (CLINK)
SO ANYWAY, UM... KO... KO...
IT'S KONDOU.

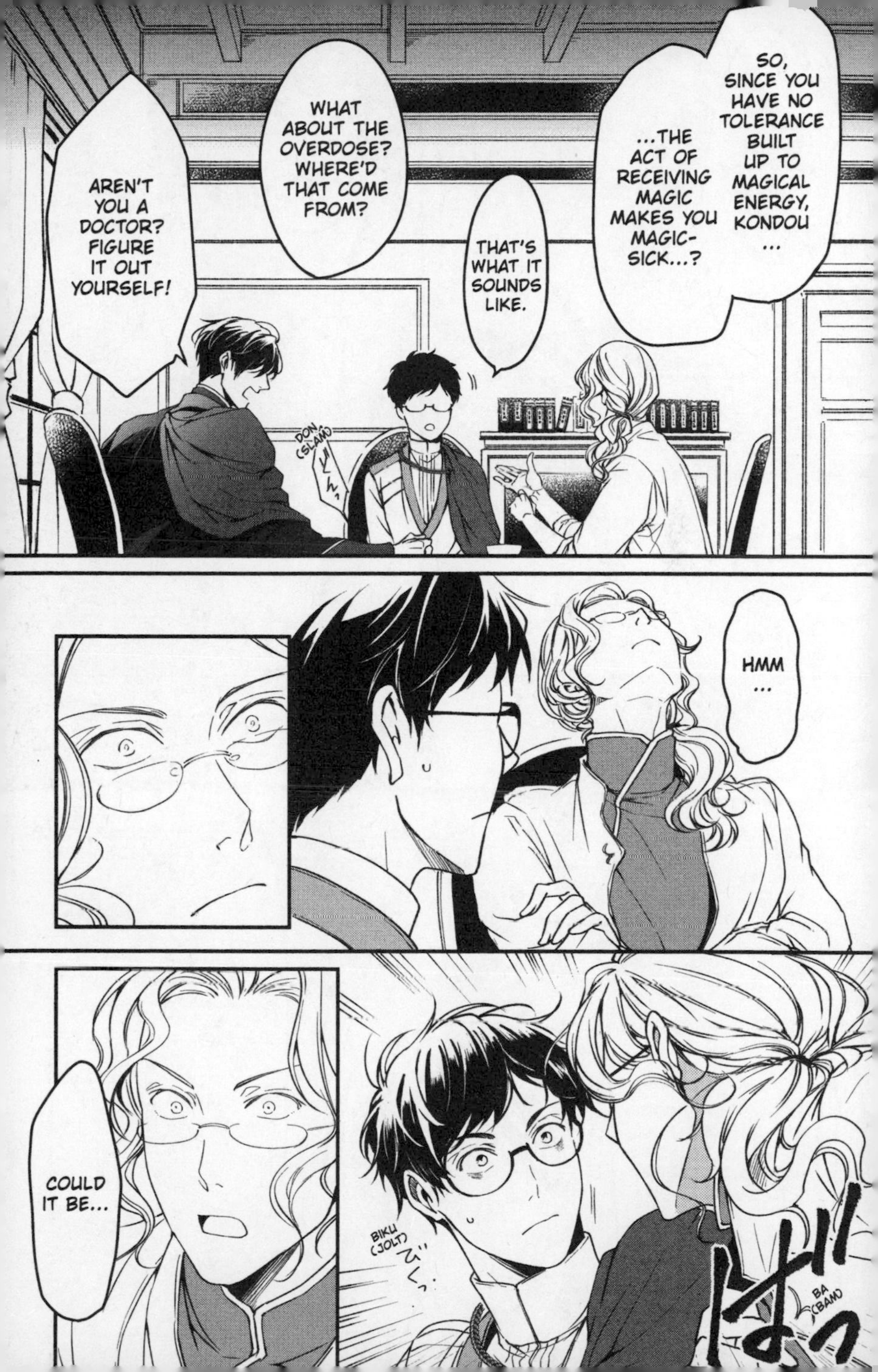
SO, SINCE YOU HAVE NO TOLERANCE BUILT UP TO MAGICAL ENERGY, KONDOU...
...THE ACT OF RECEIVING MAGIC MAKES YOU MAGIC-SICK...?
THAT'S WHAT IT SOUNDS LIKE.
WHAT ABOUT THE OVERDOSE? WHERE'D THAT COME FROM?
AREN'T YOU A DOCTOR? FIGURE IT OUT YOURSELF!
DON (SLAM)
HMM...
BA (BAM)
BIKU (JOLT)
COULD IT BE...

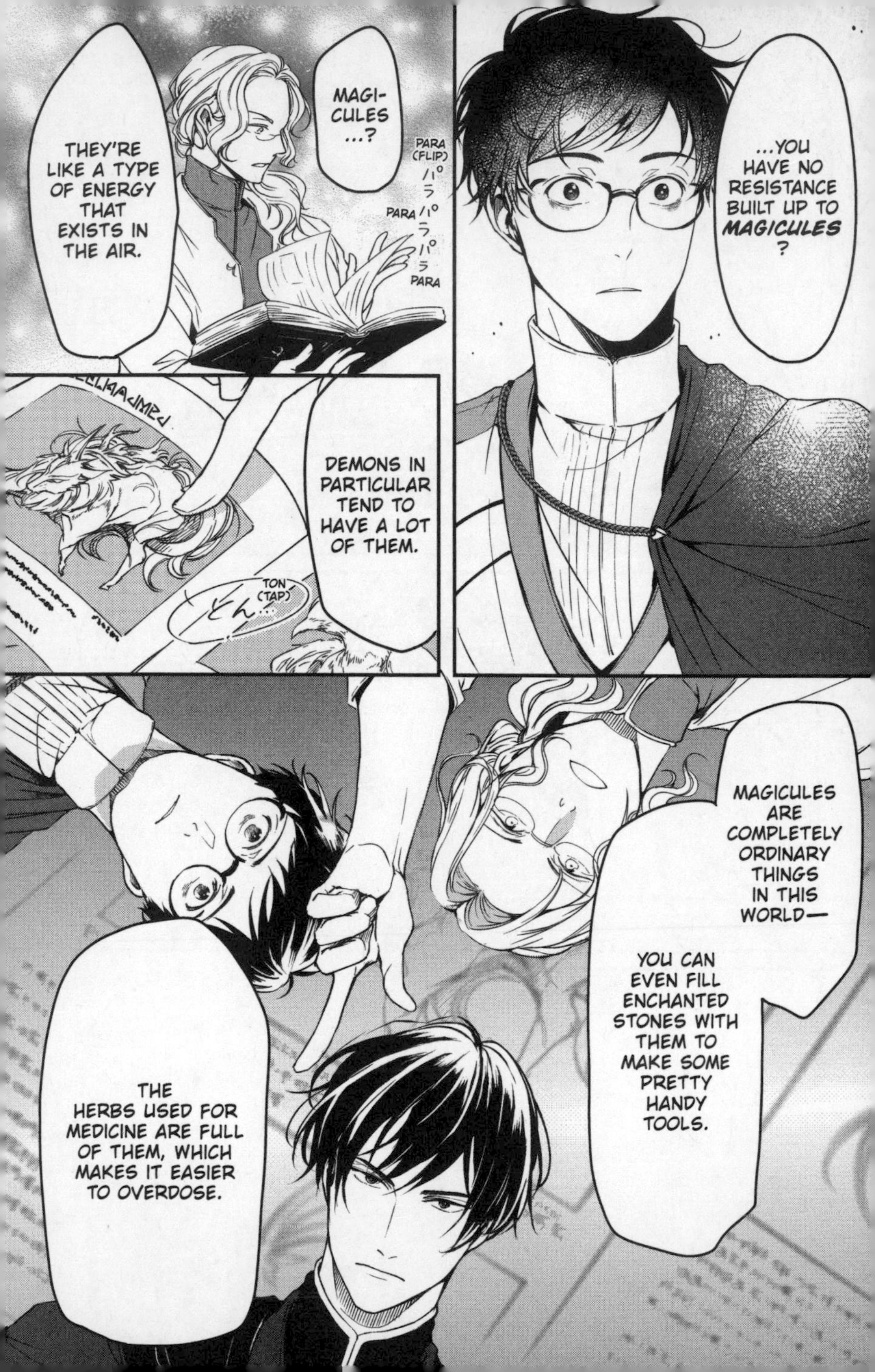
...YOU HAVE NO RESISTANCE BUILT UP TO *MAGICULES*?
MAGI-CULES ...?
PARA (FLIP) パラ
PARA パラ
パラ PARA
THEY'RE LIKE A TYPE OF ENERGY THAT EXISTS IN THE AIR.
DEMONS IN PARTICULAR TEND TO HAVE A LOT OF THEM.
TON (TAP) とん…
MAGICULES ARE COMPLETELY ORDINARY THINGS IN THIS WORLD—
YOU CAN EVEN FILL ENCHANTED STONES WITH THEM TO MAKE SOME PRETTY HANDY TOOLS.
THE HERBS USED FOR MEDICINE ARE FULL OF THEM, WHICH MAKES IT EASIER TO OVERDOSE.

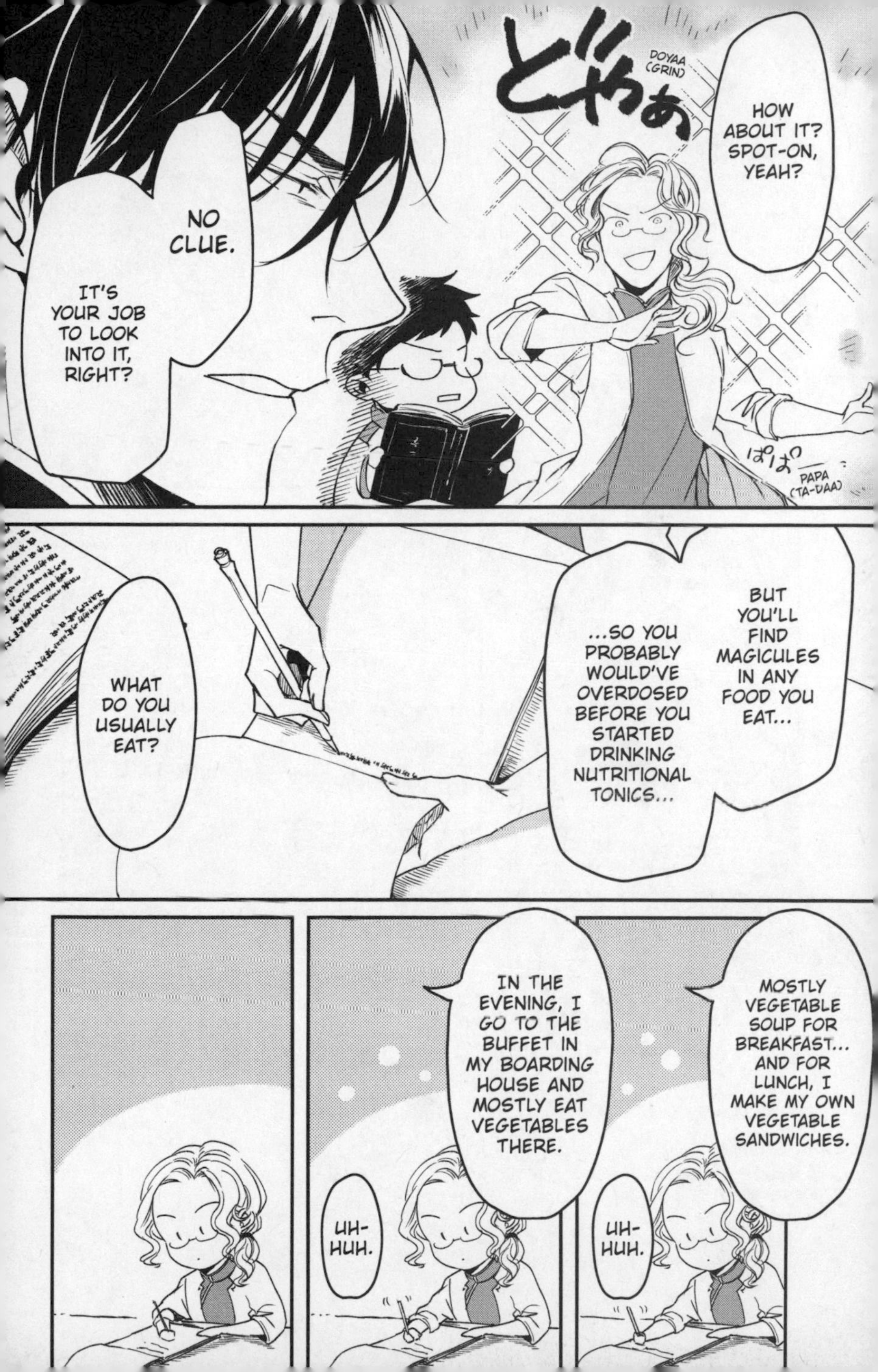
どやぁ
DOYAA (GRIN)
HOW ABOUT IT? SPOT-ON, YEAH?
ぱぱっ
PAPA (TA-DAA)
NO CLUE.
IT'S YOUR JOB TO LOOK INTO IT, RIGHT?
BUT YOU'LL FIND MAGICULES IN ANY FOOD YOU EAT...
...SO YOU PROBABLY WOULD'VE OVERDOSED BEFORE YOU STARTED DRINKING NUTRITIONAL TONICS...
WHAT DO YOU USUALLY EAT?
MOSTLY VEGETABLE SOUP FOR BREAKFAST... AND FOR LUNCH, I MAKE MY OWN VEGETABLE SANDWICHES.
UH-HUH.
IN THE EVENING, I GO TO THE BUFFET IN MY BOARDING HOUSE AND MOSTLY EAT VEGETABLES THERE.
UH-HUH.

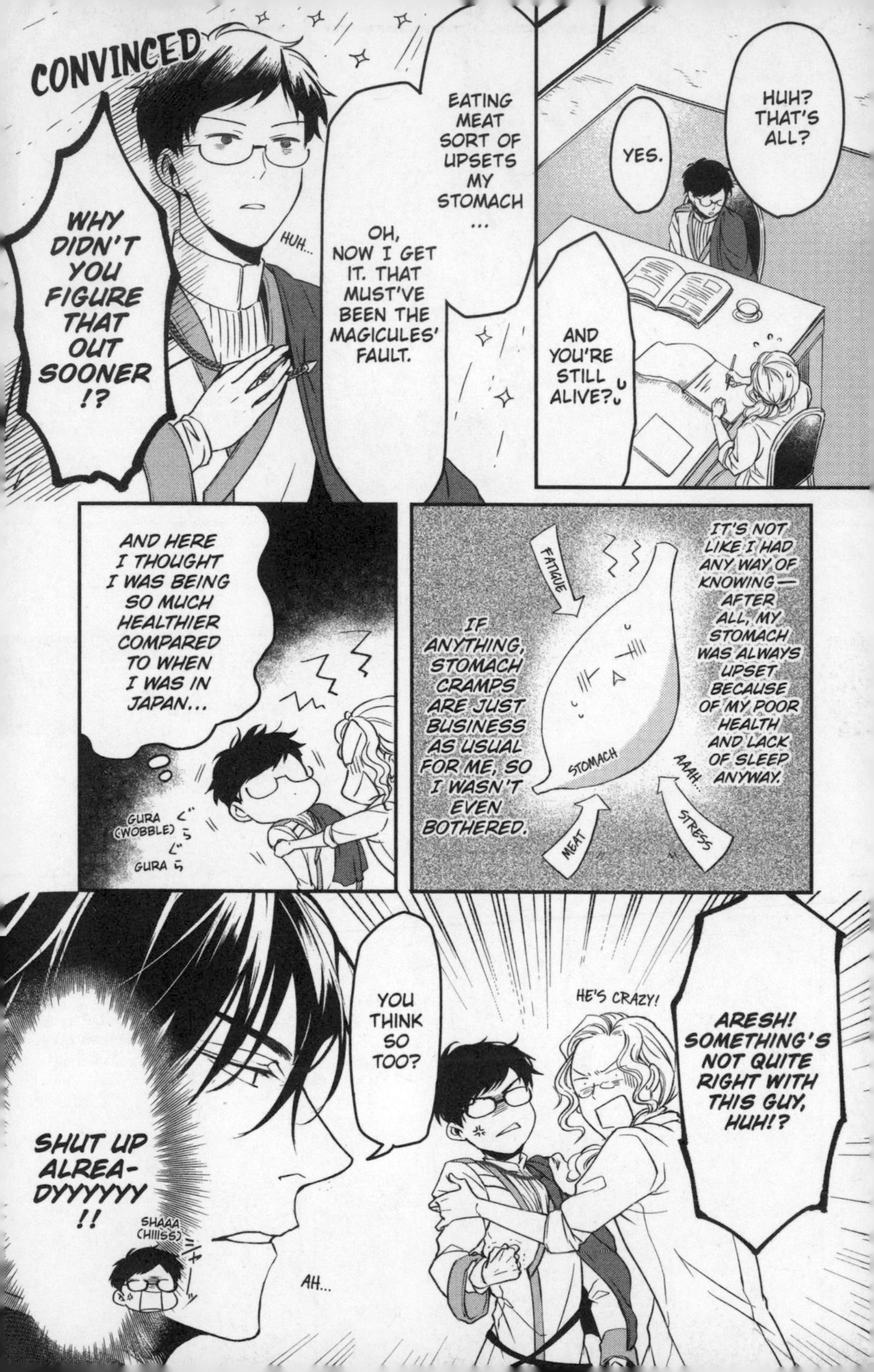
HUH? THAT'S ALL?
YES.
AND YOU'RE STILL ALIVE?
EATING MEAT SORT OF UPSETS MY STOMACH...
OH, NOW I GET IT. THAT MUST'VE BEEN THE MAGICULES' FAULT.
HUH...
CONVINCED
WHY DIDN'T YOU FIGURE THAT OUT SOONER!?
IT'S NOT LIKE I HAD ANY WAY OF KNOWING—AFTER ALL, MY STOMACH WAS ALWAYS UPSET BECAUSE OF MY POOR HEALTH AND LACK OF SLEEP ANYWAY.
FATIGUE
AAAH...
STOMACH
STRESS
MEAT
IF ANYTHING, STOMACH CRAMPS ARE JUST BUSINESS AS USUAL FOR ME, SO I WASN'T EVEN BOTHERED.
AND HERE I THOUGHT I WAS BEING SO MUCH HEALTHIER COMPARED TO WHEN I WAS IN JAPAN...
GURA (WOBBLE)
GURA
ARESH! SOMETHING'S NOT QUITE RIGHT WITH THIS GUY, HUH!?
HE'S CRAZY!
YOU THINK SO TOO?
AH...
SHUT UP ALREA-DYYYYYY!!
SHAAA (HIIISS)

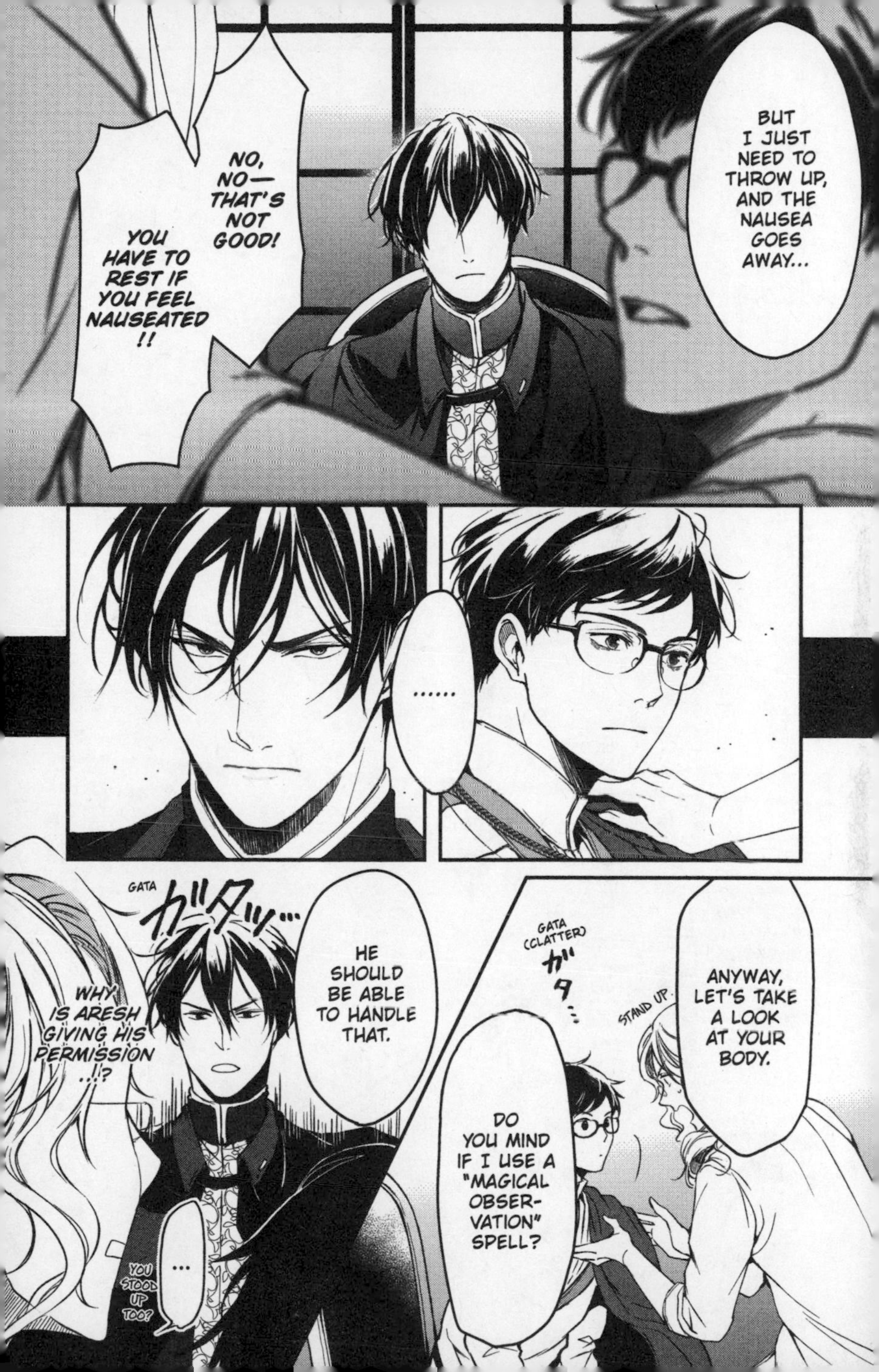
BUT I JUST NEED TO THROW UP, AND THE NAUSEA GOES AWAY...
NO, NO—THAT'S NOT GOOD!
YOU HAVE TO REST IF YOU FEEL NAUSEATED !!
......
ANYWAY, LET'S TAKE A LOOK AT YOUR BODY.
GATA (CLATTER)
ガタ…
STAND UP.
DO YOU MIND IF I USE A "MAGICAL OBSER-VATION" SPELL?
GATA
ガタッ…
HE SHOULD BE ABLE TO HANDLE THAT.
WHY IS ARESH GIVING HIS PERMISSION ..!?
...
YOU STOOD UP TOO?

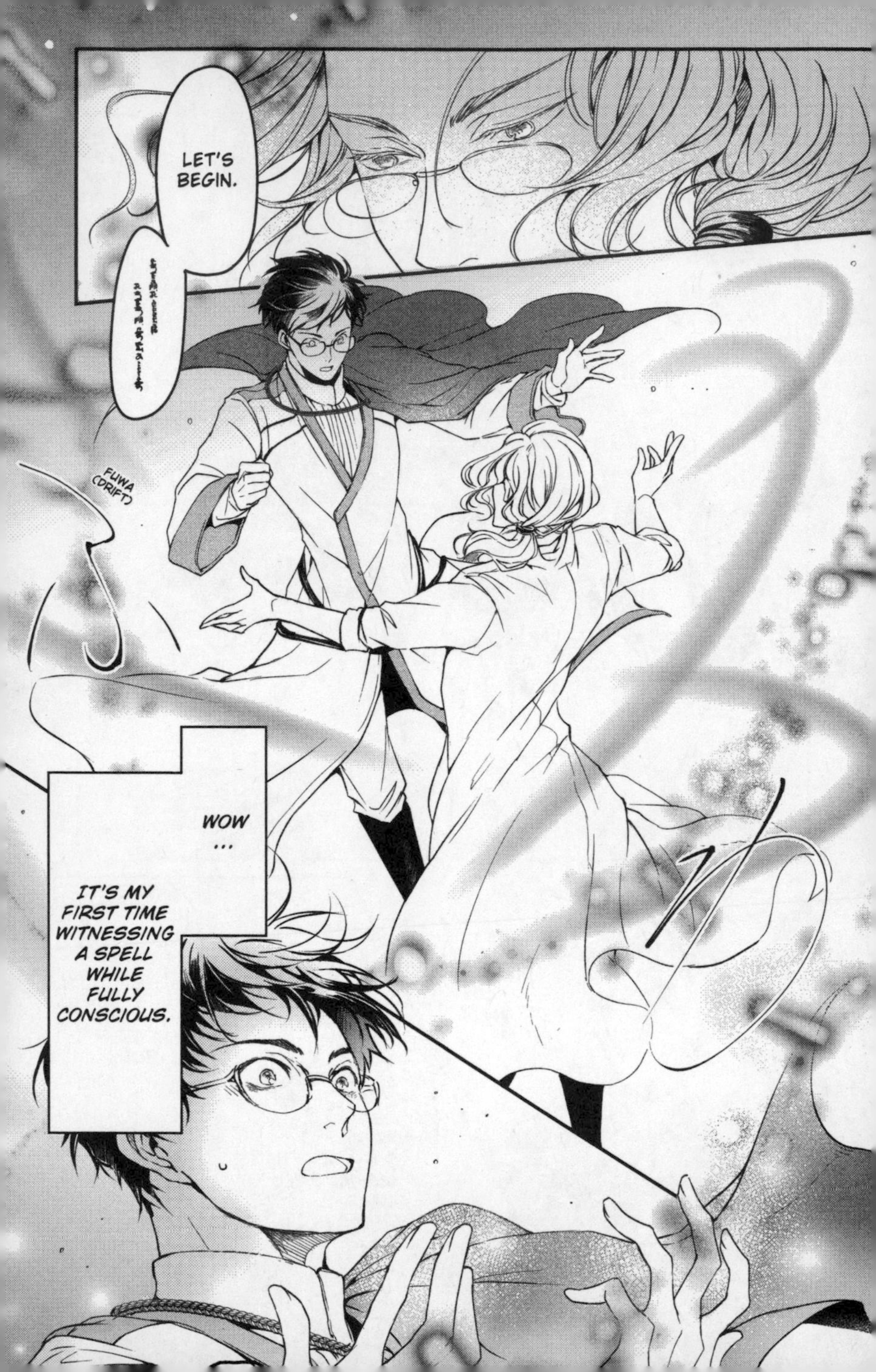
LET'S BEGIN.
FUWA (DRIFT)
WOW ...
IT'S MY FIRST TIME WITNESSING A SPELL WHILE FULLY CONSCIOUS.

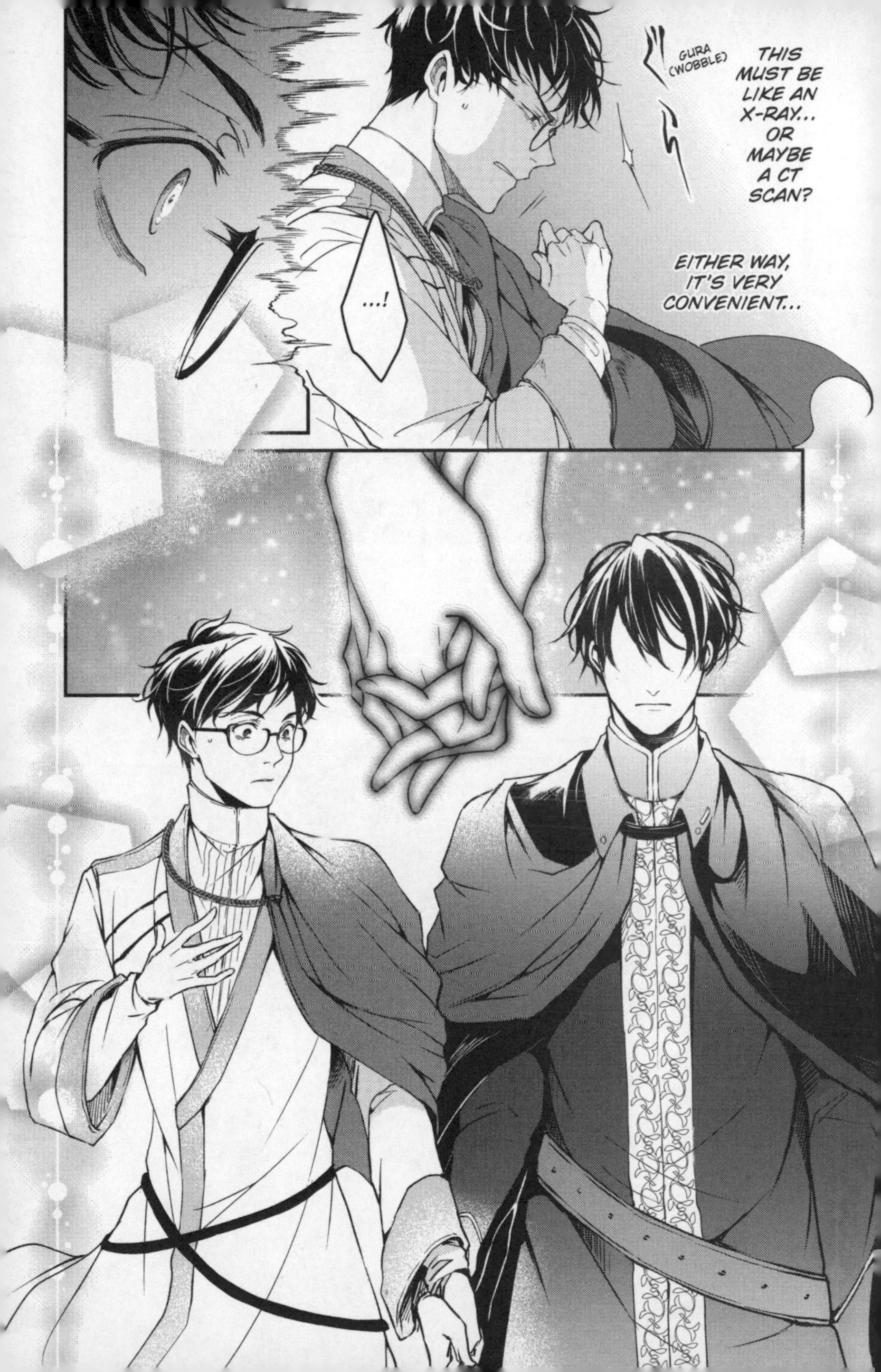
THIS MUST BE LIKE AN X-RAY... OR MAYBE A CT SCAN?
GURA (WOBBLE)
EITHER WAY, IT'S VERY CONVENIENT...
...!

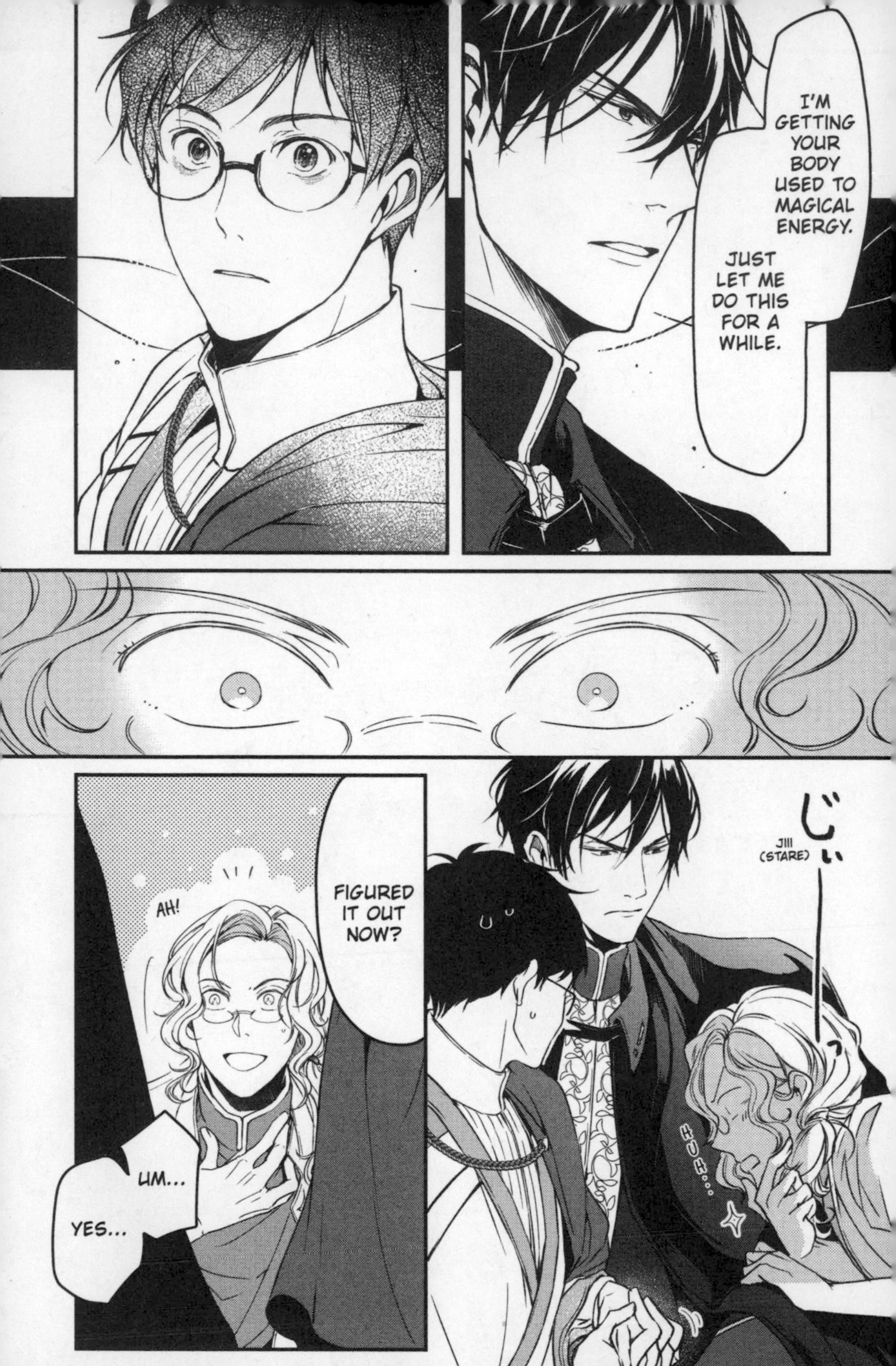
I'M GETTING YOUR BODY USED TO MAGICAL ENERGY.
JUST LET ME DO THIS FOR A WHILE.
じい
JIII (STARE)
HUH...
FIGURED IT OUT NOW?
AH!
UM...
YES...

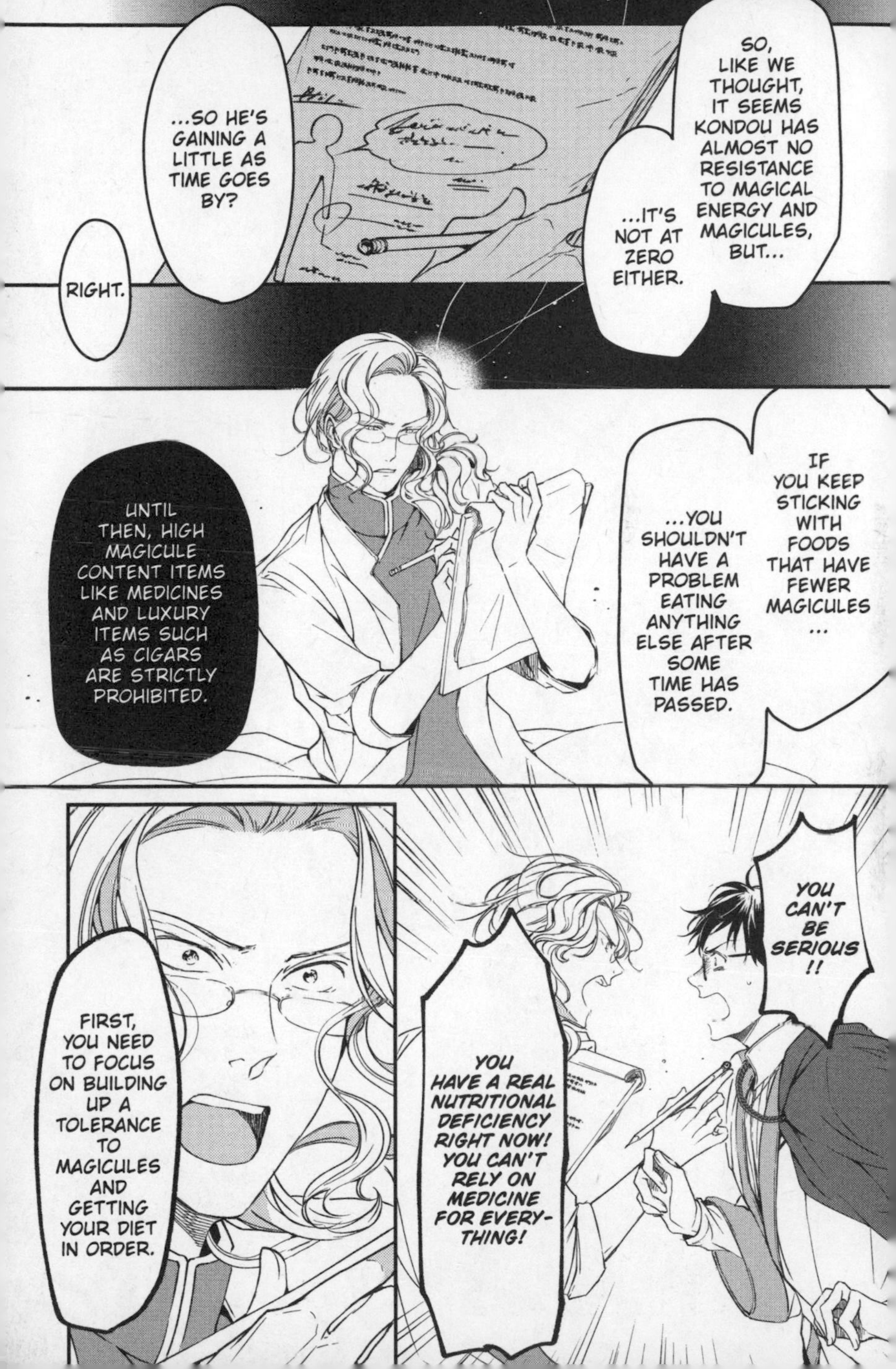
SO, LIKE WE THOUGHT, IT SEEMS KONDOU HAS ALMOST NO RESISTANCE TO MAGICAL ENERGY AND MAGICULES, BUT...
...IT'S NOT AT ZERO EITHER.
...SO HE'S GAINING A LITTLE AS TIME GOES BY?
RIGHT.
IF YOU KEEP STICKING WITH FOODS THAT HAVE FEWER MAGICULES...
...YOU SHOULDN'T HAVE A PROBLEM EATING ANYTHING ELSE AFTER SOME TIME HAS PASSED.
UNTIL THEN, HIGH MAGICULE CONTENT ITEMS LIKE MEDICINES AND LUXURY ITEMS SUCH AS CIGARS ARE STRICTLY PROHIBITED.
YOU CAN'T BE SERIOUS!!
YOU HAVE A REAL NUTRITIONAL DEFICIENCY RIGHT NOW! YOU CAN'T RELY ON MEDICINE FOR EVERY-THING!
FIRST, YOU NEED TO FOCUS ON BUILDING UP A TOLERANCE TO MAGICULES AND GETTING YOUR DIET IN ORDER.

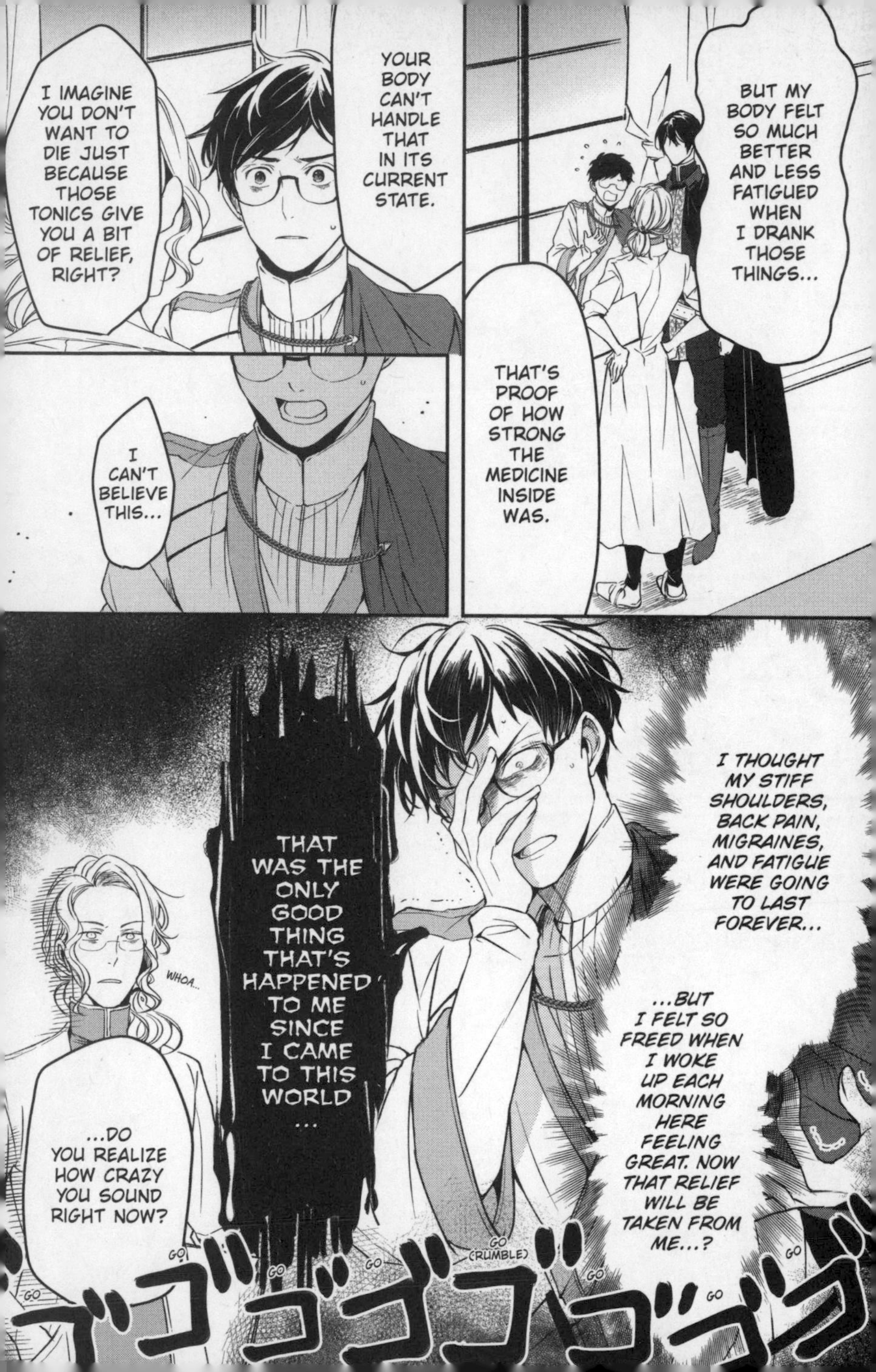
BUT MY BODY FELT SO MUCH BETTER AND LESS FATIGUED WHEN I DRANK THOSE THINGS...
THAT'S PROOF OF HOW STRONG THE MEDICINE INSIDE WAS.
YOUR BODY CAN'T HANDLE THAT IN ITS CURRENT STATE.
I IMAGINE YOU DON'T WANT TO DIE JUST BECAUSE THOSE TONICS GIVE YOU A BIT OF RELIEF, RIGHT?
I CAN'T BELIEVE THIS...
I THOUGHT MY STIFF SHOULDERS, BACK PAIN, MIGRAINES, AND FATIGUE WERE GOING TO LAST FOREVER...
...BUT I FELT SO FREED WHEN I WOKE UP EACH MORNING HERE FEELING GREAT. NOW THAT RELIEF WILL BE TAKEN FROM ME...?
THAT WAS THE ONLY GOOD THING THAT'S HAPPENED TO ME SINCE I CAME TO THIS WORLD...
WHOA...
...DO YOU REALIZE HOW CRAZY YOU SOUND RIGHT NOW?
GO GO GO GO GO GO GO GO
GO (RUMBLE)

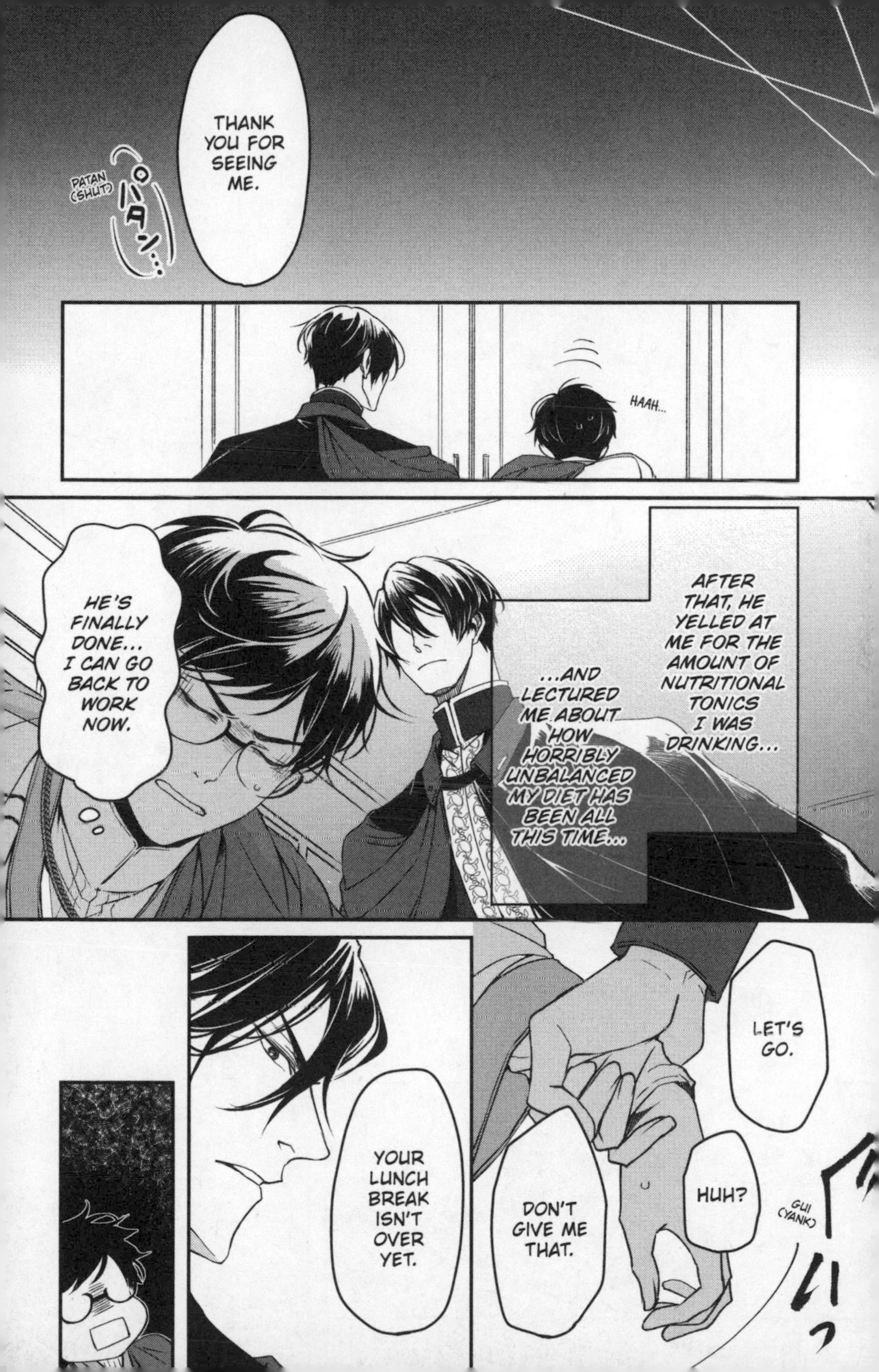
THANK YOU FOR SEEING ME.
パタン…
PATAN (SHUT)
HAAH...
AFTER THAT, HE YELLED AT ME FOR THE AMOUNT OF NUTRITIONAL TONICS I WAS DRINKING...
...AND LECTURED ME ABOUT HOW HORRIBLY UNBALANCED MY DIET HAS BEEN ALL THIS TIME...
HE'S FINALLY DONE... I CAN GO BACK TO WORK NOW.
LET'S GO.
GUI (YANK)
HUH?
DON'T GIVE ME THAT.
YOUR LUNCH BREAK ISN'T OVER YET.

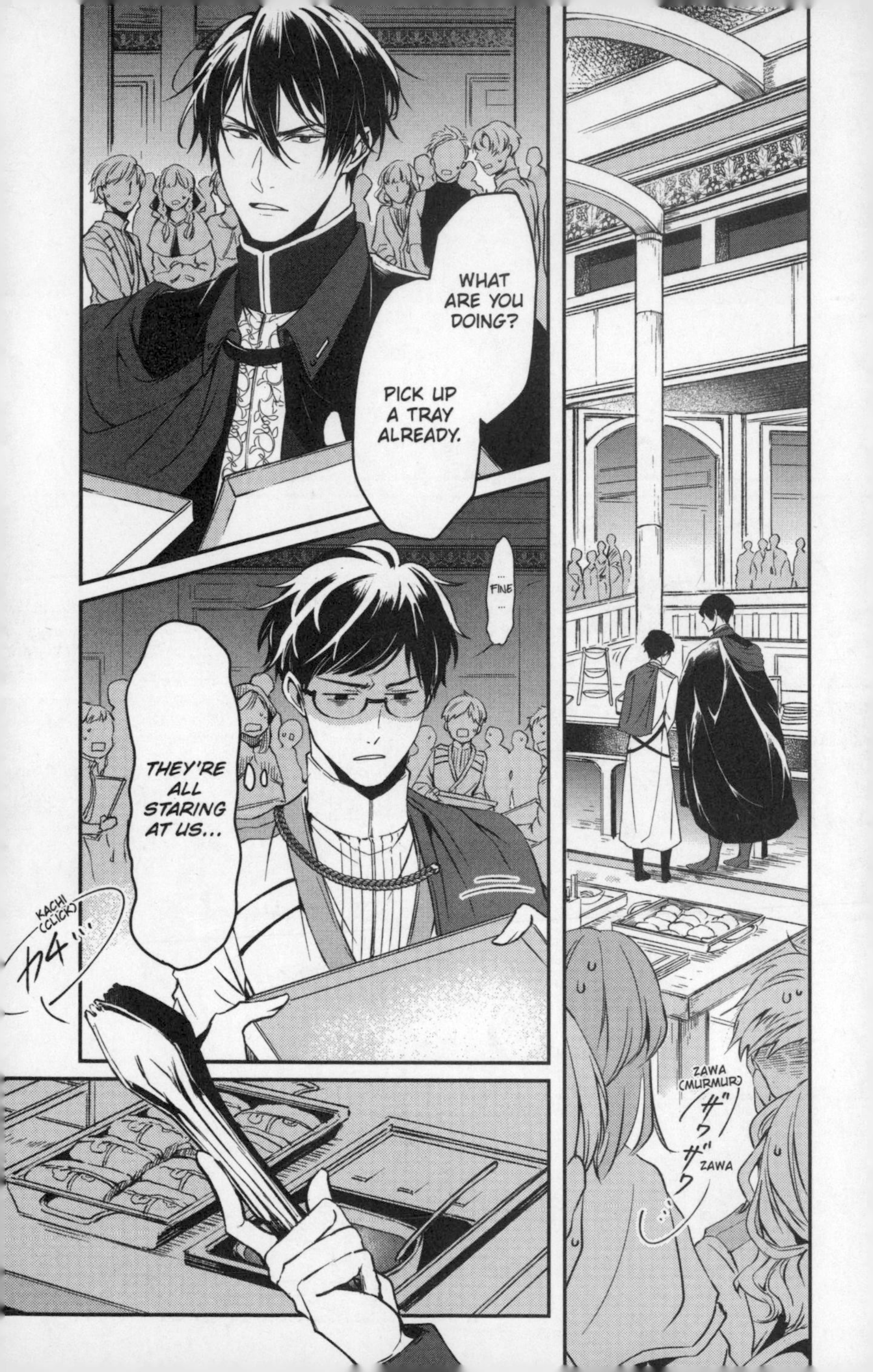
ZAWA (MURMUR)
ザワザワ
ZAWA
WHAT ARE YOU DOING?
PICK UP A TRAY ALREADY.
...FINE...
THEY'RE ALL STARING AT US...
KACHI (CLICK)
カチ

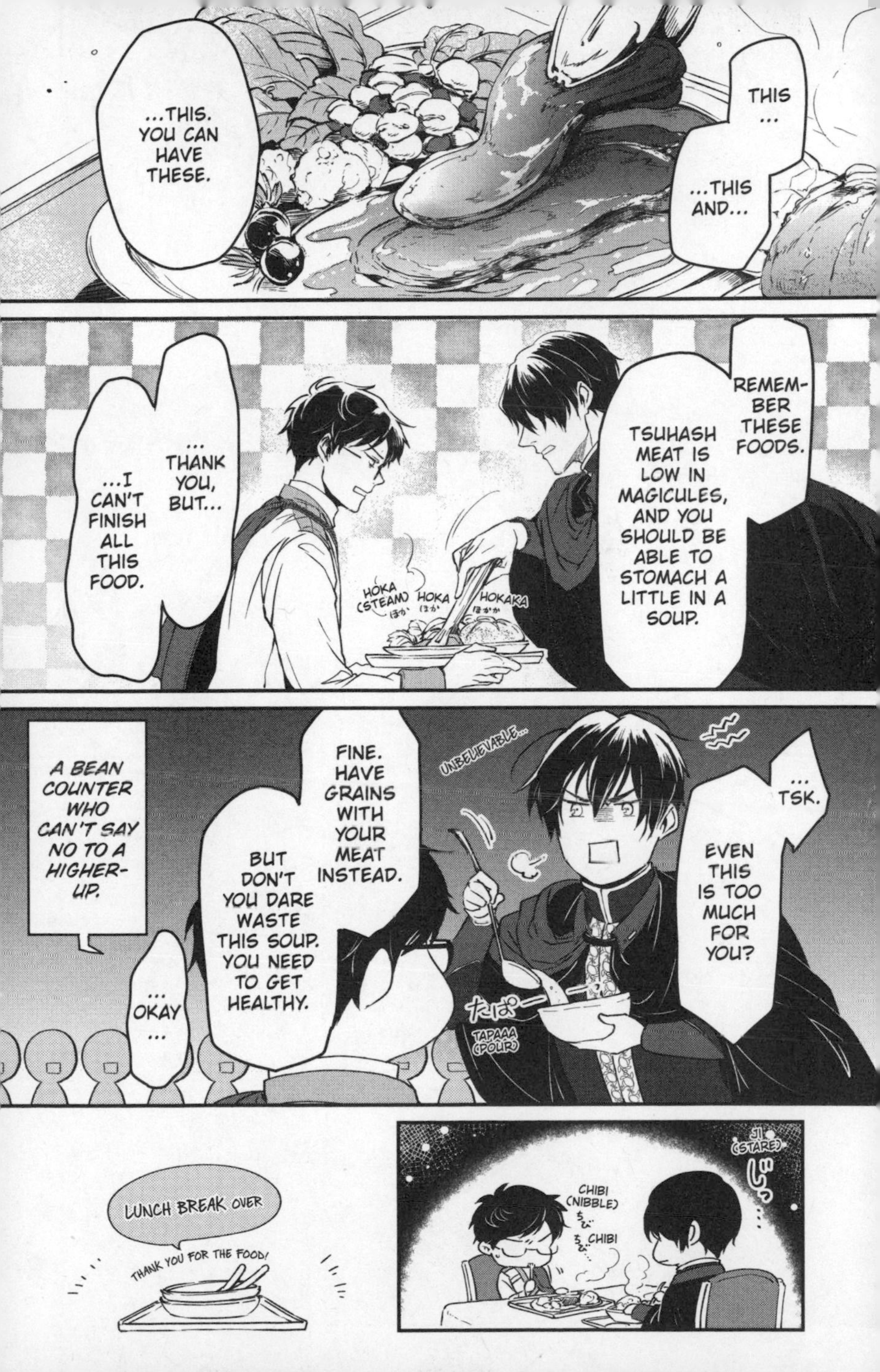
THIS ...
...THIS AND...
...THIS. YOU CAN HAVE THESE.
REMEMBER THESE FOODS.
TSUHASH MEAT IS LOW IN MAGICULES, AND YOU SHOULD BE ABLE TO STOMACH A LITTLE IN A SOUP.
HOKAKA
HOKA
HOKA (STEAM)
... THANK YOU, BUT...
...I CAN'T FINISH ALL THIS FOOD.
... TSK.
EVEN THIS IS TOO MUCH FOR YOU?
UNBELIEVABLE...
FINE. HAVE GRAINS WITH YOUR MEAT INSTEAD.
BUT DON'T YOU DARE WASTE THIS SOUP. YOU NEED TO GET HEALTHY.
TAPAAA (POUR)
... OKAY ...
A BEAN COUNTER WHO CAN'T SAY NO TO A HIGHER-UP.
JI (STARE)
CHIBI (NIBBLE)
CHIBI
LUNCH BREAK OVER
THANK YOU FOR THE FOOD!

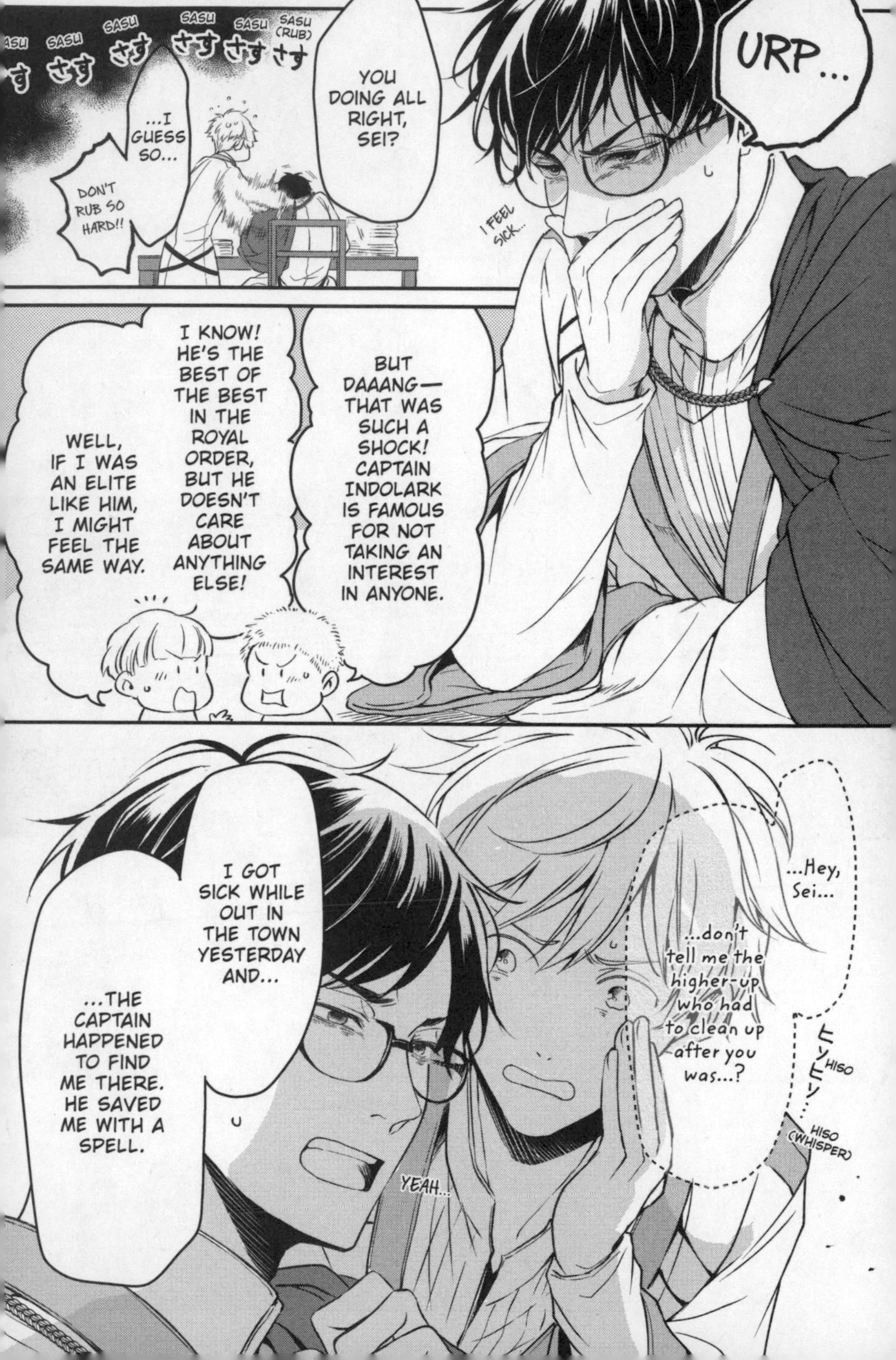
URP...
I FEEL SICK...
SASU SASU SASU SASU SASU SASU (RUB)
す さす さす さすさすさす
YOU DOING ALL RIGHT, SEI?
...I GUESS SO...
DON'T RUB SO HARD!!
BUT DAAANG—THAT WAS SUCH A SHOCK! CAPTAIN INDOLARK IS FAMOUS FOR NOT TAKING AN INTEREST IN ANYONE.
I KNOW! HE'S THE BEST OF THE BEST IN THE ROYAL ORDER, BUT HE DOESN'T CARE ABOUT ANYTHING ELSE!
WELL, IF I WAS AN ELITE LIKE HIM, I MIGHT FEEL THE SAME WAY.
...Hey, Sei...
...don't tell me the higher-up who had to clean up after you was...?
ヒソヒソ
HISO HISO (WHISPER)
I GOT SICK WHILE OUT IN THE TOWN YESTERDAY AND...
...THE CAPTAIN HAPPENED TO FIND ME THERE. HE SAVED ME WITH A SPELL.
YEAH...

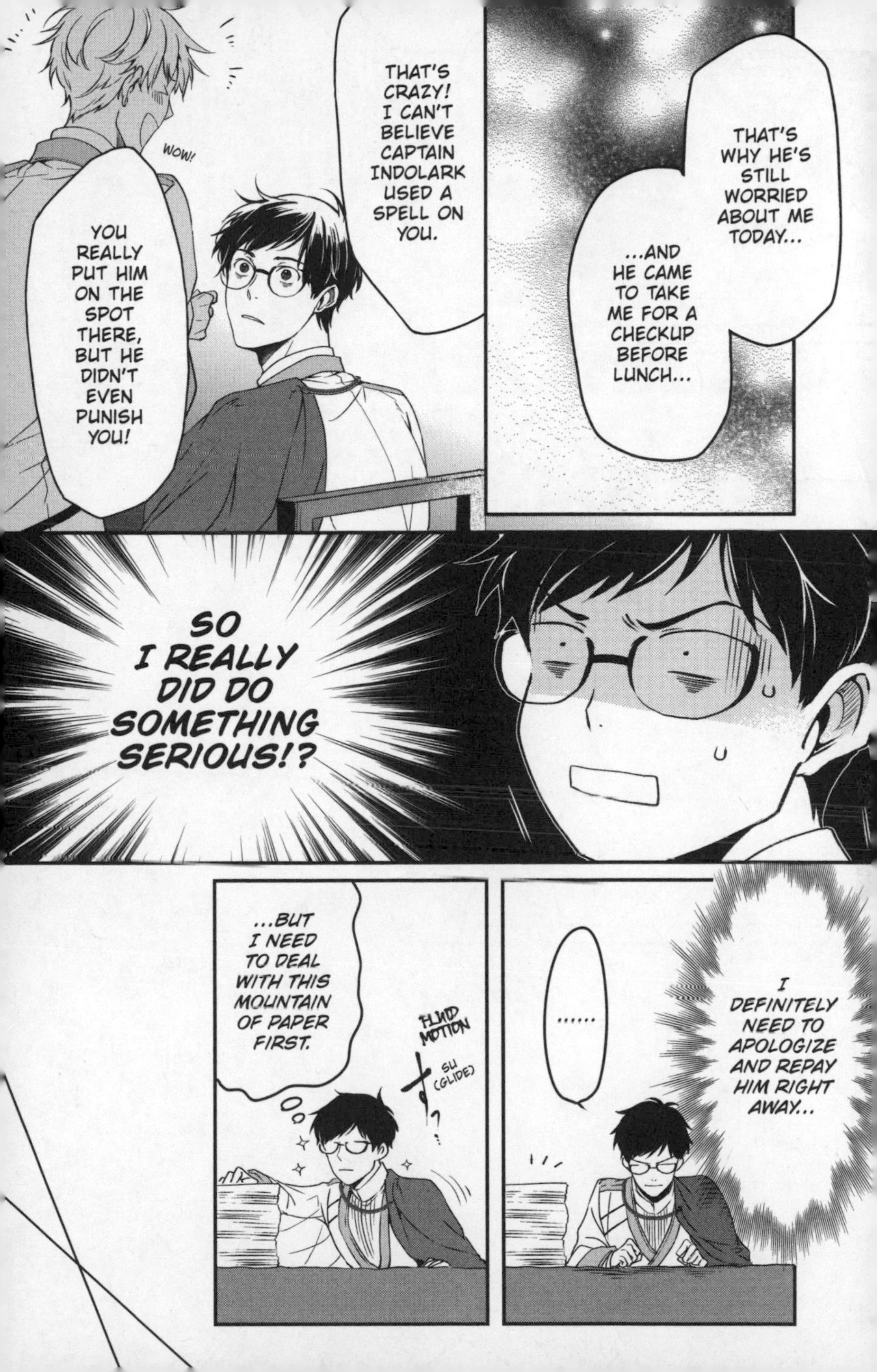

THAT'S WHY HE'S STILL WORRIED ABOUT ME TODAY...
...AND HE CAME TO TAKE ME FOR A CHECKUP BEFORE LUNCH...
THAT'S CRAZY! I CAN'T BELIEVE CAPTAIN INDOLARK USED A SPELL ON YOU.
WOW!
YOU REALLY PUT HIM ON THE SPOT THERE, BUT HE DIDN'T EVEN PUNISH YOU!
SO I REALLY DID DO SOMETHING SERIOUS!?
I DEFINITELY NEED TO APOLOGIZE AND REPAY HIM RIGHT AWAY...
......
...BUT I NEED TO DEAL WITH THIS MOUNTAIN OF PAPER FIRST.
FLUID MOTION
SU (GLIDE)

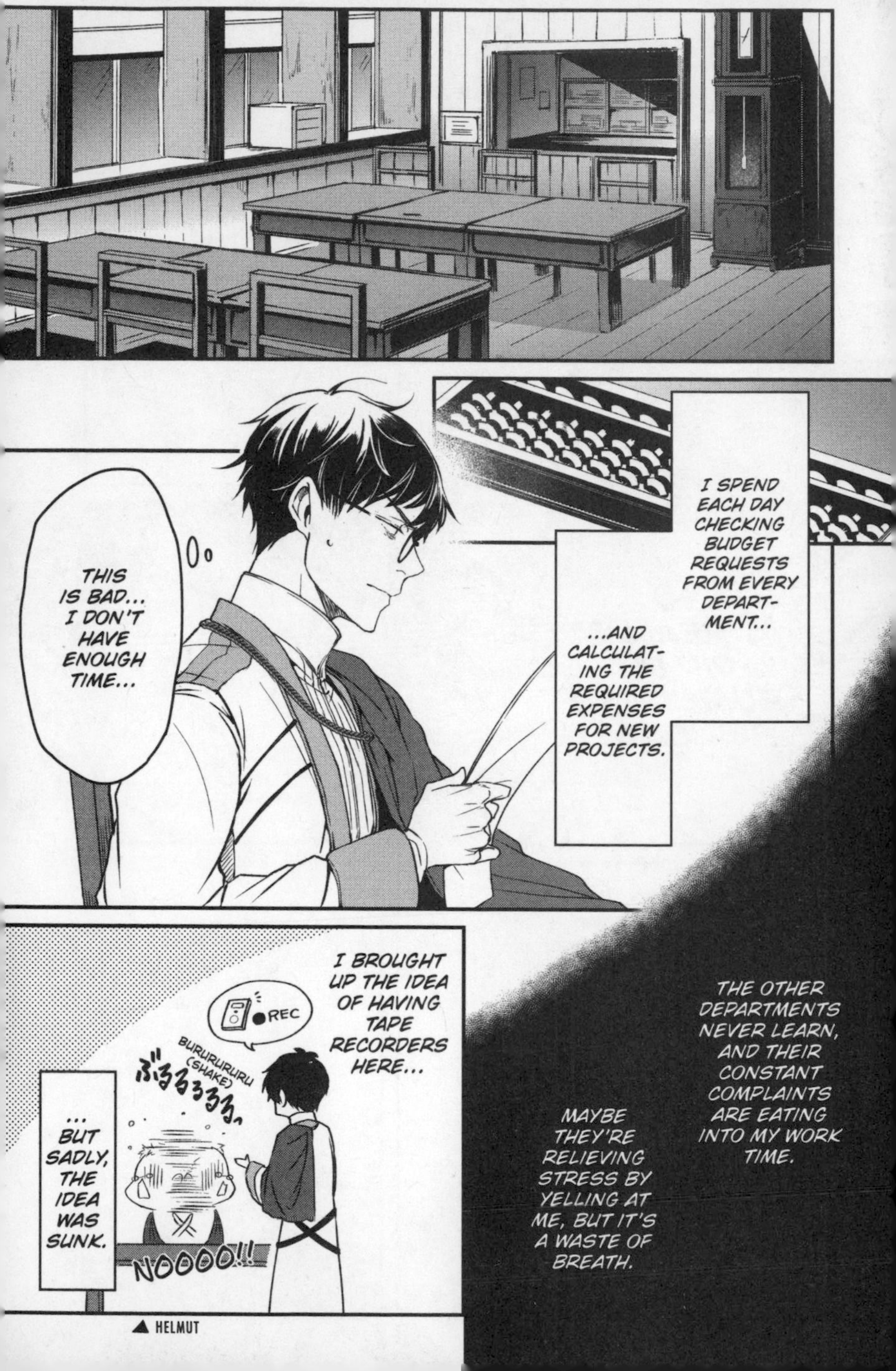
I SPEND EACH DAY CHECKING BUDGET REQUESTS FROM EVERY DEPARTMENT...
...AND CALCULATING THE REQUIRED EXPENSES FOR NEW PROJECTS.
THIS IS BAD... I DON'T HAVE ENOUGH TIME...
THE OTHER DEPARTMENTS NEVER LEARN, AND THEIR CONSTANT COMPLAINTS ARE EATING INTO MY WORK TIME.
MAYBE THEY'RE RELIEVING STRESS BY YELLING AT ME, BUT IT'S A WASTE OF BREATH.
I BROUGHT UP THE IDEA OF HAVING TAPE RECORDERS HERE...
REC
BURURURURU (SHAKE)
ぶるるるる
...BUT SADLY, THE IDEA WAS SUNK.
NOOOO!!
▲ HELMUT

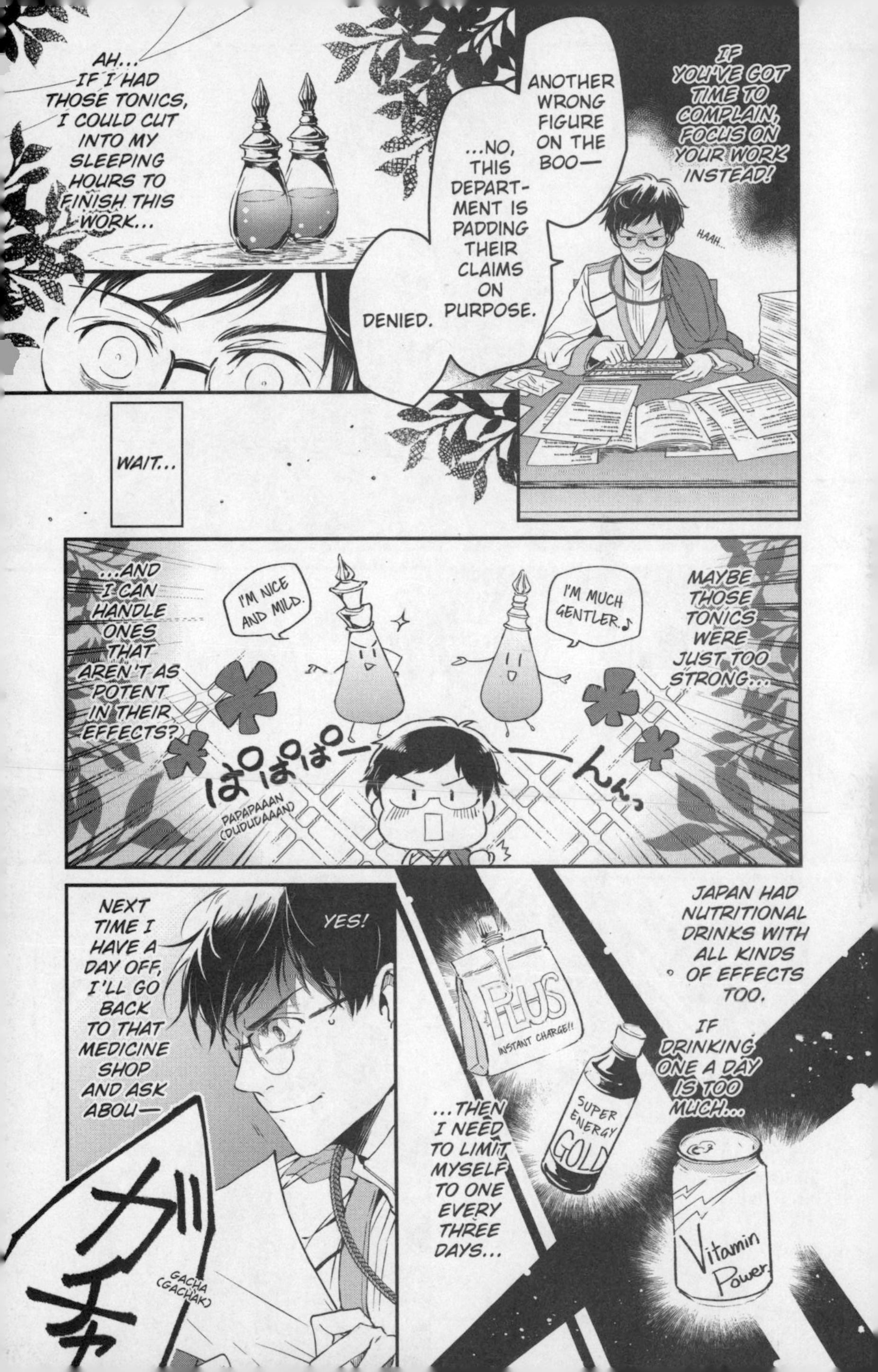
IF YOU'VE GOT TIME TO COMPLAIN, FOCUS ON YOUR WORK INSTEAD!
HAAH...
ANOTHER WRONG FIGURE ON THE BOO—
...NO, THIS DEPARTMENT IS PADDING THEIR CLAIMS ON PURPOSE.
DENIED.
AH... IF I HAD THOSE TONICS, I COULD CUT INTO MY SLEEPING HOURS TO FINISH THIS WORK...
WAIT...
MAYBE THOSE TONICS WERE JUST TOO STRONG...
I'M MUCH GENTLER.♪
I'M NICE AND MILD.
...AND I CAN HANDLE ONES THAT AREN'T AS POTENT IN THEIR EFFECTS?
ぱぱぱーーんっ
PAPAPAAAN (DUDUDAAAN)
JAPAN HAD NUTRITIONAL DRINKS WITH ALL KINDS OF EFFECTS TOO.
IF DRINKING ONE A DAY IS TOO MUCH...
...THEN I NEED TO LIMIT MYSELF TO ONE EVERY THREE DAYS...
PLUS
INSTANT CHARGE!!
SUPER ENERGY GOLD
Vitamin Power
YES!
NEXT TIME I HAVE A DAY OFF, I'LL GO BACK TO THAT MEDICINE SHOP AND ASK ABOU—
ガチャ
GACHA (GACHAK)

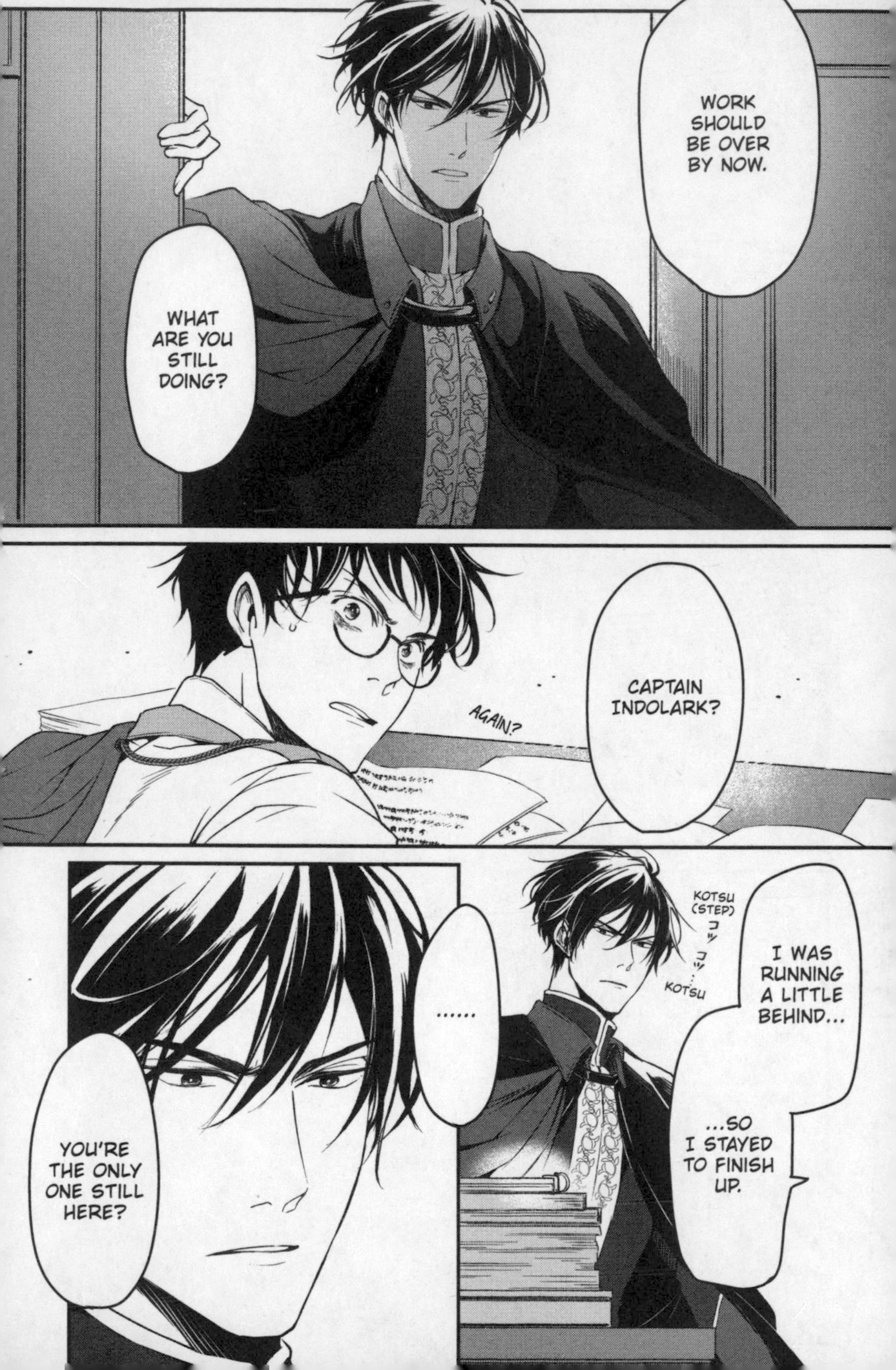
WORK SHOULD BE OVER BY NOW.
WHAT ARE YOU STILL DOING?
CAPTAIN INDOLARK?
AGAIN?
KOTSU (STEP)
コツ
コツ
KOTSU
I WAS RUNNING A LITTLE BEHIND...
...SO I STAYED TO FINISH UP.
......
YOU'RE THE ONLY ONE STILL HERE?

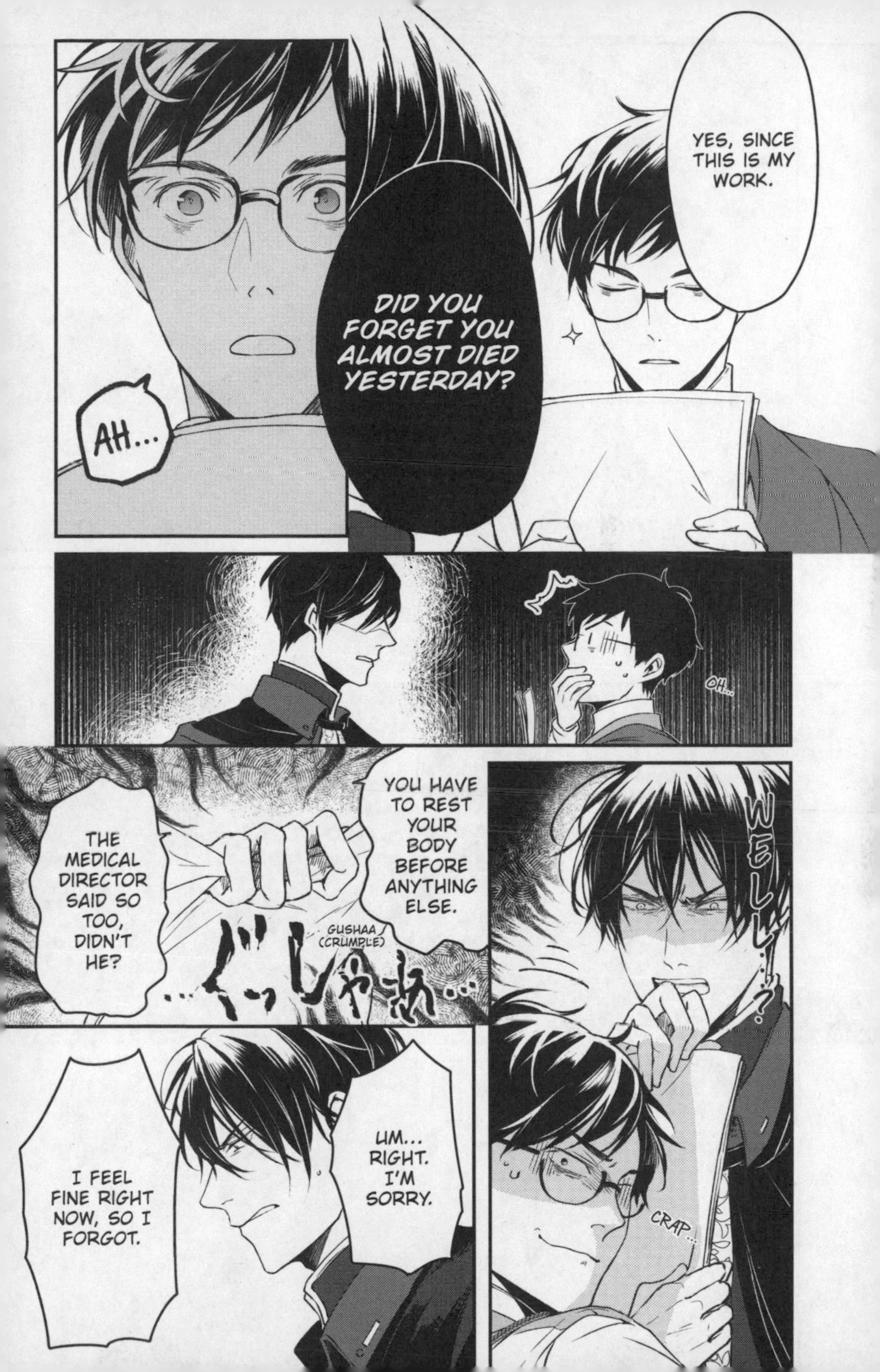
YES, SINCE THIS IS MY WORK.
DID YOU FORGET YOU ALMOST DIED YESTERDAY?
AH...
OH...
WELL...?
YOU HAVE TO REST YOUR BODY BEFORE ANYTHING ELSE.
THE MEDICAL DIRECTOR SAID SO TOO, DIDN'T HE?
GUSHAA (CRUMPLE)
CRAP...
UM... RIGHT. I'M SORRY.
I FEEL FINE RIGHT NOW, SO I FORGOT.

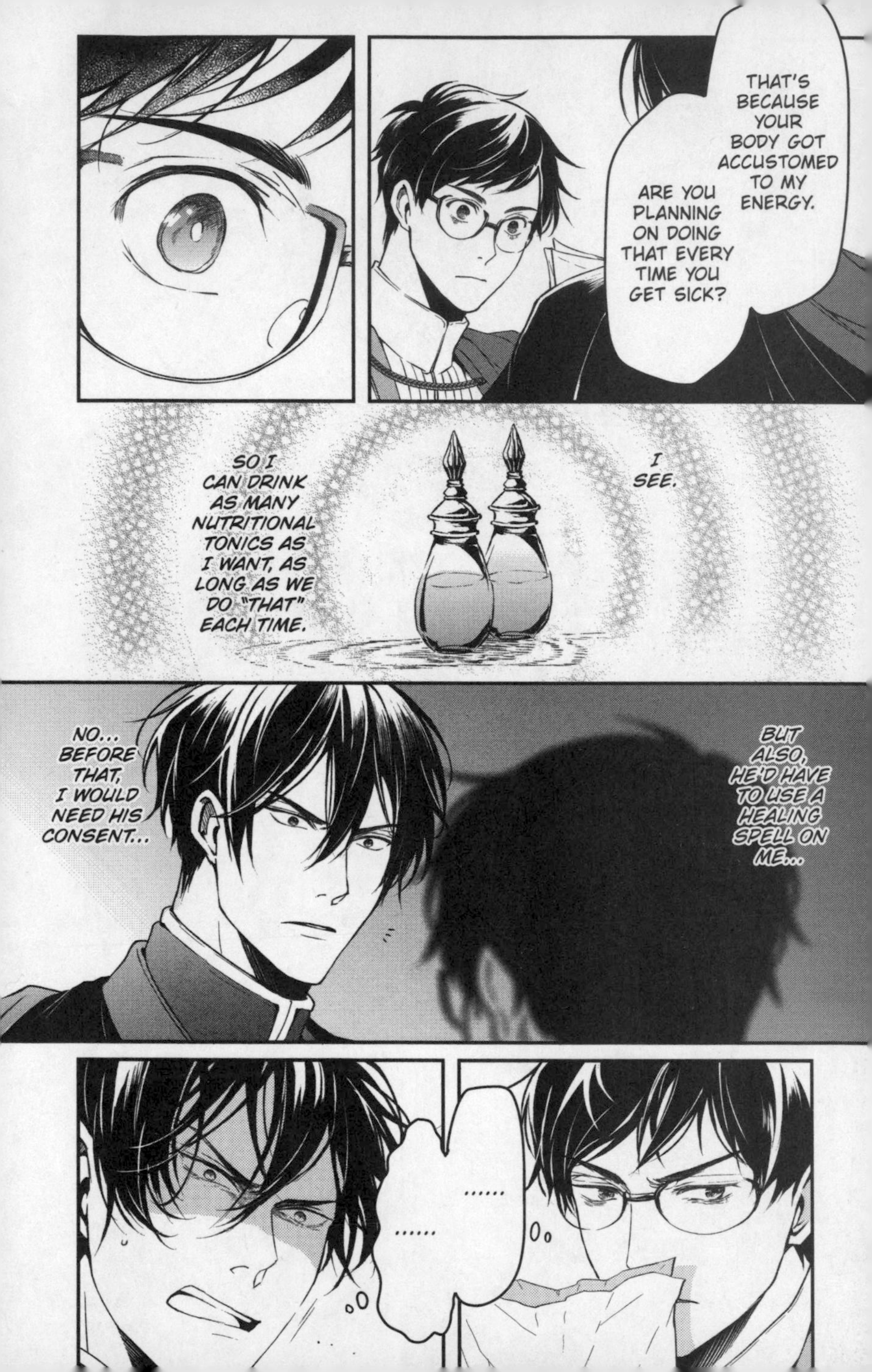
THAT'S BECAUSE YOUR BODY GOT ACCUSTOMED TO MY ENERGY.
ARE YOU PLANNING ON DOING THAT EVERY TIME YOU GET SICK?
I SEE.
SO I CAN DRINK AS MANY NUTRITIONAL TONICS AS I WANT, AS LONG AS WE DO "THAT" EACH TIME.
BUT ALSO, HE'D HAVE TO USE A HEALING SPELL ON ME...
NO... BEFORE THAT, I WOULD NEED HIS CONSENT...
......
......

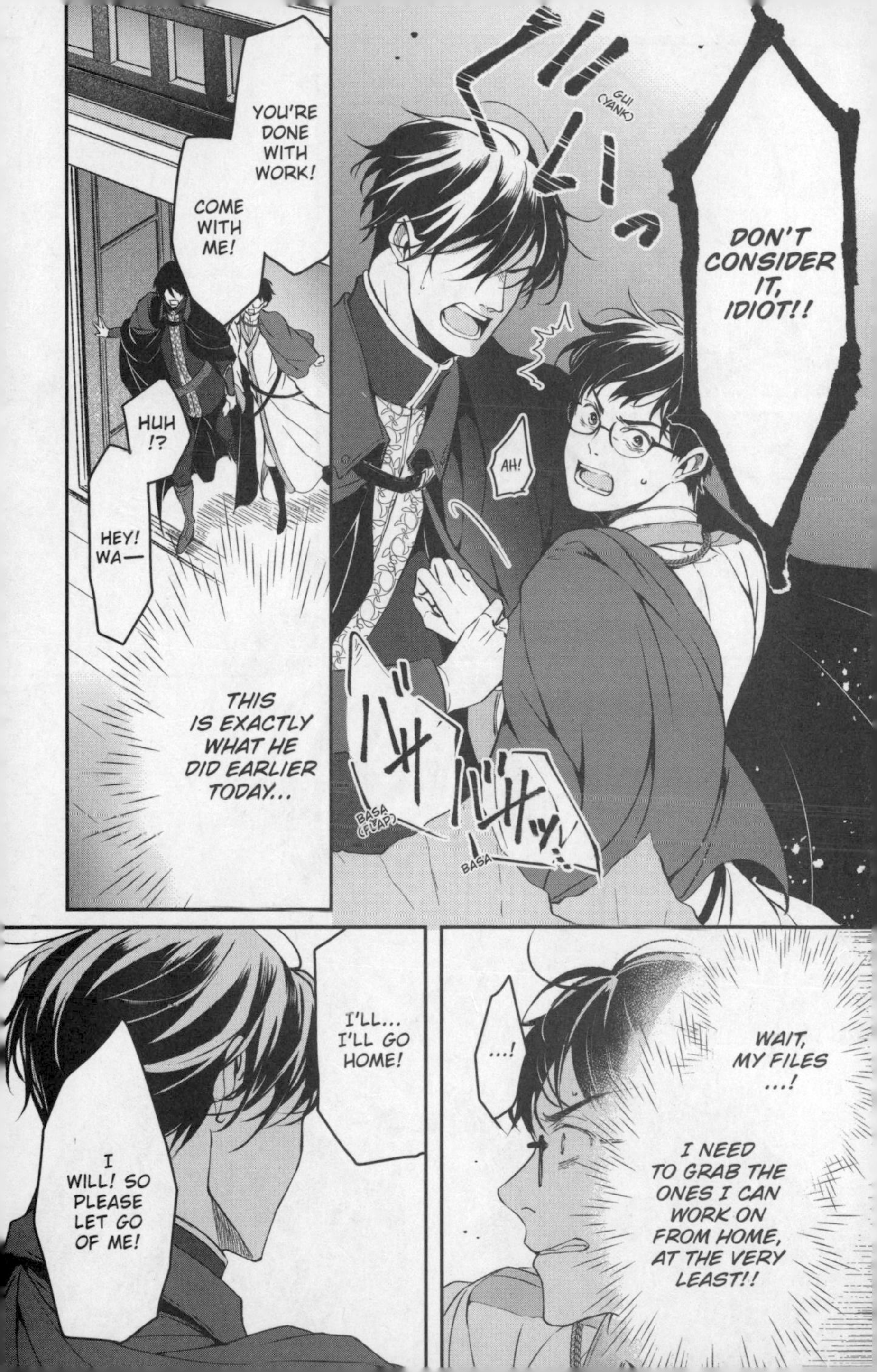
GUI (YANK)
DON'T CONSIDER IT, IDIOT!!
AH!
BASA (FLAP)
BASA
YOU'RE DONE WITH WORK!
COME WITH ME!
HUH !?
HEY! WA—
THIS IS EXACTLY WHAT HE DID EARLIER TODAY...
...!
WAIT, MY FILES ...!
I NEED TO GRAB THE ONES I CAN WORK ON FROM HOME, AT THE VERY LEAST!!
I'LL... I'LL GO HOME!
I WILL! SO PLEASE LET GO OF ME!

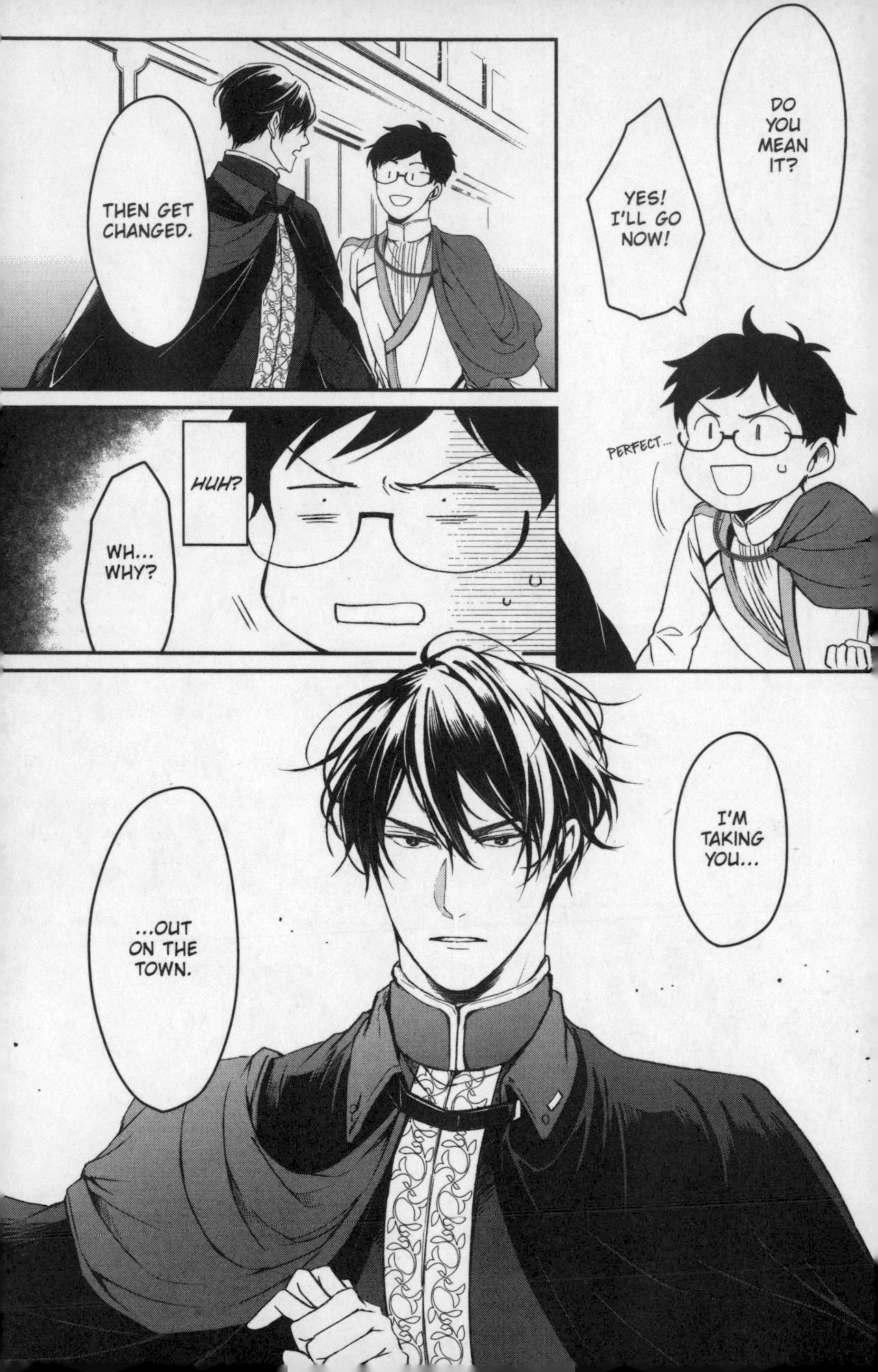
DO YOU MEAN IT?
YES! I'LL GO NOW!
PERFECT...
THEN GET CHANGED.
HUH?
WH... WHY?
I'M TAKING YOU...
...OUT ON THE TOWN.

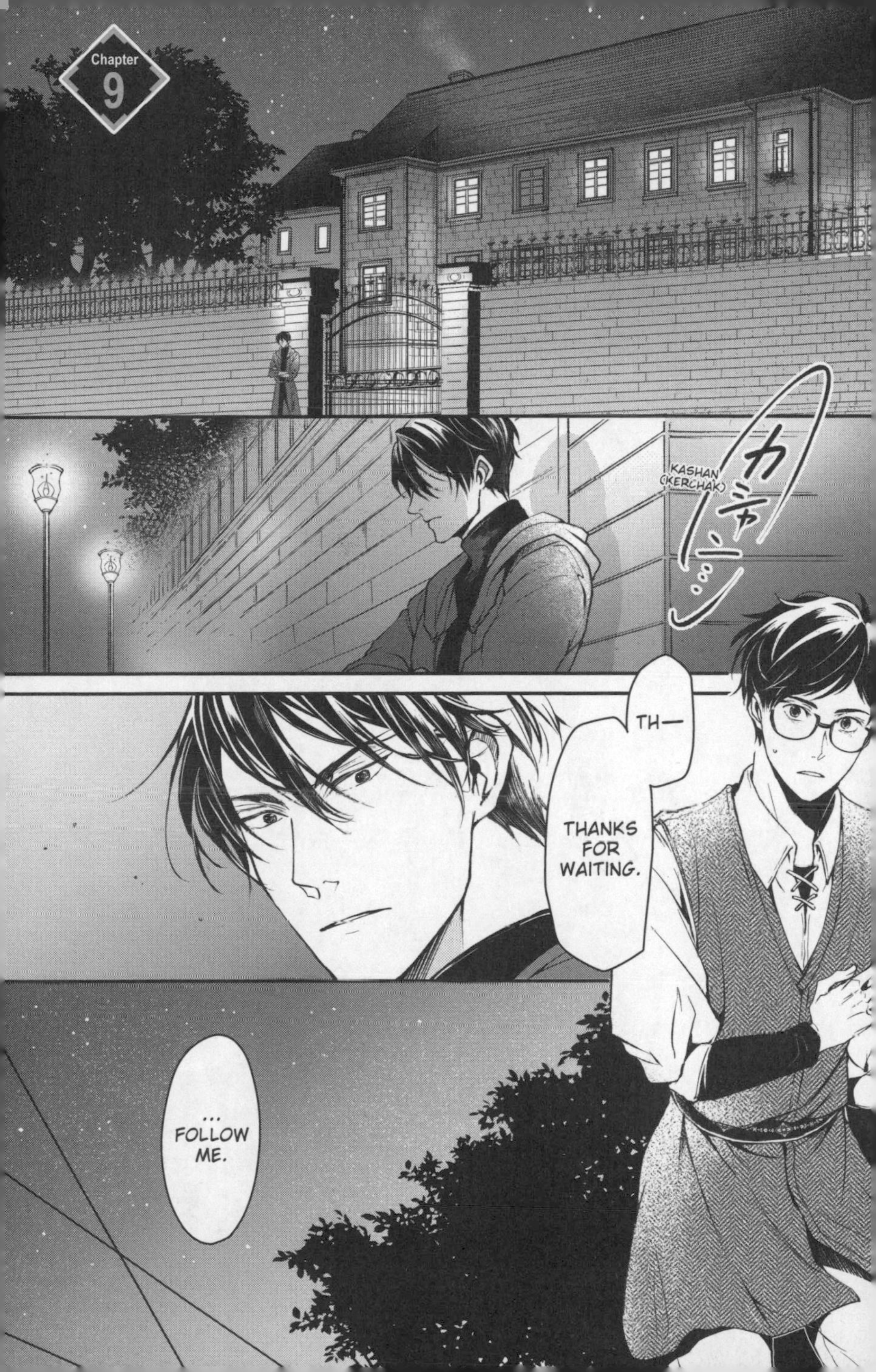
Chapter 9
カシャン…
KASHAN (KERCHAK)
TH—
THANKS FOR WAITING.
... FOLLOW ME.

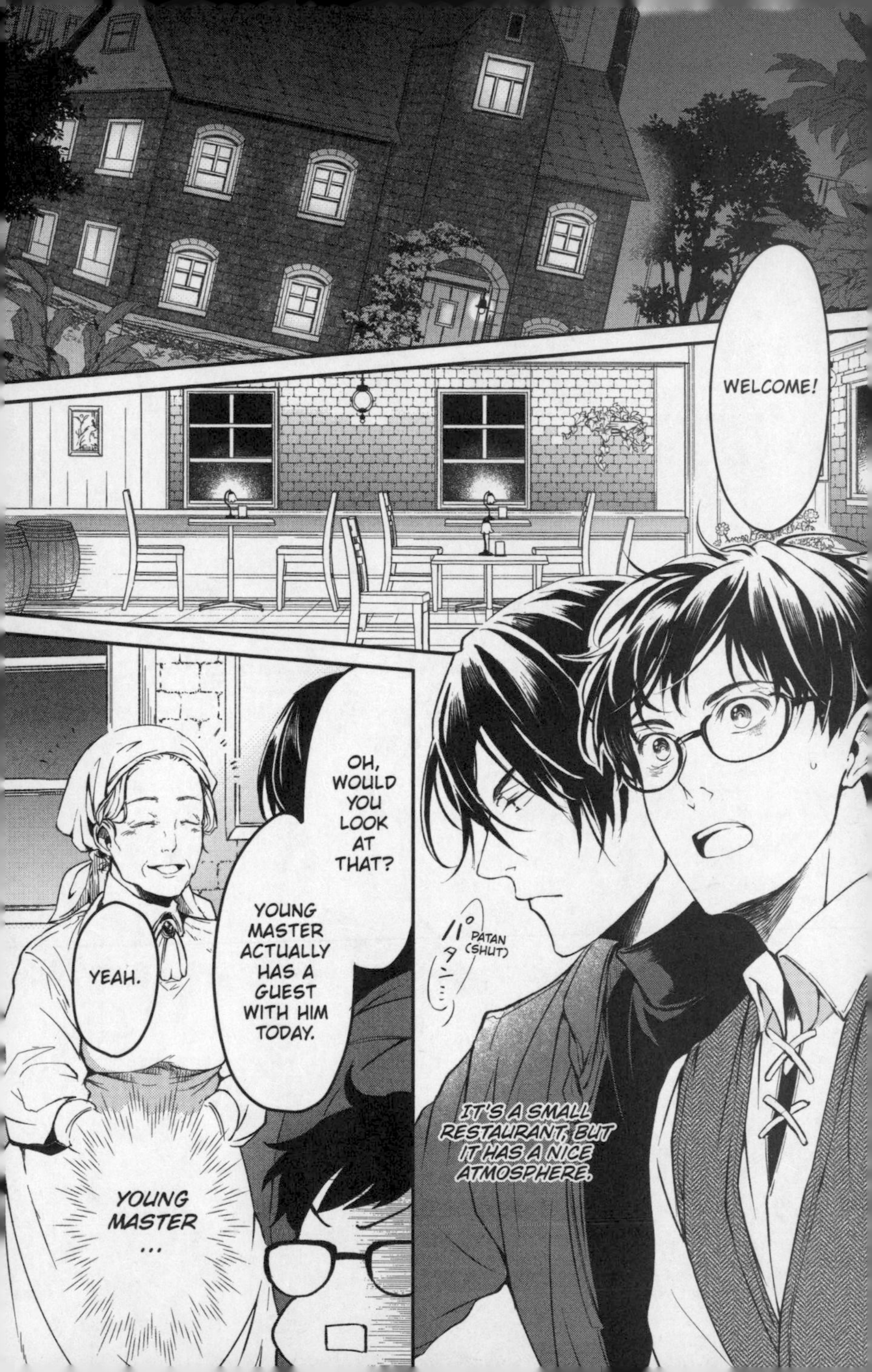
WELCOME!
PATAN (SHUT)
IT'S A SMALL RESTAURANT, BUT IT HAS A NICE ATMOSPHERE.
OH, WOULD YOU LOOK AT THAT?
YOUNG MASTER ACTUALLY HAS A GUEST WITH HIM TODAY.
YEAH.
YOUNG MASTER...

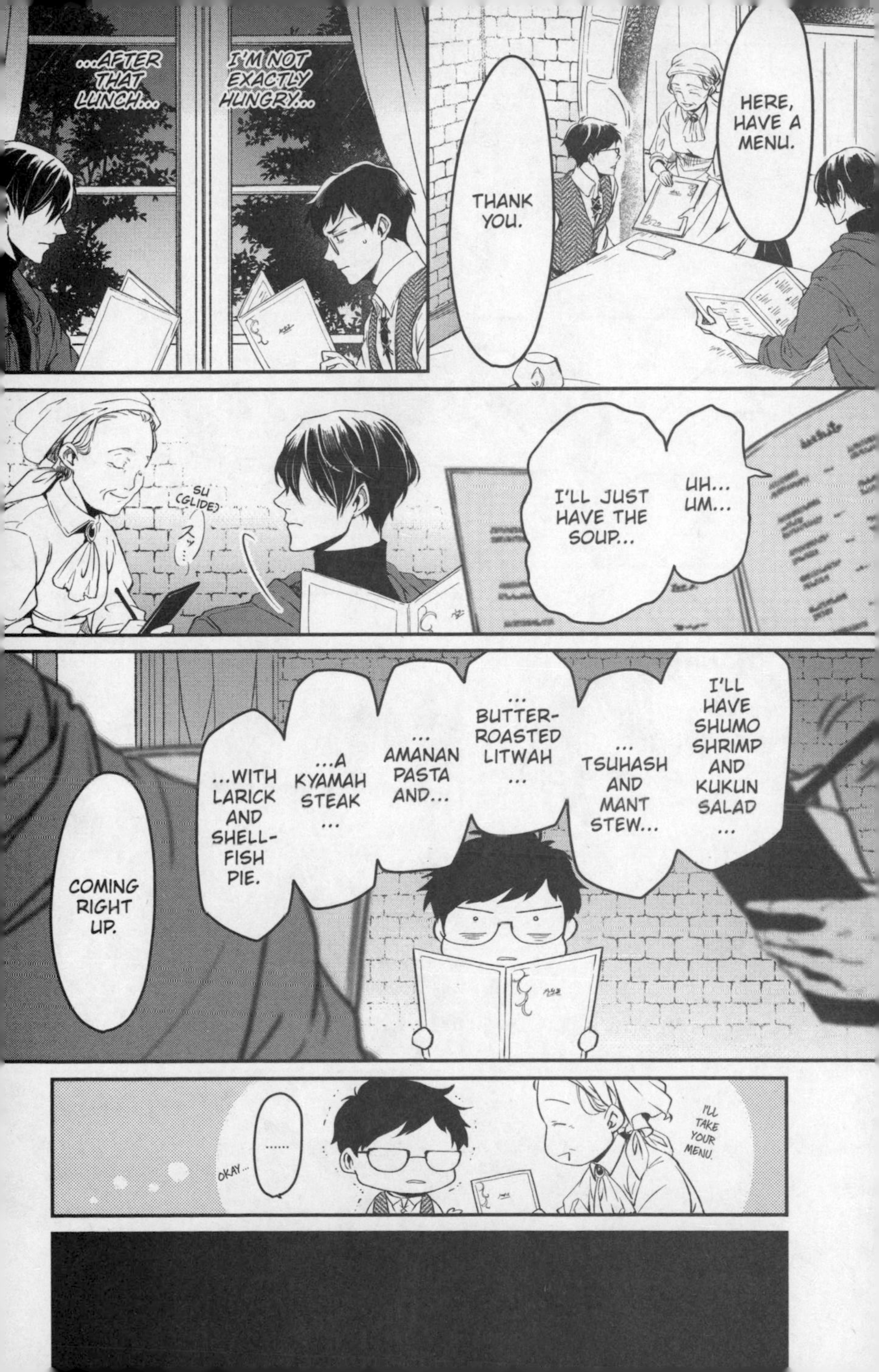
HERE, HAVE A MENU.
THANK YOU.
I'M NOT EXACTLY HUNGRY...
...AFTER THAT LUNCH...
UH... UM...
I'LL JUST HAVE THE SOUP...
SU (GLIDE)
スッ…
I'LL HAVE SHUMO SHRIMP AND KUKUN SALAD...
...TSUHASH AND MANT STEW...
...BUTTER-ROASTED LITWAH...
...AMANAN PASTA AND...
...A KYAMAH STEAK...
...WITH LARICK AND SHELL-FISH PIE.
COMING RIGHT UP.
I'LL TAKE YOUR MENU.
......
OKAY...

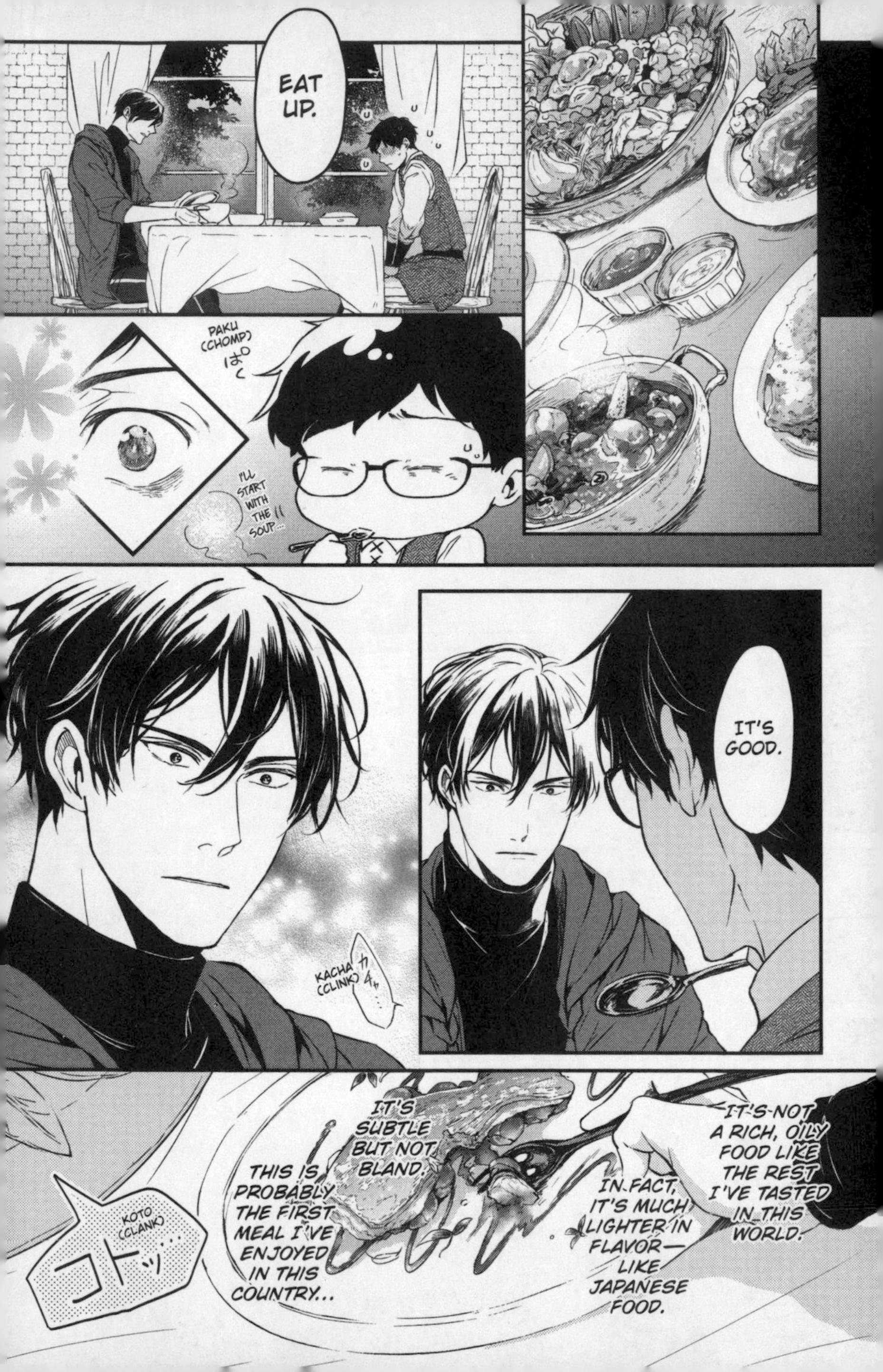
EAT UP.
PAKU (CHOMP)
ぱく
I'LL START WITH THE SOUP...
IT'S GOOD.
KACHA (CLINK)
カチャ
IT'S NOT A RICH, OILY FOOD LIKE THE REST I'VE TASTED IN THIS WORLD.
IN FACT, IT'S MUCH LIGHTER IN FLAVOR—LIKE JAPANESE FOOD.
IT'S SUBTLE BUT NOT BLAND.
THIS IS PROBABLY THE FIRST MEAL I'VE ENJOYED IN THIS COUNTRY...
KOTO (CLANK)
コトッ

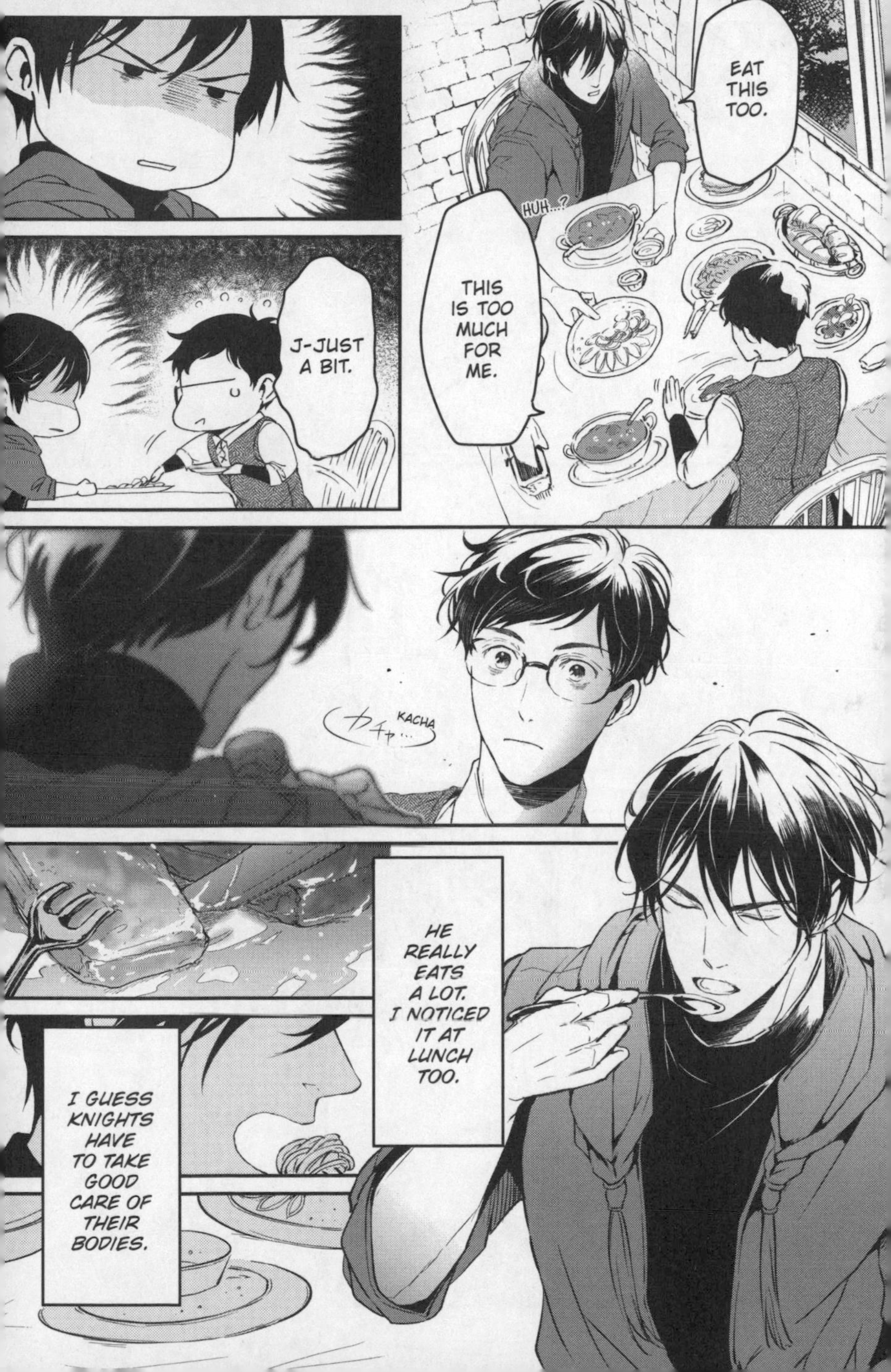
EAT THIS TOO.
HUH...?
THIS IS TOO MUCH FOR ME.
J-JUST A BIT.
カチャ…
KACHA
HE REALLY EATS A LOT. I NOTICED IT AT LUNCH TOO.
I GUESS KNIGHTS HAVE TO TAKE GOOD CARE OF THEIR BODIES.

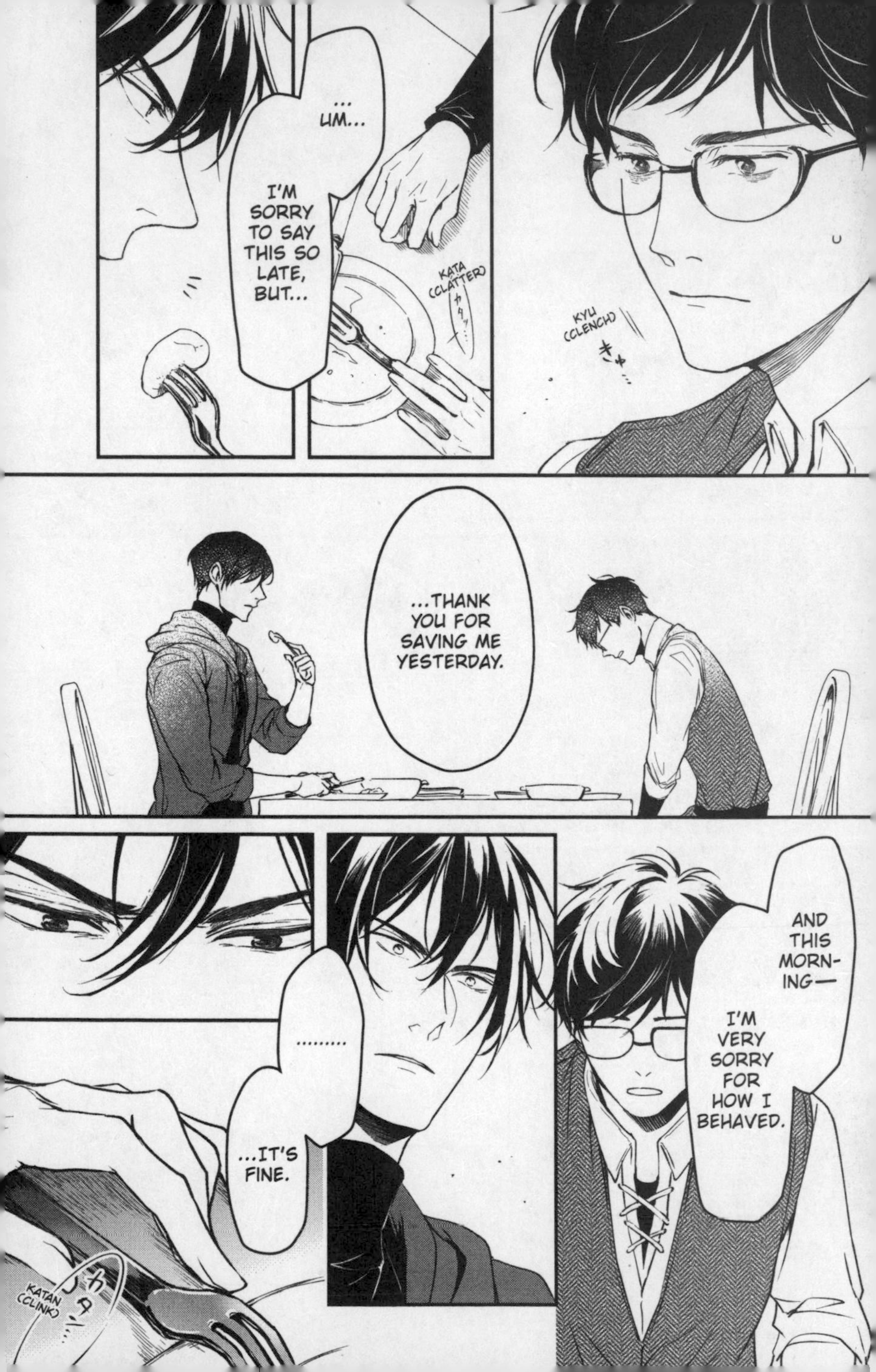
KYU (CLENCH)
きゅ…
KATA (CLATTER)
カタッ…
... UM...
I'M SORRY TO SAY THIS SO LATE, BUT...
...THANK YOU FOR SAVING ME YESTERDAY.
AND THIS MORN-ING—
I'M VERY SORRY FOR HOW I BEHAVED.
....
...IT'S FINE.
KATAN (CLINK)
カタン…

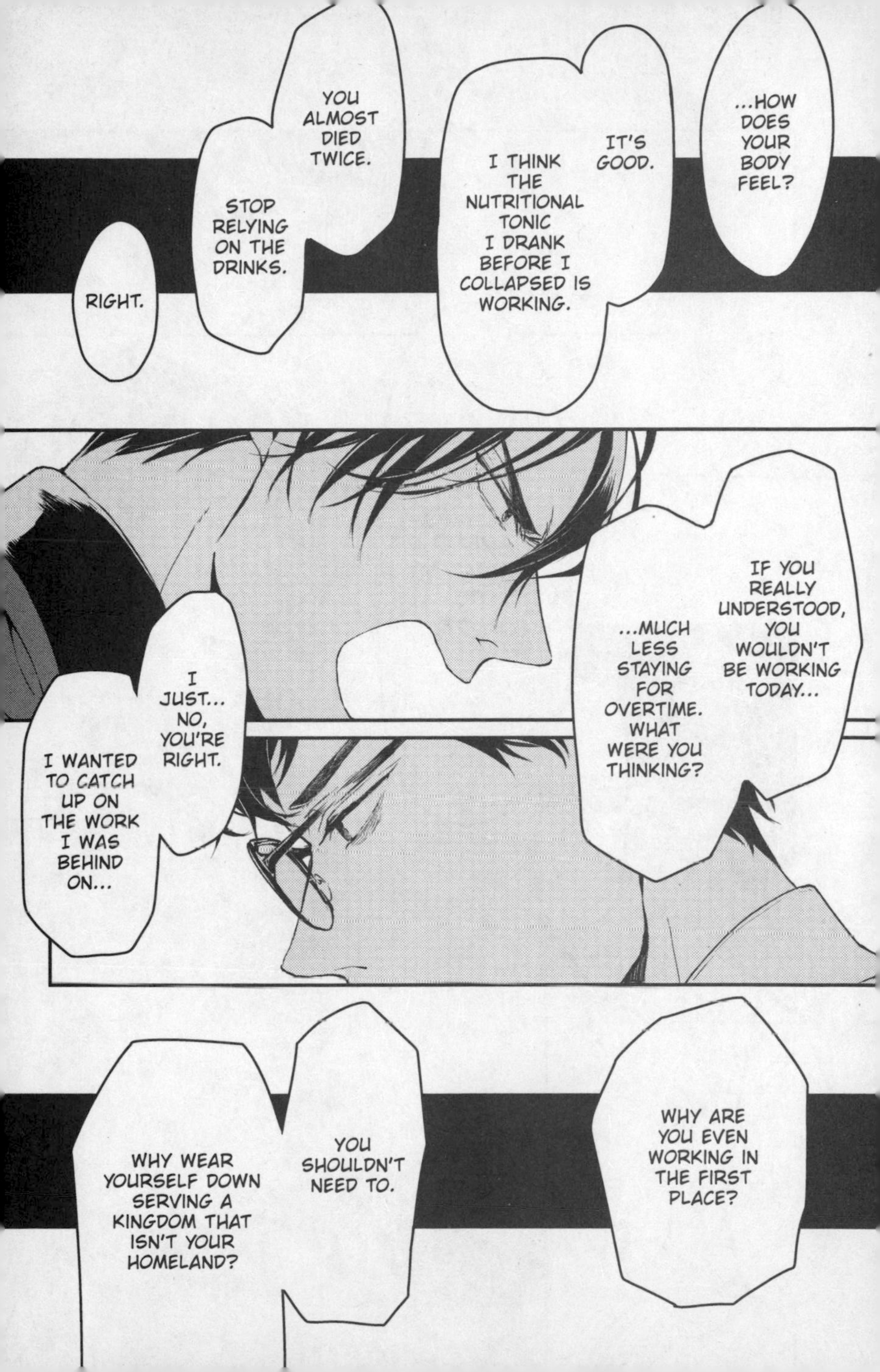
...HOW DOES YOUR BODY FEEL?
IT'S GOOD.
I THINK THE NUTRITIONAL TONIC I DRANK BEFORE I COLLAPSED IS WORKING.
YOU ALMOST DIED TWICE.
STOP RELYING ON THE DRINKS.
RIGHT.
IF YOU REALLY UNDERSTOOD, YOU WOULDN'T BE WORKING TODAY...
...MUCH LESS STAYING FOR OVERTIME. WHAT WERE YOU THINKING?
I JUST... NO, YOU'RE RIGHT.
I WANTED TO CATCH UP ON THE WORK I WAS BEHIND ON...
WHY ARE YOU EVEN WORKING IN THE FIRST PLACE?
YOU SHOULDN'T NEED TO.
WHY WEAR YOURSELF DOWN SERVING A KINGDOM THAT ISN'T YOUR HOMELAND?

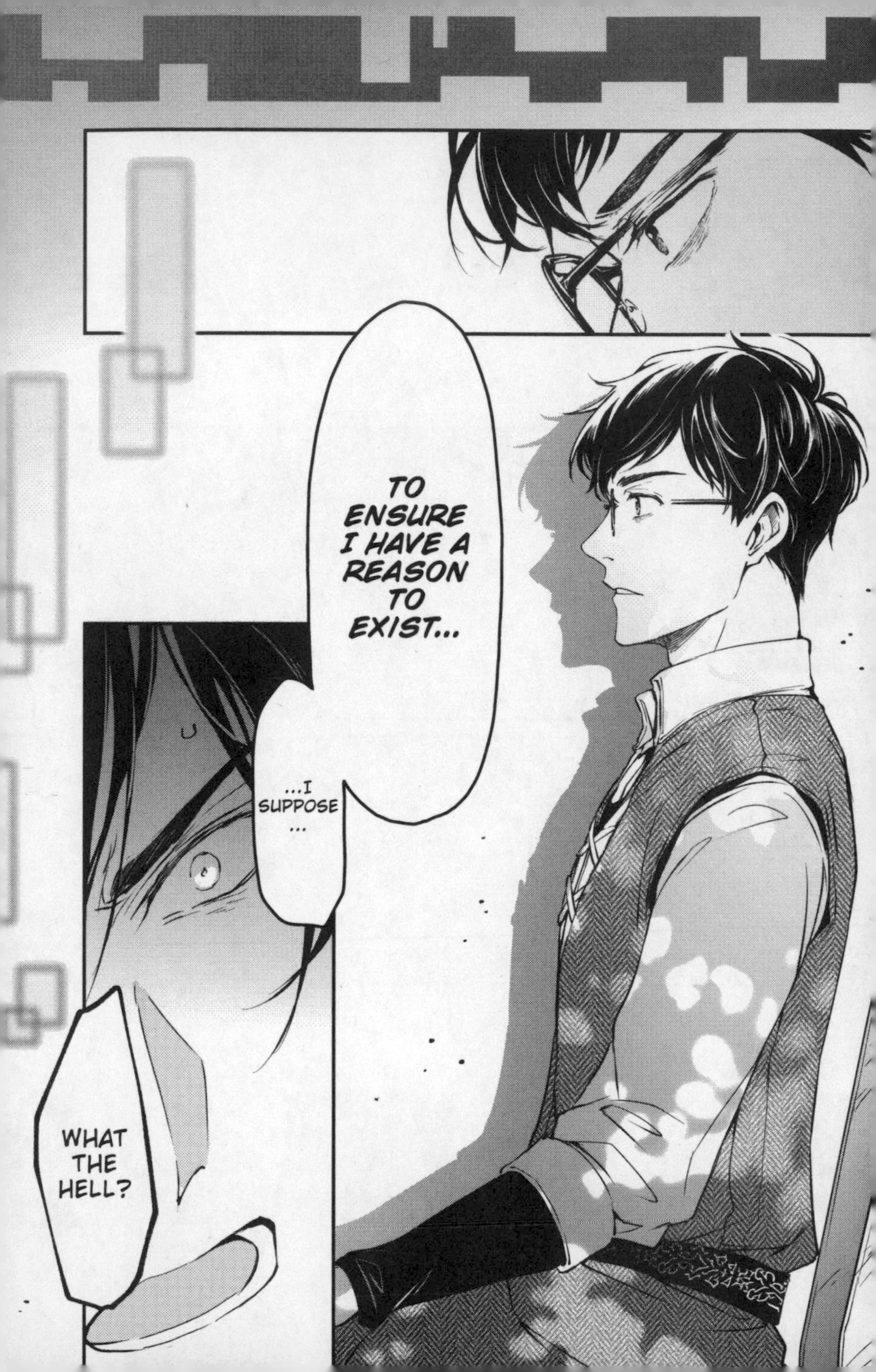
TO ENSURE I HAVE A REASON TO EXIST...
...I SUPPOSE ...
WHAT THE HELL?

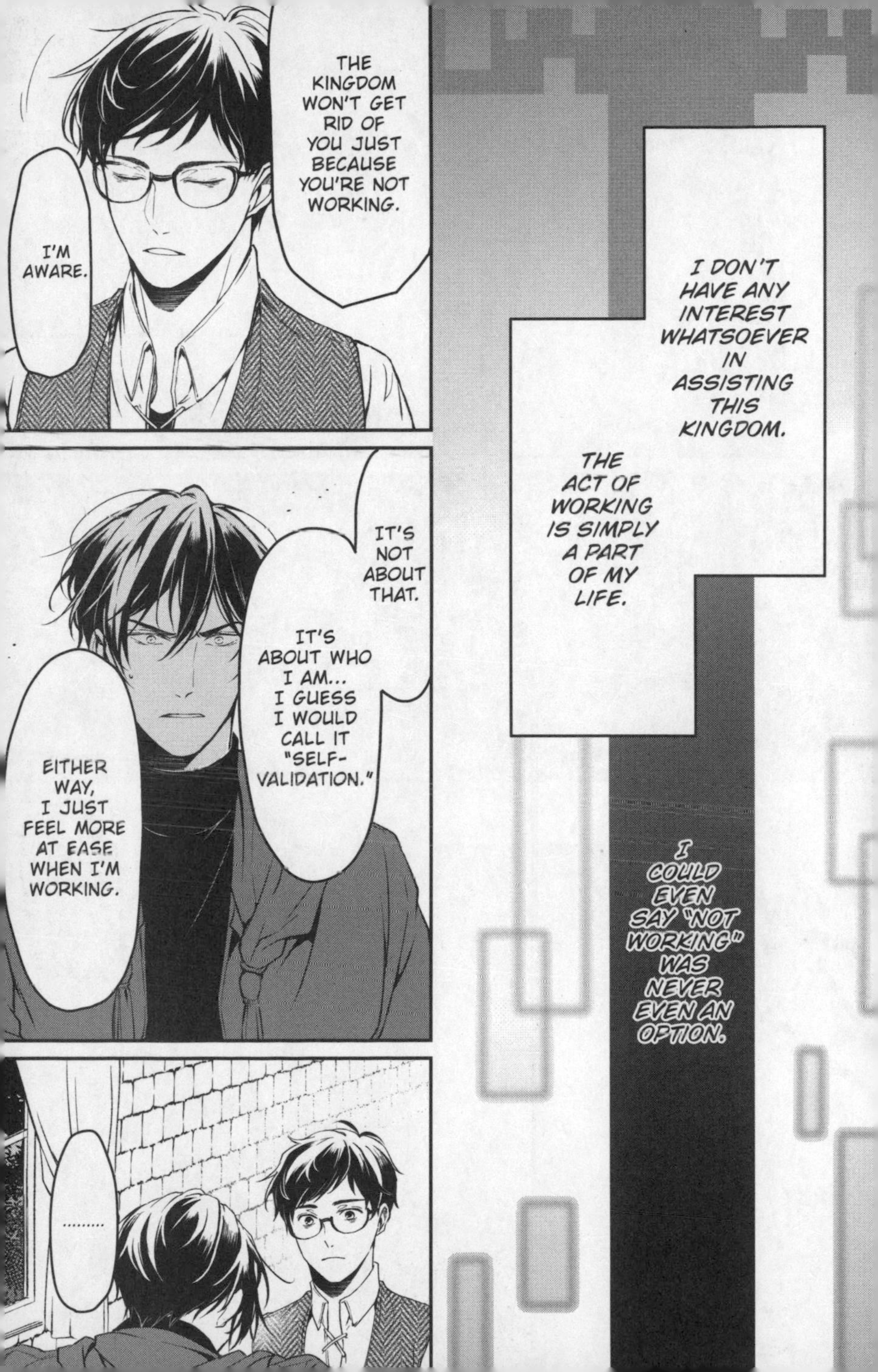
I DON'T HAVE ANY INTEREST WHATSOEVER IN ASSISTING THIS KINGDOM.
THE ACT OF WORKING IS SIMPLY A PART OF MY LIFE.
I COULD EVEN SAY "NOT WORKING" WAS NEVER EVEN AN OPTION.
THE KINGDOM WON'T GET RID OF YOU JUST BECAUSE YOU'RE NOT WORKING.
I'M AWARE.
IT'S NOT ABOUT THAT.
IT'S ABOUT WHO I AM... I GUESS I WOULD CALL IT "SELF-VALIDATION."
EITHER WAY, I JUST FEEL MORE AT EASE WHEN I'M WORKING.
....

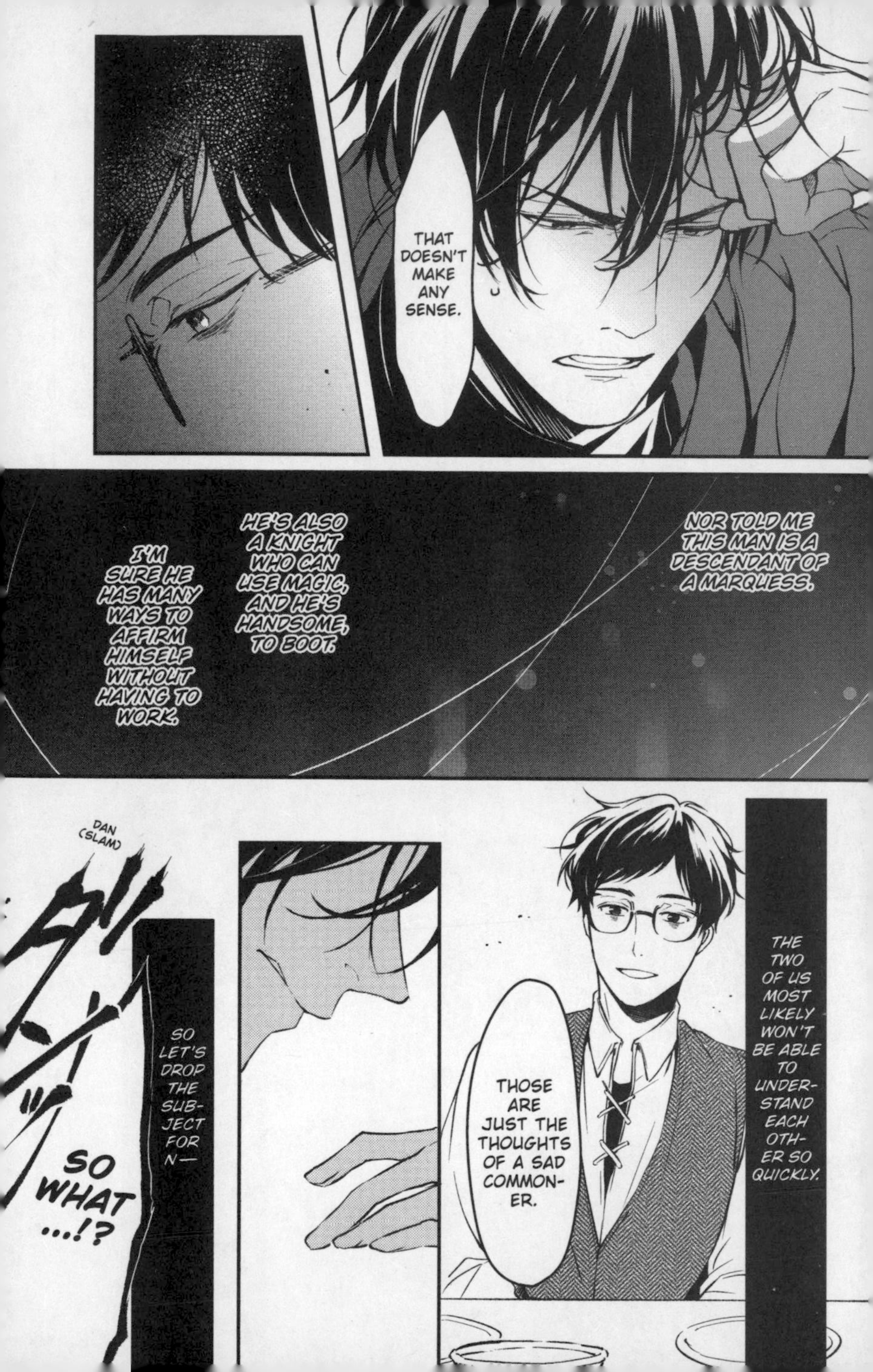
THAT DOESN'T MAKE ANY SENSE.
NOR TOLD ME THIS MAN IS A DESCENDANT OF A MARQUESS.
HE'S ALSO A KNIGHT WHO CAN USE MAGIC, AND HE'S HANDSOME, TO BOOT.
I'M SURE HE HAS MANY WAYS TO AFFIRM HIMSELF WITHOUT HAVING TO WORK.
THE TWO OF US MOST LIKELY WON'T BE ABLE TO UNDER-STAND EACH OTH-ER SO QUICKLY.
THOSE ARE JUST THE THOUGHTS OF A SAD COMMON-ER.
SO LET'S DROP THE SUB-JECT FOR N—
DAN (SLAM)
SO WHAT ...!?

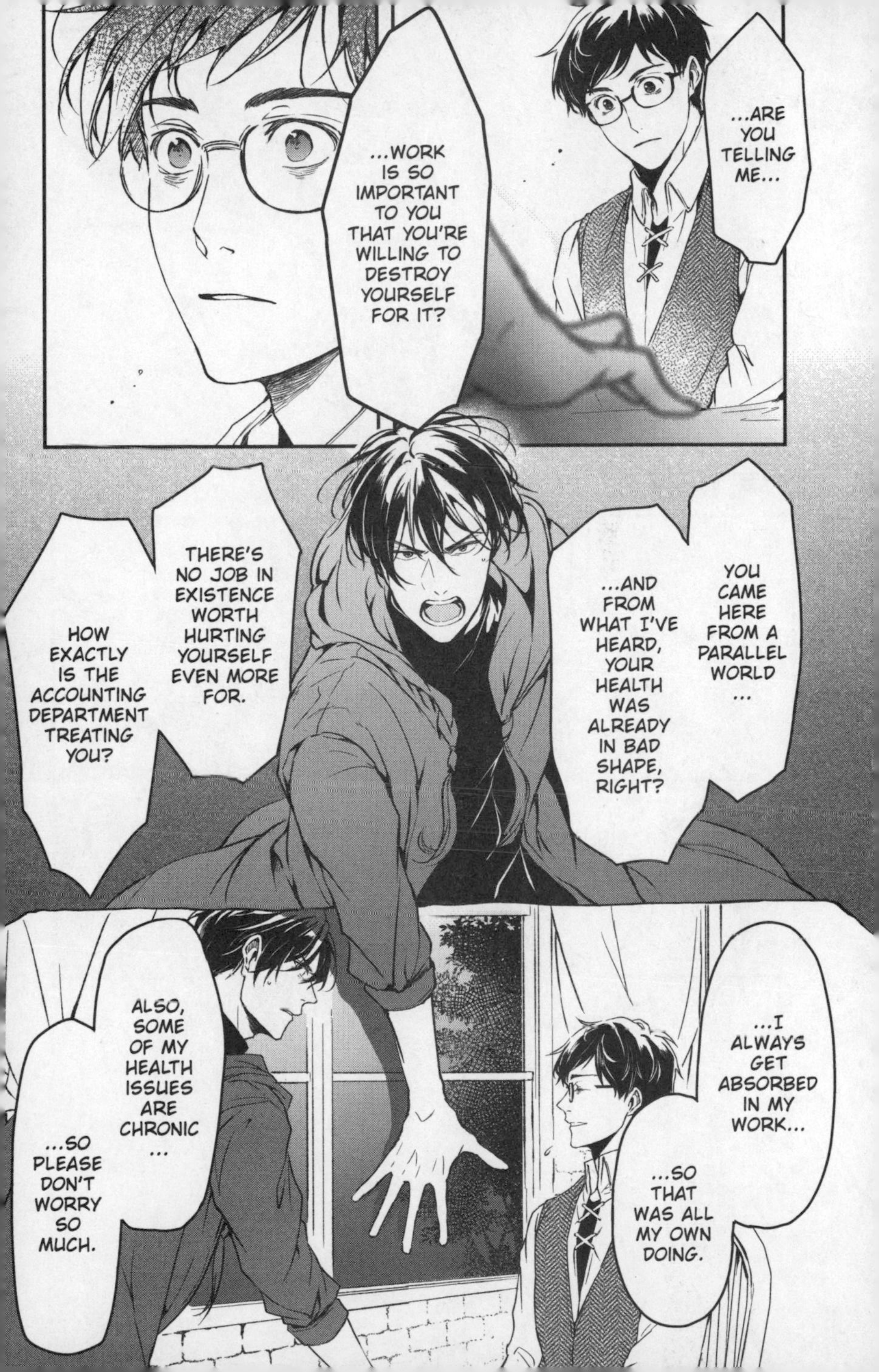
...ARE YOU TELLING ME...
...WORK IS SO IMPORTANT TO YOU THAT YOU'RE WILLING TO DESTROY YOURSELF FOR IT?
YOU CAME HERE FROM A PARALLEL WORLD...
...AND FROM WHAT I'VE HEARD, YOUR HEALTH WAS ALREADY IN BAD SHAPE, RIGHT?
THERE'S NO JOB IN EXISTENCE WORTH HURTING YOURSELF EVEN MORE FOR.
HOW EXACTLY IS THE ACCOUNTING DEPARTMENT TREATING YOU?
...I ALWAYS GET ABSORBED IN MY WORK...
...SO THAT WAS ALL MY OWN DOING.
ALSO, SOME OF MY HEALTH ISSUES ARE CHRONIC...
...SO PLEASE DON'T WORRY SO MUCH.

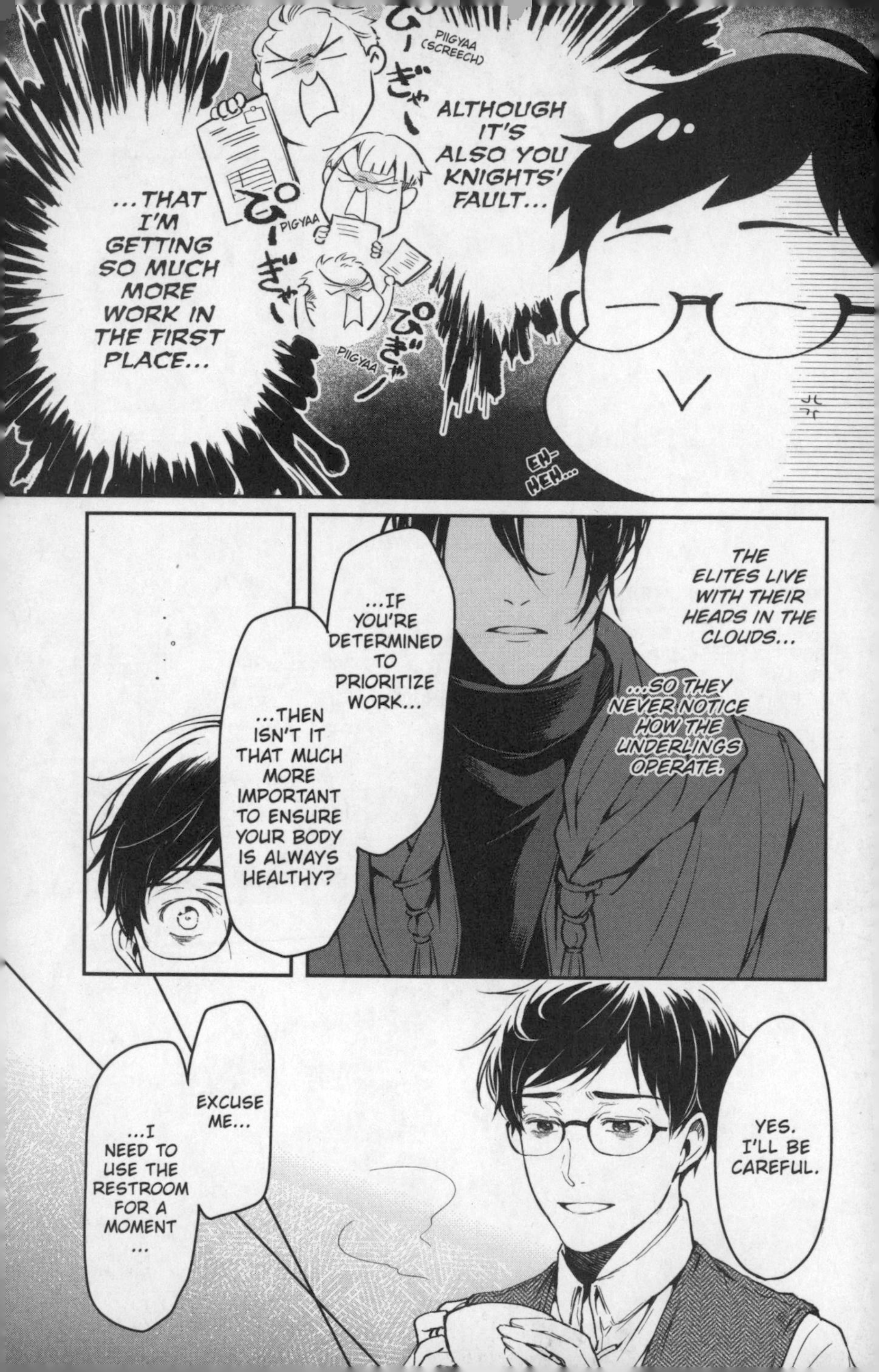

ぴーぎゃー
PIIGYAA (SCREECH)
ALTHOUGH IT'S ALSO YOU KNIGHTS' FAULT...
...THAT I'M GETTING SO MUCH MORE WORK IN THE FIRST PLACE...
ぴーぎゃー
PIIGYAA
ぴぎゃー
PIIGYAA
EH-HEH...
THE ELITES LIVE WITH THEIR HEADS IN THE CLOUDS...
...SO THEY NEVER NOTICE HOW THE UNDERLINGS OPERATE.
...IF YOU'RE DETERMINED TO PRIORITIZE WORK...
...THEN ISN'T IT THAT MUCH MORE IMPORTANT TO ENSURE YOUR BODY IS ALWAYS HEALTHY?
YES. I'LL BE CAREFUL.
EXCUSE ME...
...I NEED TO USE THE RESTROOM FOR A MOMENT...

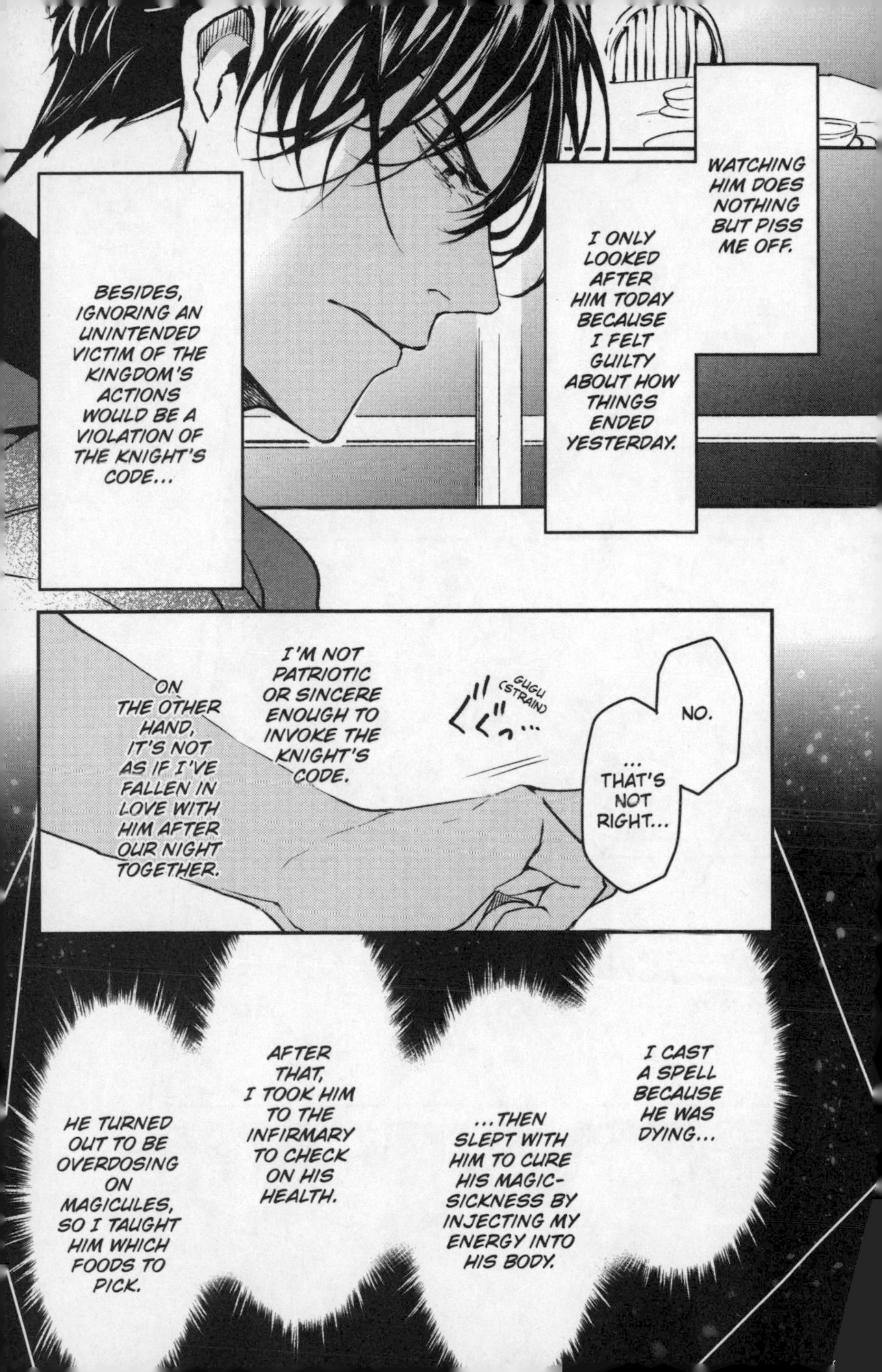
WATCHING HIM DOES NOTHING BUT PISS ME OFF.
I ONLY LOOKED AFTER HIM TODAY BECAUSE I FELT GUILTY ABOUT HOW THINGS ENDED YESTERDAY.
BESIDES, IGNORING AN UNINTENDED VICTIM OF THE KINGDOM'S ACTIONS WOULD BE A VIOLATION OF THE KNIGHT'S CODE...
NO.
...THAT'S NOT RIGHT...
GUGU (STRAIN)
ぐぐっ…
I'M NOT PATRIOTIC OR SINCERE ENOUGH TO INVOKE THE KNIGHT'S CODE.
ON THE OTHER HAND, IT'S NOT AS IF I'VE FALLEN IN LOVE WITH HIM AFTER OUR NIGHT TOGETHER.
I CAST A SPELL BECAUSE HE WAS DYING...
...THEN SLEPT WITH HIM TO CURE HIS MAGIC-SICKNESS BY INJECTING MY ENERGY INTO HIS BODY.
AFTER THAT, I TOOK HIM TO THE INFIRMARY TO CHECK ON HIS HEALTH.
HE TURNED OUT TO BE OVERDOSING ON MAGICULES, SO I TAUGHT HIM WHICH FOODS TO PICK.

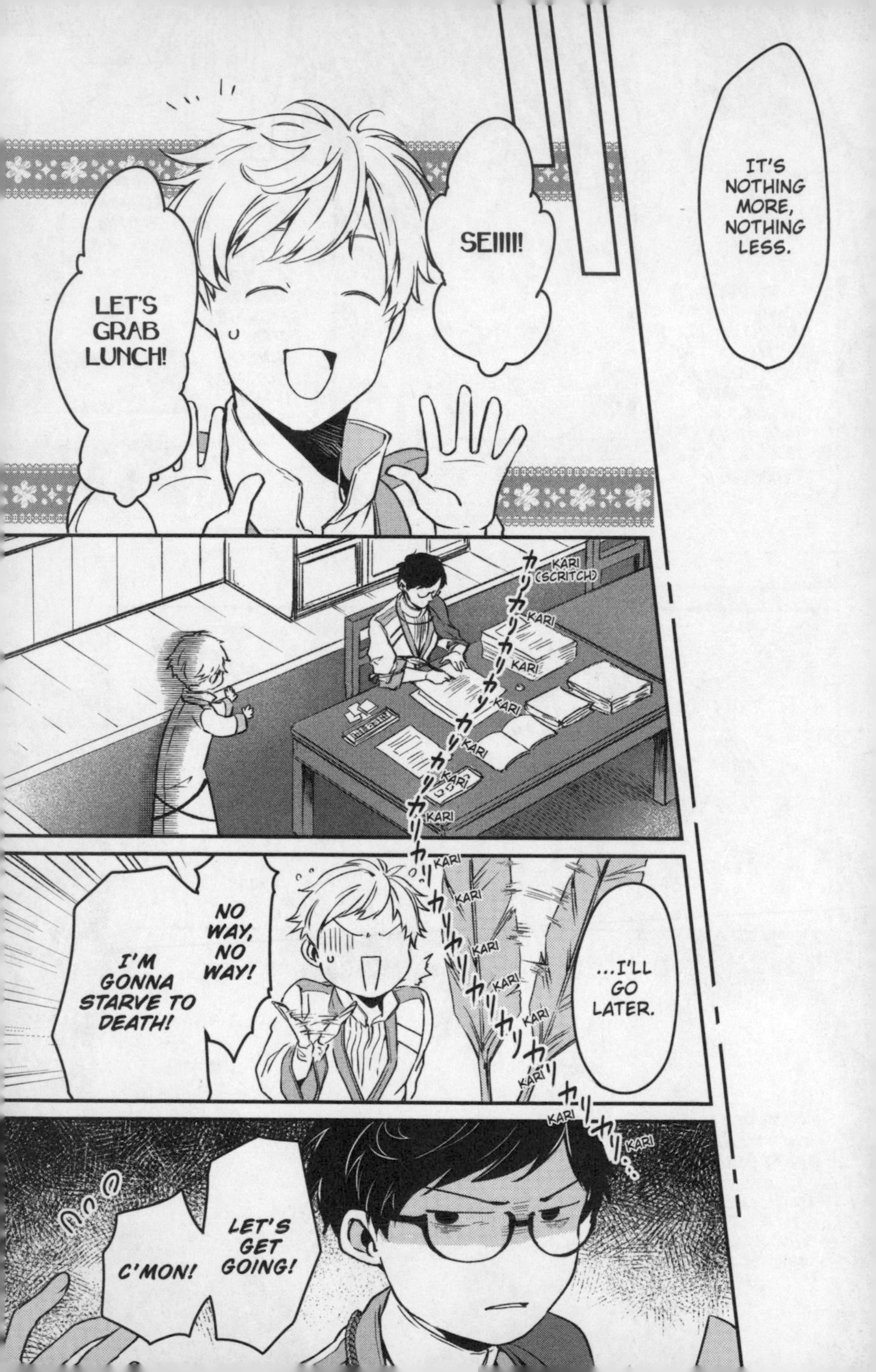
IT'S NOTHING MORE, NOTHING LESS.
SEIIIII!
LET'S GRAB LUNCH!
KARI (SCRITCH)
KARI
KARI
KARI
KARI
KARI
KARI
...I'LL GO LATER.
KARI
KARI
KARI
KARI
KARI
NO WAY, NO WAY!
I'M GONNA STARVE TO DEATH!
KARI
KARI
LET'S GET GOING!
C'MON!

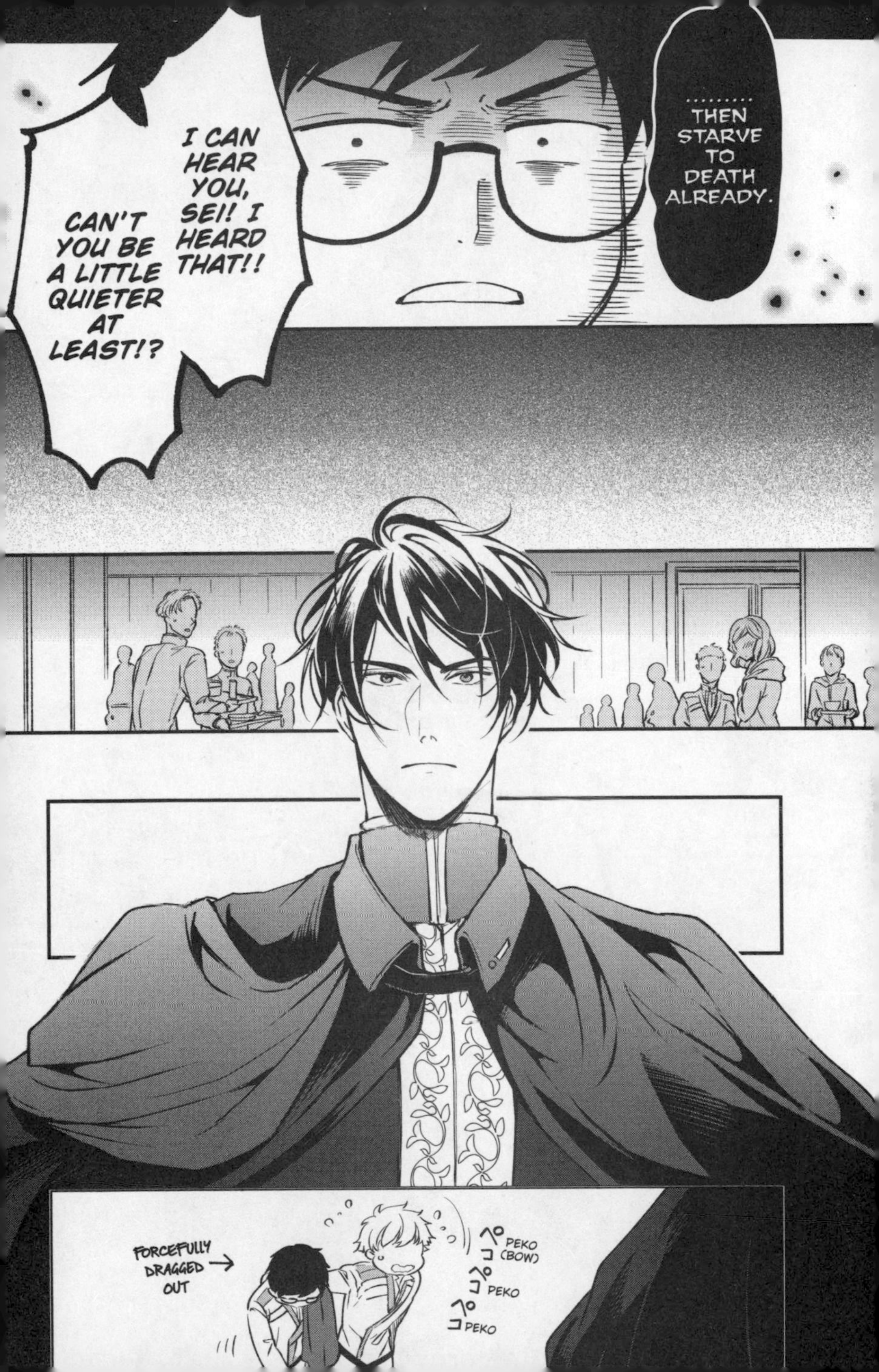
....
THEN STARVE TO DEATH ALREADY.
I CAN HEAR YOU, SEI! I HEARD THAT!!
CAN'T YOU BE A LITTLE QUIETER AT LEAST!?
PEKO (BOW)
PEKO
PEKO
FORCEFULLY DRAGGED OUT

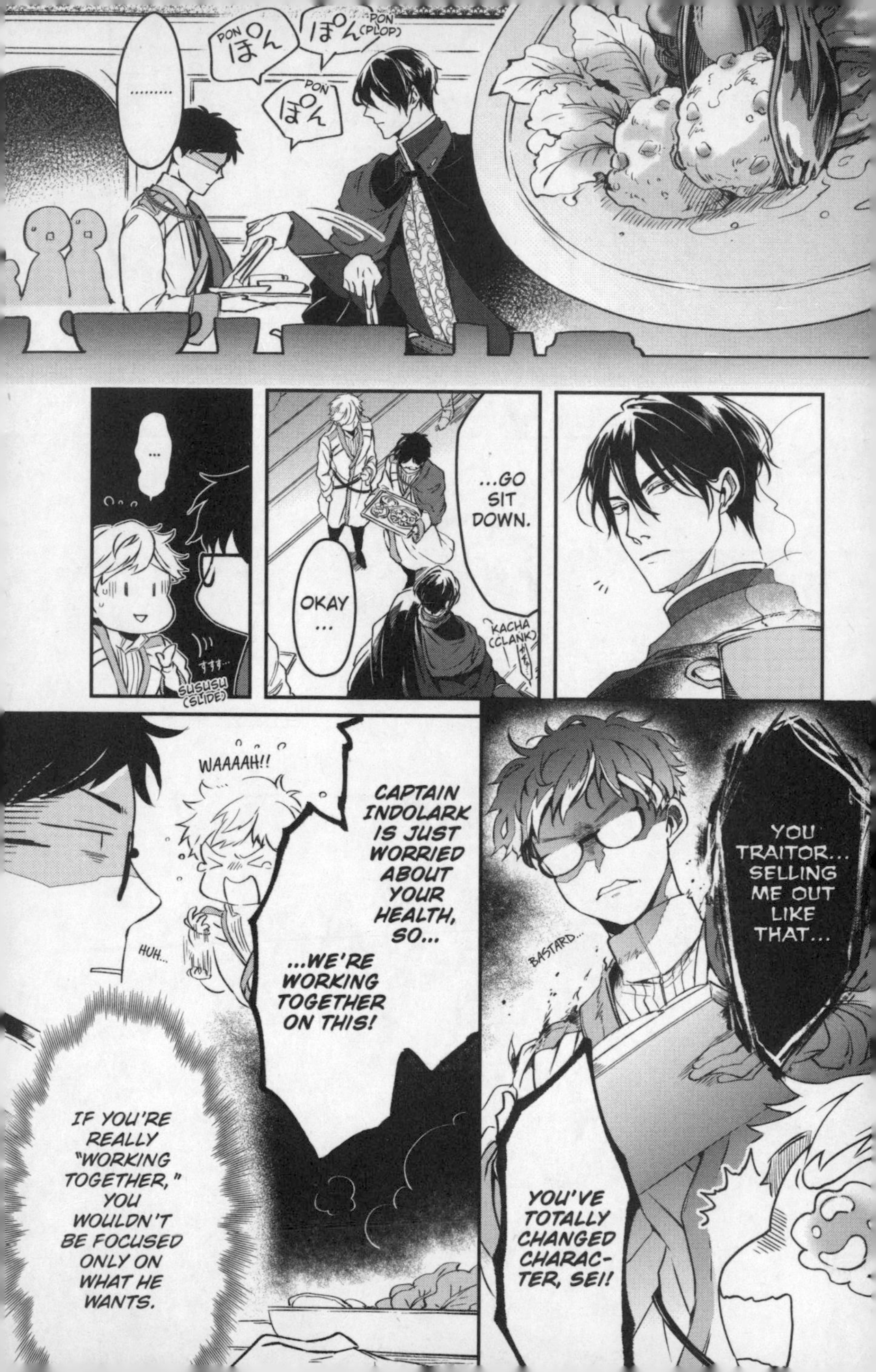
PON (PLOP) ぽん
PON ぽん
PON ぽん
....
KACHA (CLANK) ガチャ
...GO SIT DOWN.
OKAY ...
...
SUSUSU (SLIDE) すすす...
YOU TRAITOR... SELLING ME OUT LIKE THAT...
BASTARD...
YOU'VE TOTALLY CHANGED CHARAC-TER, SEI!
CAPTAIN INDOLARK IS JUST WORRIED ABOUT YOUR HEALTH, SO...
WAAAAH!!
...WE'RE WORKING TOGETHER ON THIS!
HUH...
IF YOU'RE REALLY "WORKING TOGETHER," YOU WOULDN'T BE FOCUSED ONLY ON WHAT HE WANTS.

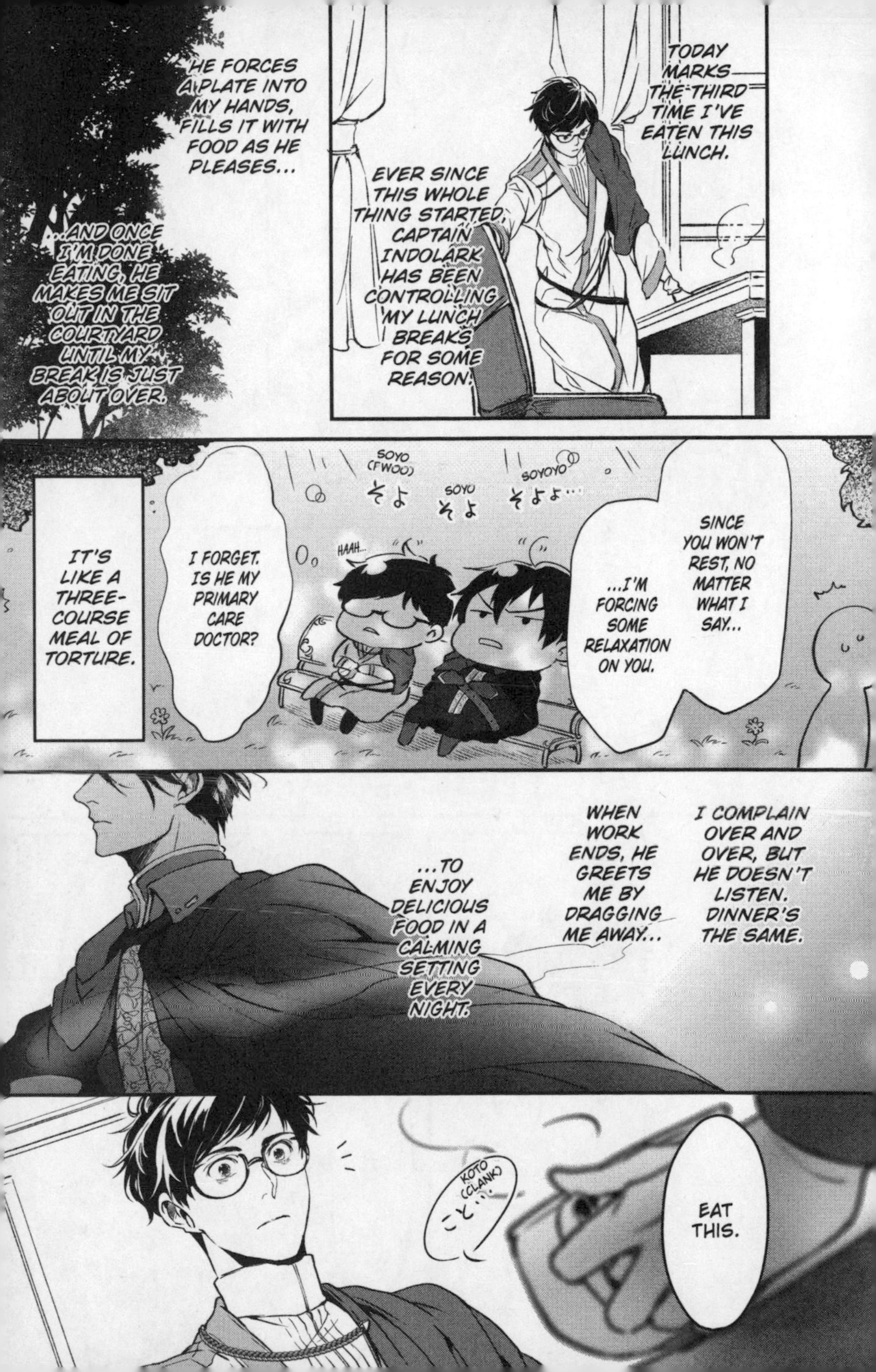
TODAY MARKS THE THIRD TIME I'VE EATEN THIS LUNCH.
EVER SINCE THIS WHOLE THING STARTED, CAPTAIN INDOLARK HAS BEEN CONTROLLING MY LUNCH BREAKS FOR SOME REASON.
HE FORCES A PLATE INTO MY HANDS, FILLS IT WITH FOOD AS HE PLEASES...
...AND ONCE I'M DONE EATING, HE MAKES ME SIT OUT IN THE COURTYARD UNTIL MY BREAK IS JUST ABOUT OVER.
そよよ… SOYOYO
そよ SOYO
そよ SOYO (FWOO)
SINCE YOU WON'T REST, NO MATTER WHAT I SAY...
...I'M FORCING SOME RELAXATION ON YOU.
HAAH...
I FORGET. IS HE MY PRIMARY CARE DOCTOR?
IT'S LIKE A THREE-COURSE MEAL OF TORTURE.
I COMPLAIN OVER AND OVER, BUT HE DOESN'T LISTEN. DINNER'S THE SAME.
WHEN WORK ENDS, HE GREETS ME BY DRAGGING ME AWAY...
...TO ENJOY DELICIOUS FOOD IN A CALMING SETTING EVERY NIGHT.
EAT THIS.
こと… KOTO (CLANK)

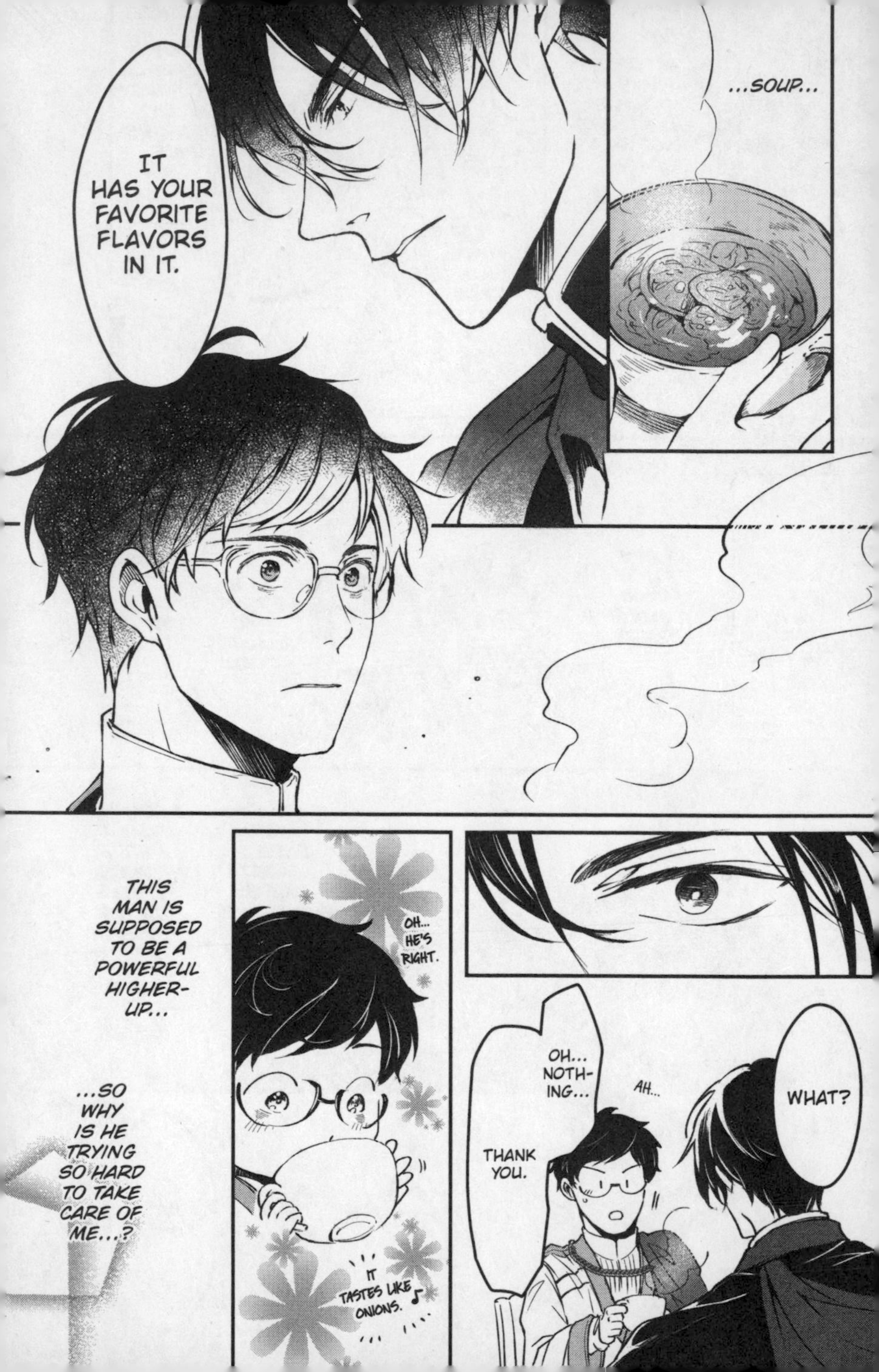
...SOUP...
IT HAS YOUR FAVORITE FLAVORS IN IT.
WHAT?
AH...
OH... NOTHING...
THANK YOU.
OH... HE'S RIGHT.
IT TASTES LIKE ONIONS. ♪
THIS MAN IS SUPPOSED TO BE A POWERFUL HIGHER-UP...
...SO WHY IS HE TRYING SO HARD TO TAKE CARE OF ME...?

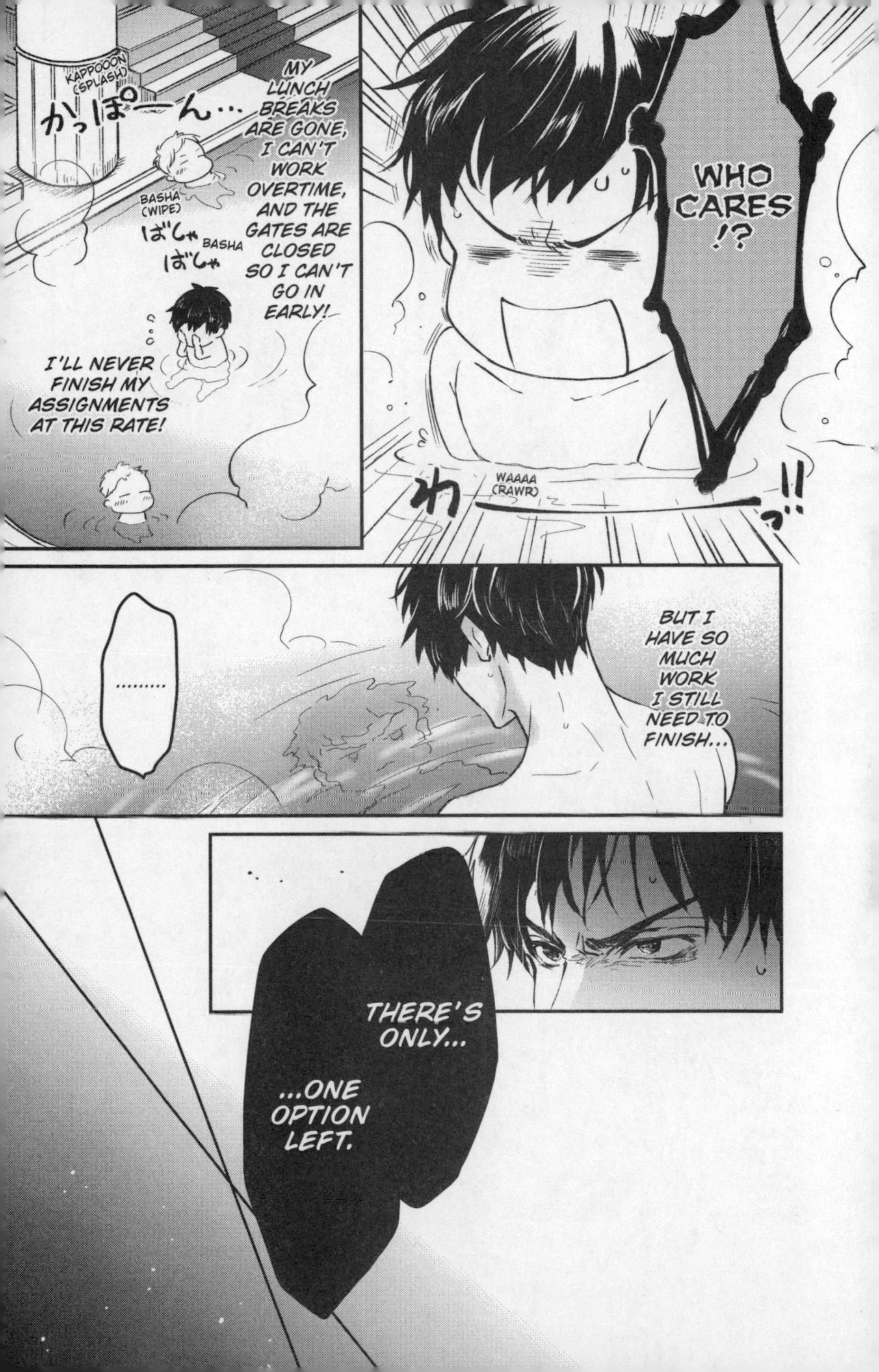
WHO CARES!?
WAAAA (RAWR)
わーっ!!
MY LUNCH BREAKS ARE GONE, I CAN'T WORK OVERTIME, AND THE GATES ARE CLOSED SO I CAN'T GO IN EARLY!
KAPPOOON (SPLASH)
かっぽーん…
BASHA (WIPE)
ばしゃ
BASHA
ばしゃ
I'LL NEVER FINISH MY ASSIGNMENTS AT THIS RATE!
BUT I HAVE SO MUCH WORK I STILL NEED TO FINISH...
....
...
THERE'S ONLY...
...ONE OPTION LEFT.

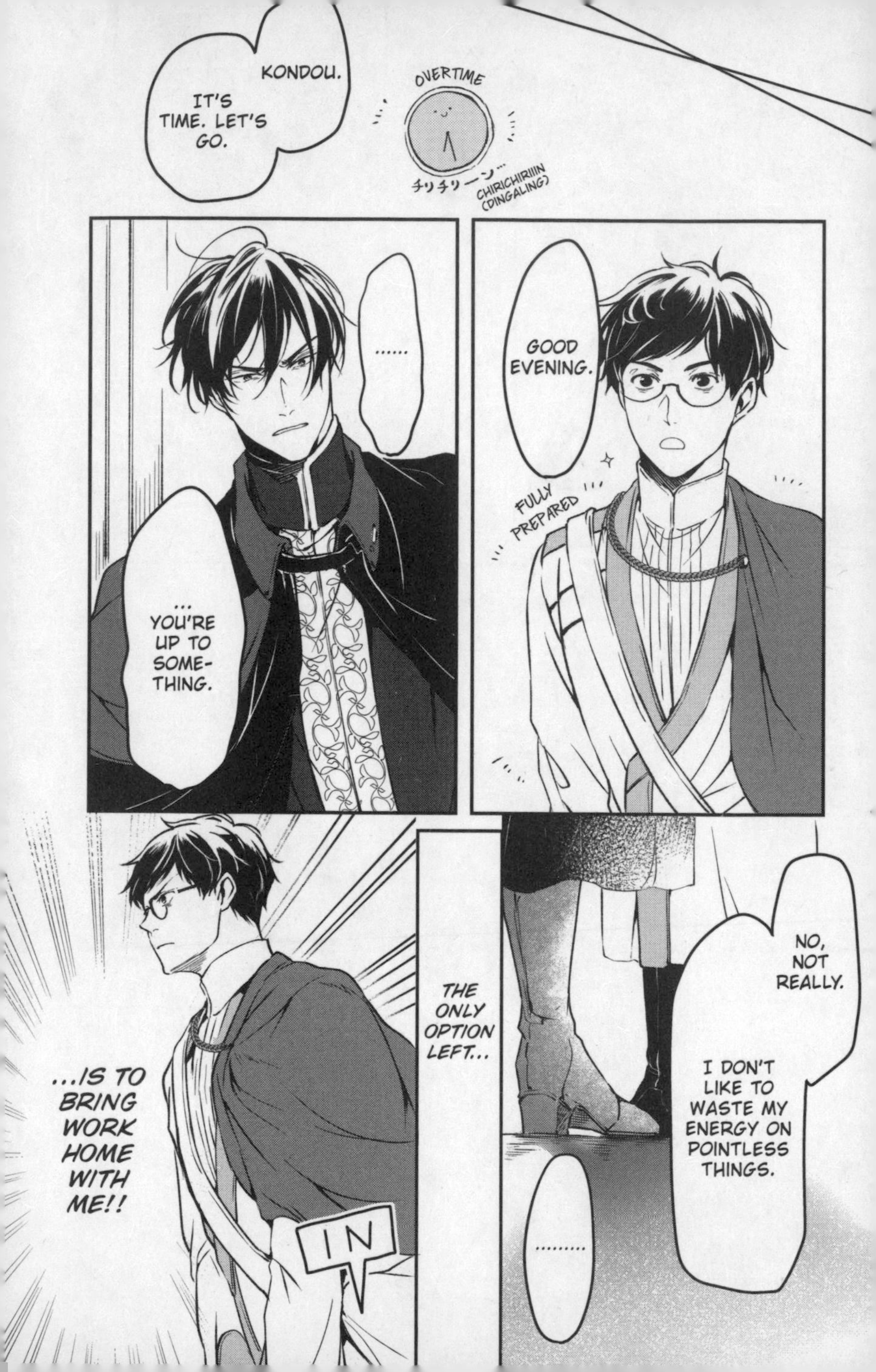
OVERTIME
チリチリーン…
CHIRICHIRIIIN (DINGALING)
KONDOU.
IT'S TIME. LET'S GO.
GOOD EVENING.
FULLY PREPARED
......
... YOU'RE UP TO SOME-THING.
NO, NOT REALLY.
I DON'T LIKE TO WASTE MY ENERGY ON POINTLESS THINGS.
....
THE ONLY OPTION LEFT...
...IS TO BRING WORK HOME WITH ME!!
IN

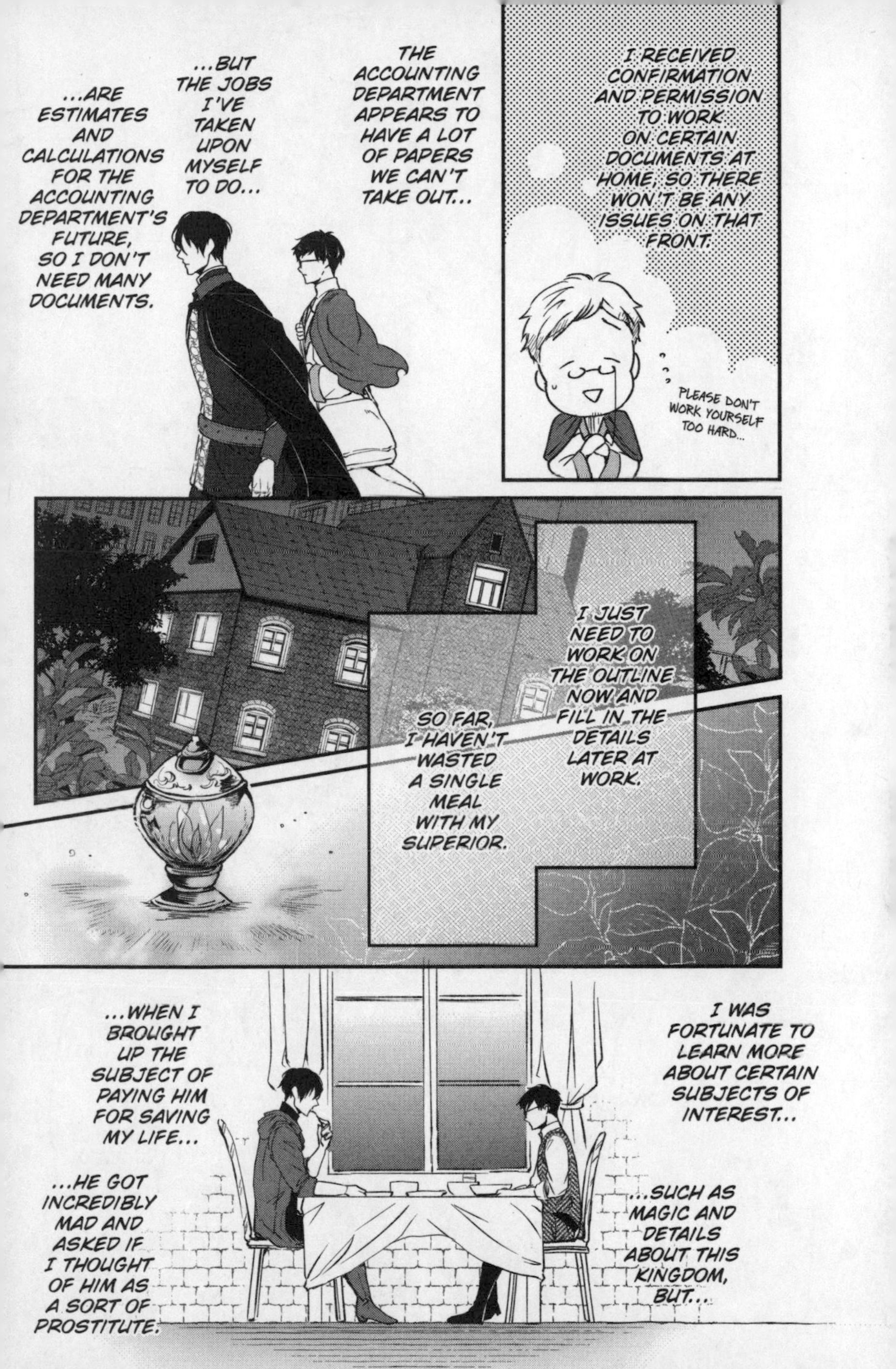
I RECEIVED CONFIRMATION AND PERMISSION TO WORK ON CERTAIN DOCUMENTS AT HOME, SO THERE WON'T BE ANY ISSUES ON THAT FRONT.
PLEASE DON'T WORK YOURSELF TOO HARD...
THE ACCOUNTING DEPARTMENT APPEARS TO HAVE A LOT OF PAPERS WE CAN'T TAKE OUT...
...BUT THE JOBS I'VE TAKEN UPON MYSELF TO DO...
...ARE ESTIMATES AND CALCULATIONS FOR THE ACCOUNTING DEPARTMENT'S FUTURE, SO I DON'T NEED MANY DOCUMENTS.
I JUST NEED TO WORK ON THE OUTLINE NOW AND FILL IN THE DETAILS LATER AT WORK.
SO FAR, I HAVEN'T WASTED A SINGLE MEAL WITH MY SUPERIOR.
I WAS FORTUNATE TO LEARN MORE ABOUT CERTAIN SUBJECTS OF INTEREST...
...SUCH AS MAGIC AND DETAILS ABOUT THIS KINGDOM, BUT...
...WHEN I BROUGHT UP THE SUBJECT OF PAYING HIM FOR SAVING MY LIFE...
...HE GOT INCREDIBLY MAD AND ASKED IF I THOUGHT OF HIM AS A SORT OF PROSTITUTE.

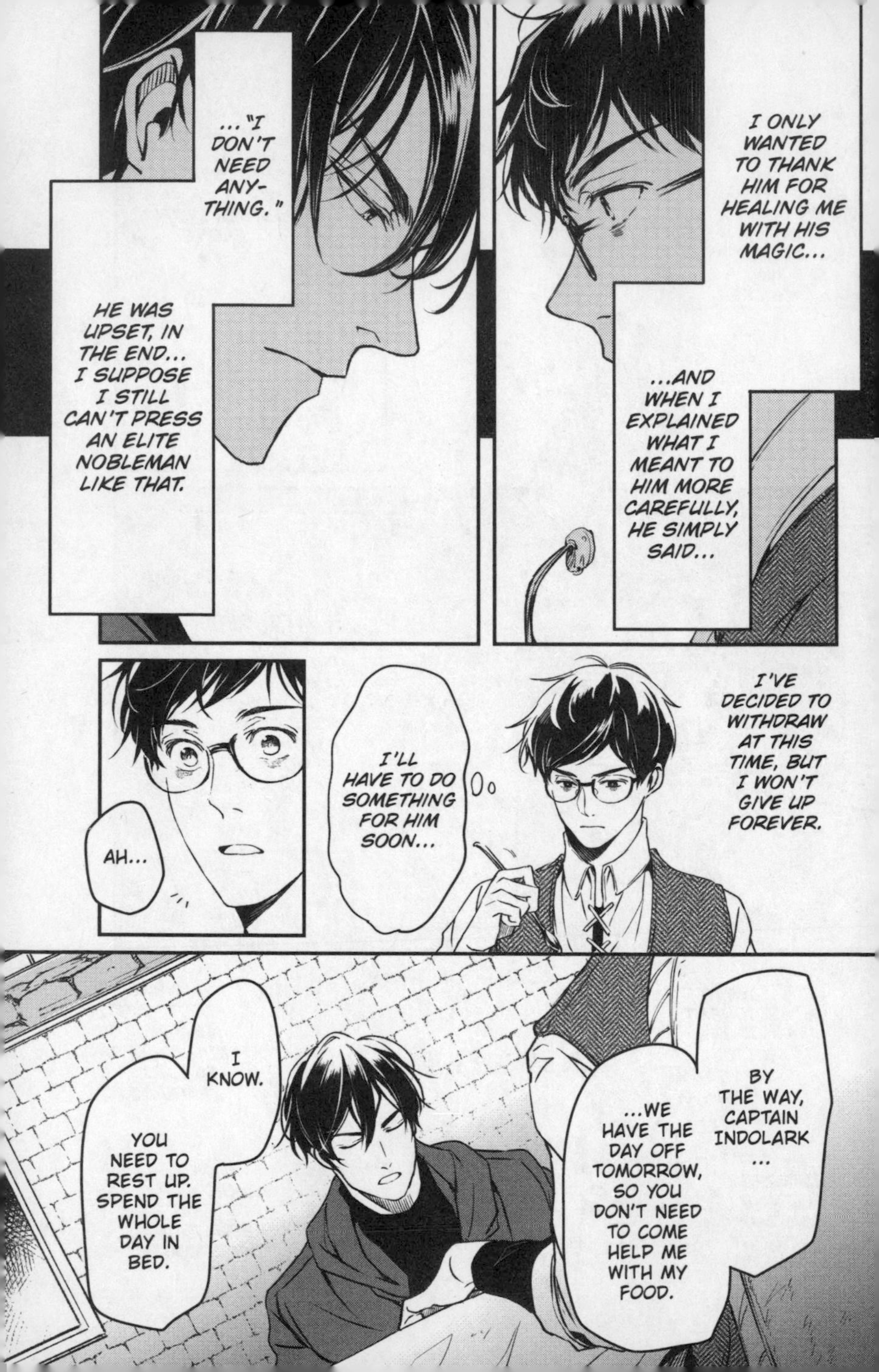
I ONLY WANTED TO THANK HIM FOR HEALING ME WITH HIS MAGIC...
...AND WHEN I EXPLAINED WHAT I MEANT TO HIM MORE CAREFULLY, HE SIMPLY SAID...
..."I DON'T NEED ANYTHING."
HE WAS UPSET, IN THE END... I SUPPOSE I STILL CAN'T PRESS AN ELITE NOBLEMAN LIKE THAT.
I'VE DECIDED TO WITHDRAW AT THIS TIME, BUT I WON'T GIVE UP FOREVER.
I'LL HAVE TO DO SOMETHING FOR HIM SOON...
AH...
BY THE WAY, CAPTAIN INDOLARK ...
...WE HAVE THE DAY OFF TOMORROW, SO YOU DON'T NEED TO COME HELP ME WITH MY FOOD.
I KNOW.
YOU NEED TO REST UP. SPEND THE WHOLE DAY IN BED.

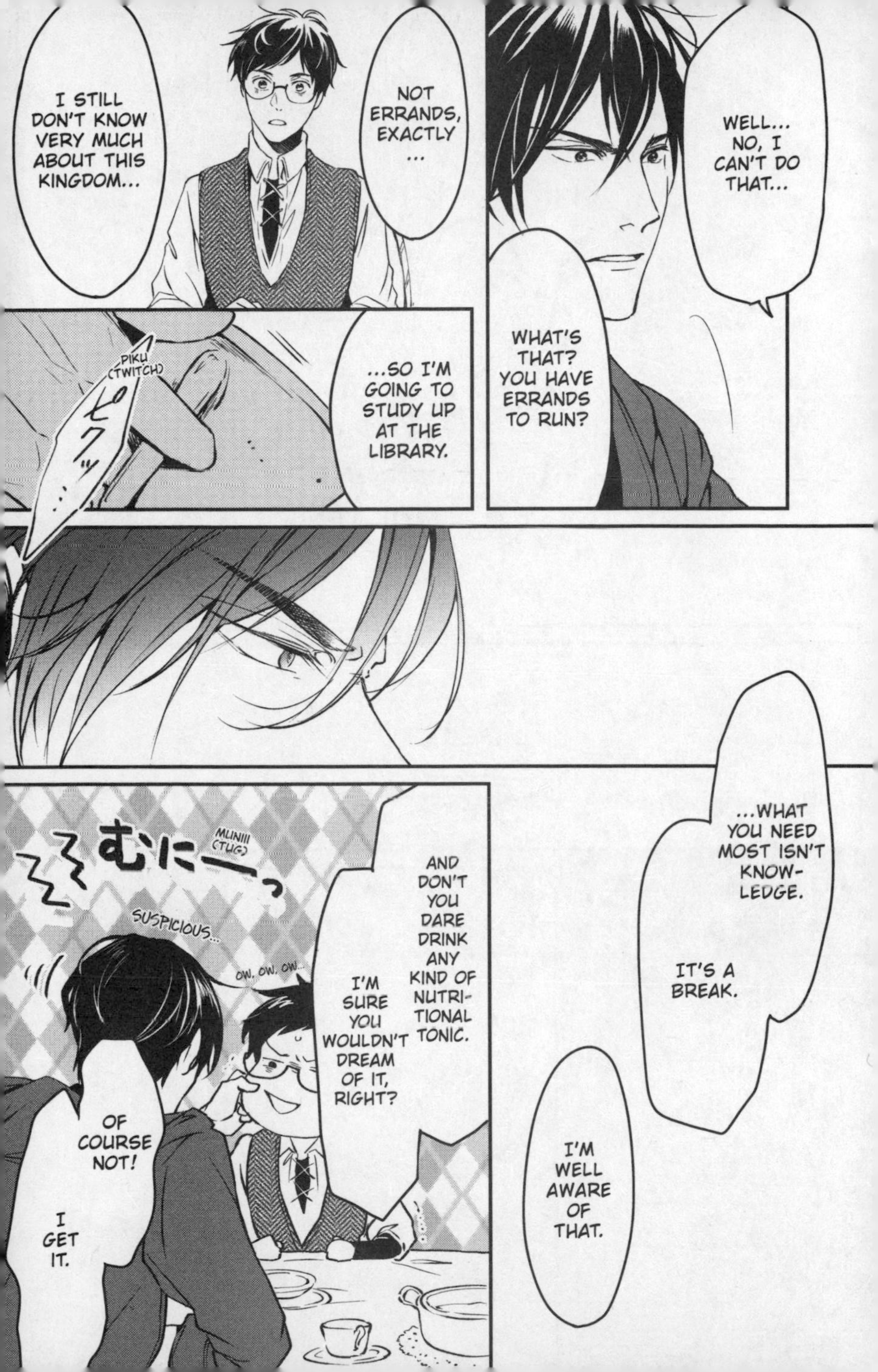
WELL... NO, I CAN'T DO THAT...
WHAT'S THAT? YOU HAVE ERRANDS TO RUN?
NOT ERRANDS, EXACTLY ...
I STILL DON'T KNOW VERY MUCH ABOUT THIS KINGDOM...
...SO I'M GOING TO STUDY UP AT THE LIBRARY.
PIKU (TWITCH)
ピクッ
...WHAT YOU NEED MOST ISN'T KNOW-LEDGE.
IT'S A BREAK.
I'M WELL AWARE OF THAT.
AND DON'T YOU DARE DRINK ANY KIND OF NUTRI-TIONAL TONIC.
I'M SURE YOU WOULDN'T DREAM OF IT, RIGHT?
MUNIII (TUG)
むにーっ
SUSPICIOUS...
OW, OW, OW...
OF COURSE NOT!
I GET IT.

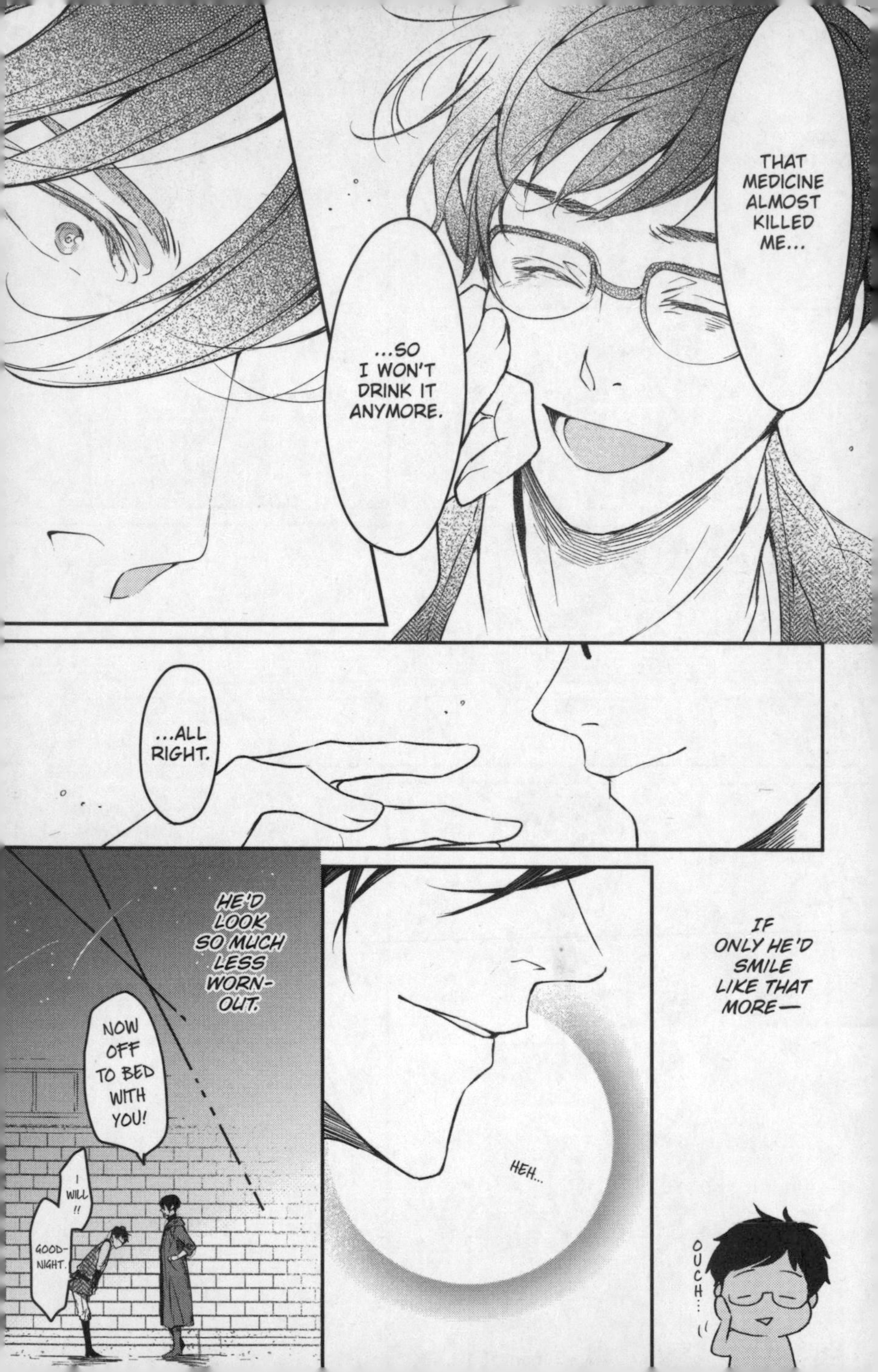
THAT MEDICINE ALMOST KILLED ME...
...SO I WON'T DRINK IT ANYMORE.
...ALL RIGHT.
IF ONLY HE'D SMILE LIKE THAT MORE—
OUCH...
HEH...
HE'D LOOK SO MUCH LESS WORN-OUT.
NOW OFF TO BED WITH YOU!
I WILL!!
GOOD-NIGHT.

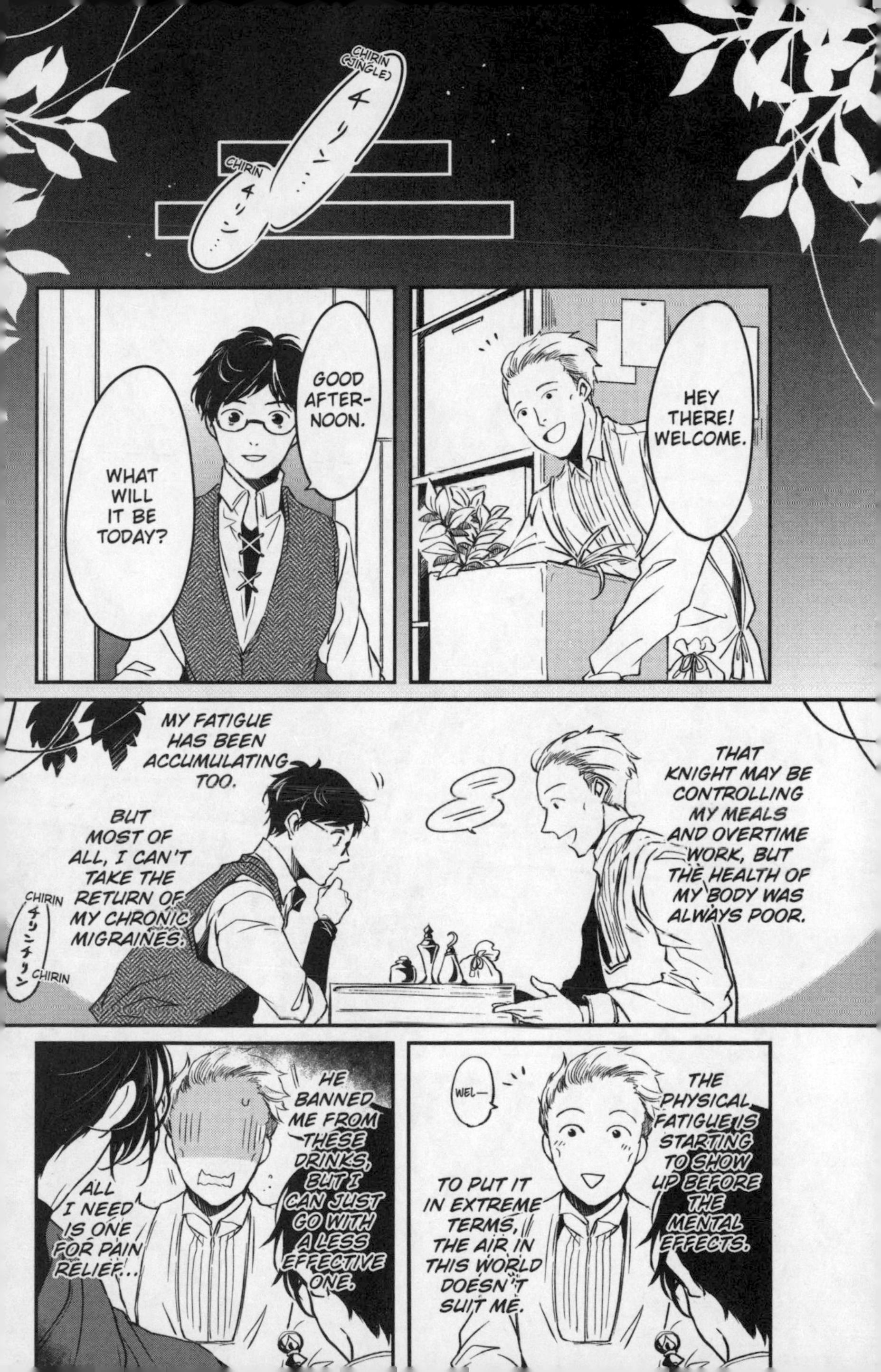
CHIRIN (JINGLE)
チリン…
CHIRIN
チリン…
HEY THERE! WELCOME.
GOOD AFTERNOON.
WHAT WILL IT BE TODAY?
THAT KNIGHT MAY BE CONTROLLING MY MEALS AND OVERTIME WORK, BUT THE HEALTH OF MY BODY WAS ALWAYS POOR.
MY FATIGUE HAS BEEN ACCUMULATING TOO.
BUT MOST OF ALL, I CAN'T TAKE THE RETURN OF MY CHRONIC MIGRAINES.
CHIRIN チリンチリン CHIRIN
THE PHYSICAL FATIGUE IS STARTING TO SHOW UP BEFORE THE MENTAL EFFECTS.
WEL—
TO PUT IT IN EXTREME TERMS, THE AIR IN THIS WORLD DOESN'T SUIT ME.
HE BANNED ME FROM THESE DRINKS, BUT I CAN JUST GO WITH A LESS EFFECTIVE ONE.
ALL I NEED IS ONE FOR PAIN RELIEF...

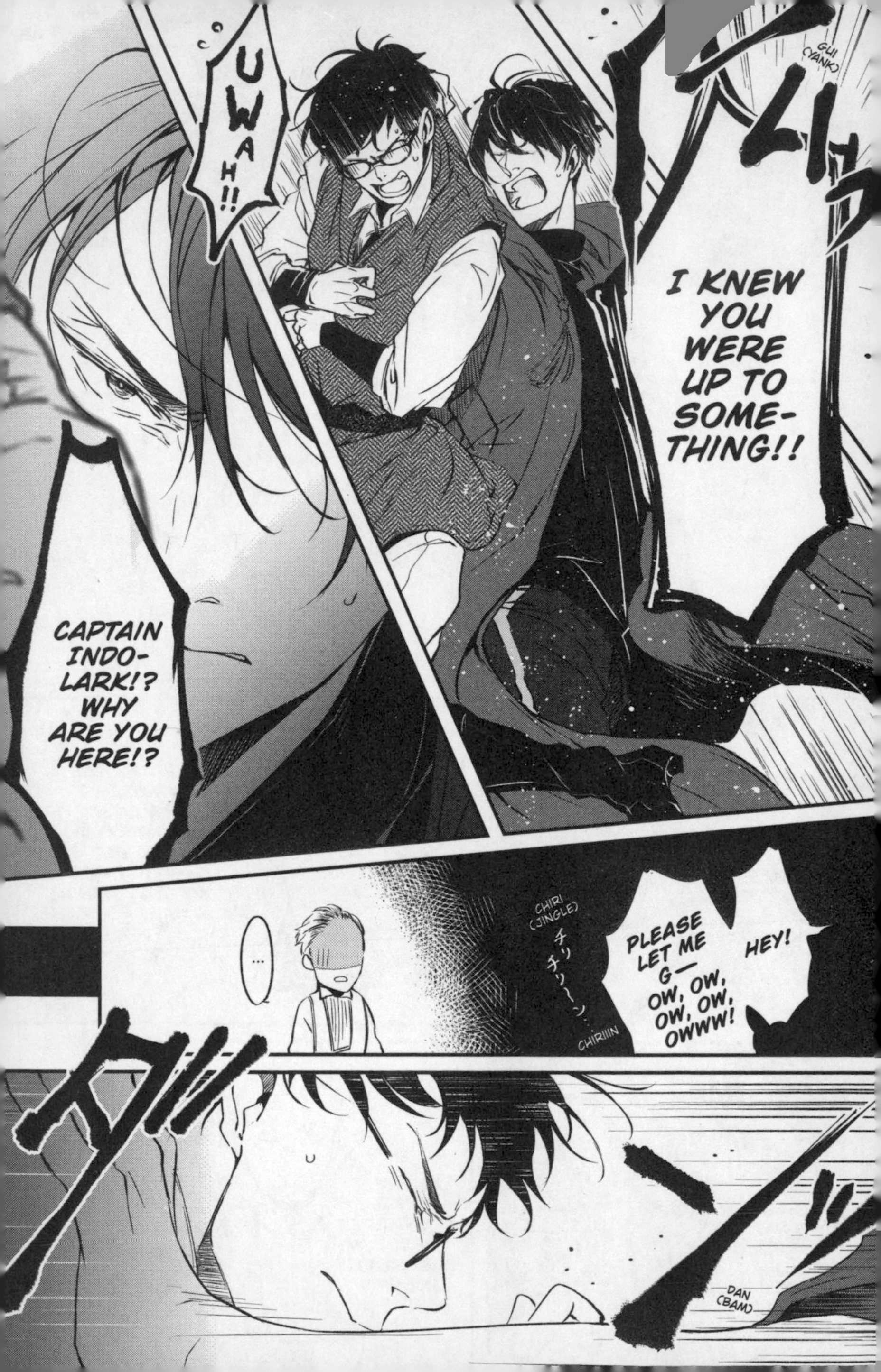
GUI (YANK)
I KNEW YOU WERE UP TO SOME-THING!!
UWAH!!
CAPTAIN INDO-LARK!? WHY ARE YOU HERE!?
HEY!
PLEASE LET ME G— OW, OW, OW, OWWW!
CHIRI (JINGLE)
チリ チリ〜ン…
CHIRIIN
...
DAN (BAM)

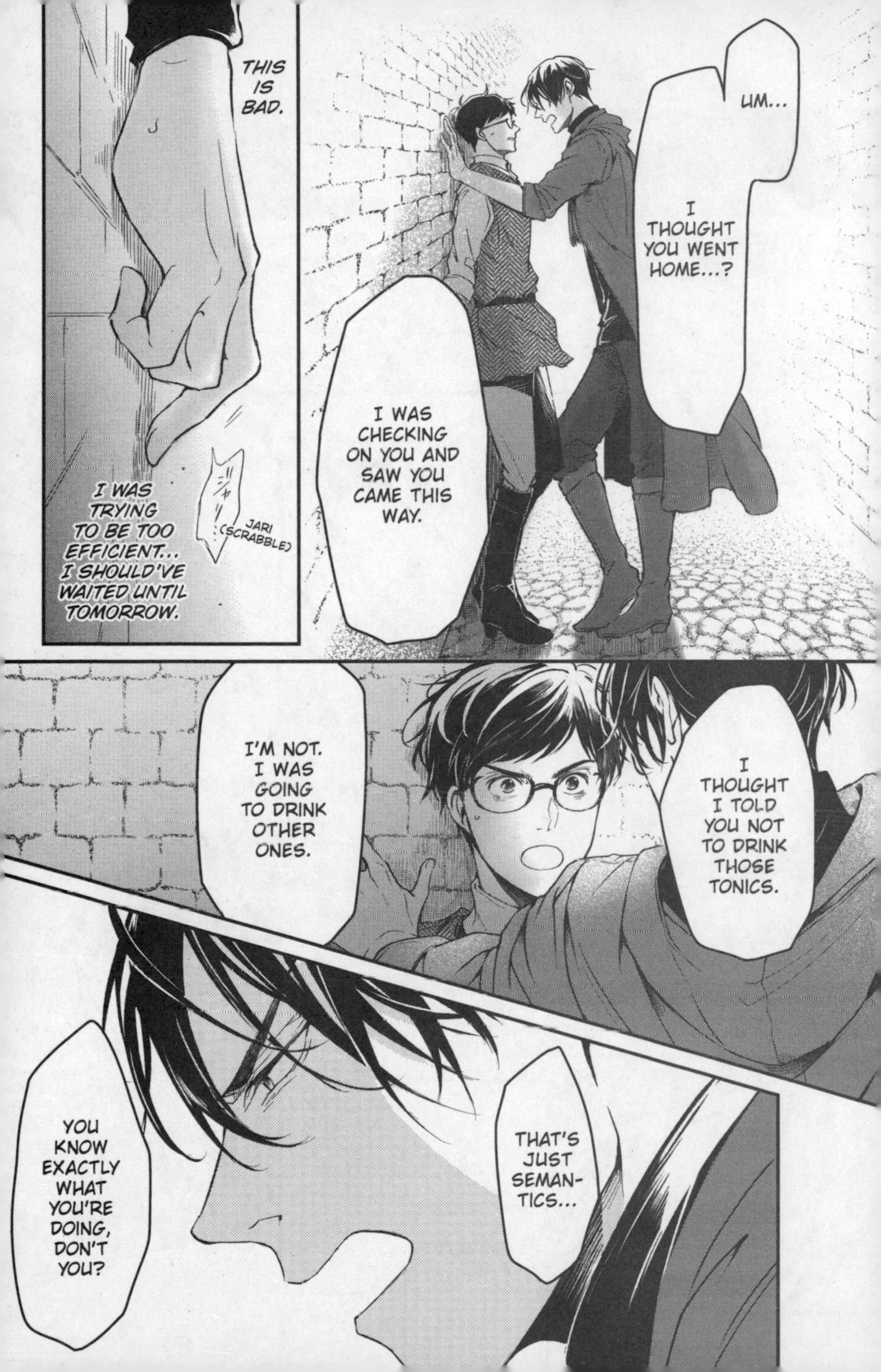
UM...
I THOUGHT YOU WENT HOME...?
I WAS CHECKING ON YOU AND SAW YOU CAME THIS WAY.
THIS IS BAD.
JARI (SCRABBLE)
I WAS TRYING TO BE TOO EFFICIENT... I SHOULD'VE WAITED UNTIL TOMORROW.
I THOUGHT I TOLD YOU NOT TO DRINK THOSE TONICS.
I'M NOT. I WAS GOING TO DRINK OTHER ONES.
THAT'S JUST SEMAN-TICS...
YOU KNOW EXACTLY WHAT YOU'RE DOING, DON'T YOU?

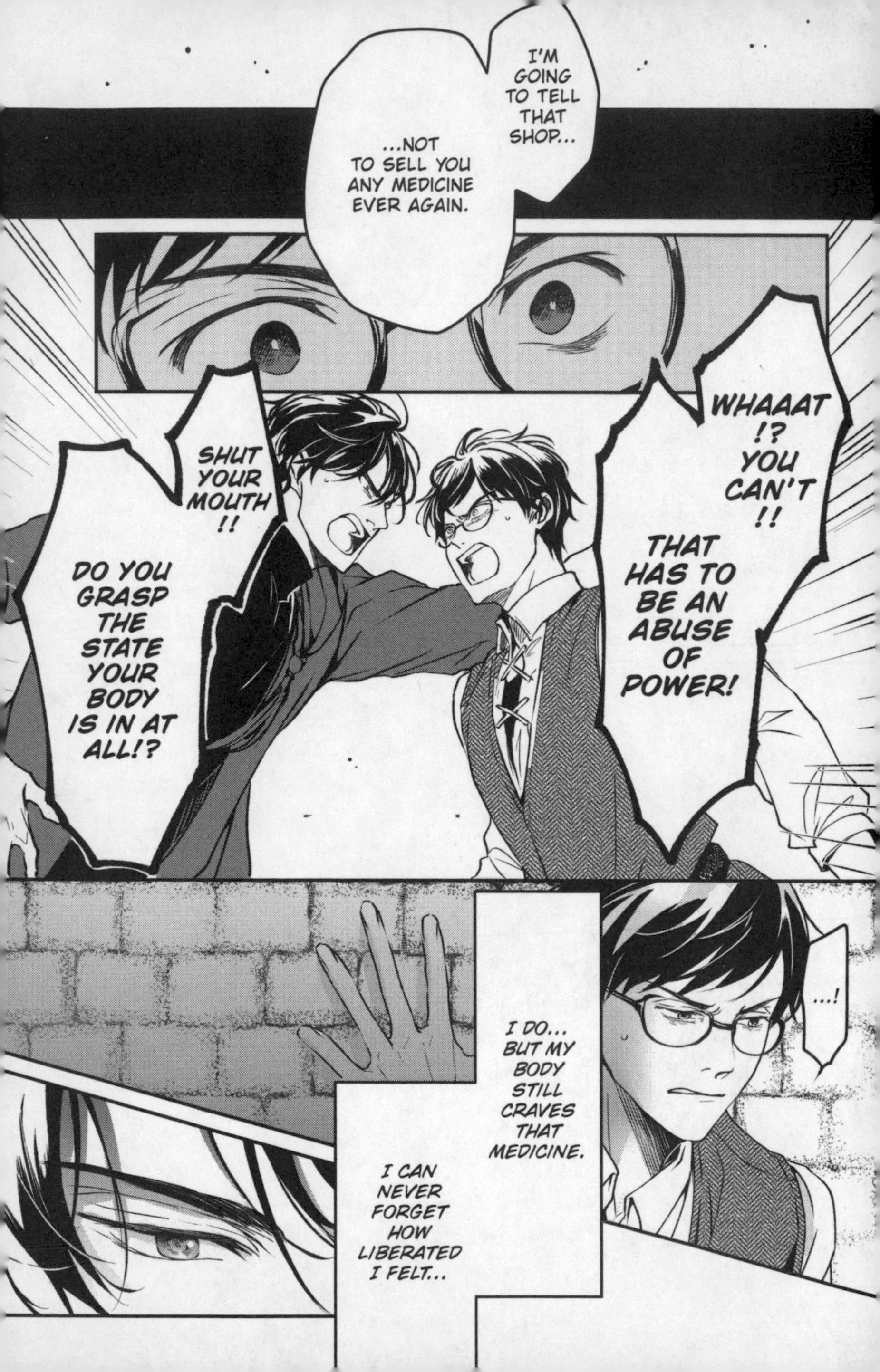
I'M GOING TO TELL THAT SHOP...
...NOT TO SELL YOU ANY MEDICINE EVER AGAIN.
WHAAAT!? YOU CAN'T!!
THAT HAS TO BE AN ABUSE OF POWER!
SHUT YOUR MOUTH!!
DO YOU GRASP THE STATE YOUR BODY IS IN AT ALL!?
...!
I DO... BUT MY BODY STILL CRAVES THAT MEDICINE.
I CAN NEVER FORGET HOW LIBERATED I FELT...

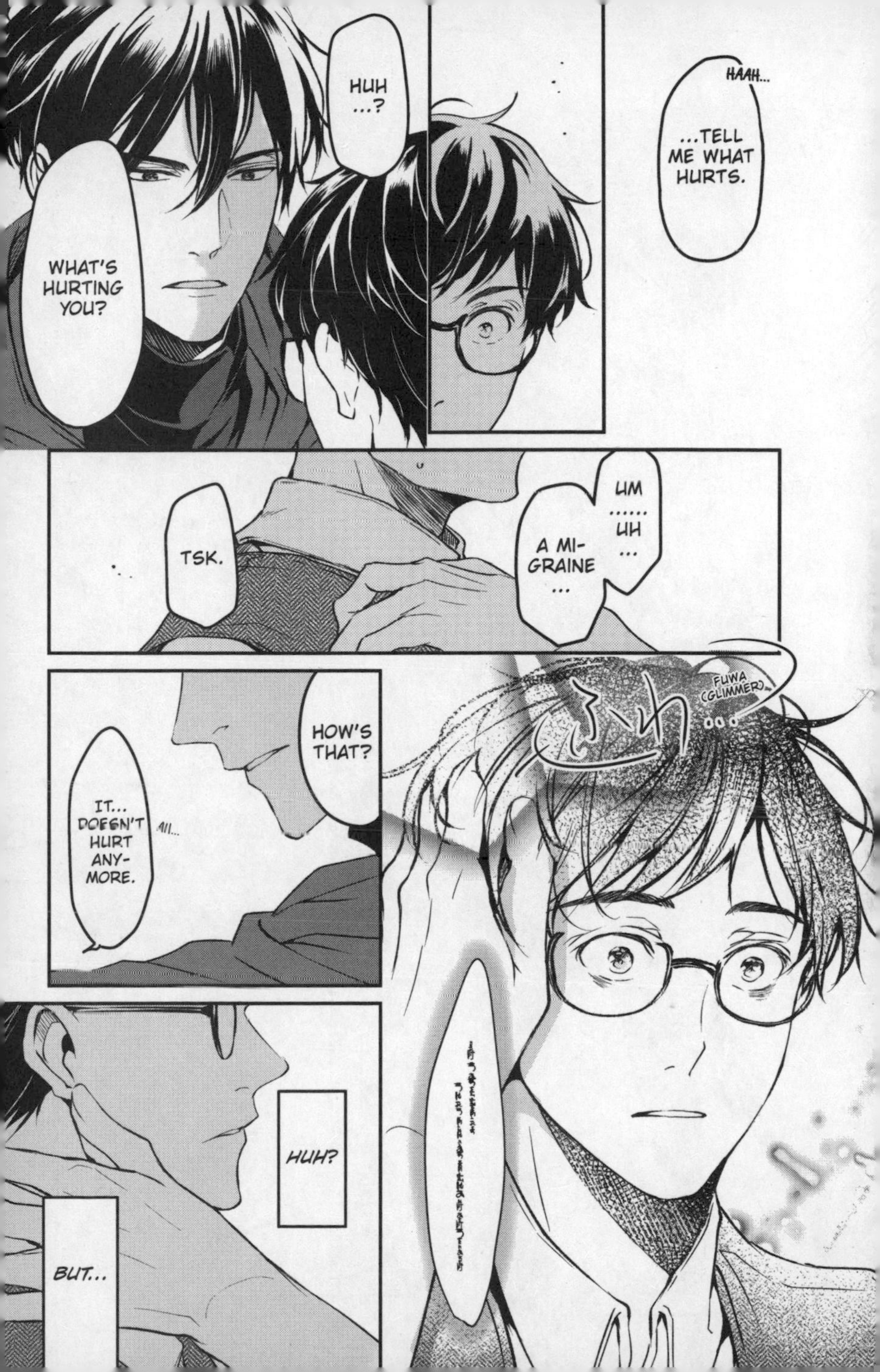
HAAH...
...TELL ME WHAT HURTS.
HUH ...?
WHAT'S HURTING YOU?
UM ...... UH ...
A MI-GRAINE ...
TSK.
FUWA (GLIMMER)
HOW'S THAT?
IT... DOESN'T HURT ANY-MORE.
AH...
HUH?
BUT...

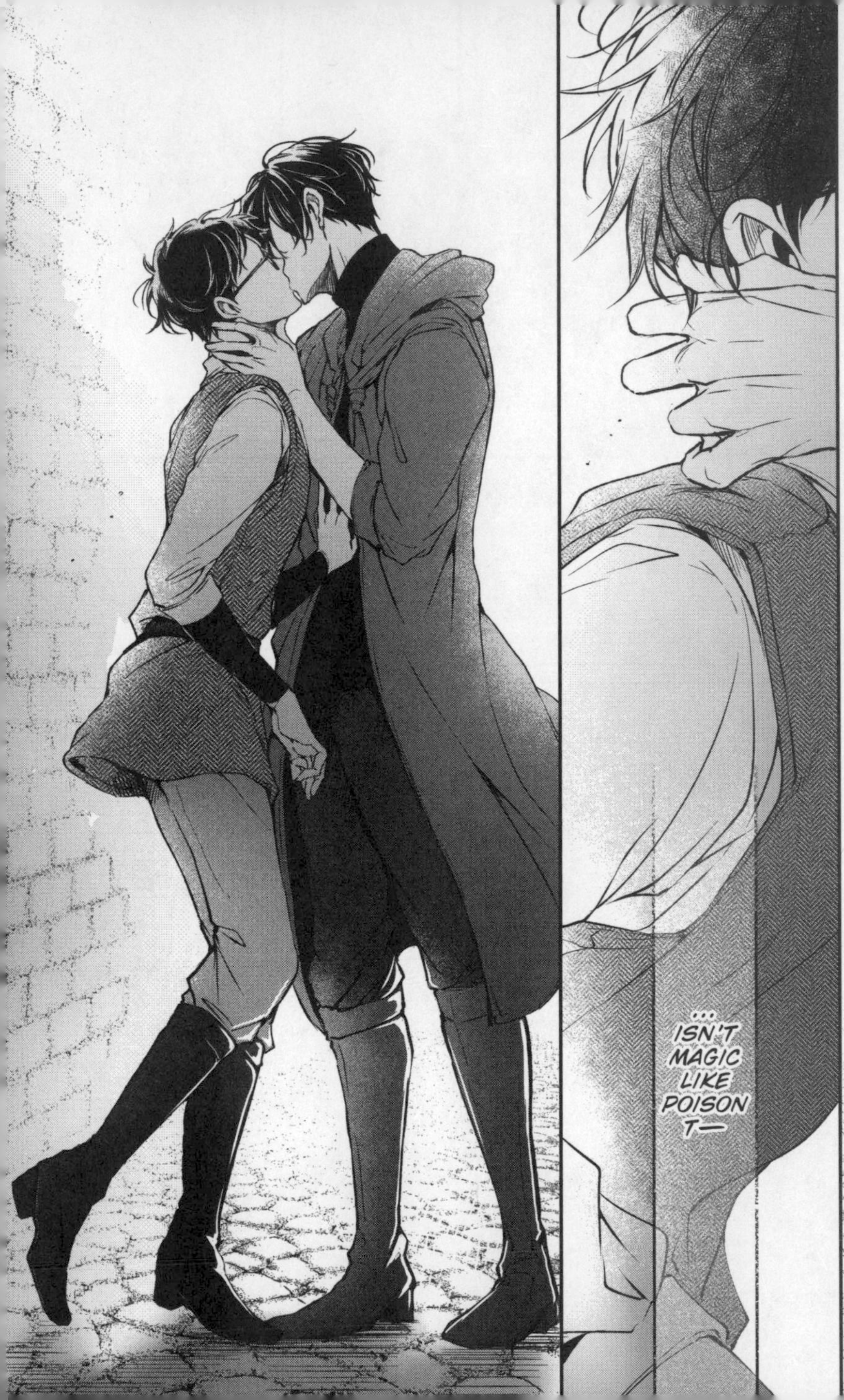
...ISN'T MAGIC LIKE POISON T—

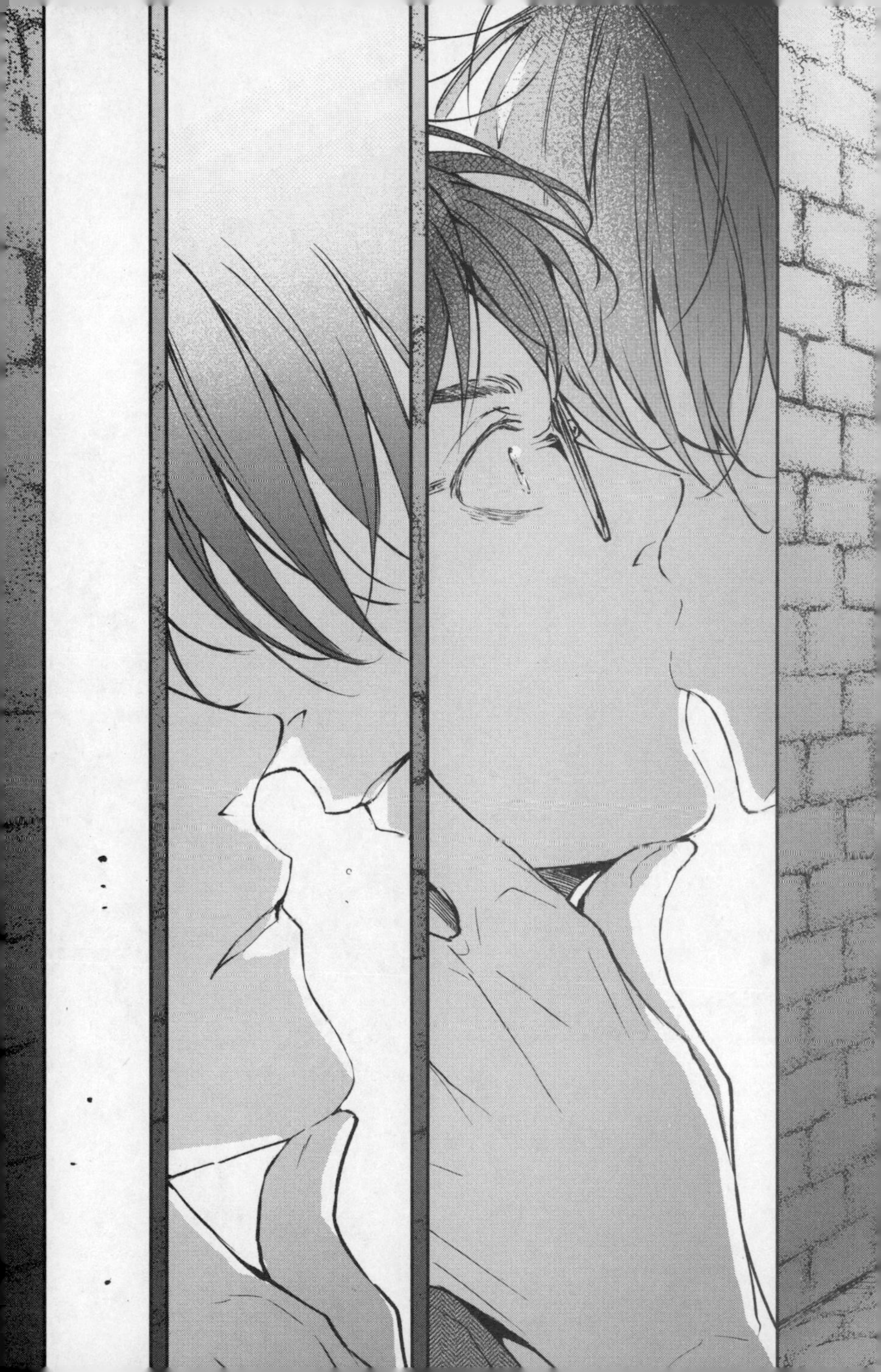
...

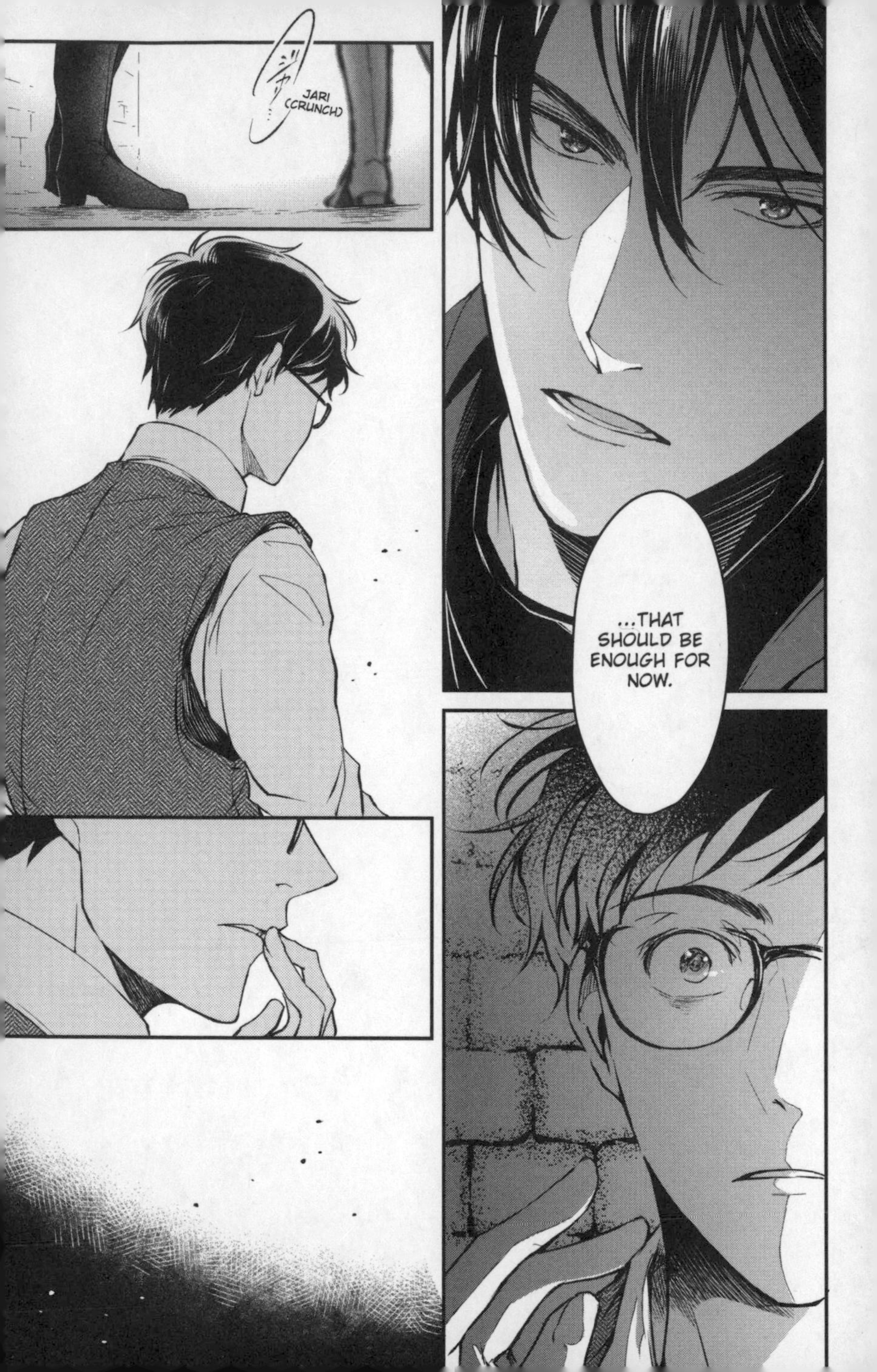
...THAT SHOULD BE ENOUGH FOR NOW.
ジャリ…
JARI (CRUNCH)

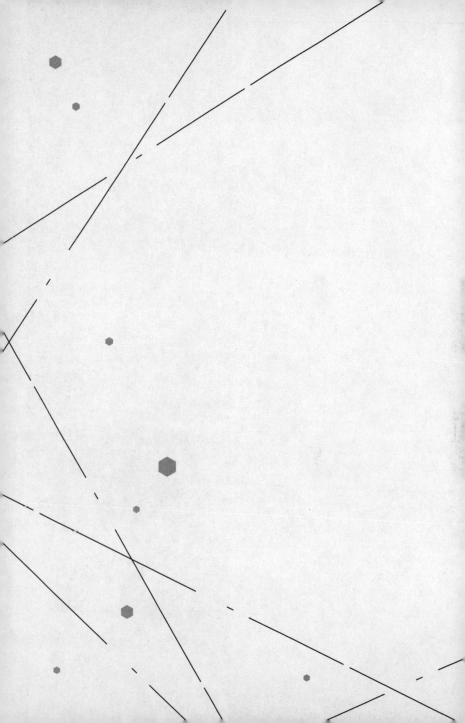

The Other World's Books Depend on the Bean Counter

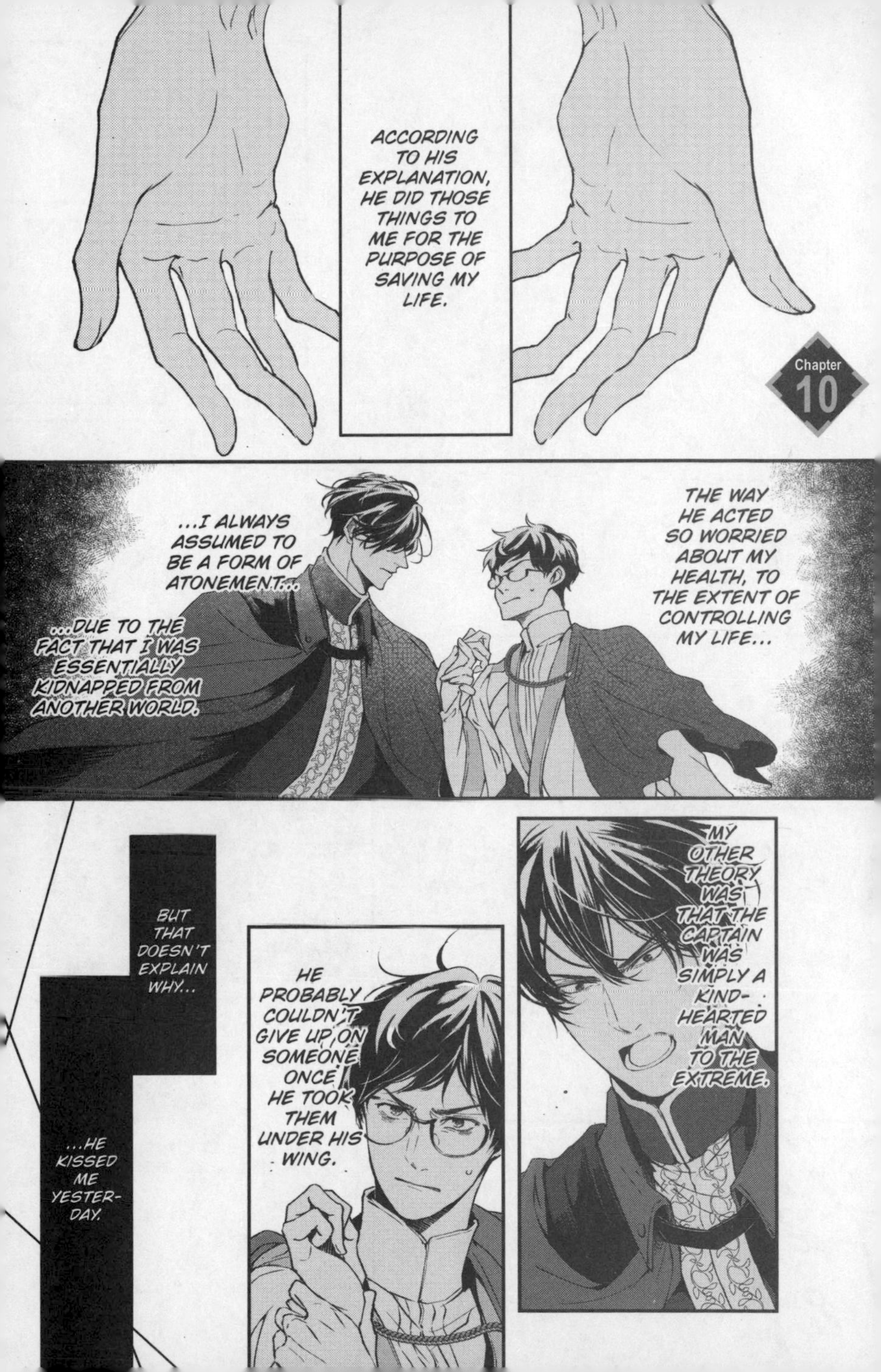
ACCORDING TO HIS EXPLANATION, HE DID THOSE THINGS TO ME FOR THE PURPOSE OF SAVING MY LIFE.
Chapter 10
THE WAY HE ACTED SO WORRIED ABOUT MY HEALTH, TO THE EXTENT OF CONTROLLING MY LIFE...
...I ALWAYS ASSUMED TO BE A FORM OF ATONEMENT...
...DUE TO THE FACT THAT I WAS ESSENTIALLY KIDNAPPED FROM ANOTHER WORLD.
MY OTHER THEORY WAS THAT THE CAPTAIN WAS SIMPLY A KIND-HEARTED MAN TO THE EXTREME.
HE PROBABLY COULDN'T GIVE UP ON SOMEONE ONCE HE TOOK THEM UNDER HIS WING.
BUT THAT DOESN'T EXPLAIN WHY...
...HE KISSED ME YESTER-DAY.

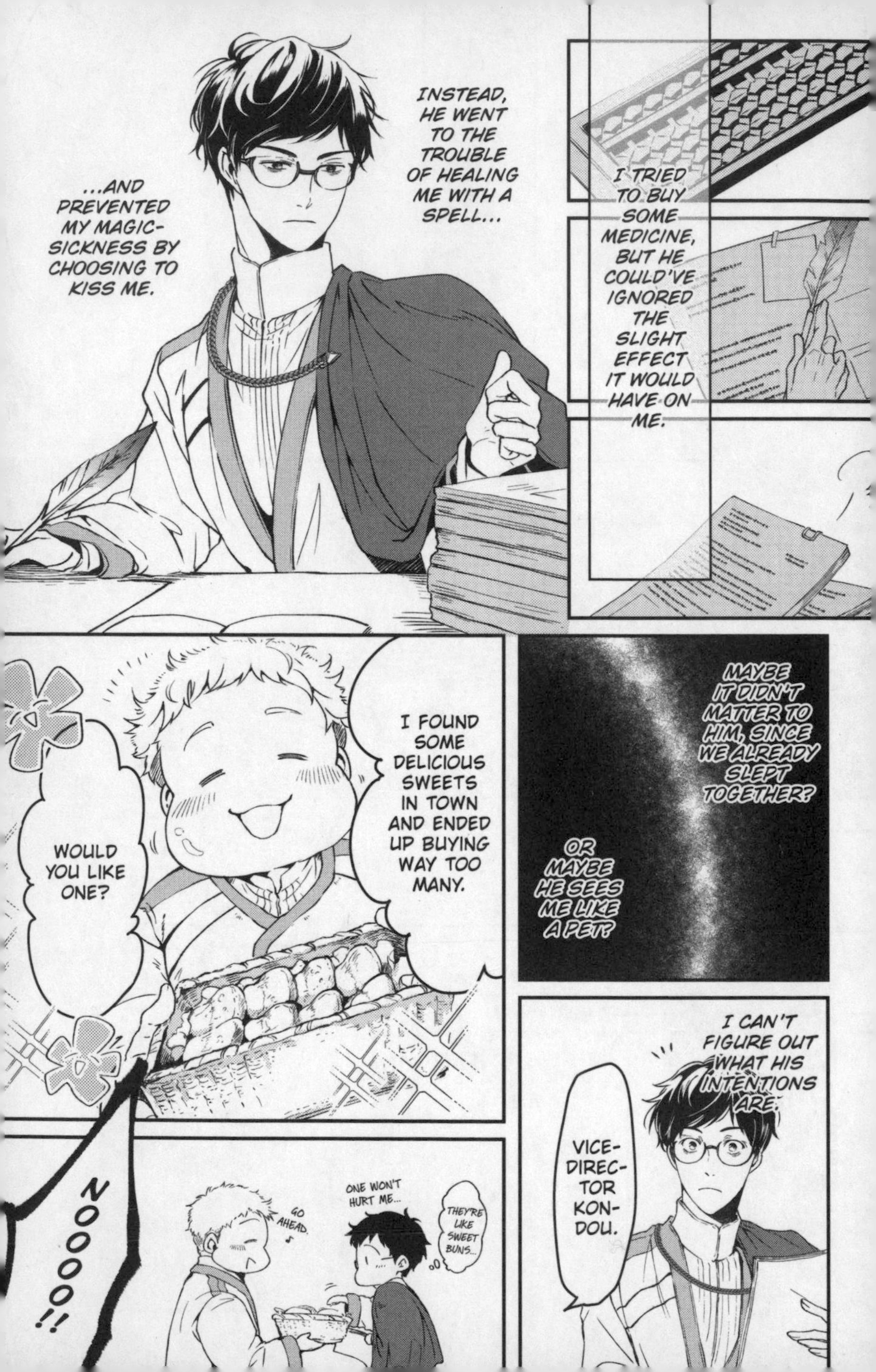
I TRIED TO BUY SOME MEDICINE, BUT HE COULD'VE IGNORED THE SLIGHT EFFECT IT WOULD HAVE ON ME.
INSTEAD, HE WENT TO THE TROUBLE OF HEALING ME WITH A SPELL...
...AND PREVENTED MY MAGIC-SICKNESS BY CHOOSING TO KISS ME.
MAYBE IT DIDN'T MATTER TO HIM, SINCE WE ALREADY SLEPT TOGETHER?
OR MAYBE HE SEES ME LIKE A PET?
I CAN'T FIGURE OUT WHAT HIS INTENTIONS ARE.
VICE-DIRECTOR KONDOU.
I FOUND SOME DELICIOUS SWEETS IN TOWN AND ENDED UP BUYING WAY TOO MANY.
WOULD YOU LIKE ONE?
ONE WON'T HURT ME...
THEY'RE LIKE SWEET BUNS...
GO AHEAD. ♪
NOOOOO!!

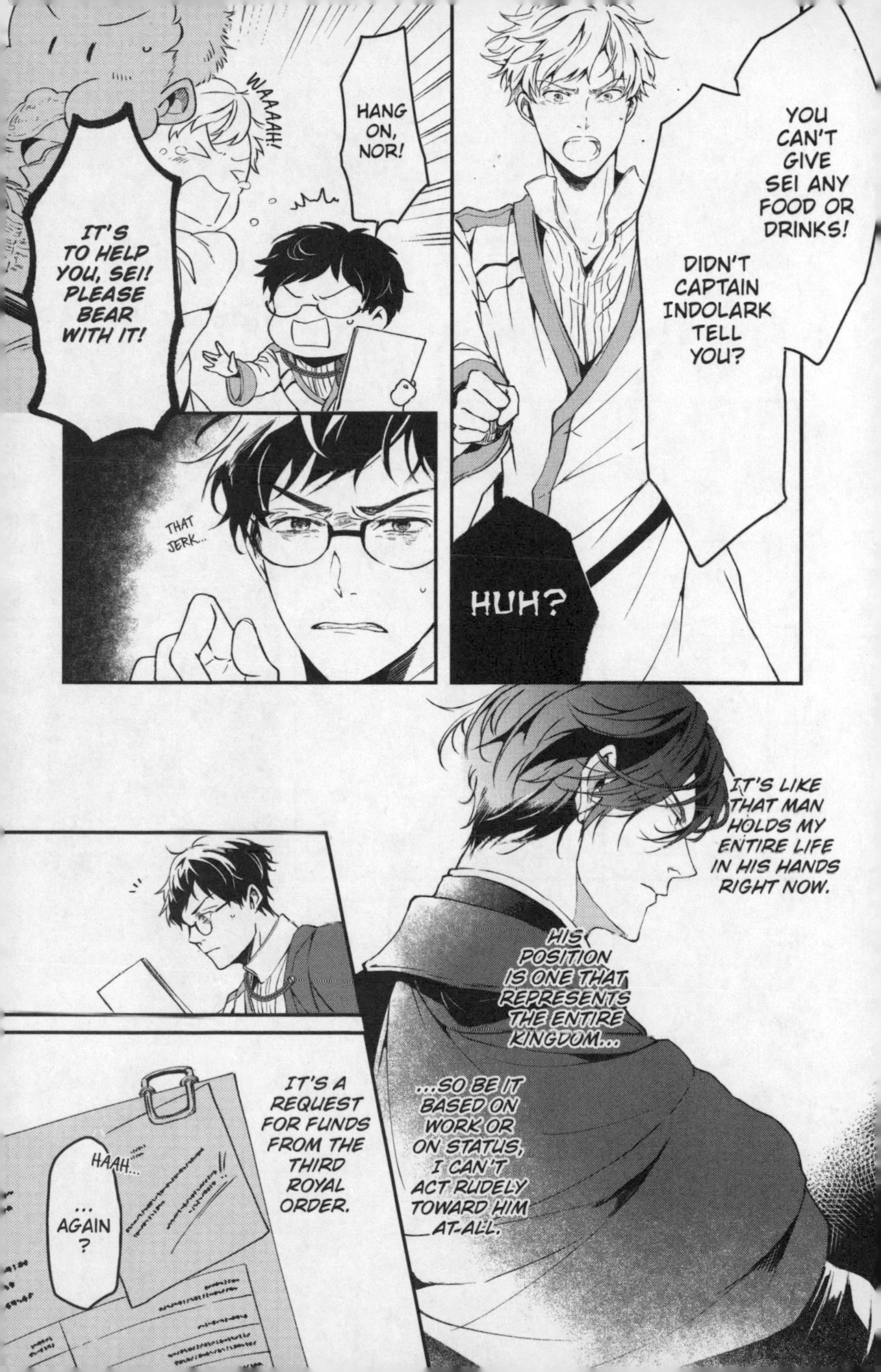
YOU CAN'T GIVE SEI ANY FOOD OR DRINKS!
DIDN'T CAPTAIN INDOLARK TELL YOU?
HANG ON, NOR!
WAAAAH!
IT'S TO HELP YOU, SEI! PLEASE BEAR WITH IT!
HUH?
THAT JERK...
IT'S LIKE THAT MAN HOLDS MY ENTIRE LIFE IN HIS HANDS RIGHT NOW.
HIS POSITION IS ONE THAT REPRESENTS THE ENTIRE KINGDOM...
...SO BE IT BASED ON WORK OR ON STATUS, I CAN'T ACT RUDELY TOWARD HIM AT ALL.
IT'S A REQUEST FOR FUNDS FROM THE THIRD ROYAL ORDER.
HAAH...
...AGAIN?

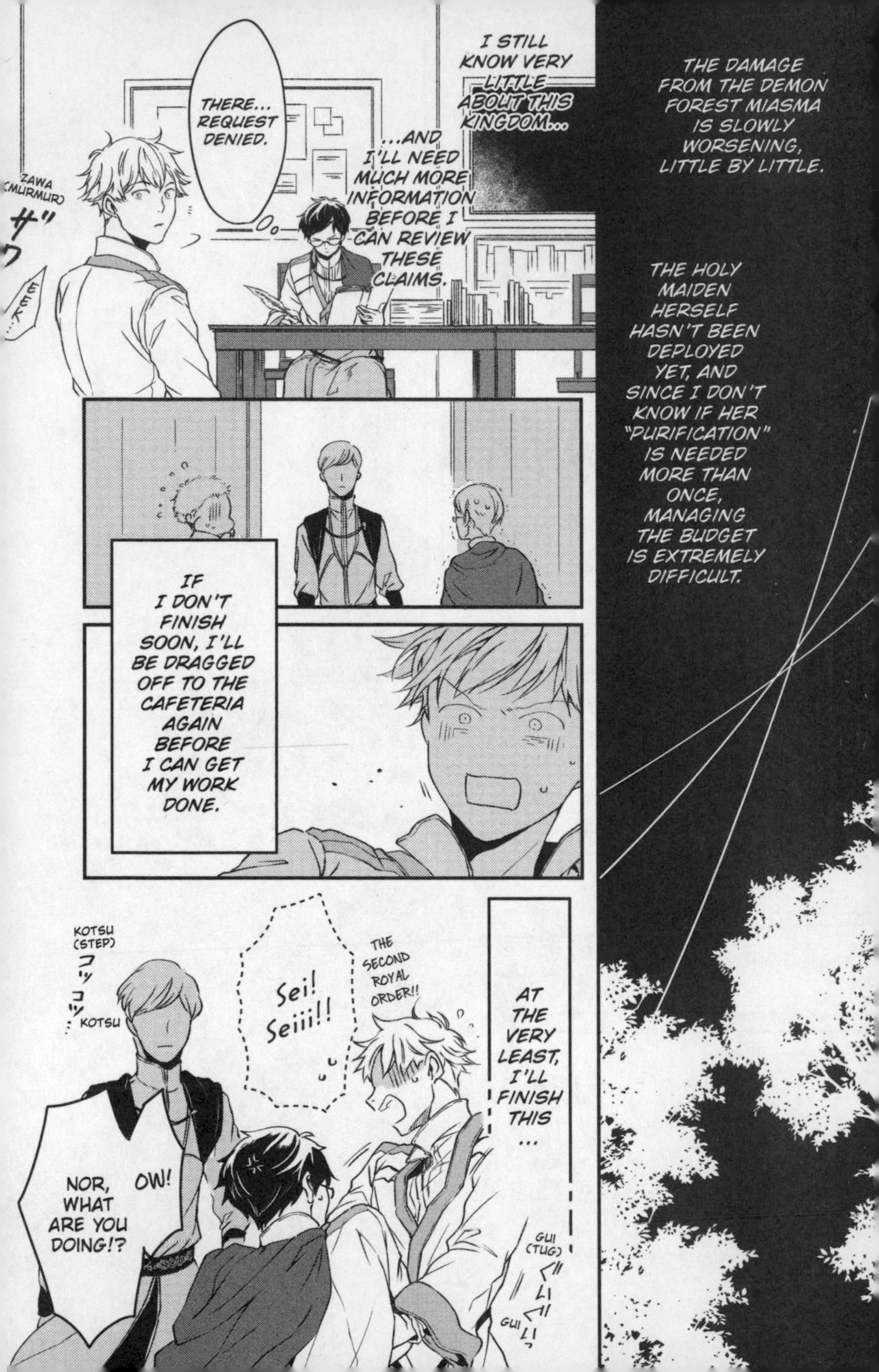
THE DAMAGE FROM THE DEMON FOREST MIASMA IS SLOWLY WORSENING, LITTLE BY LITTLE.
THE HOLY MAIDEN HERSELF HASN'T BEEN DEPLOYED YET, AND SINCE I DON'T KNOW IF HER "PURIFICATION" IS NEEDED MORE THAN ONCE, MANAGING THE BUDGET IS EXTREMELY DIFFICULT.
I STILL KNOW VERY LITTLE ABOUT THIS KINGDOM...
...AND I'LL NEED MUCH MORE INFORMATION BEFORE I CAN REVIEW THESE CLAIMS.
THERE... REQUEST DENIED.
ZAWA (MURMUR)
ザワ
EEK...
IF I DON'T FINISH SOON, I'LL BE DRAGGED OFF TO THE CAFETERIA AGAIN BEFORE I CAN GET MY WORK DONE.
AT THE VERY LEAST, I'LL FINISH THIS...
THE SECOND ROYAL ORDER!!
Sei! Seiii!!
KOTSU (STEP)
コッ コッ
KOTSU
NOR, WHAT ARE YOU DOING!?
OW!
GUI (TUG)
ぐい ぐい
GUI

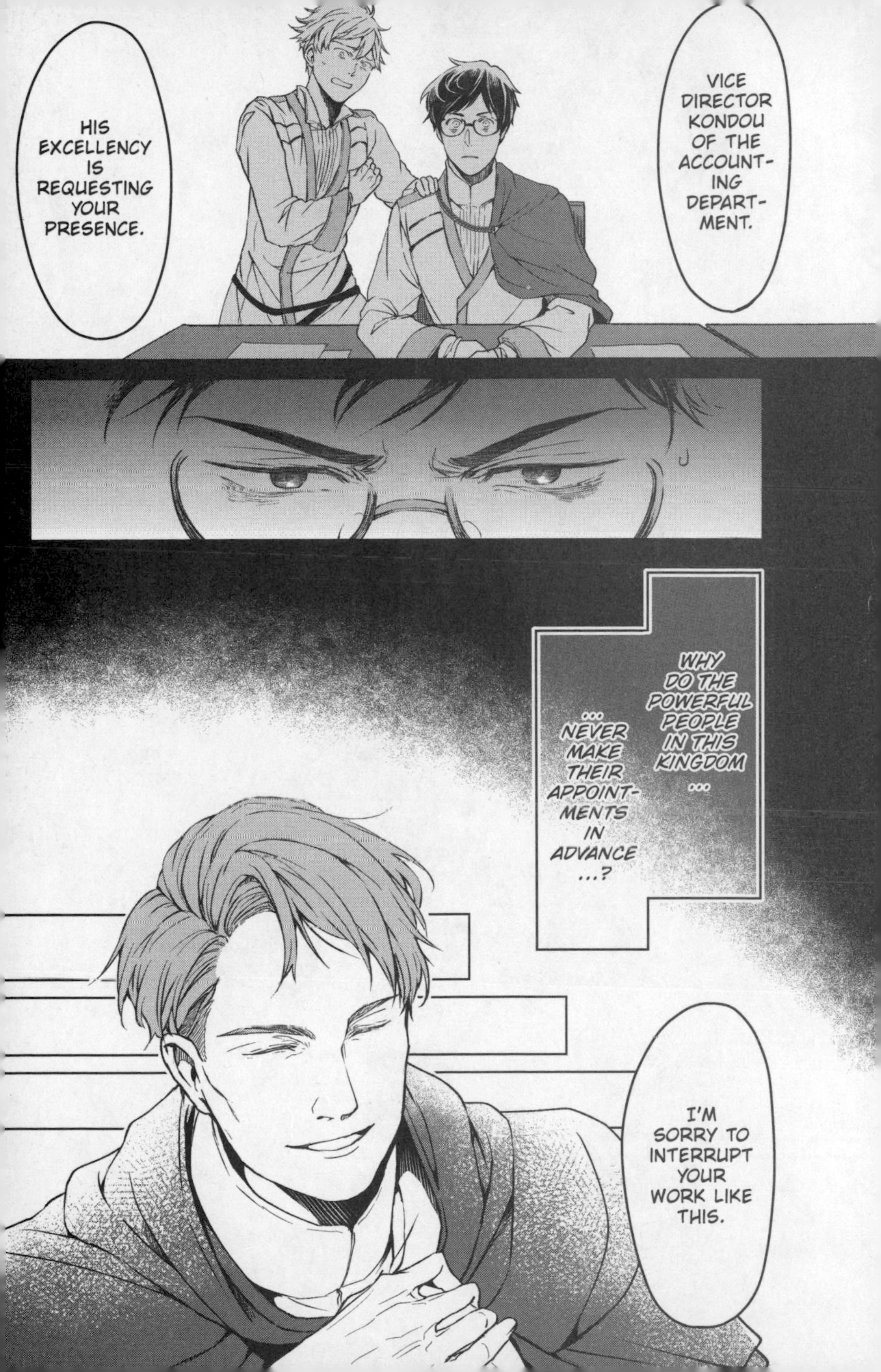
VICE DIRECTOR KONDOU OF THE ACCOUNTING DEPARTMENT.
HIS EXCELLENCY IS REQUESTING YOUR PRESENCE.
WHY DO THE POWERFUL PEOPLE IN THIS KINGDOM ...
... NEVER MAKE THEIR APPOINTMENTS IN ADVANCE ...?
I'M SORRY TO INTERRUPT YOUR WORK LIKE THIS.

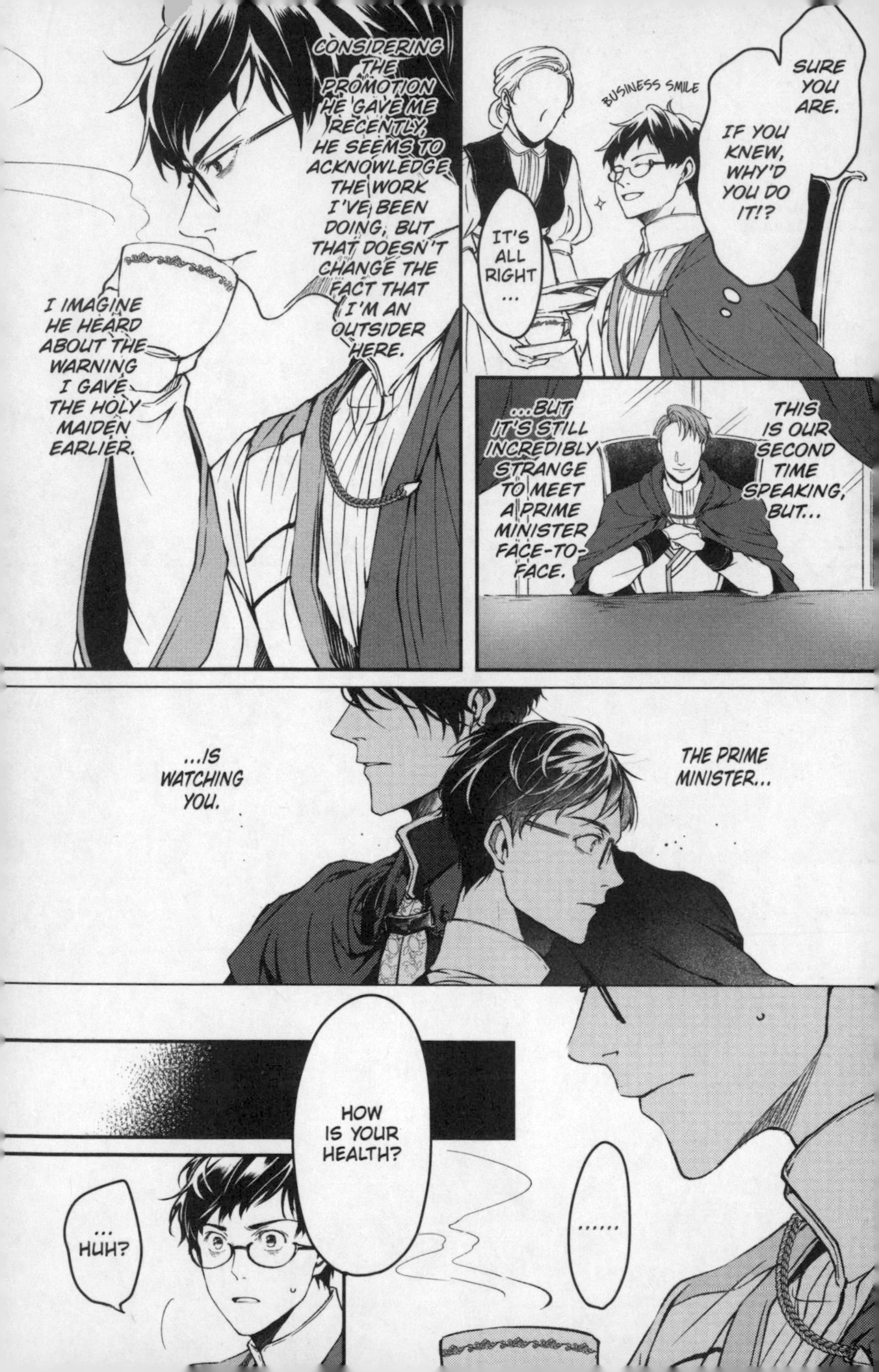
SURE YOU ARE.
IF YOU KNEW, WHY'D YOU DO IT!?
BUSINESS SMILE
IT'S ALL RIGHT...
THIS IS OUR SECOND TIME SPEAKING, BUT...
...BUT IT'S STILL INCREDIBLY STRANGE TO MEET A PRIME MINISTER FACE-TO-FACE.
CONSIDERING THE PROMOTION HE GAVE ME RECENTLY, HE SEEMS TO ACKNOWLEDGE THE WORK I'VE BEEN DOING, BUT THAT DOESN'T CHANGE THE FACT THAT I'M AN OUTSIDER HERE.
I IMAGINE HE HEARD ABOUT THE WARNING I GAVE THE HOLY MAIDEN EARLIER.
THE PRIME MINISTER...
...IS WATCHING YOU.
......
HOW IS YOUR HEALTH?
...HUH?

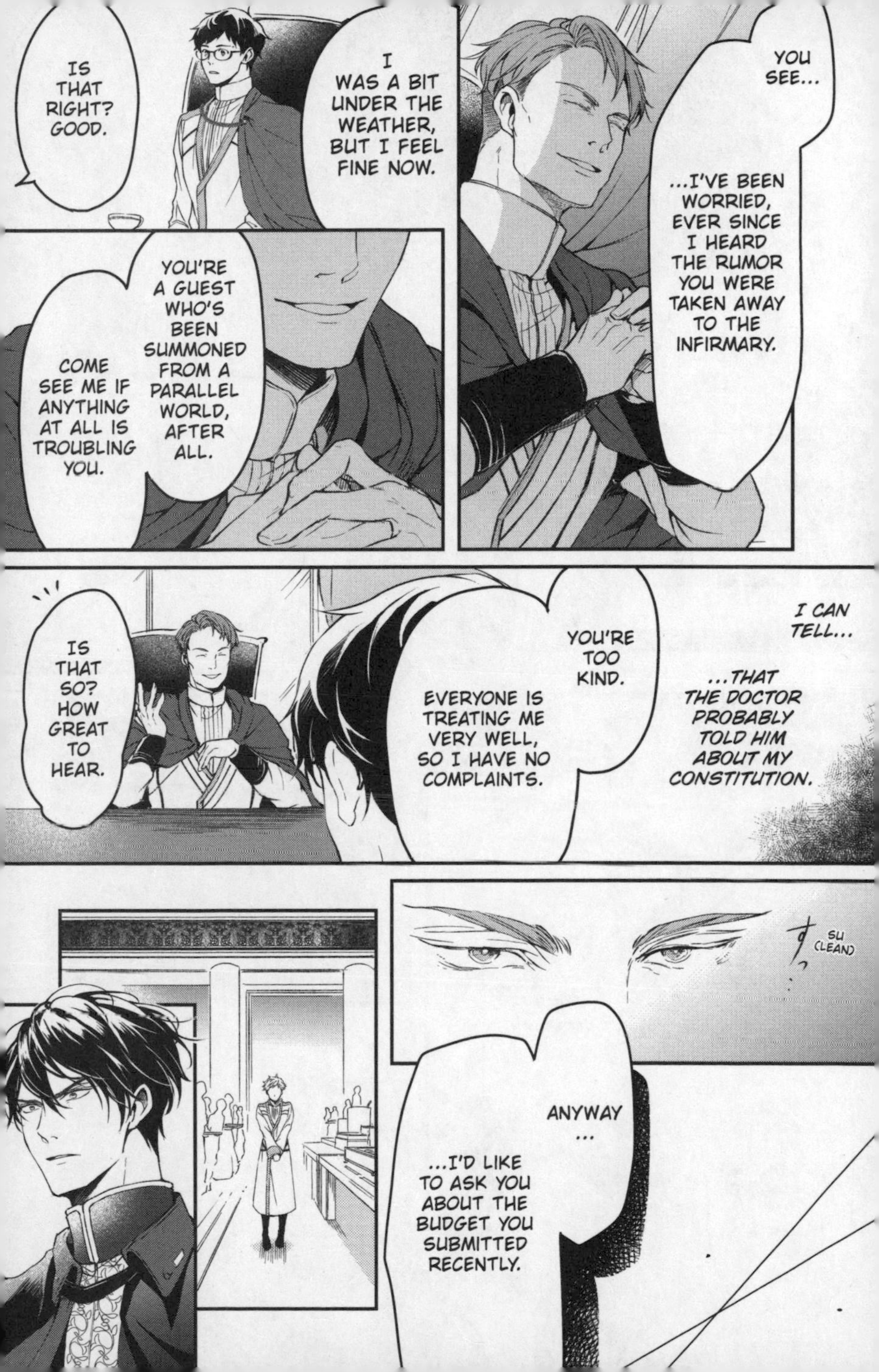
YOU SEE...
...I'VE BEEN WORRIED, EVER SINCE I HEARD THE RUMOR YOU WERE TAKEN AWAY TO THE INFIRMARY.
I WAS A BIT UNDER THE WEATHER, BUT I FEEL FINE NOW.
IS THAT RIGHT? GOOD.
YOU'RE A GUEST WHO'S BEEN SUMMONED FROM A PARALLEL WORLD, AFTER ALL.
COME SEE ME IF ANYTHING AT ALL IS TROUBLING YOU.
I CAN TELL...
...THAT THE DOCTOR PROBABLY TOLD HIM ABOUT MY CONSTITUTION.
YOU'RE TOO KIND.
EVERYONE IS TREATING ME VERY WELL, SO I HAVE NO COMPLAINTS.
IS THAT SO? HOW GREAT TO HEAR.
SU (LEAN)
ANYWAY...
...I'D LIKE TO ASK YOU ABOUT THE BUDGET YOU SUBMITTED RECENTLY.

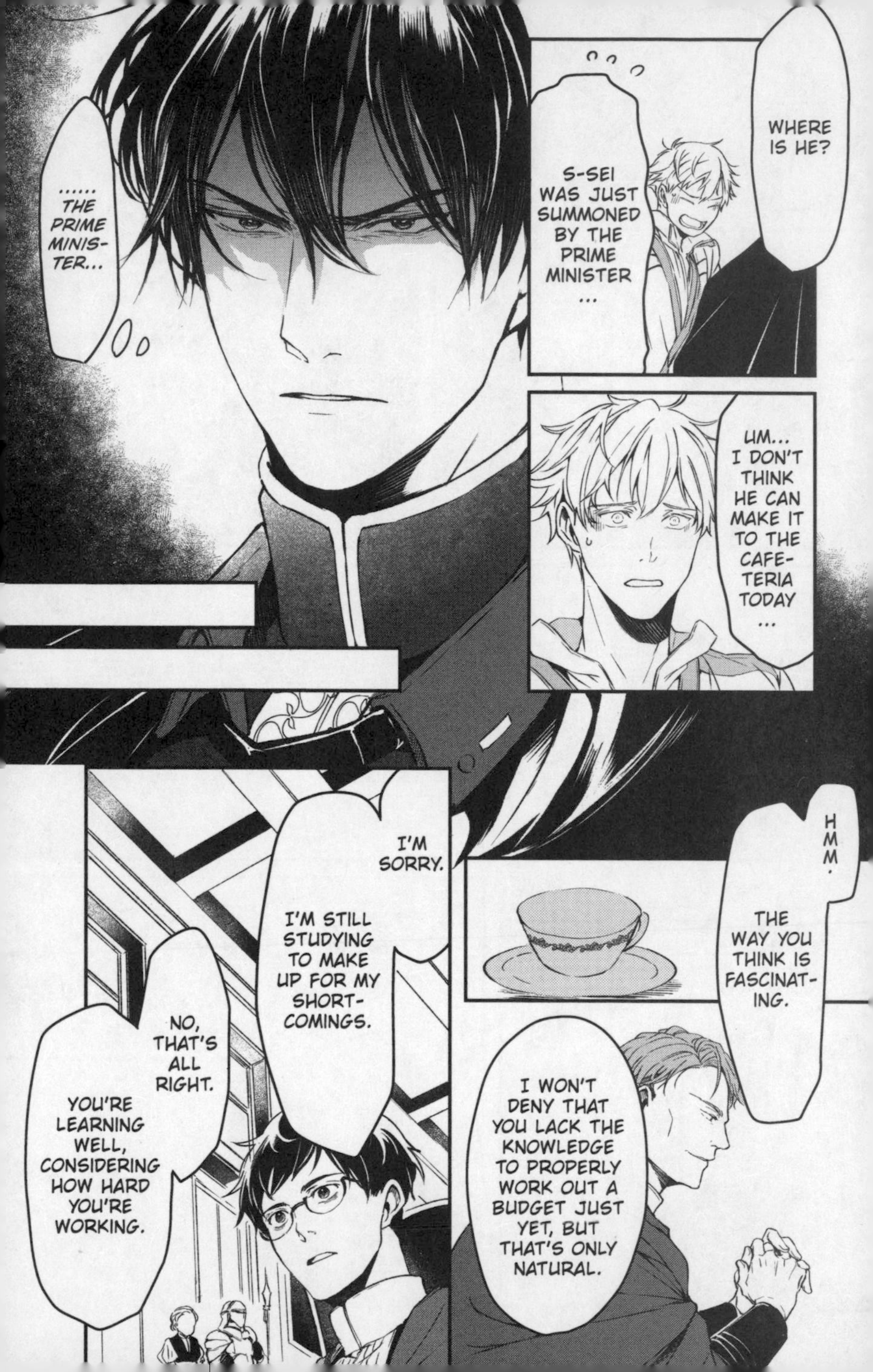
WHERE IS HE?
S-SEI WAS JUST SUMMONED BY THE PRIME MINISTER...
UM... I DON'T THINK HE CAN MAKE IT TO THE CAFETERIA TODAY...
......THE PRIME MINISTER...
HMM.
THE WAY YOU THINK IS FASCINATING.
I WON'T DENY THAT YOU LACK THE KNOWLEDGE TO PROPERLY WORK OUT A BUDGET JUST YET, BUT THAT'S ONLY NATURAL.
I'M SORRY.
I'M STILL STUDYING TO MAKE UP FOR MY SHORTCOMINGS.
NO, THAT'S ALL RIGHT.
YOU'RE LEARNING WELL, CONSIDERING HOW HARD YOU'RE WORKING.

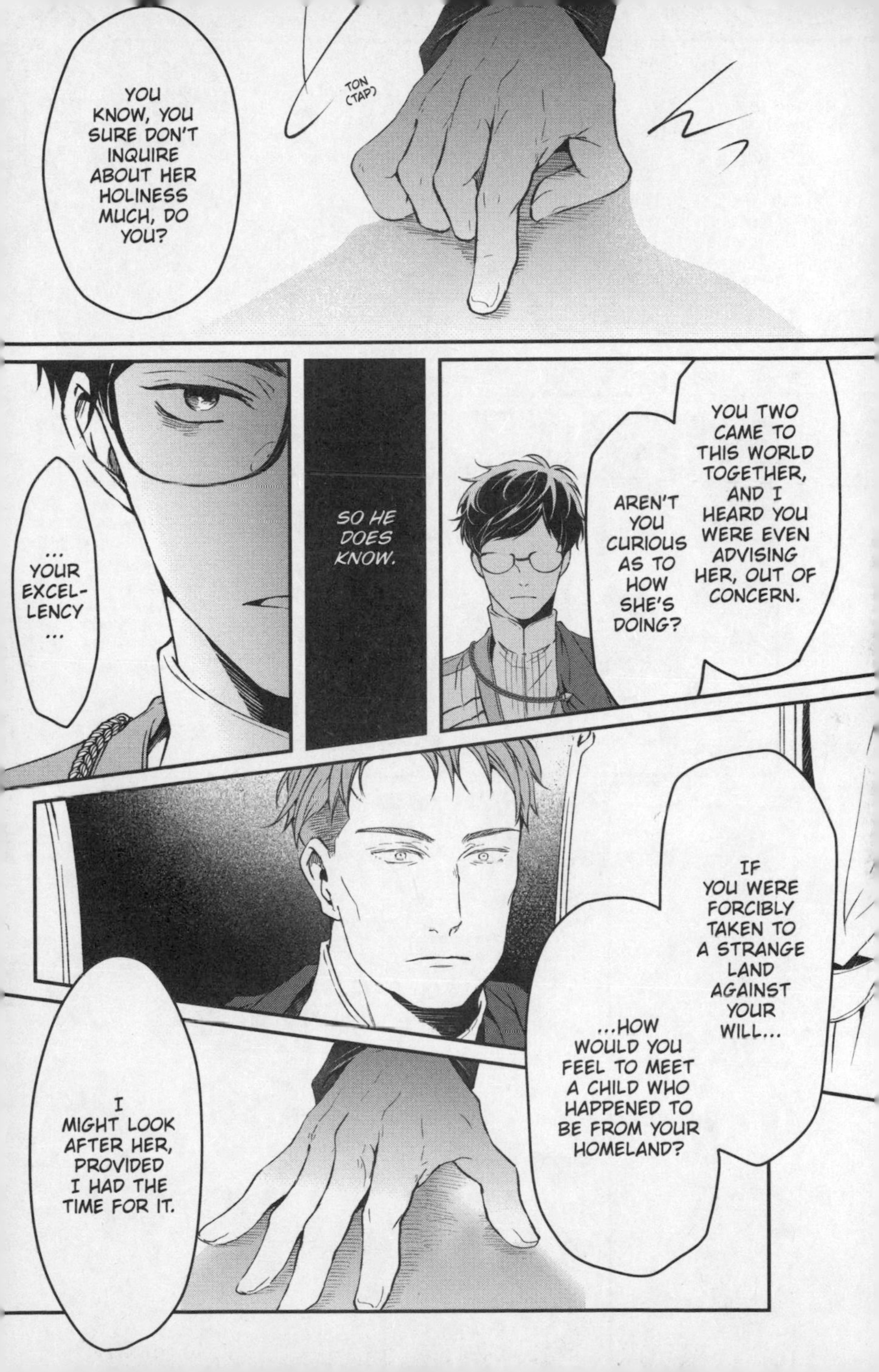
TON (TAP)
YOU KNOW, YOU SURE DON'T INQUIRE ABOUT HER HOLINESS MUCH, DO YOU?
YOU TWO CAME TO THIS WORLD TOGETHER, AND I HEARD YOU WERE EVEN ADVISING HER, OUT OF CONCERN.
AREN'T YOU CURIOUS AS TO HOW SHE'S DOING?
SO HE DOES KNOW.
... YOUR EXCEL-LENCY ...
IF YOU WERE FORCIBLY TAKEN TO A STRANGE LAND AGAINST YOUR WILL...
...HOW WOULD YOU FEEL TO MEET A CHILD WHO HAPPENED TO BE FROM YOUR HOMELAND?
I MIGHT LOOK AFTER HER, PROVIDED I HAD THE TIME FOR IT.

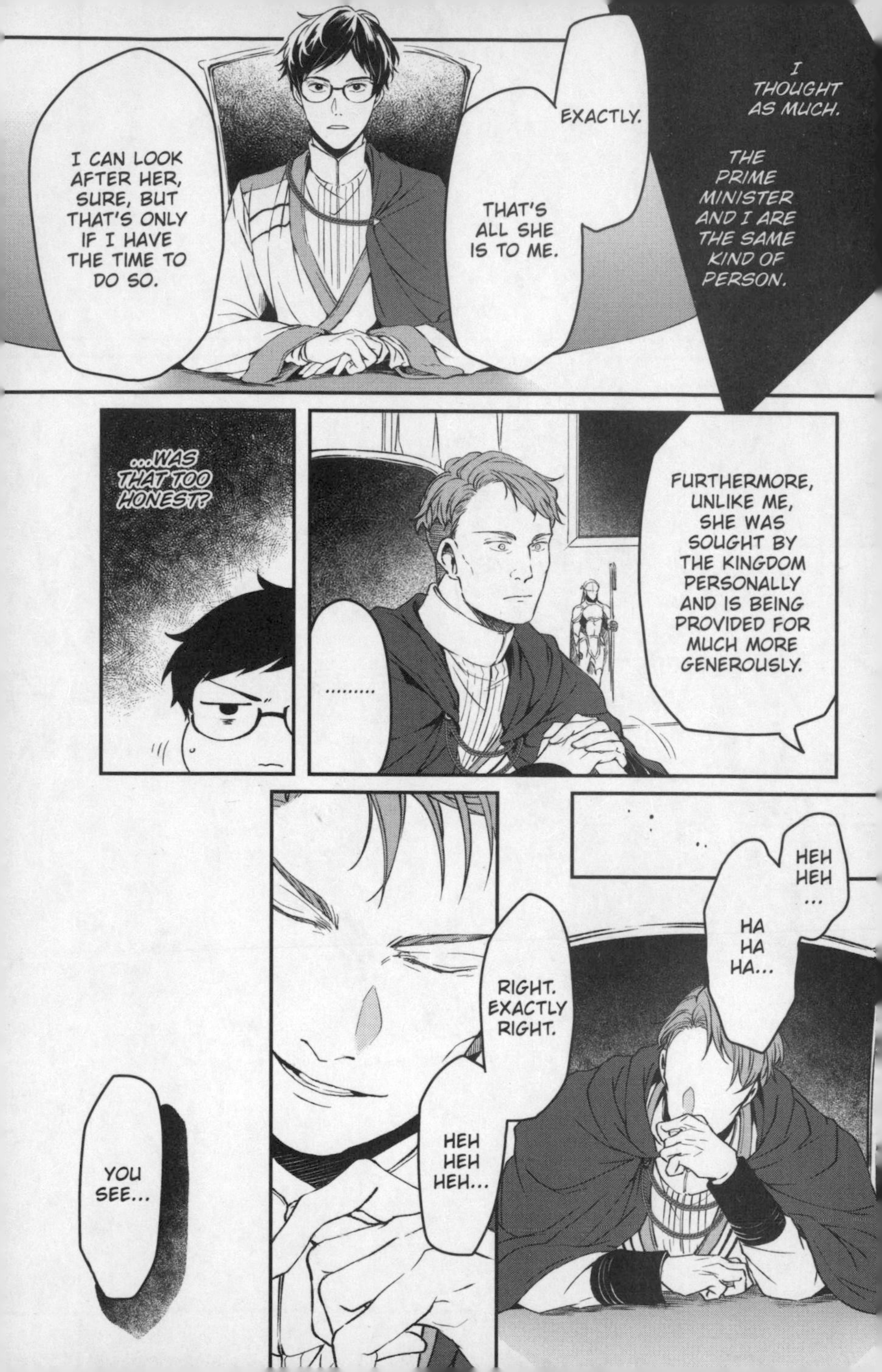
I THOUGHT AS MUCH.
THE PRIME MINISTER AND I ARE THE SAME KIND OF PERSON.
EXACTLY.
THAT'S ALL SHE IS TO ME.
I CAN LOOK AFTER HER, SURE, BUT THAT'S ONLY IF I HAVE THE TIME TO DO SO.
FURTHERMORE, UNLIKE ME, SHE WAS SOUGHT BY THE KINGDOM PERSONALLY AND IS BEING PROVIDED FOR MUCH MORE GENEROUSLY.
....
...WAS THAT TOO HONEST?
HEH HEH ...
HA HA HA...
RIGHT. EXACTLY RIGHT.
HEH HEH HEH...
YOU SEE...

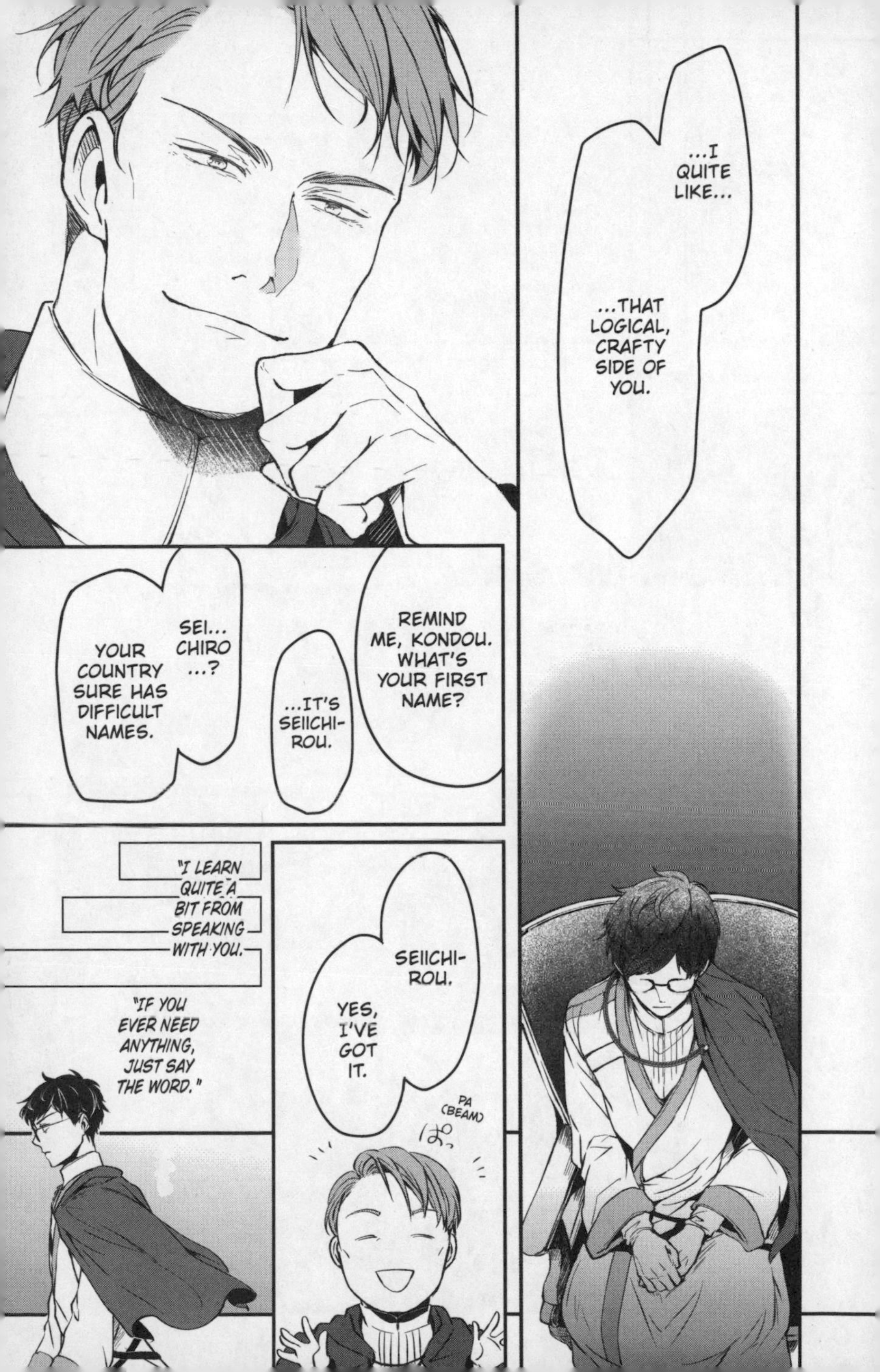
...I QUITE LIKE...
...THAT LOGICAL, CRAFTY SIDE OF YOU.
REMIND ME, KONDOU. WHAT'S YOUR FIRST NAME?
...IT'S SEIICHI-ROU.
SEI... CHIRO ...?
YOUR COUNTRY SURE HAS DIFFICULT NAMES.
SEIICHI-ROU.
YES, I'VE GOT IT.
PA (BEAM)
ぱっ
"I LEARN QUITE A BIT FROM SPEAKING WITH YOU.
"IF YOU EVER NEED ANYTHING, JUST SAY THE WORD."

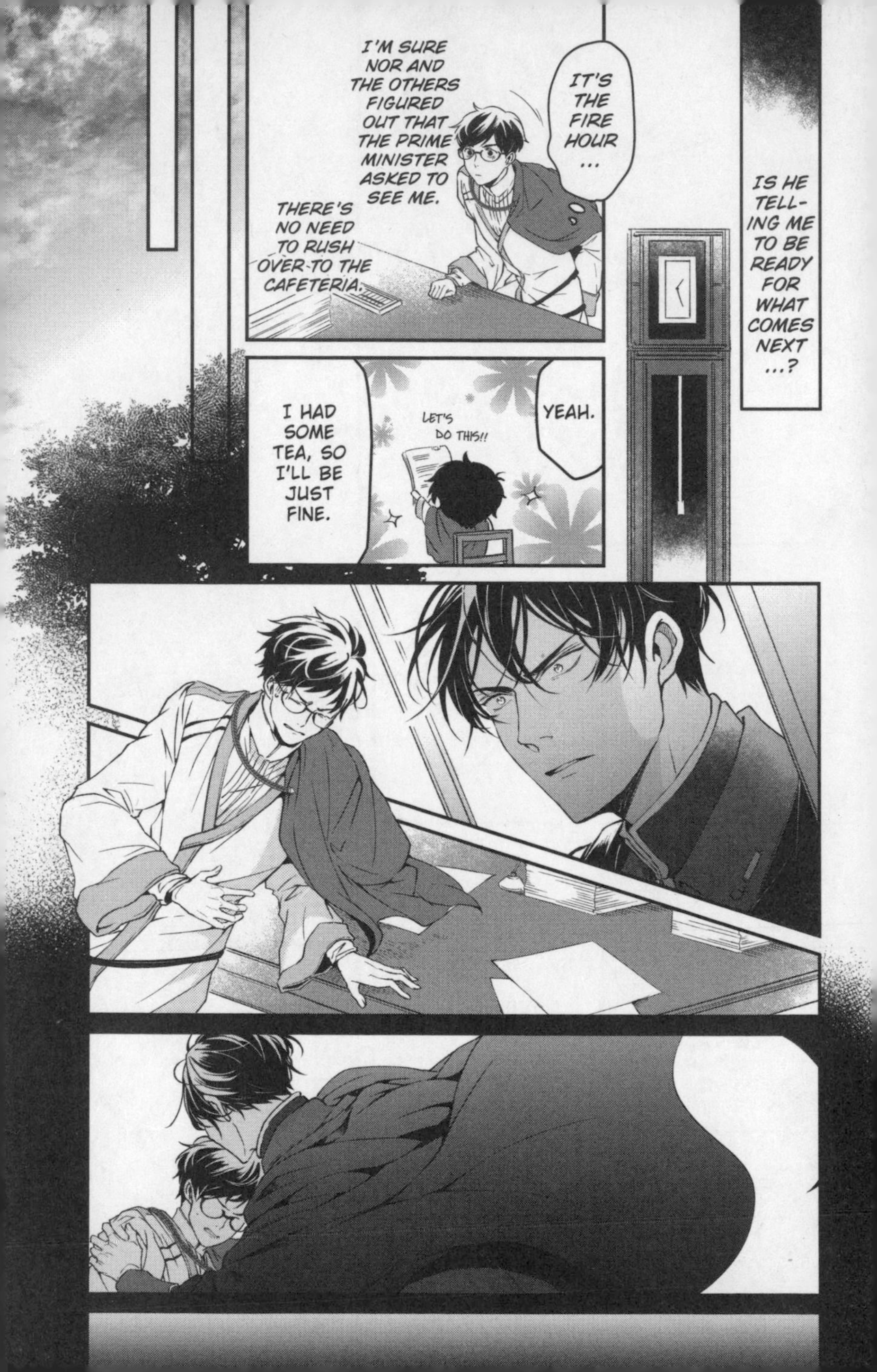
IS HE TELLING ME TO BE READY FOR WHAT COMES NEXT ...?
IT'S THE FIRE HOUR ...
I'M SURE NOR AND THE OTHERS FIGURED OUT THAT THE PRIME MINISTER ASKED TO SEE ME.
THERE'S NO NEED TO RUSH OVER TO THE CAFETERIA.
YEAH.
LET'S DO THIS!!
I HAD SOME TEA, SO I'LL BE JUST FINE.

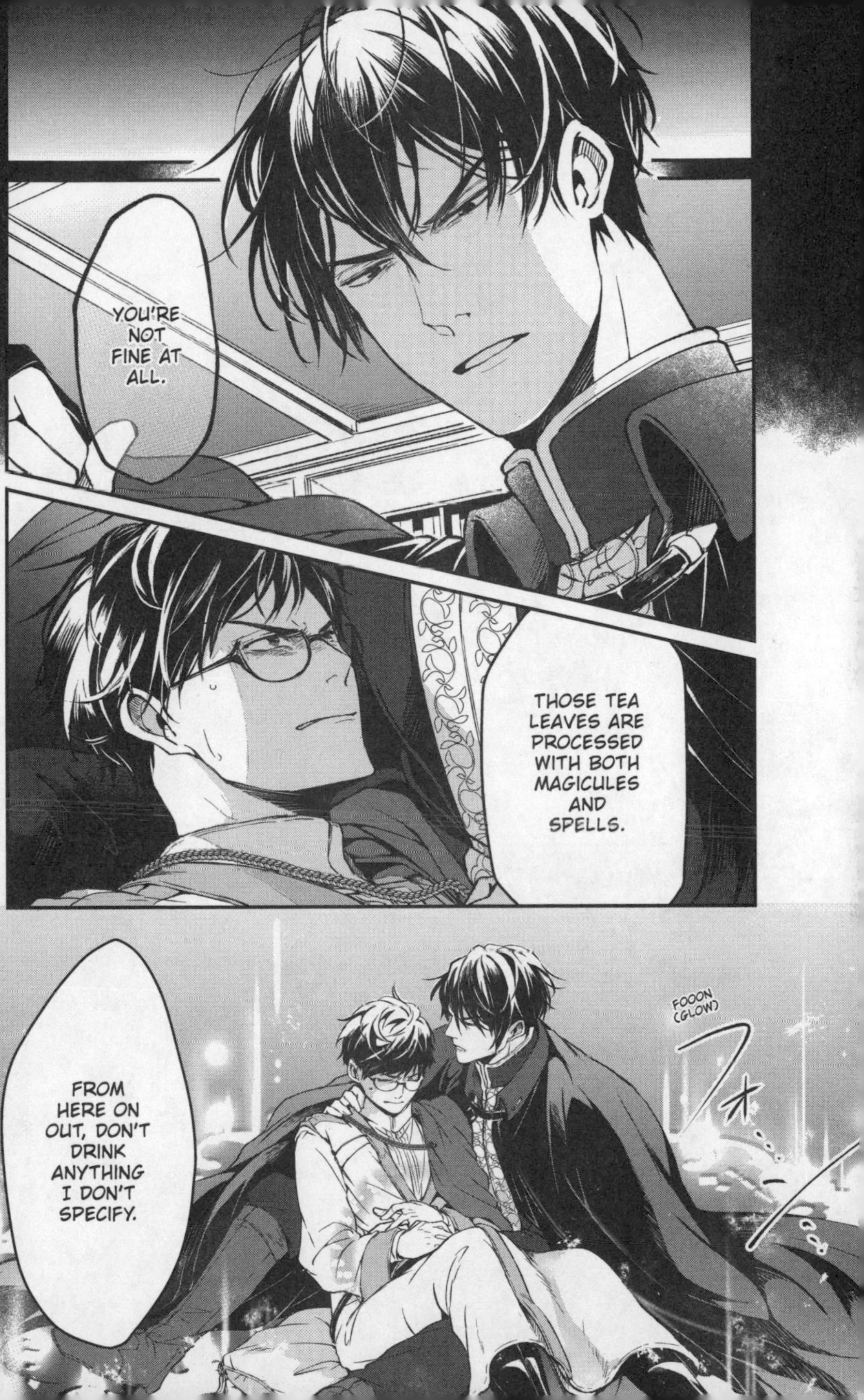
YOU'RE NOT FINE AT ALL.
THOSE TEA LEAVES ARE PROCESSED WITH BOTH MAGICULES AND SPELLS.
FOOON (GLOW)
FROM HERE ON OUT, DON'T DRINK ANYTHING I DON'T SPECIFY.

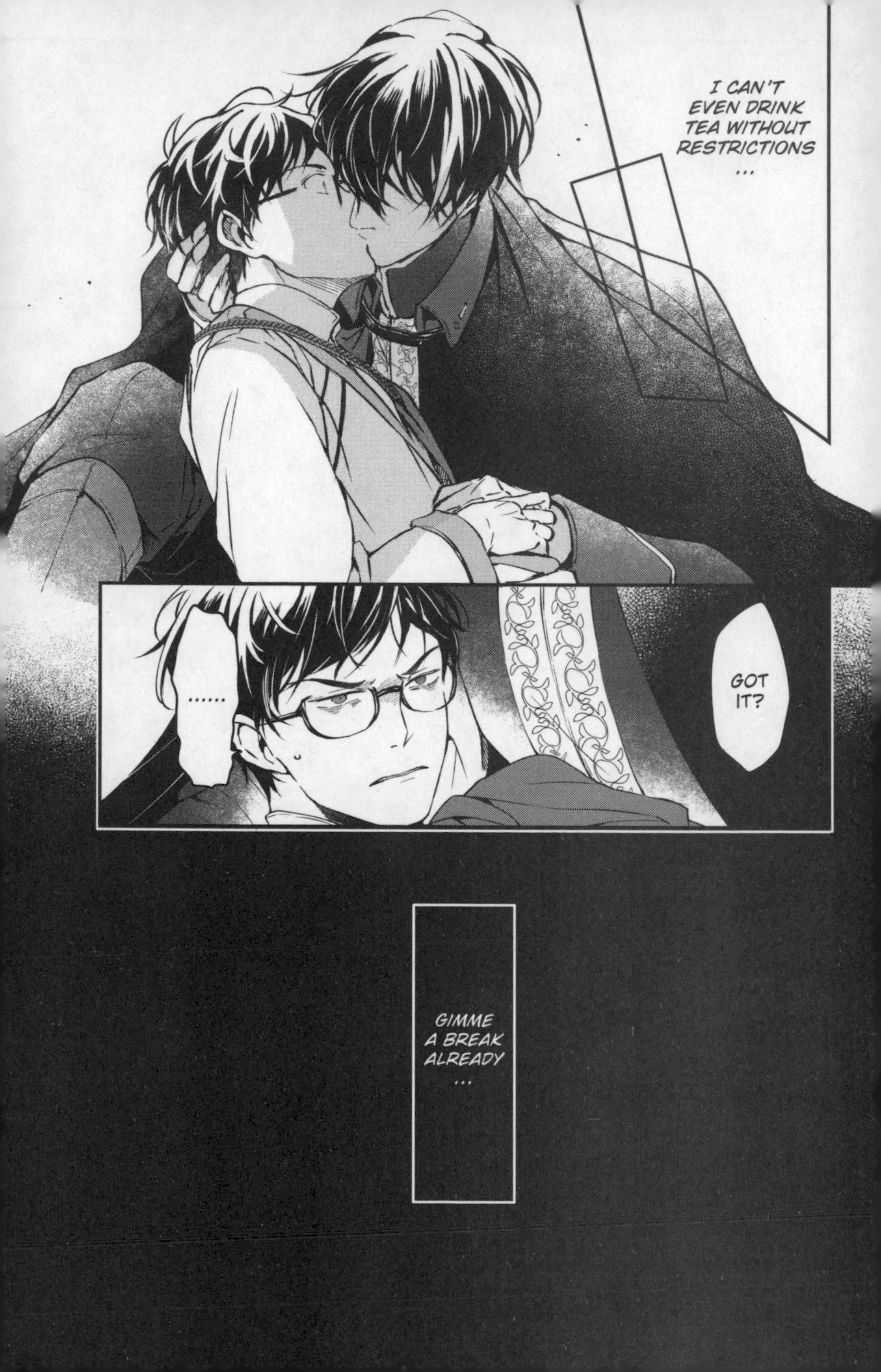
I CAN'T EVEN DRINK TEA WITHOUT RESTRICTIONS ...
GOT IT?
......
GIMME A BREAK ALREADY ...

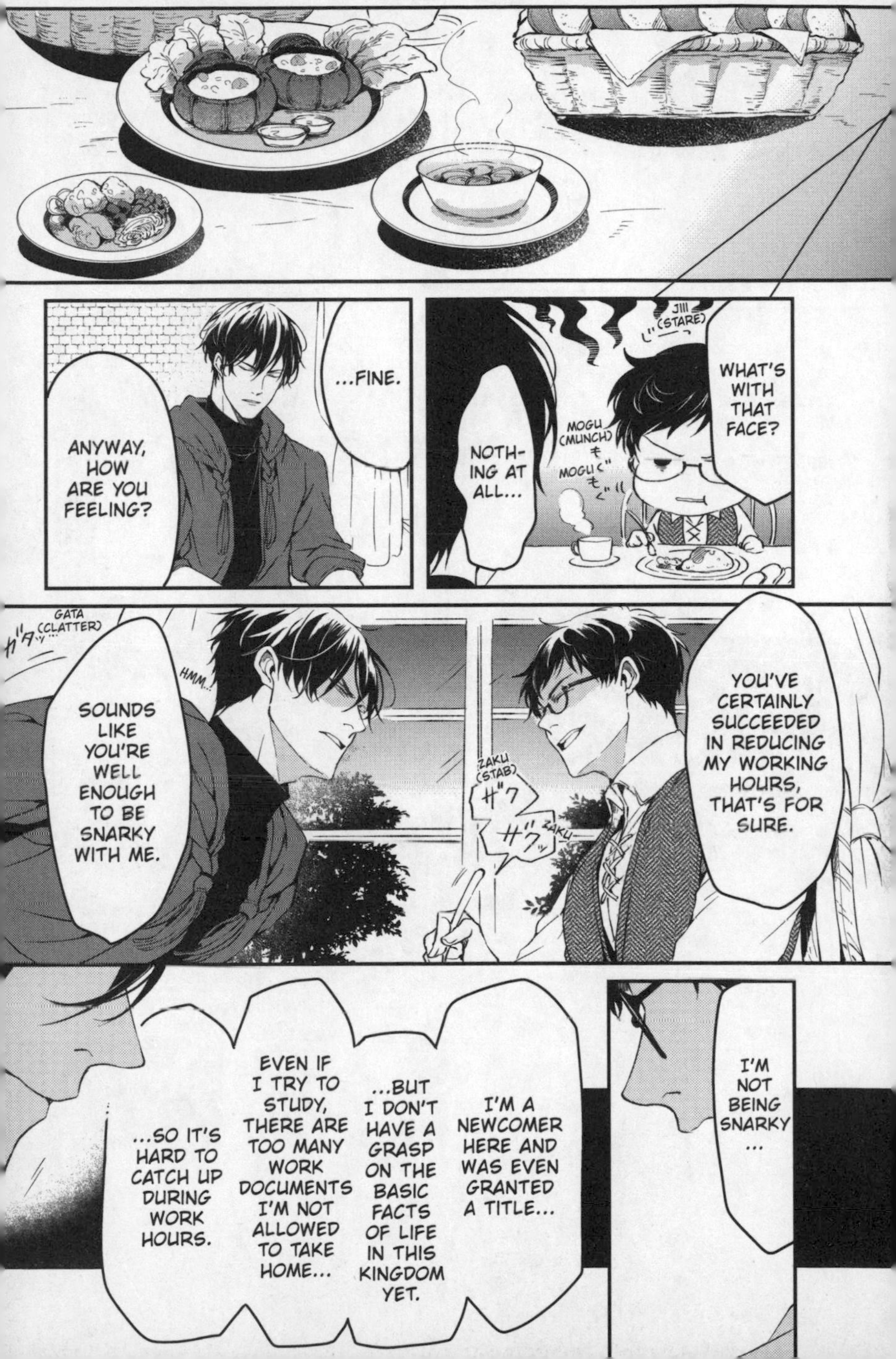
JIII (STARE)
WHAT'S WITH THAT FACE?
MOGU (MUNCH) MOGU
NOTH-ING AT ALL...
...FINE.
ANYWAY, HOW ARE YOU FEELING?
YOU'VE CERTAINLY SUCCEEDED IN REDUCING MY WORKING HOURS, THAT'S FOR SURE.
ZAKU (STAB)
ZAKU
HMM...
SOUNDS LIKE YOU'RE WELL ENOUGH TO BE SNARKY WITH ME.
GATA (CLATTER)
I'M NOT BEING SNARKY...
I'M A NEWCOMER HERE AND WAS EVEN GRANTED A TITLE...
...BUT I DON'T HAVE A GRASP ON THE BASIC FACTS OF LIFE IN THIS KINGDOM YET.
EVEN IF I TRY TO STUDY, THERE ARE TOO MANY WORK DOCUMENTS I'M NOT ALLOWED TO TAKE HOME...
...SO IT'S HARD TO CATCH UP DURING WORK HOURS.

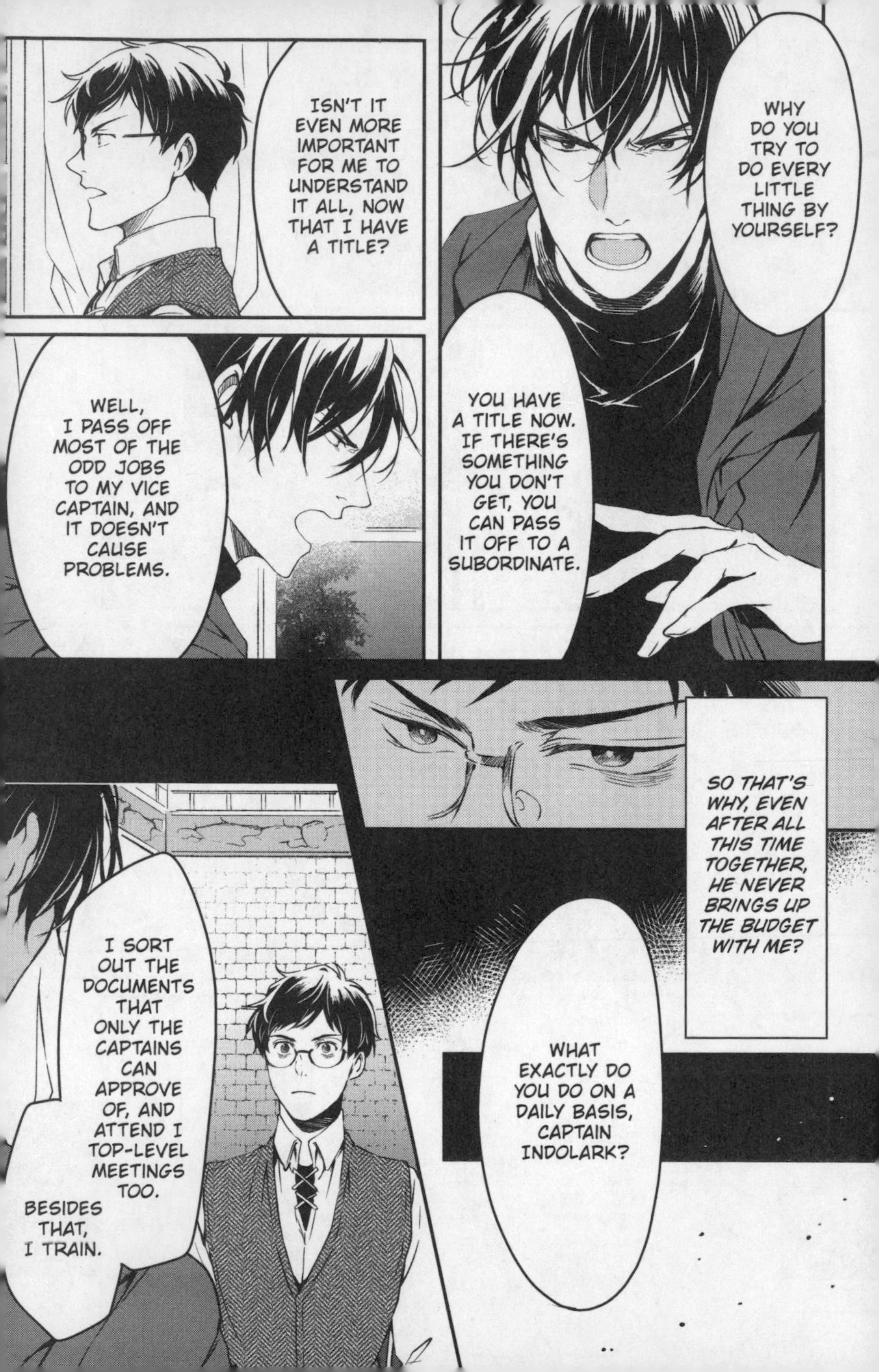
WHY DO YOU TRY TO DO EVERY LITTLE THING BY YOURSELF?
YOU HAVE A TITLE NOW. IF THERE'S SOMETHING YOU DON'T GET, YOU CAN PASS IT OFF TO A SUBORDINATE.
ISN'T IT EVEN MORE IMPORTANT FOR ME TO UNDERSTAND IT ALL, NOW THAT I HAVE A TITLE?
WELL, I PASS OFF MOST OF THE ODD JOBS TO MY VICE CAPTAIN, AND IT DOESN'T CAUSE PROBLEMS.
SO THAT'S WHY, EVEN AFTER ALL THIS TIME TOGETHER, HE NEVER BRINGS UP THE BUDGET WITH ME?
WHAT EXACTLY DO YOU DO ON A DAILY BASIS, CAPTAIN INDOLARK?
I SORT OUT THE DOCUMENTS THAT ONLY THE CAPTAINS CAN APPROVE OF, AND ATTEND I TOP-LEVEL MEETINGS TOO.
BESIDES THAT, I TRAIN.

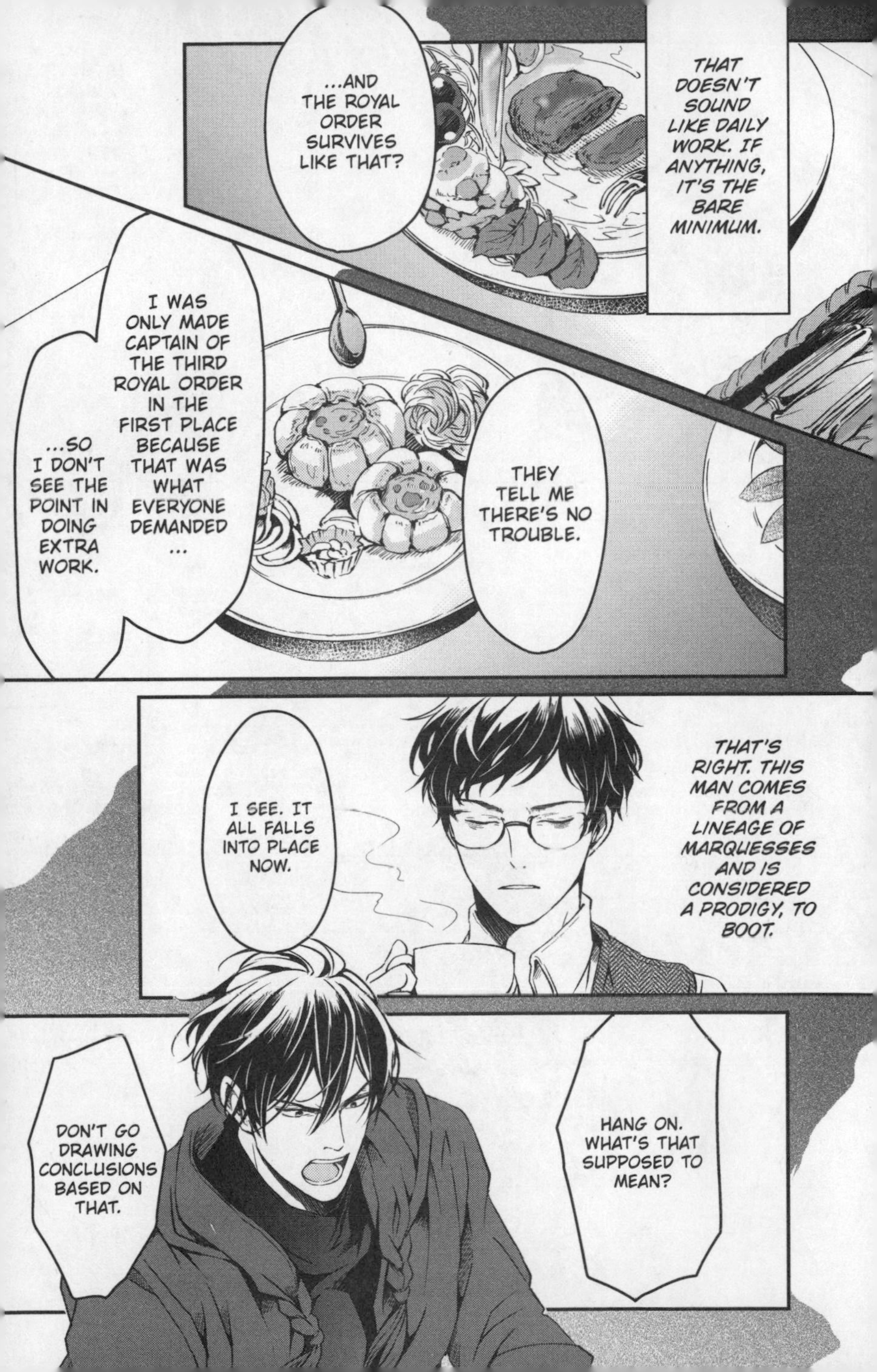
THAT DOESN'T SOUND LIKE DAILY WORK. IF ANYTHING, IT'S THE BARE MINIMUM.
...AND THE ROYAL ORDER SURVIVES LIKE THAT?
THEY TELL ME THERE'S NO TROUBLE.
I WAS ONLY MADE CAPTAIN OF THE THIRD ROYAL ORDER IN THE FIRST PLACE BECAUSE THAT WAS WHAT EVERYONE DEMANDED...
...SO I DON'T SEE THE POINT IN DOING EXTRA WORK.
I SEE. IT ALL FALLS INTO PLACE NOW.
THAT'S RIGHT. THIS MAN COMES FROM A LINEAGE OF MARQUESSES AND IS CONSIDERED A PRODIGY, TO BOOT.
HANG ON. WHAT'S THAT SUPPOSED TO MEAN?
DON'T GO DRAWING CONCLUSIONS BASED ON THAT.

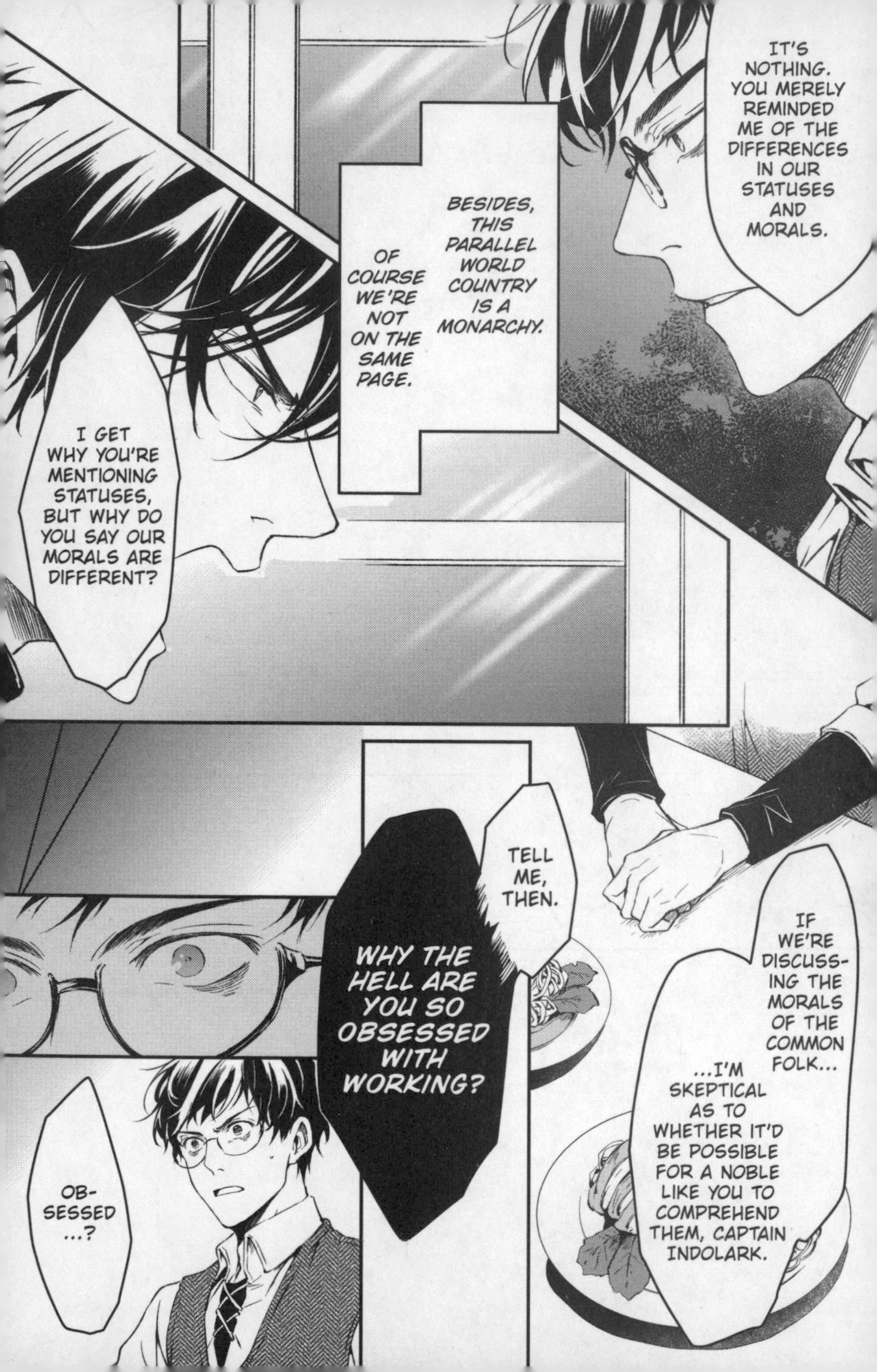
IT'S NOTHING. YOU MERELY REMINDED ME OF THE DIFFERENCES IN OUR STATUSES AND MORALS.
BESIDES, THIS PARALLEL WORLD COUNTRY IS A MONARCHY.
OF COURSE WE'RE NOT ON THE SAME PAGE.
I GET WHY YOU'RE MENTIONING STATUSES, BUT WHY DO YOU SAY OUR MORALS ARE DIFFERENT?
IF WE'RE DISCUSS-ING THE MORALS OF THE COMMON FOLK...
...I'M SKEPTICAL AS TO WHETHER IT'D BE POSSIBLE FOR A NOBLE LIKE YOU TO COMPREHEND THEM, CAPTAIN INDOLARK.
TELL ME, THEN.
WHY THE HELL ARE YOU SO OBSESSED WITH WORKING?
OB-SESSED ...?

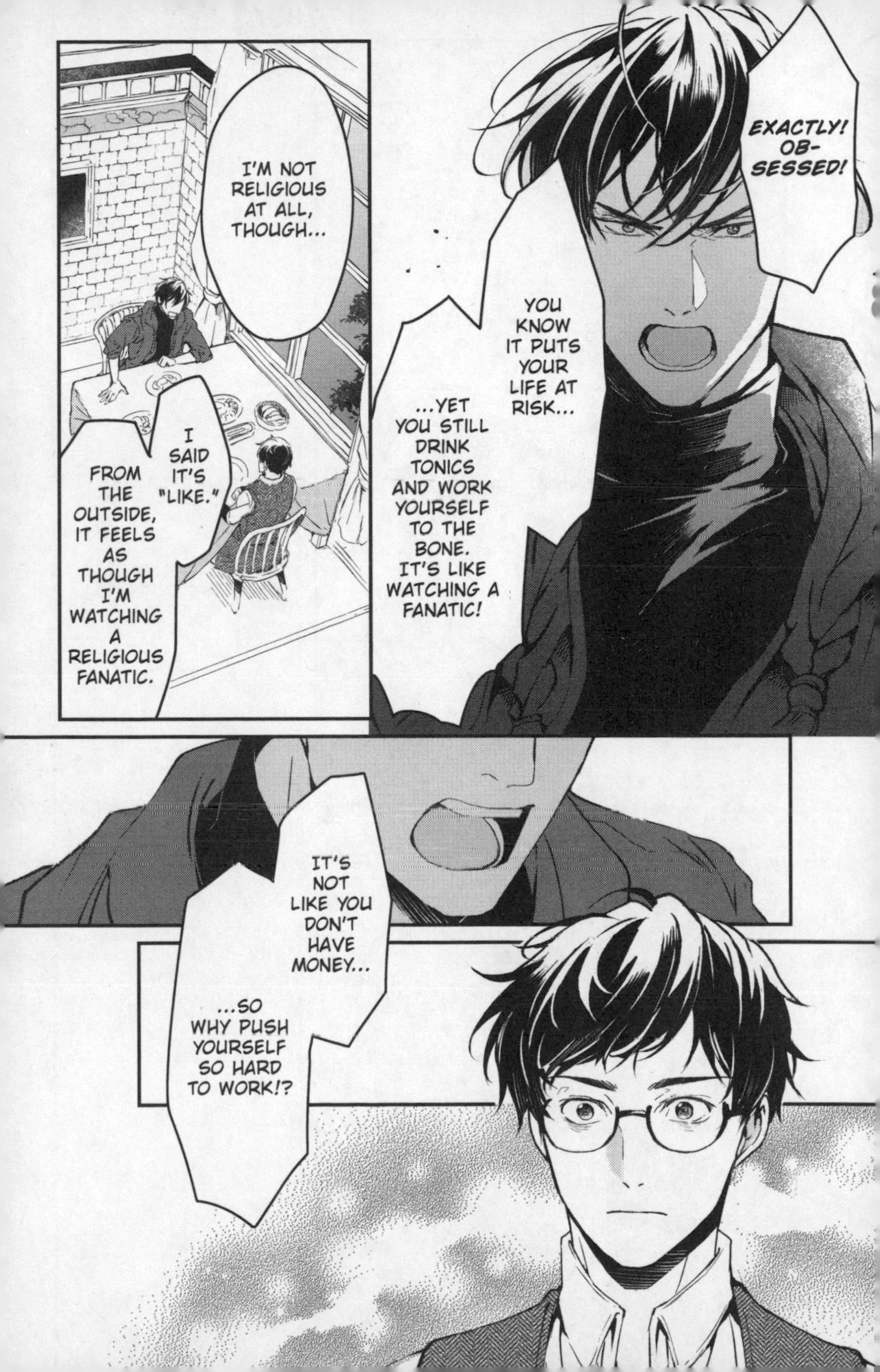
EXACTLY! OB-SESSED!
YOU KNOW IT PUTS YOUR LIFE AT RISK...
...YET YOU STILL DRINK TONICS AND WORK YOURSELF TO THE BONE. IT'S LIKE WATCHING A FANATIC!
I'M NOT RELIGIOUS AT ALL, THOUGH...
I SAID IT'S "LIKE."
FROM THE OUTSIDE, IT FEELS AS THOUGH I'M WATCHING A RELIGIOUS FANATIC.
IT'S NOT LIKE YOU DON'T HAVE MONEY...
...SO WHY PUSH YOURSELF SO HARD TO WORK!?

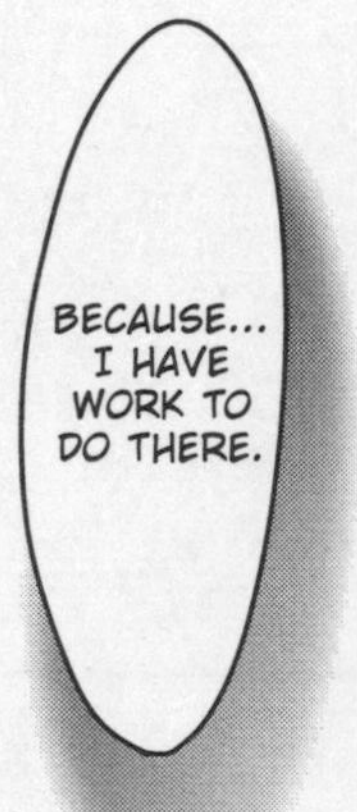
BECAUSE... I HAVE WORK TO DO THERE.

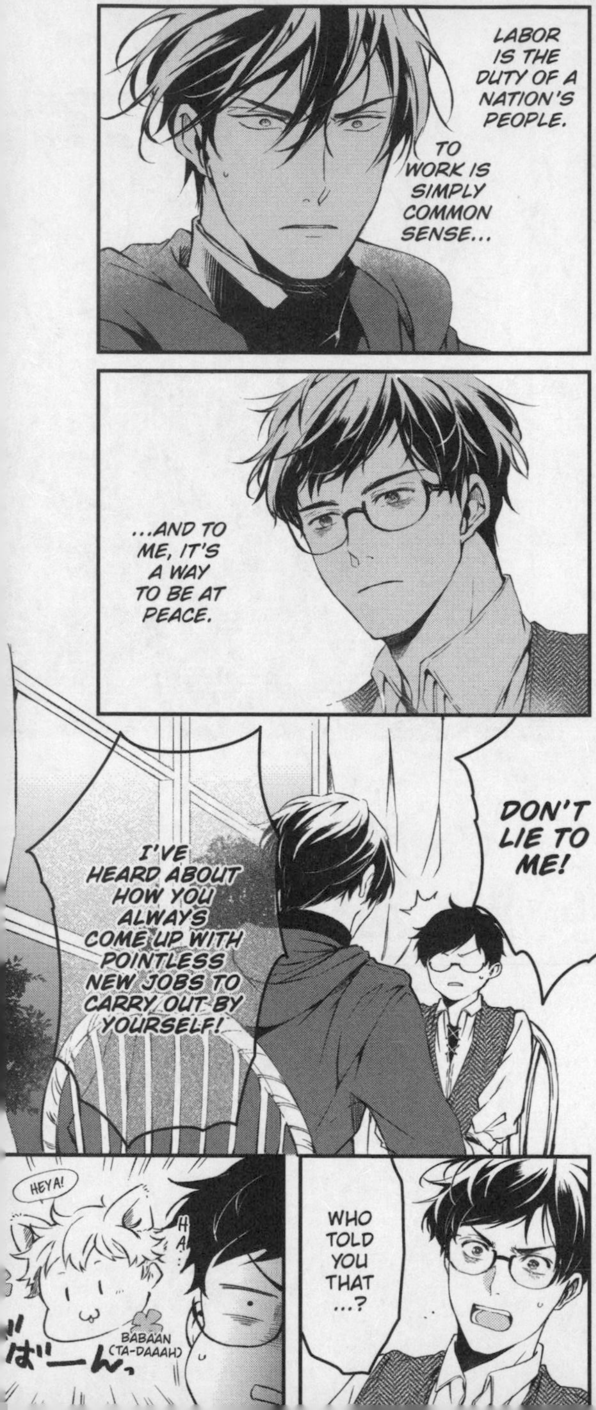
LABOR IS THE DUTY OF A NATION'S PEOPLE.
TO WORK IS SIMPLY COMMON SENSE...
...AND TO ME, IT'S A WAY TO BE AT PEACE.
DON'T LIE TO ME!
I'VE HEARD ABOUT HOW YOU ALWAYS COME UP WITH POINTLESS NEW JOBS TO CARRY OUT BY YOURSELF!
WHO TOLD YOU THAT...?
HEYA!
HA...
BABAAN (TA-DAAAH)
ばーん

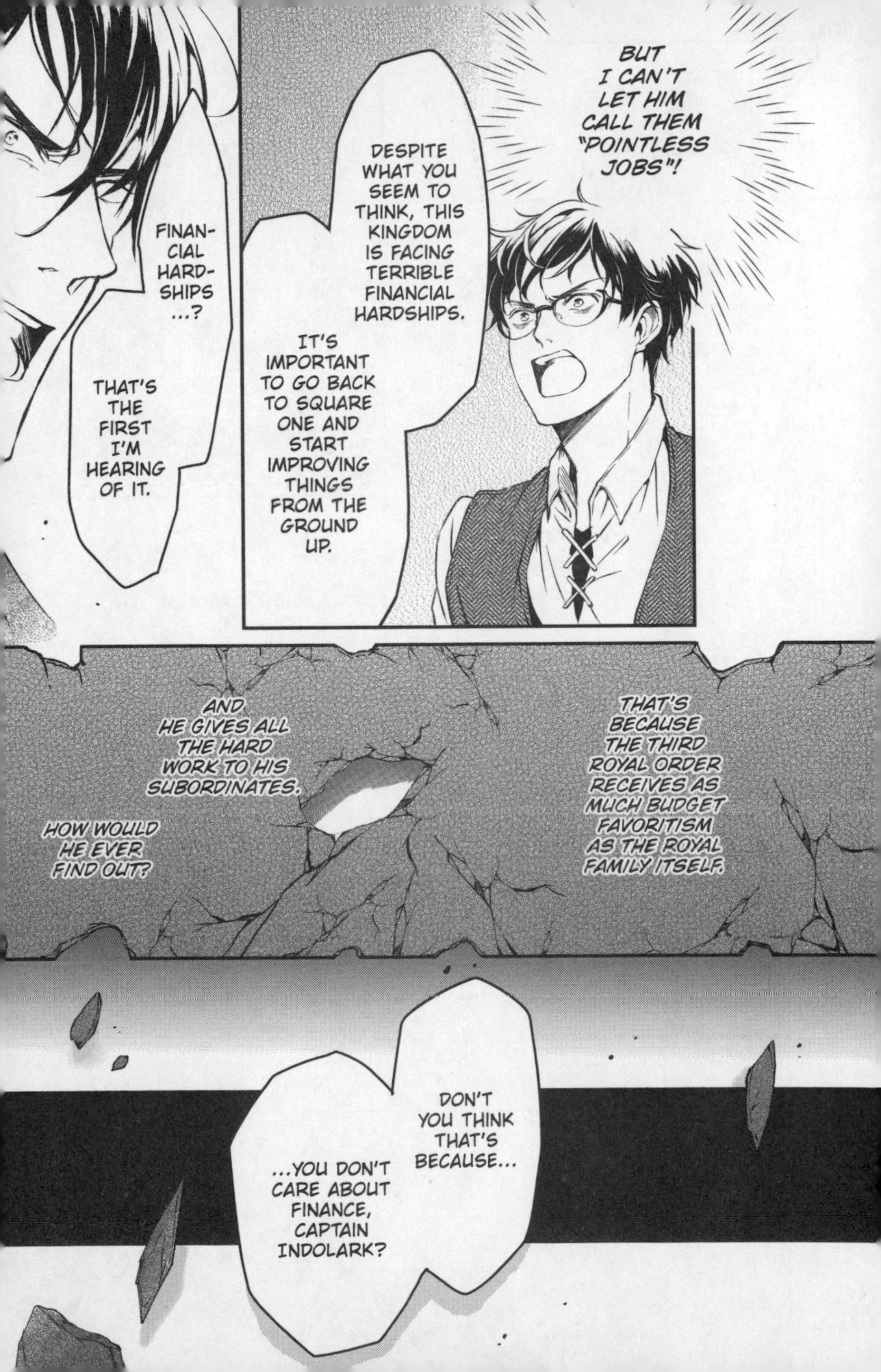
BUT I CAN'T LET HIM CALL THEM "POINTLESS JOBS"!
DESPITE WHAT YOU SEEM TO THINK, THIS KINGDOM IS FACING TERRIBLE FINANCIAL HARDSHIPS.
IT'S IMPORTANT TO GO BACK TO SQUARE ONE AND START IMPROVING THINGS FROM THE GROUND UP.
FINAN-CIAL HARD-SHIPS ...?
THAT'S THE FIRST I'M HEARING OF IT.
THAT'S BECAUSE THE THIRD ROYAL ORDER RECEIVES AS MUCH BUDGET FAVORITISM AS THE ROYAL FAMILY ITSELF.
AND HE GIVES ALL THE HARD WORK TO HIS SUBORDINATES.
HOW WOULD HE EVER FIND OUT?
DON'T YOU THINK THAT'S BECAUSE...
...YOU DON'T CARE ABOUT FINANCE, CAPTAIN INDOLARK?

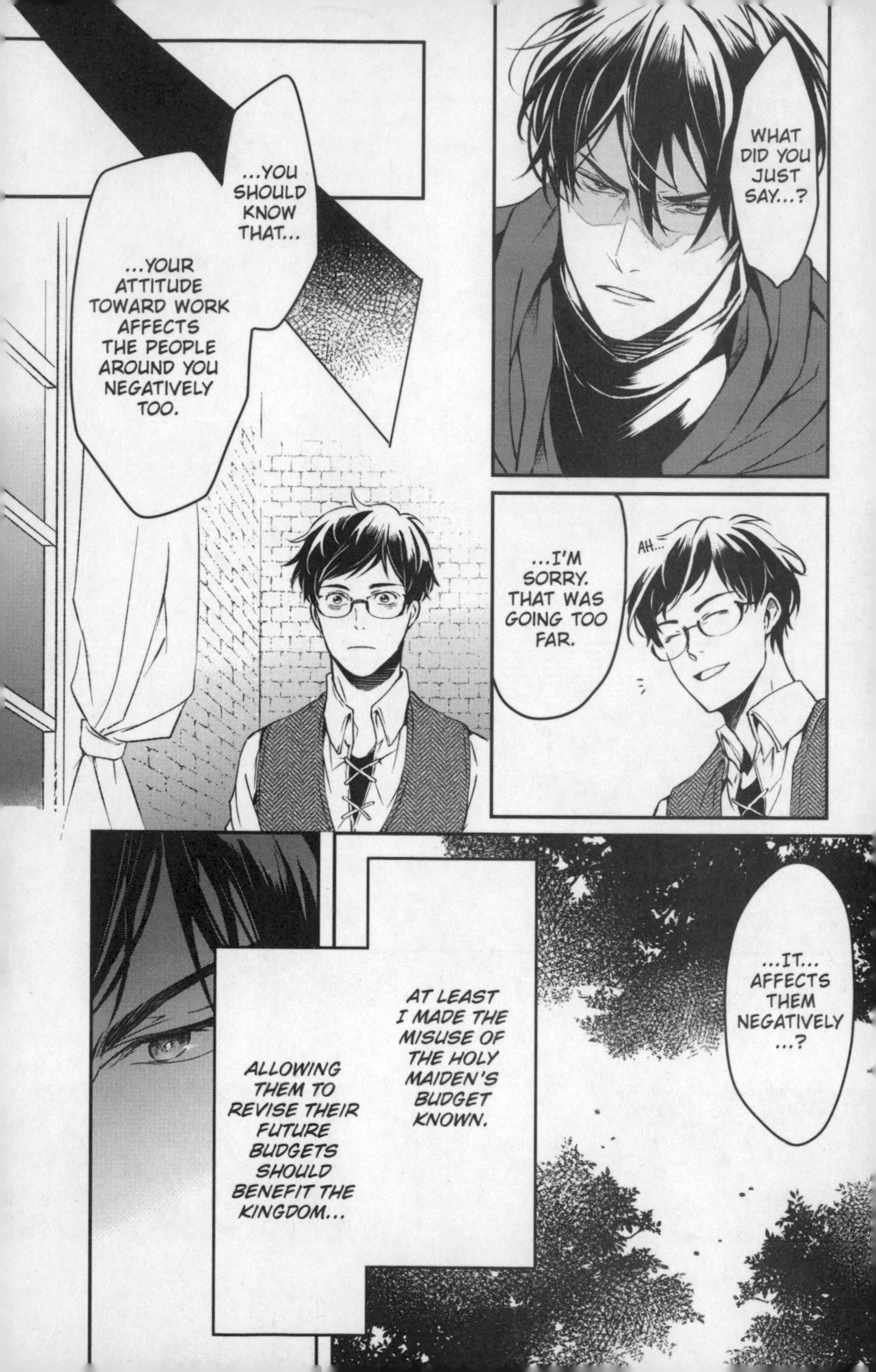
...YOU SHOULD KNOW THAT...
...YOUR ATTITUDE TOWARD WORK AFFECTS THE PEOPLE AROUND YOU NEGATIVELY TOO.
WHAT DID YOU JUST SAY...?
AH...
...I'M SORRY. THAT WAS GOING TOO FAR.
...IT... AFFECTS THEM NEGATIVELY ...?
AT LEAST I MADE THE MISUSE OF THE HOLY MAIDEN'S BUDGET KNOWN.
ALLOWING THEM TO REVISE THEIR FUTURE BUDGETS SHOULD BENEFIT THE KINGDOM...

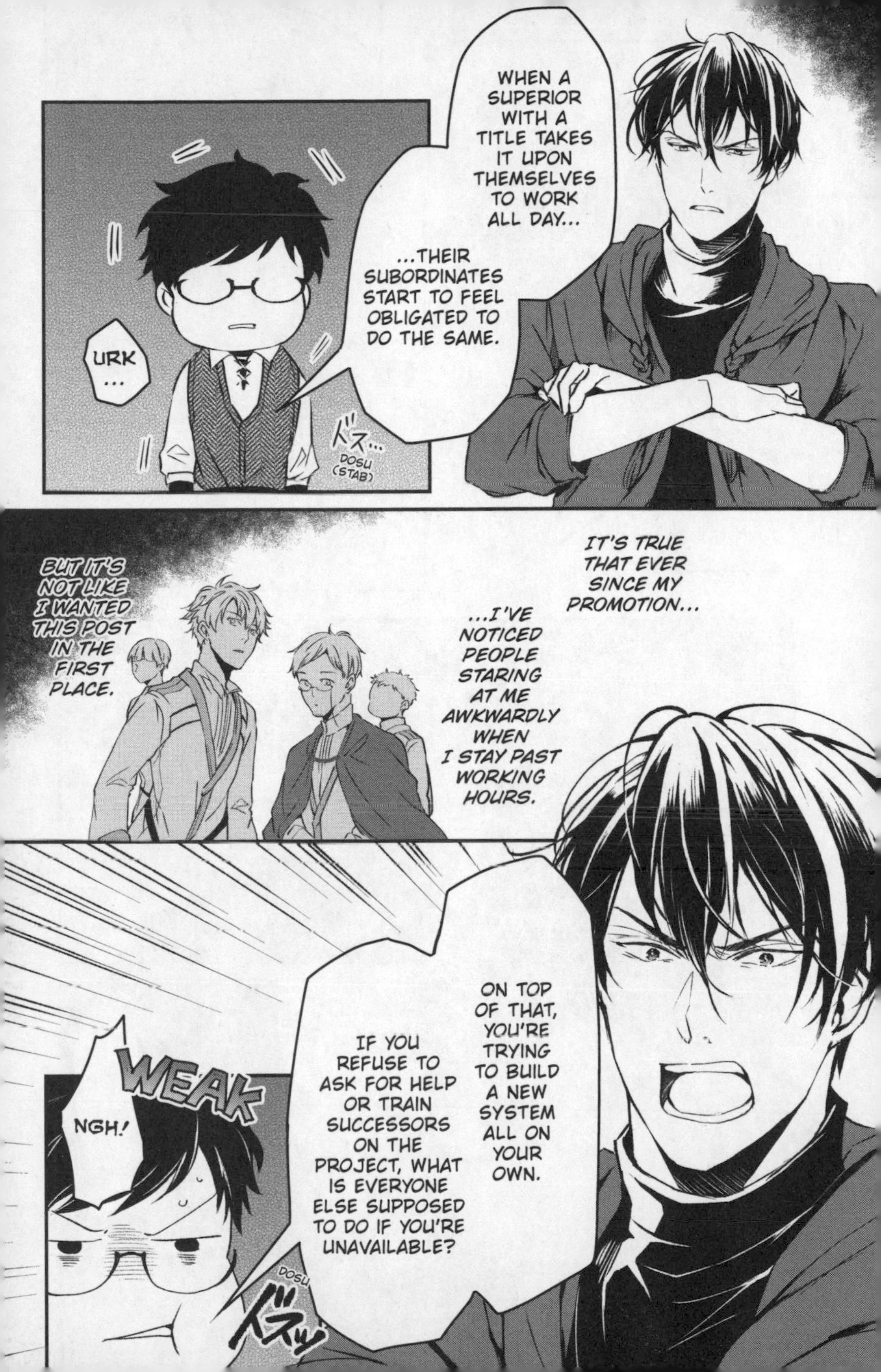
WHEN A SUPERIOR WITH A TITLE TAKES IT UPON THEMSELVES TO WORK ALL DAY...
...THEIR SUBORDINATES START TO FEEL OBLIGATED TO DO THE SAME.
URK...
ドス... DOSU (STAB)
IT'S TRUE THAT EVER SINCE MY PROMOTION...
...I'VE NOTICED PEOPLE STARING AT ME AWKWARDLY WHEN I STAY PAST WORKING HOURS.
BUT IT'S NOT LIKE I WANTED THIS POST IN THE FIRST PLACE.
ON TOP OF THAT, YOU'RE TRYING TO BUILD A NEW SYSTEM ALL ON YOUR OWN.
IF YOU REFUSE TO ASK FOR HELP OR TRAIN SUCCESSORS ON THE PROJECT, WHAT IS EVERYONE ELSE SUPPOSED TO DO IF YOU'RE UNAVAILABLE?
WEAK
NGH!
DOSU ドスッ

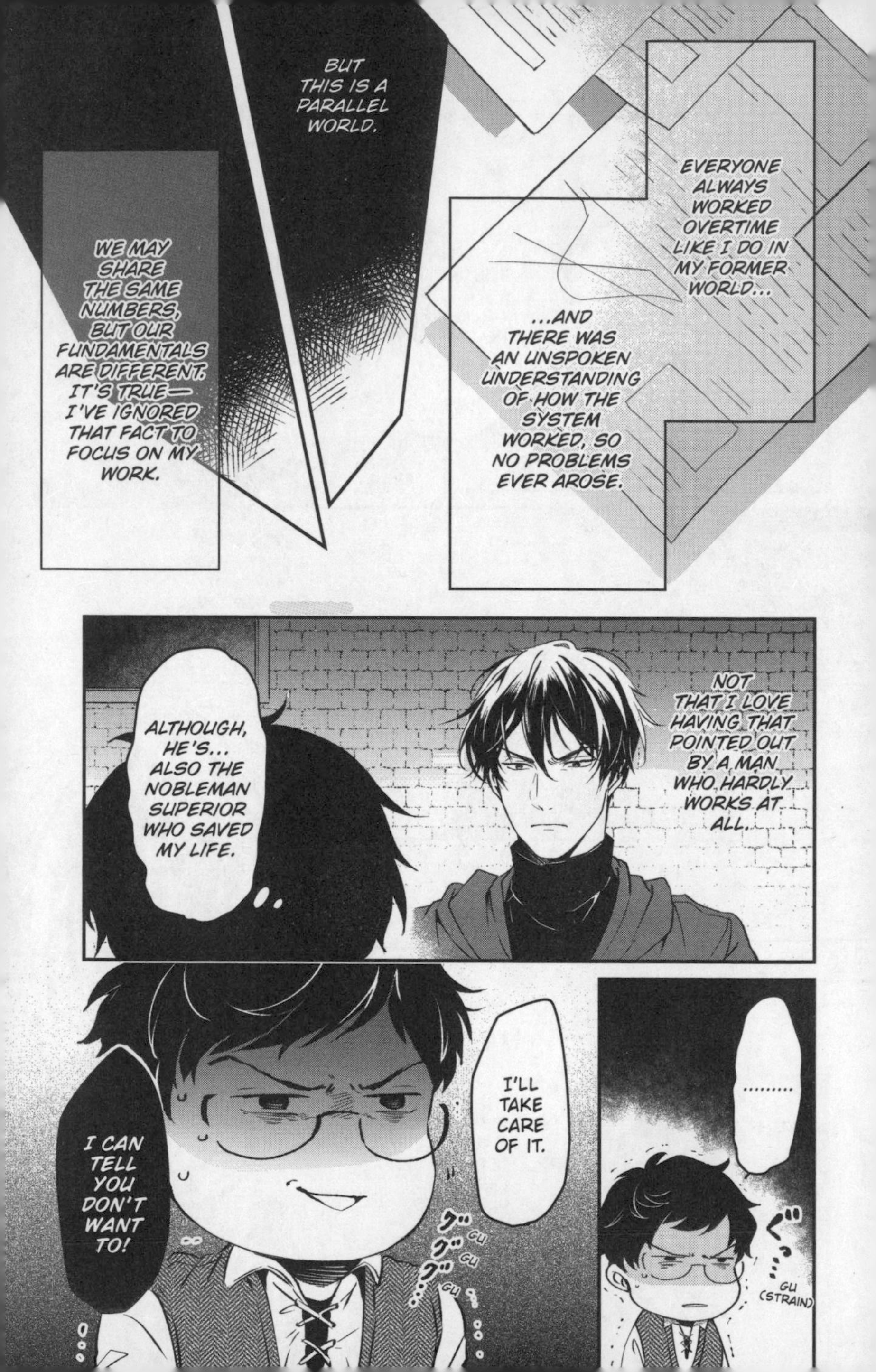
EVERYONE ALWAYS WORKED OVERTIME LIKE I DO IN MY FORMER WORLD...
...AND THERE WAS AN UNSPOKEN UNDERSTANDING OF HOW THE SYSTEM WORKED, SO NO PROBLEMS EVER AROSE.
BUT THIS IS A PARALLEL WORLD.
WE MAY SHARE THE SAME NUMBERS, BUT OUR FUNDAMENTALS ARE DIFFERENT. IT'S TRUE—I'VE IGNORED THAT FACT TO FOCUS ON MY WORK.
NOT THAT I LOVE HAVING THAT POINTED OUT BY A MAN WHO HARDLY WORKS AT ALL.
ALTHOUGH, HE'S... ALSO THE NOBLEMAN SUPERIOR WHO SAVED MY LIFE.
....
GU (STRAIN)
I'LL TAKE CARE OF IT.
I CAN TELL YOU DON'T WANT TO!
GU GU GU

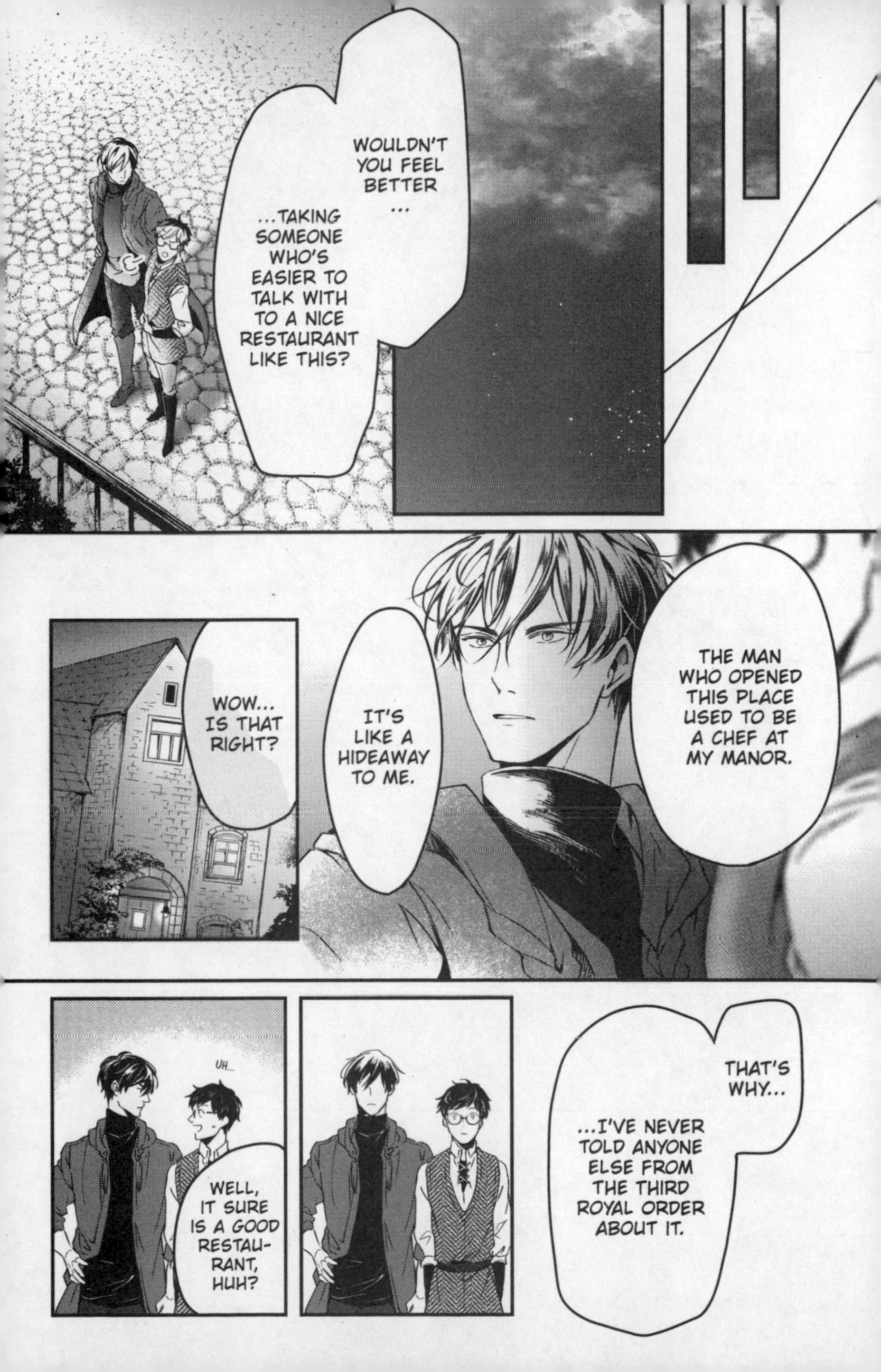
WOULDN'T YOU FEEL BETTER ...
...TAKING SOMEONE WHO'S EASIER TO TALK WITH TO A NICE RESTAURANT LIKE THIS?
THE MAN WHO OPENED THIS PLACE USED TO BE A CHEF AT MY MANOR.
IT'S LIKE A HIDEAWAY TO ME.
WOW... IS THAT RIGHT?
THAT'S WHY...
...I'VE NEVER TOLD ANYONE ELSE FROM THE THIRD ROYAL ORDER ABOUT IT.
UH...
WELL, IT SURE IS A GOOD RESTAU-RANT, HUH?

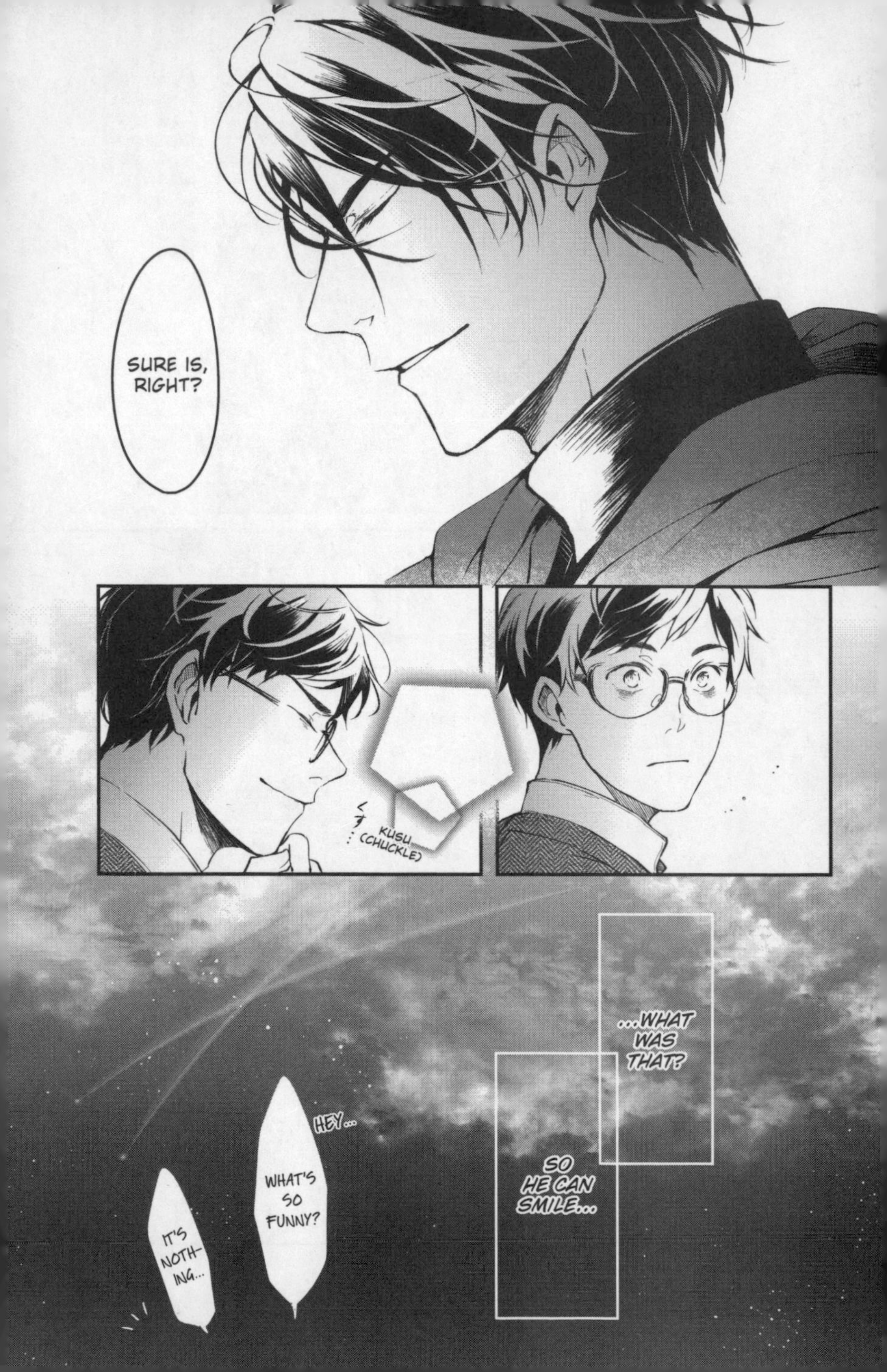
SURE IS, RIGHT?
KUSU (CHUCKLE)
...WHAT WAS THAT?
SO HE CAN SMILE...
HEY...
WHAT'S SO FUNNY?
IT'S NOTHING...

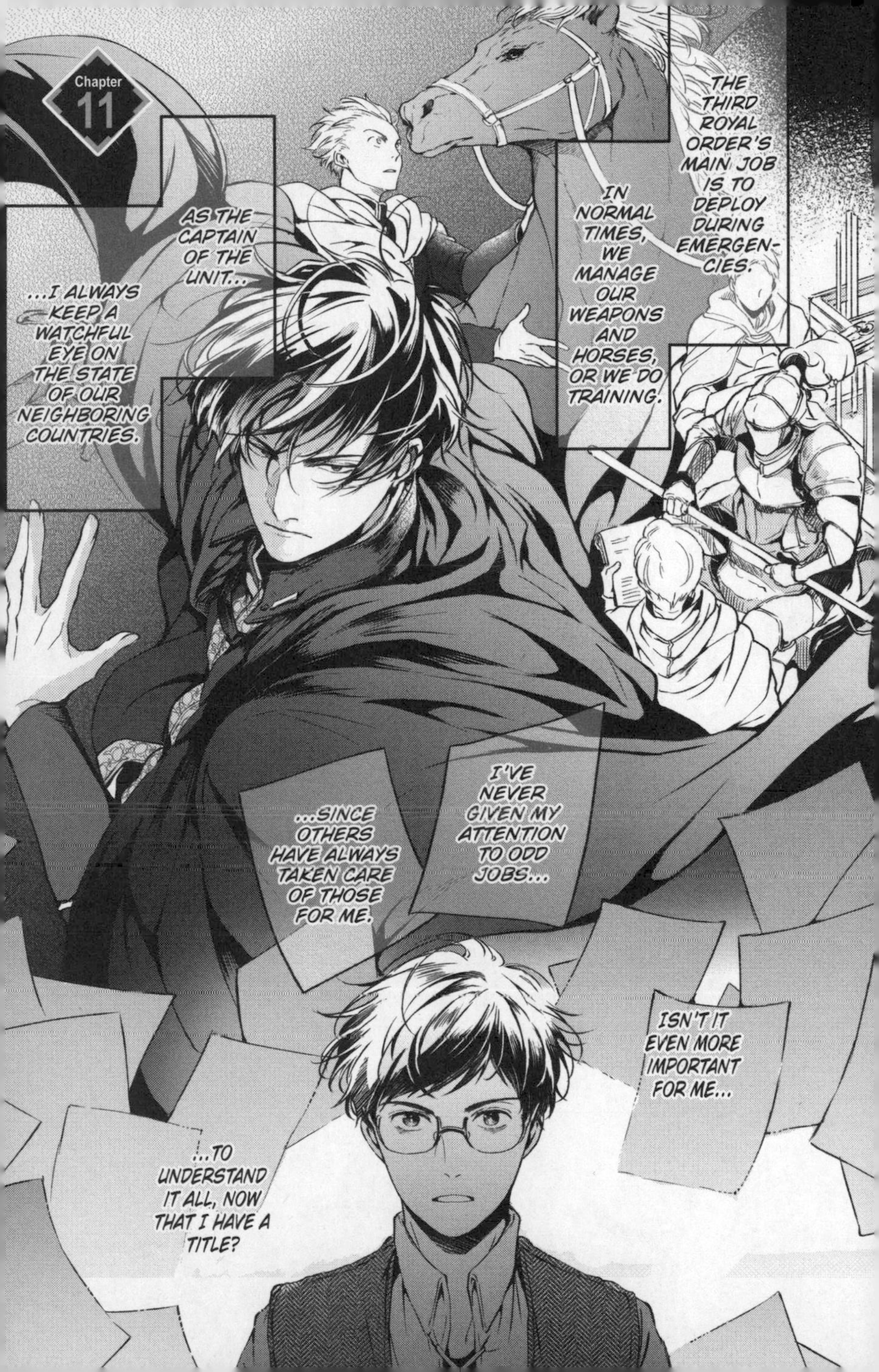
Chapter 11
THE THIRD ROYAL ORDER'S MAIN JOB IS TO DEPLOY DURING EMERGENCIES.
IN NORMAL TIMES, WE MANAGE OUR WEAPONS AND HORSES, OR WE DO TRAINING.
AS THE CAPTAIN OF THE UNIT...
...I ALWAYS KEEP A WATCHFUL EYE ON THE STATE OF OUR NEIGHBORING COUNTRIES.
I'VE NEVER GIVEN MY ATTENTION TO ODD JOBS...
...SINCE OTHERS HAVE ALWAYS TAKEN CARE OF THOSE FOR ME.
ISN'T IT EVEN MORE IMPORTANT FOR ME...
...TO UNDERSTAND IT ALL, NOW THAT I HAVE A TITLE?

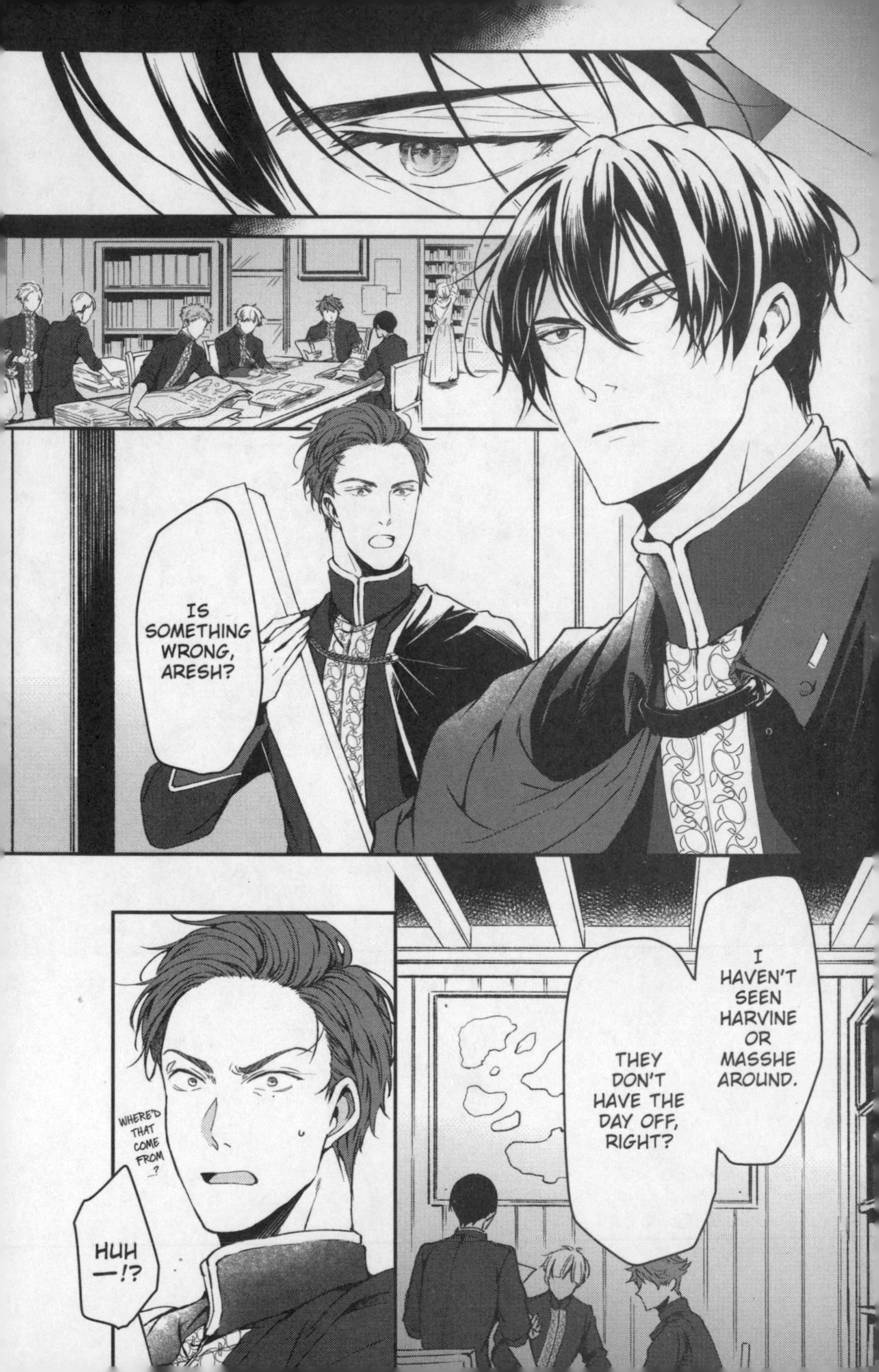
IS SOMETHING WRONG, ARESH?
I HAVEN'T SEEN HARVINE OR MASSHE AROUND.
THEY DON'T HAVE THE DAY OFF, RIGHT?
HUH—!?
WHERE'D THAT COME FROM ...?

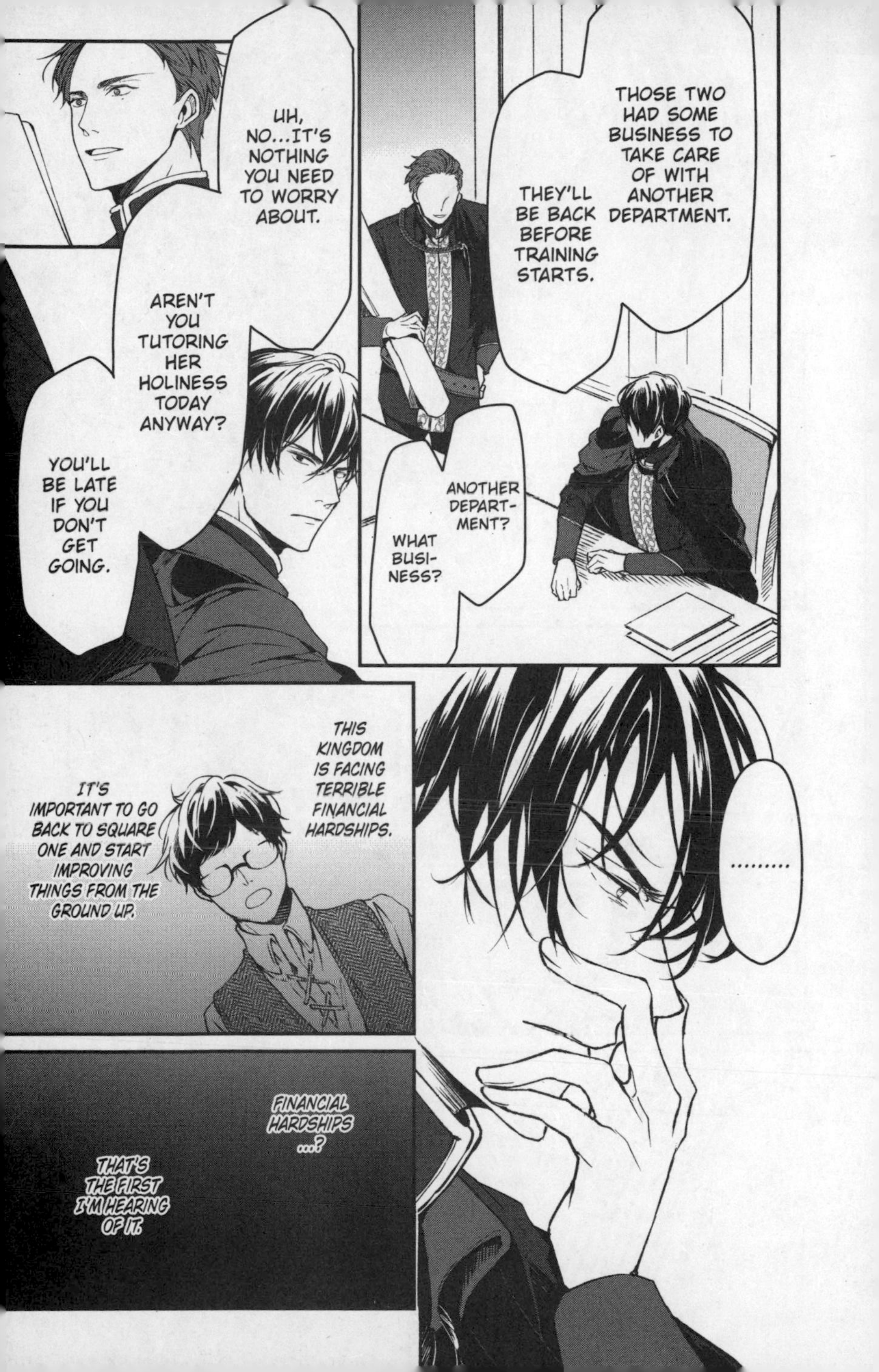
THOSE TWO HAD SOME BUSINESS TO TAKE CARE OF WITH ANOTHER DEPARTMENT.
THEY'LL BE BACK BEFORE TRAINING STARTS.
ANOTHER DEPARTMENT?
WHAT BUSINESS?
UH, NO...IT'S NOTHING YOU NEED TO WORRY ABOUT.
AREN'T YOU TUTORING HER HOLINESS TODAY ANYWAY?
YOU'LL BE LATE IF YOU DON'T GET GOING.
....
THIS KINGDOM IS FACING TERRIBLE FINANCIAL HARDSHIPS.
IT'S IMPORTANT TO GO BACK TO SQUARE ONE AND START IMPROVING THINGS FROM THE GROUND UP.
FINANCIAL HARDSHIPS ...?
THAT'S THE FIRST I'M HEARING OF IT.

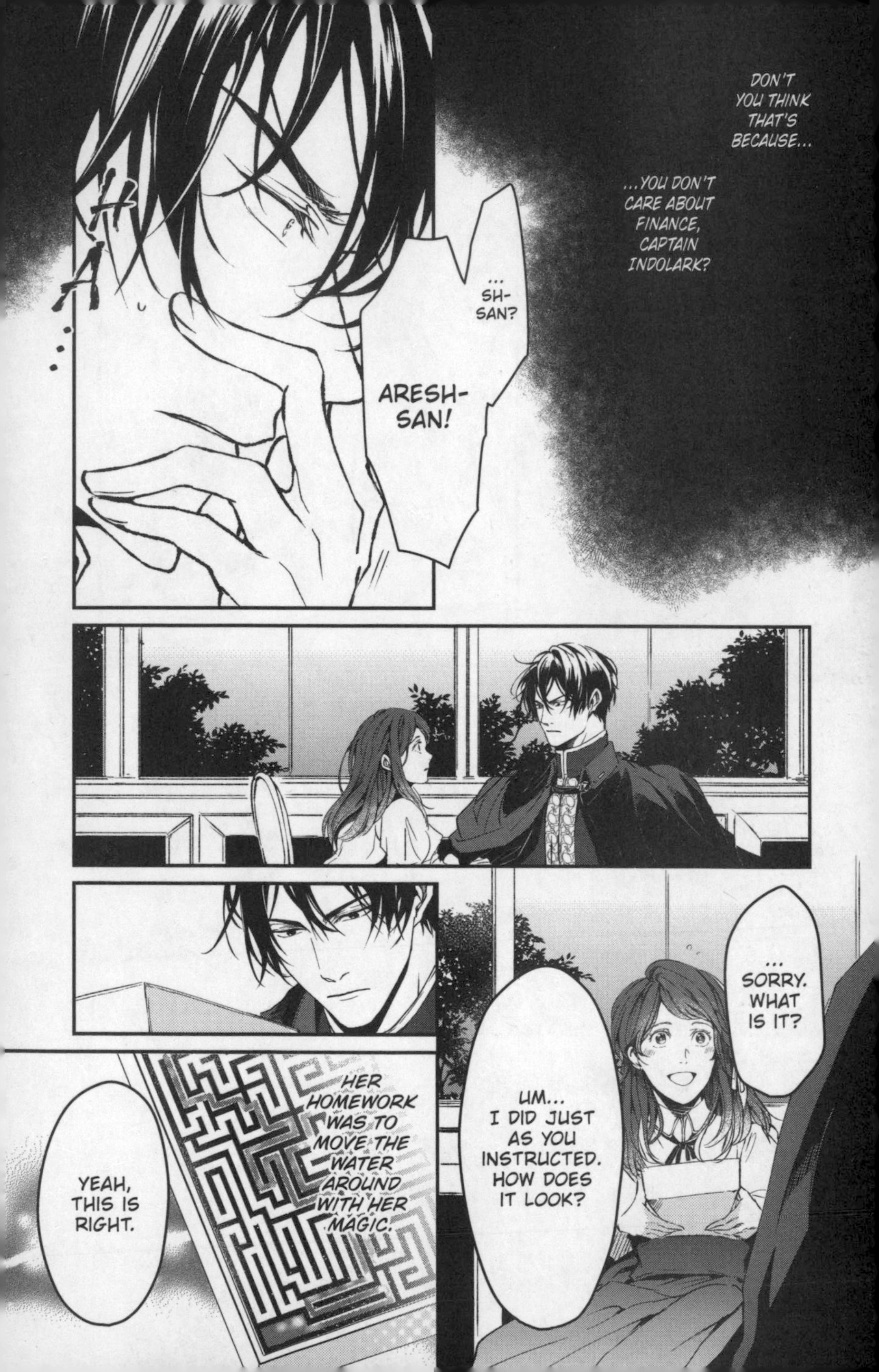
DON'T YOU THINK THAT'S BECAUSE...
...YOU DON'T CARE ABOUT FINANCE, CAPTAIN INDOLARK?
HA...
... SH- SAN?
ARESH-SAN!
... SORRY. WHAT IS IT?
UM... I DID JUST AS YOU INSTRUCTED. HOW DOES IT LOOK?
HER HOMEWORK WAS TO MOVE THE WATER AROUND WITH HER MAGIC.
YEAH, THIS IS RIGHT.

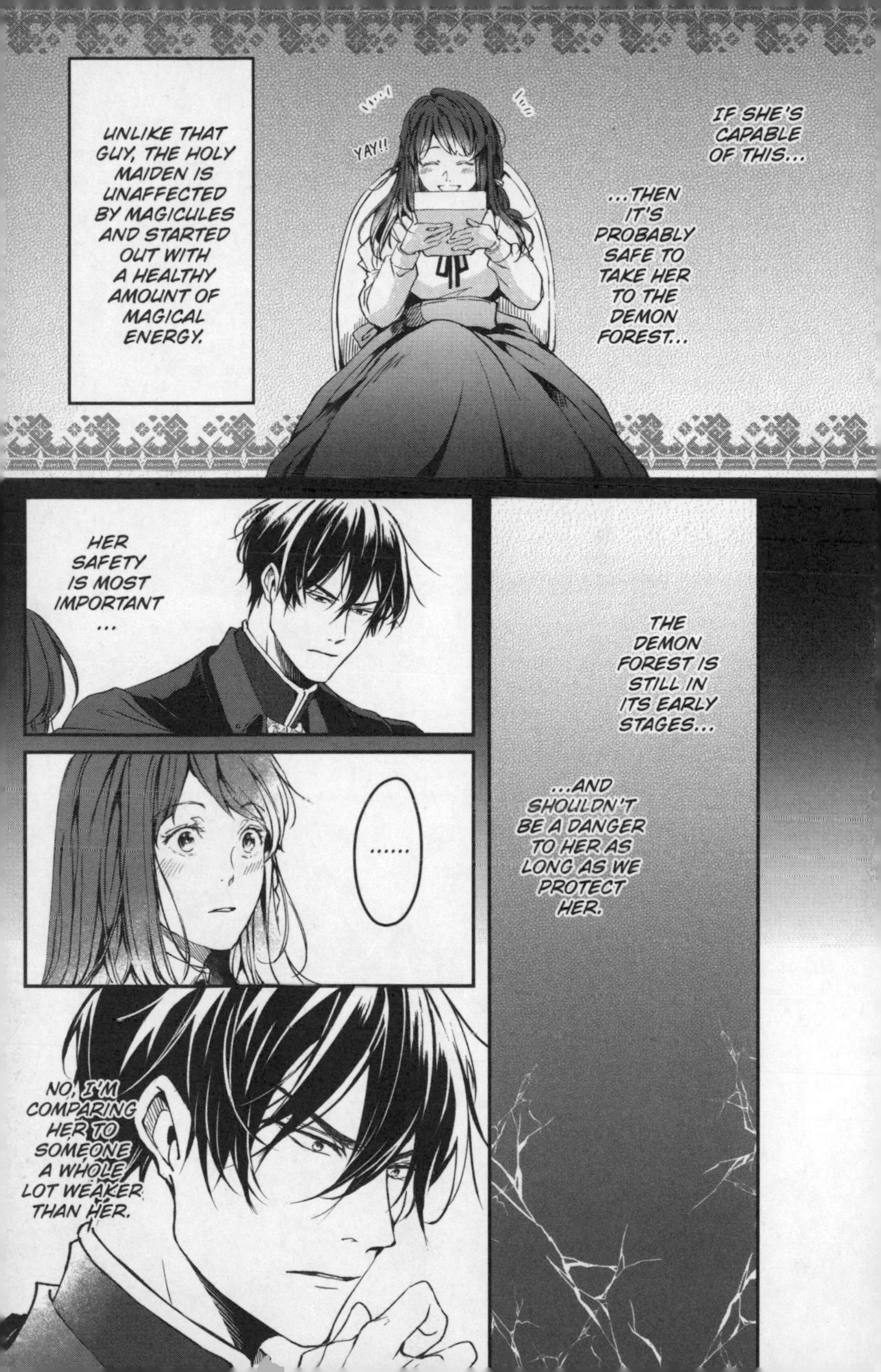
IF SHE'S CAPABLE OF THIS...
...THEN IT'S PROBABLY SAFE TO TAKE HER TO THE DEMON FOREST...
YAY!!
UNLIKE THAT GUY, THE HOLY MAIDEN IS UNAFFECTED BY MAGICULES AND STARTED OUT WITH A HEALTHY AMOUNT OF MAGICAL ENERGY.
THE DEMON FOREST IS STILL IN ITS EARLY STAGES...
...AND SHOULDN'T BE A DANGER TO HER AS LONG AS WE PROTECT HER.
HER SAFETY IS MOST IMPORTANT...
......
NO, I'M COMPARING HER TO SOMEONE A WHOLE LOT WEAKER THAN HER.

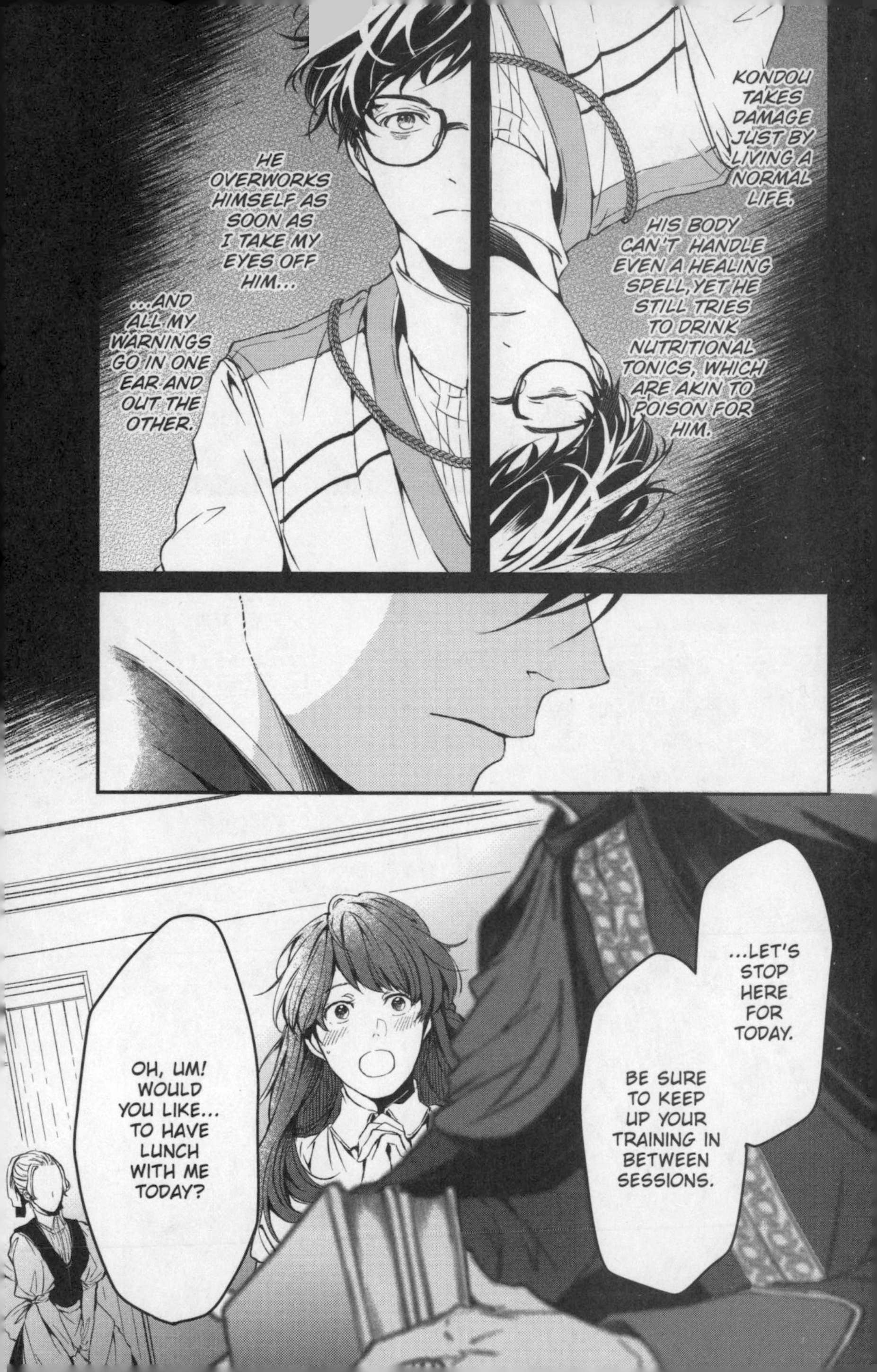
KONDOU TAKES DAMAGE JUST BY LIVING A NORMAL LIFE.
HIS BODY CAN'T HANDLE EVEN A HEALING SPELL, YET HE STILL TRIES TO DRINK NUTRITIONAL TONICS, WHICH ARE AKIN TO POISON FOR HIM.
HE OVERWORKS HIMSELF AS SOON AS I TAKE MY EYES OFF HIM...
...AND ALL MY WARNINGS GO IN ONE EAR AND OUT THE OTHER.
...LET'S STOP HERE FOR TODAY.
BE SURE TO KEEP UP YOUR TRAINING IN BETWEEN SESSIONS.
OH, UM! WOULD YOU LIKE... TO HAVE LUNCH WITH ME TODAY?

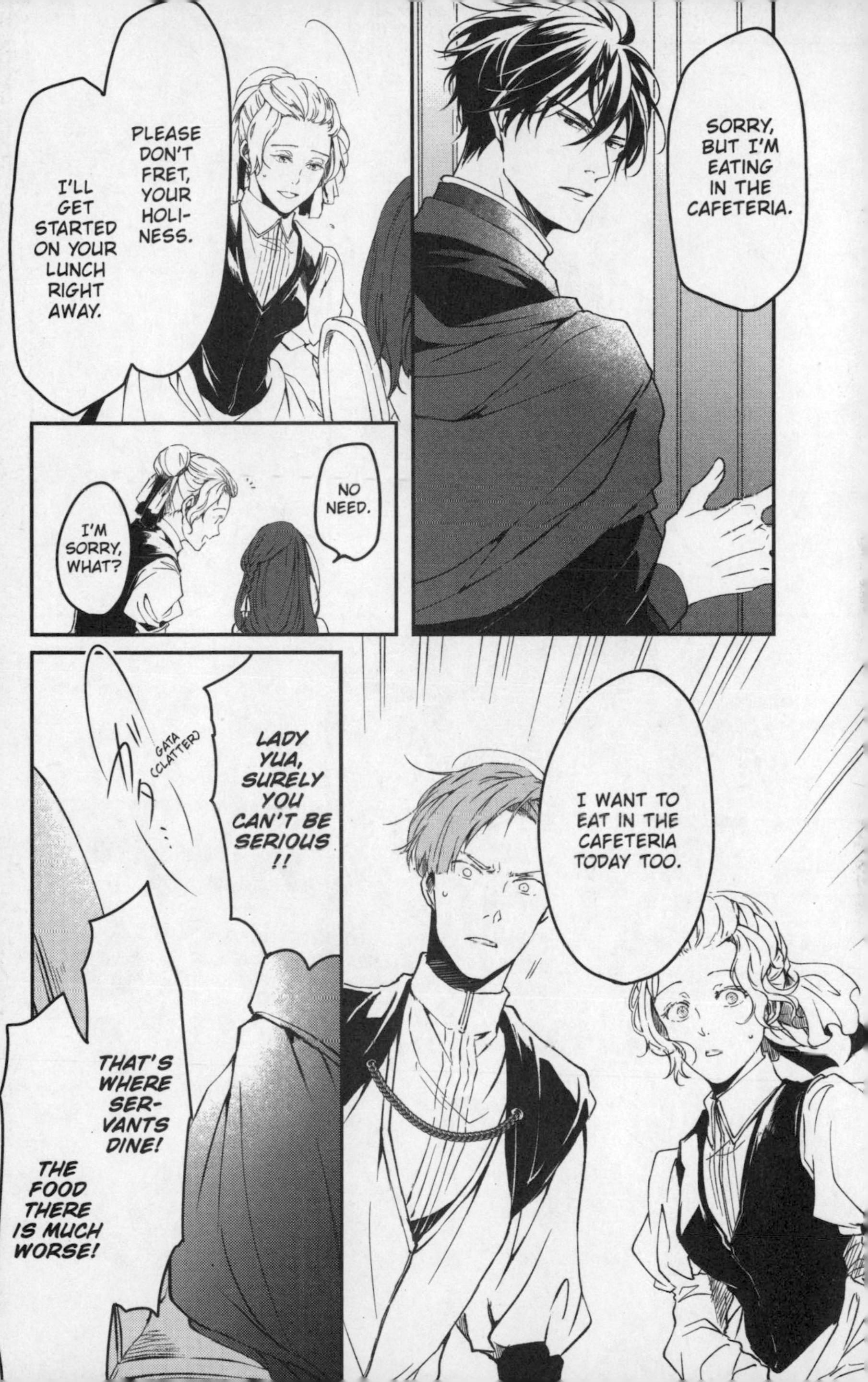
SORRY, BUT I'M EATING IN THE CAFETERIA.
PLEASE DON'T FRET, YOUR HOLINESS.
I'LL GET STARTED ON YOUR LUNCH RIGHT AWAY.
NO NEED.
I'M SORRY, WHAT?
I WANT TO EAT IN THE CAFETERIA TODAY TOO.
GATA (CLATTER)
LADY YUA, SURELY YOU CAN'T BE SERIOUS!!
THAT'S WHERE SER-VANTS DINE!
THE FOOD THERE IS MUCH WORSE!

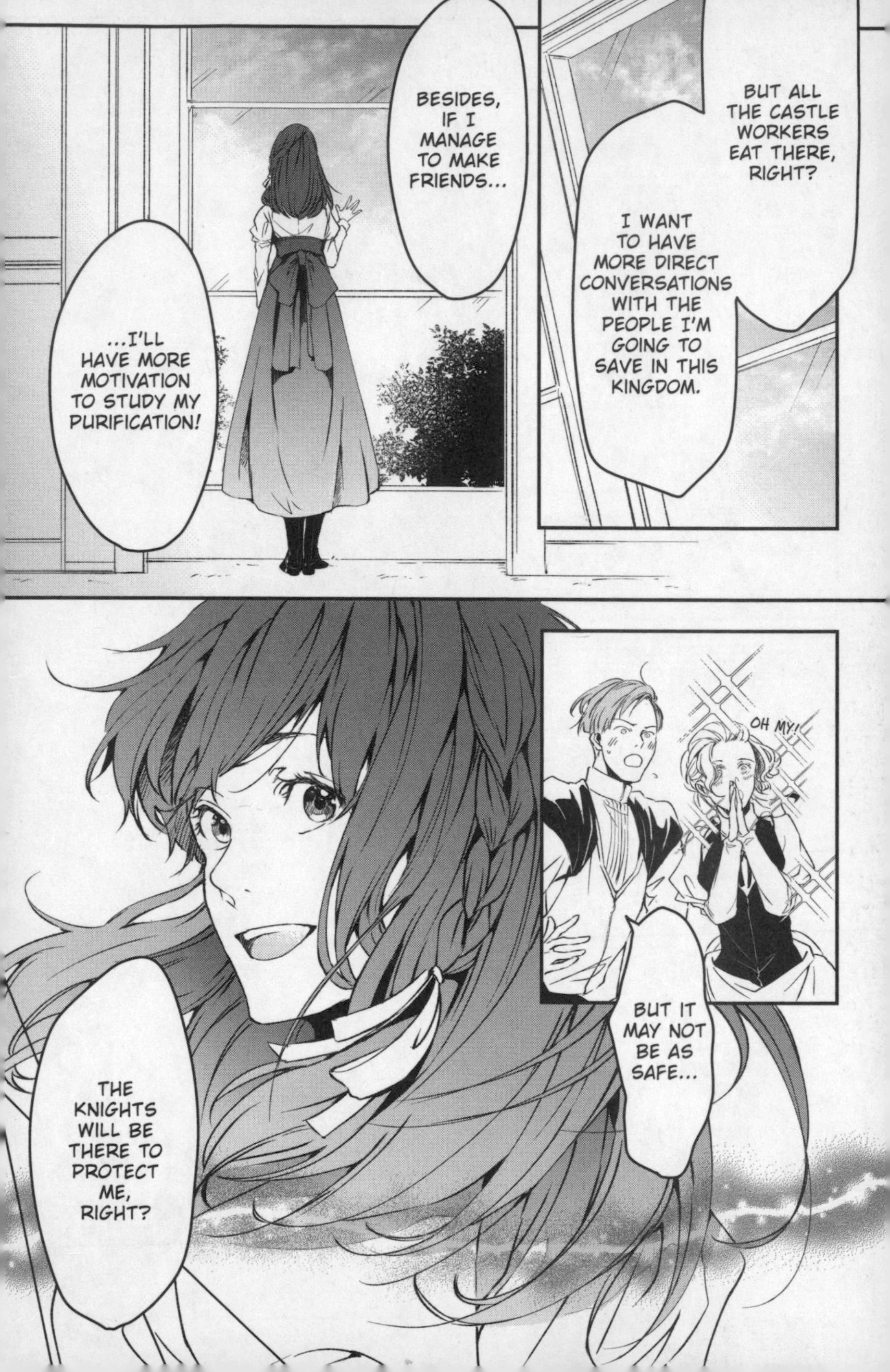
BUT ALL THE CASTLE WORKERS EAT THERE, RIGHT?
I WANT TO HAVE MORE DIRECT CONVERSATIONS WITH THE PEOPLE I'M GOING TO SAVE IN THIS KINGDOM.
BESIDES, IF I MANAGE TO MAKE FRIENDS...
...I'LL HAVE MORE MOTIVATION TO STUDY MY PURIFICATION!
OH MY!
BUT IT MAY NOT BE AS SAFE...
THE KNIGHTS WILL BE THERE TO PROTECT ME, RIGHT?

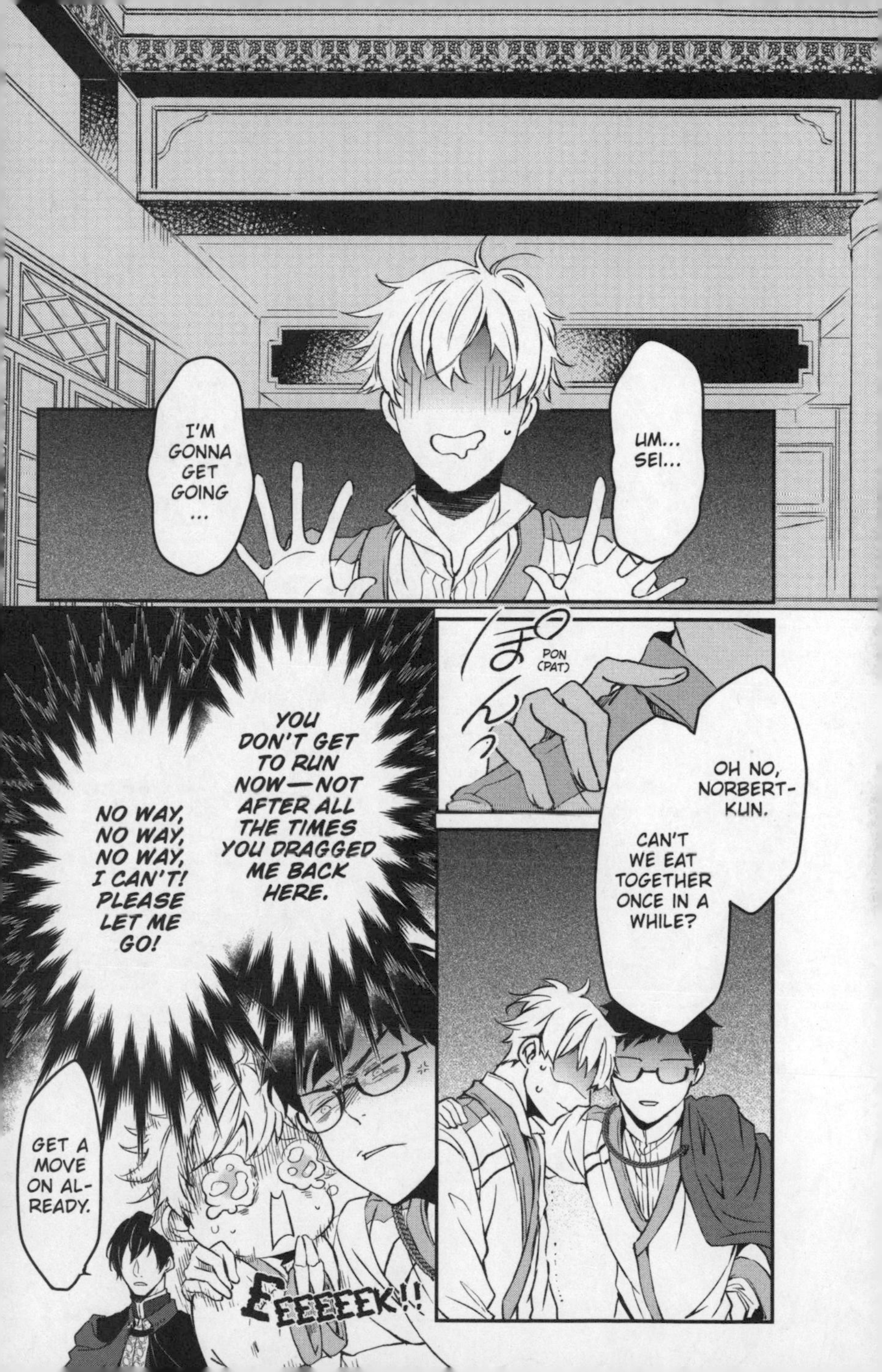
UM... SEI...
I'M GONNA GET GOING...
ぽんっ
PON (PAT)
OH NO, NORBERT-KUN.
CAN'T WE EAT TOGETHER ONCE IN A WHILE?
YOU DON'T GET TO RUN NOW—NOT AFTER ALL THE TIMES YOU DRAGGED ME BACK HERE.
NO WAY, NO WAY, NO WAY, I CAN'T! PLEASE LET ME GO!
GET A MOVE ON AL-READY.
EEEEEEK!!

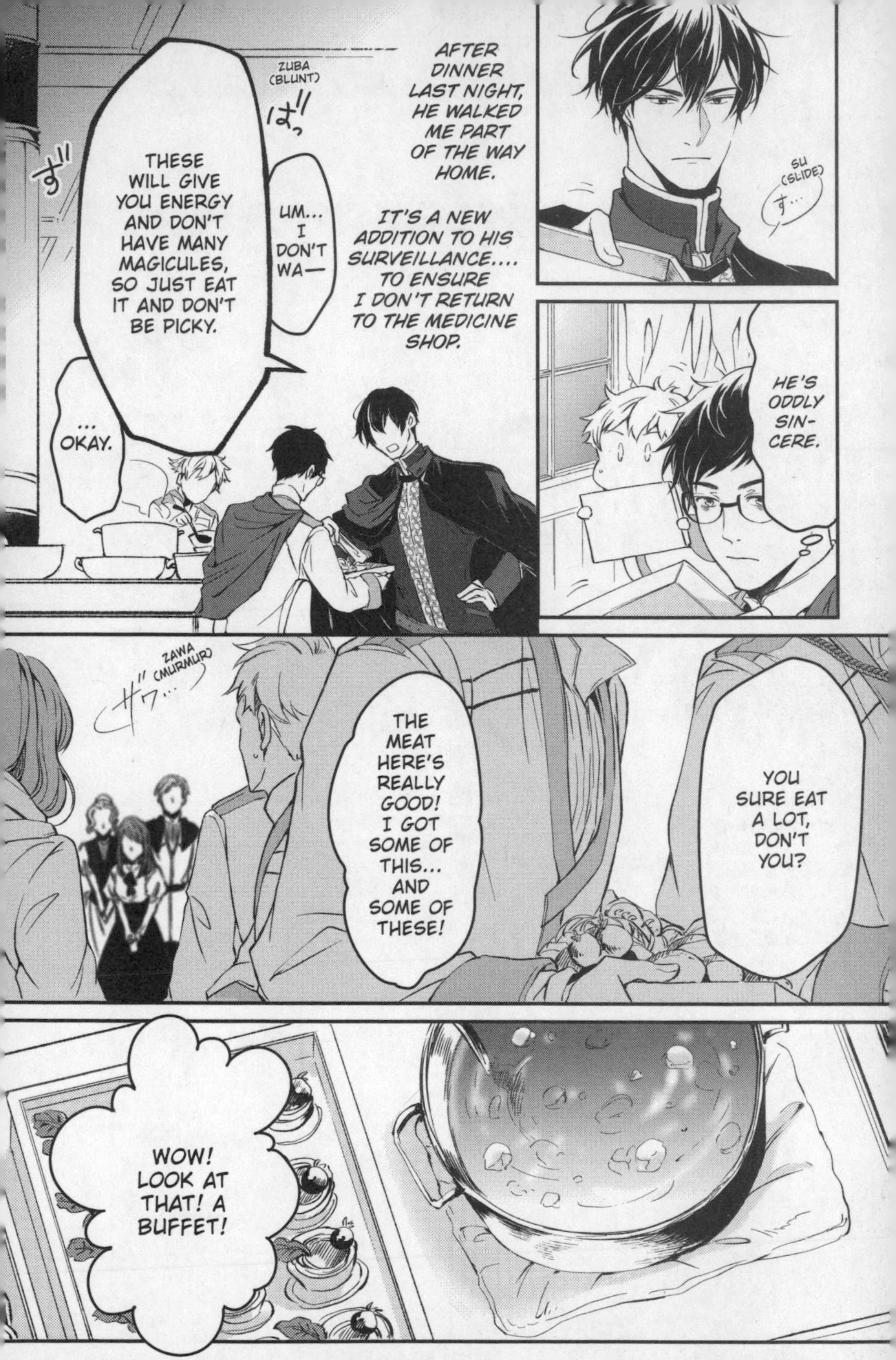
AFTER DINNER LAST NIGHT, HE WALKED ME PART OF THE WAY HOME.
IT'S A NEW ADDITION TO HIS SURVEILLANCE.... TO ENSURE I DON'T RETURN TO THE MEDICINE SHOP.
SU (SLIDE)
す…
HE'S ODDLY SIN-CERE.
ZUBA (BLUNT)
ばっ
UM... I DON'T WA—
THESE WILL GIVE YOU ENERGY AND DON'T HAVE MANY MAGICULES, SO JUST EAT IT AND DON'T BE PICKY.
ず
...OKAY.
YOU SURE EAT A LOT, DON'T YOU?
THE MEAT HERE'S REALLY GOOD! I GOT SOME OF THIS... AND SOME OF THESE!
ZAWA (MURMUR)
ザワ…
WOW! LOOK AT THAT! A BUFFET!

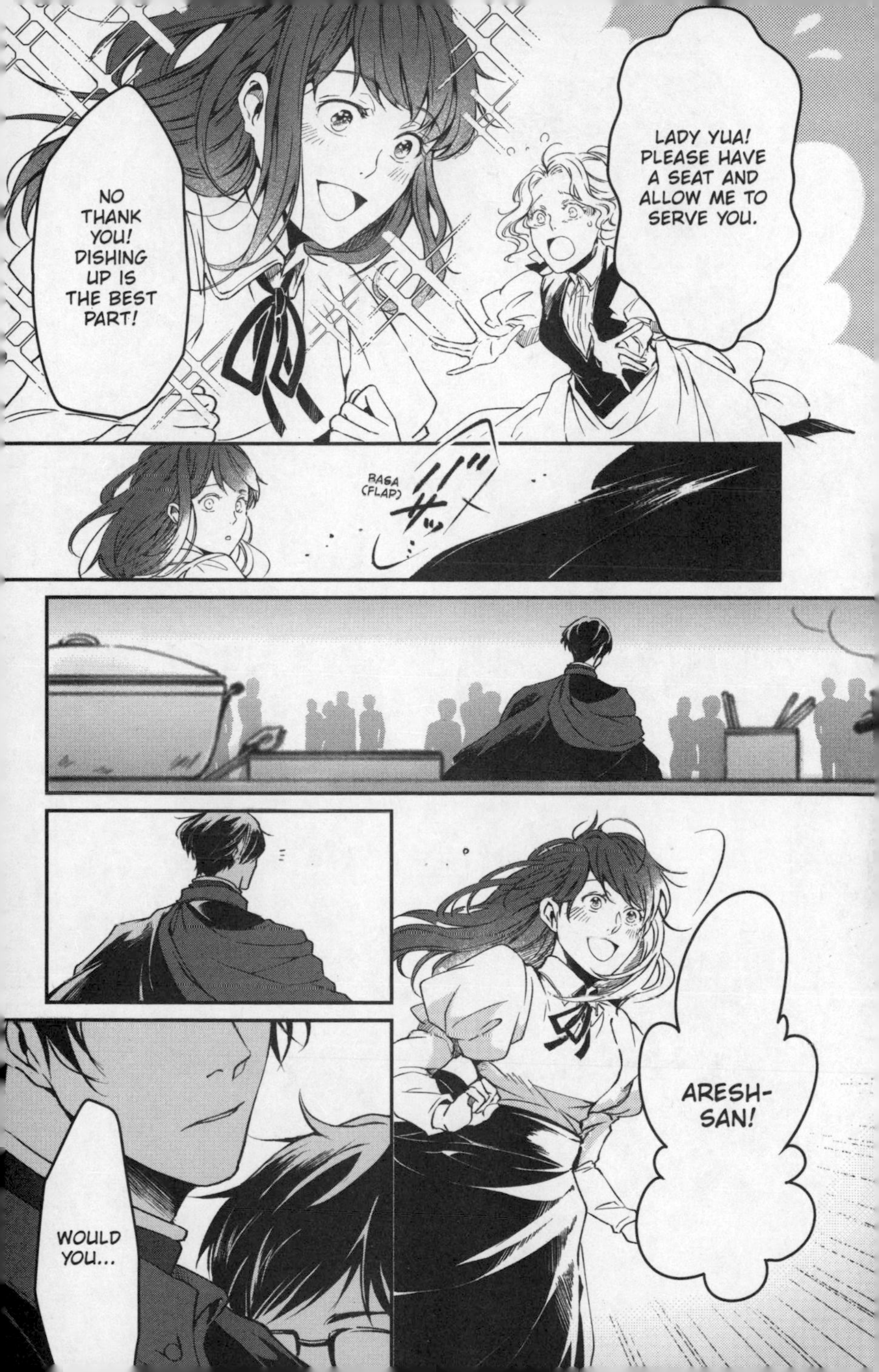
LADY YUA! PLEASE HAVE A SEAT AND ALLOW ME TO SERVE YOU.
NO THANK YOU! DISHING UP IS THE BEST PART!
BASA (FLAP)
ARESH-SAN!
WOULD YOU...

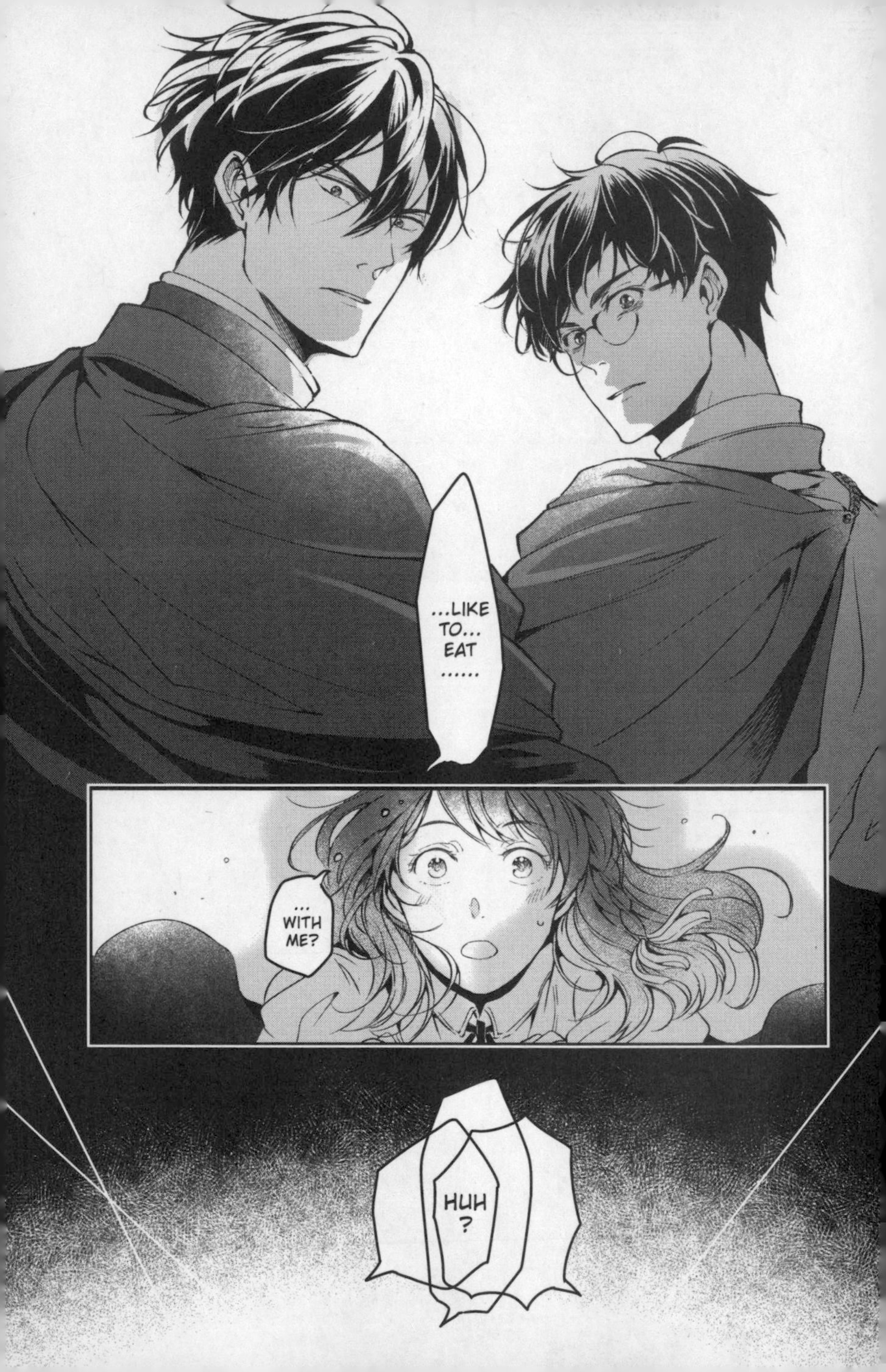
...LIKE TO... EAT ......
... WITH ME?
HUH ?

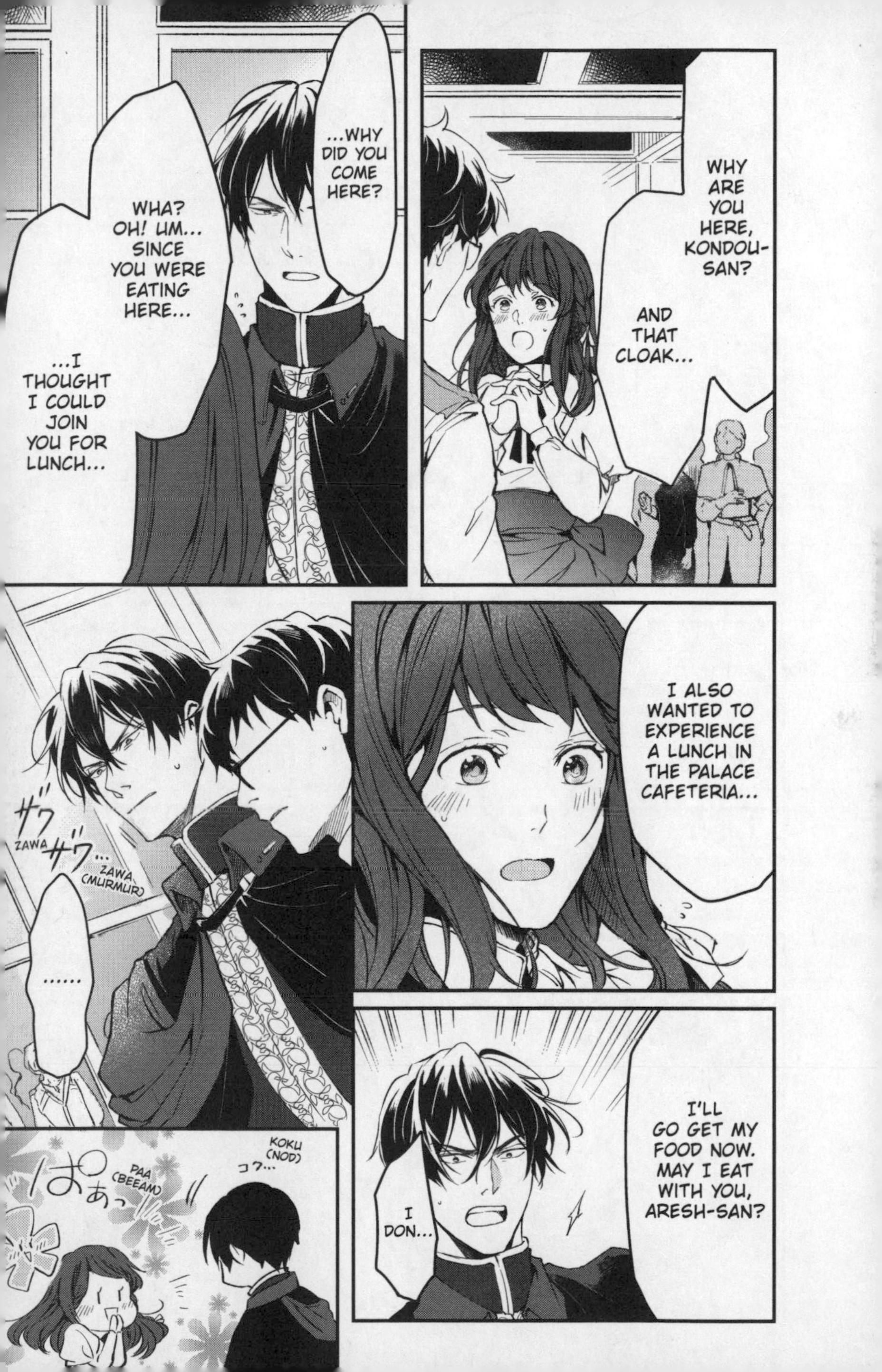
WHY ARE YOU HERE, KONDOU-SAN?
AND THAT CLOAK...
...WHY DID YOU COME HERE?
WHA? OH! UM... SINCE YOU WERE EATING HERE...
...I THOUGHT I COULD JOIN YOU FOR LUNCH...
I ALSO WANTED TO EXPERIENCE A LUNCH IN THE PALACE CAFETERIA...
I'LL GO GET MY FOOD NOW. MAY I EAT WITH YOU, ARESH-SAN?
I DON...
ザワ ZAWA ザワ... ZAWA (MURMUR)
......
ぱあっ PAA (BEEAM)
コク... KOKU (NOD)

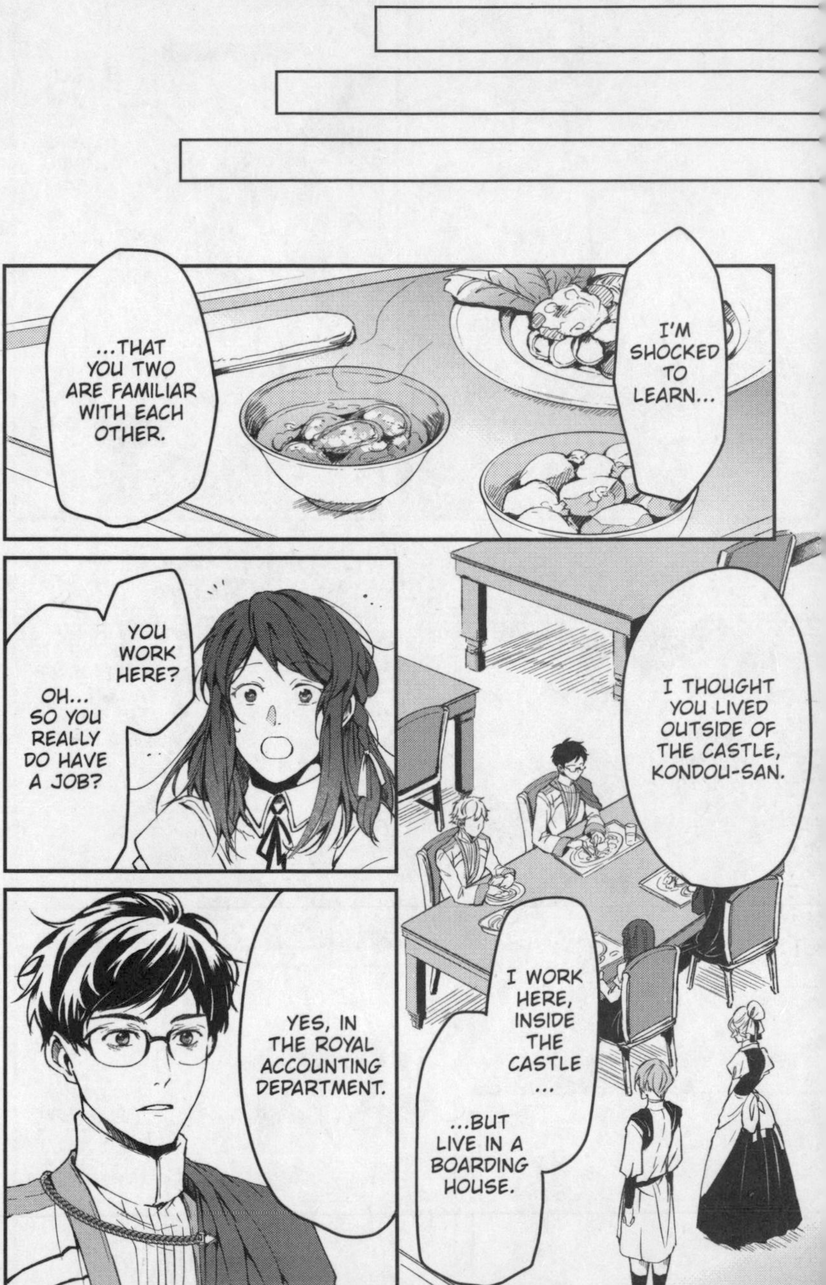
I'M SHOCKED TO LEARN...
...THAT YOU TWO ARE FAMILIAR WITH EACH OTHER.
I THOUGHT YOU LIVED OUTSIDE OF THE CASTLE, KONDOU-SAN.
I WORK HERE, INSIDE THE CASTLE ...
...BUT LIVE IN A BOARDING HOUSE.
YOU WORK HERE?
OH... SO YOU REALLY DO HAVE A JOB?
YES, IN THE ROYAL ACCOUNTING DEPARTMENT.

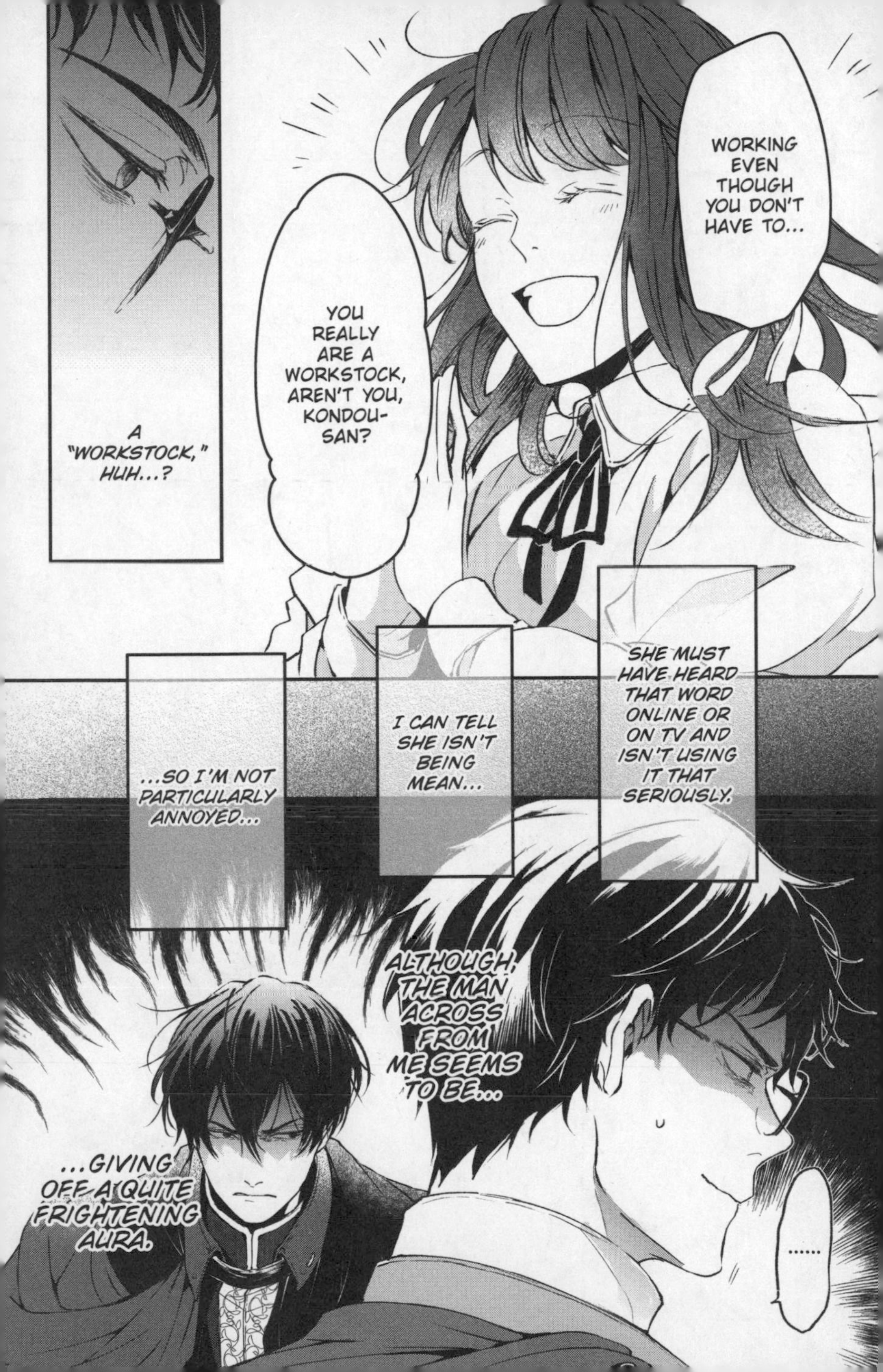
WORKING EVEN THOUGH YOU DON'T HAVE TO...
YOU REALLY ARE A WORKSTOCK, AREN'T YOU, KONDOU-SAN?
A "WORKSTOCK," HUH...?
SHE MUST HAVE HEARD THAT WORD ONLINE OR ON TV AND ISN'T USING IT THAT SERIOUSLY.
I CAN TELL SHE ISN'T BEING MEAN...
...SO I'M NOT PARTICULARLY ANNOYED...
ALTHOUGH, THE MAN ACROSS FROM ME SEEMS TO BE...
......
...GIVING OFF A QUITE FRIGHTENING AURA.

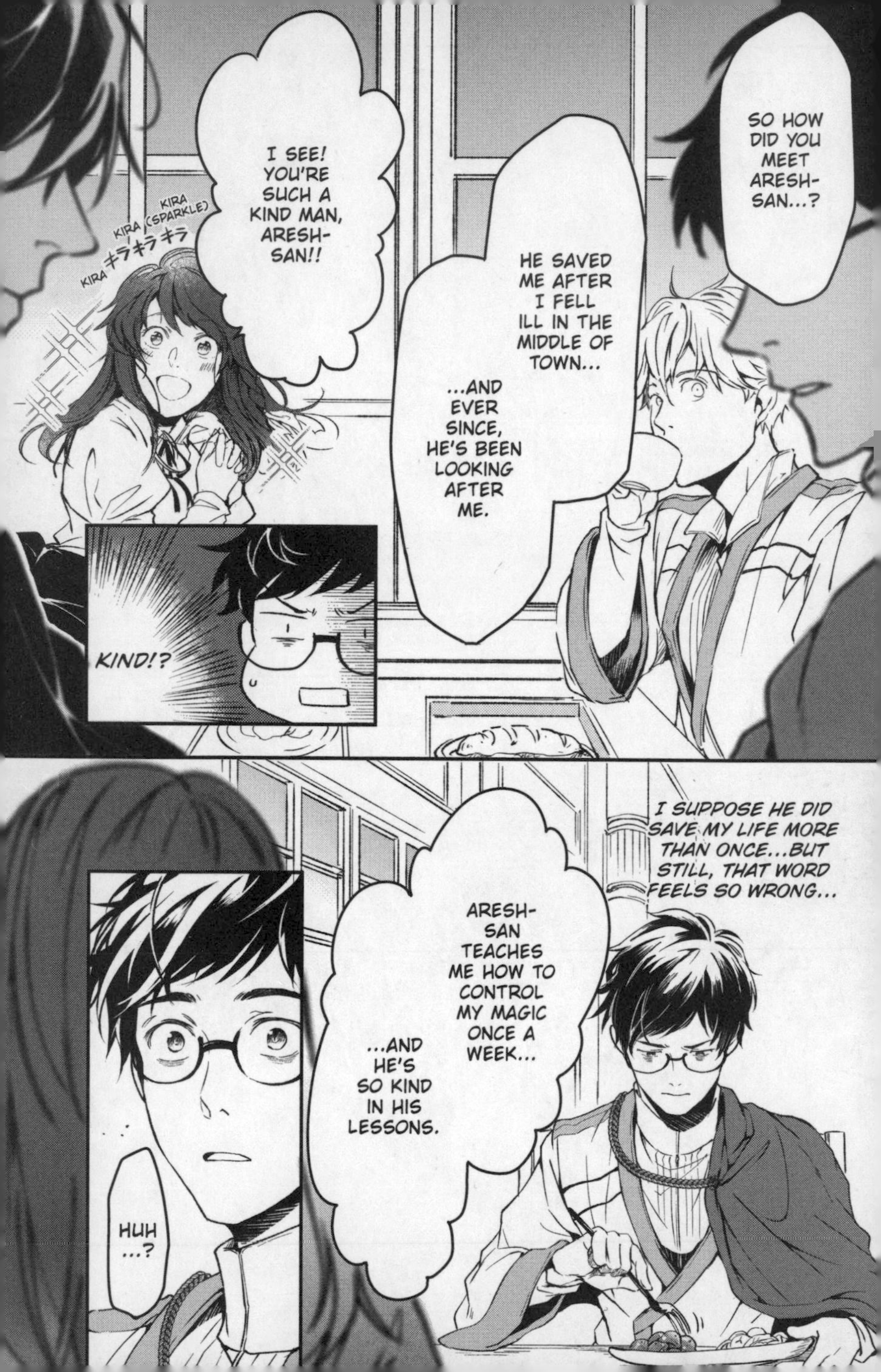
SO HOW DID YOU MEET ARESH-SAN...?
HE SAVED ME AFTER I FELL ILL IN THE MIDDLE OF TOWN...
...AND EVER SINCE, HE'S BEEN LOOKING AFTER ME.
I SEE! YOU'RE SUCH A KIND MAN, ARESH-SAN!!
キラキラキラ
KIRA KIRA KIRA (SPARKLE)
KIND!?
I SUPPOSE HE DID SAVE MY LIFE MORE THAN ONCE...BUT STILL, THAT WORD FEELS SO WRONG...
ARESH-SAN TEACHES ME HOW TO CONTROL MY MAGIC ONCE A WEEK...
...AND HE'S SO KIND IN HIS LESSONS.
HUH...?

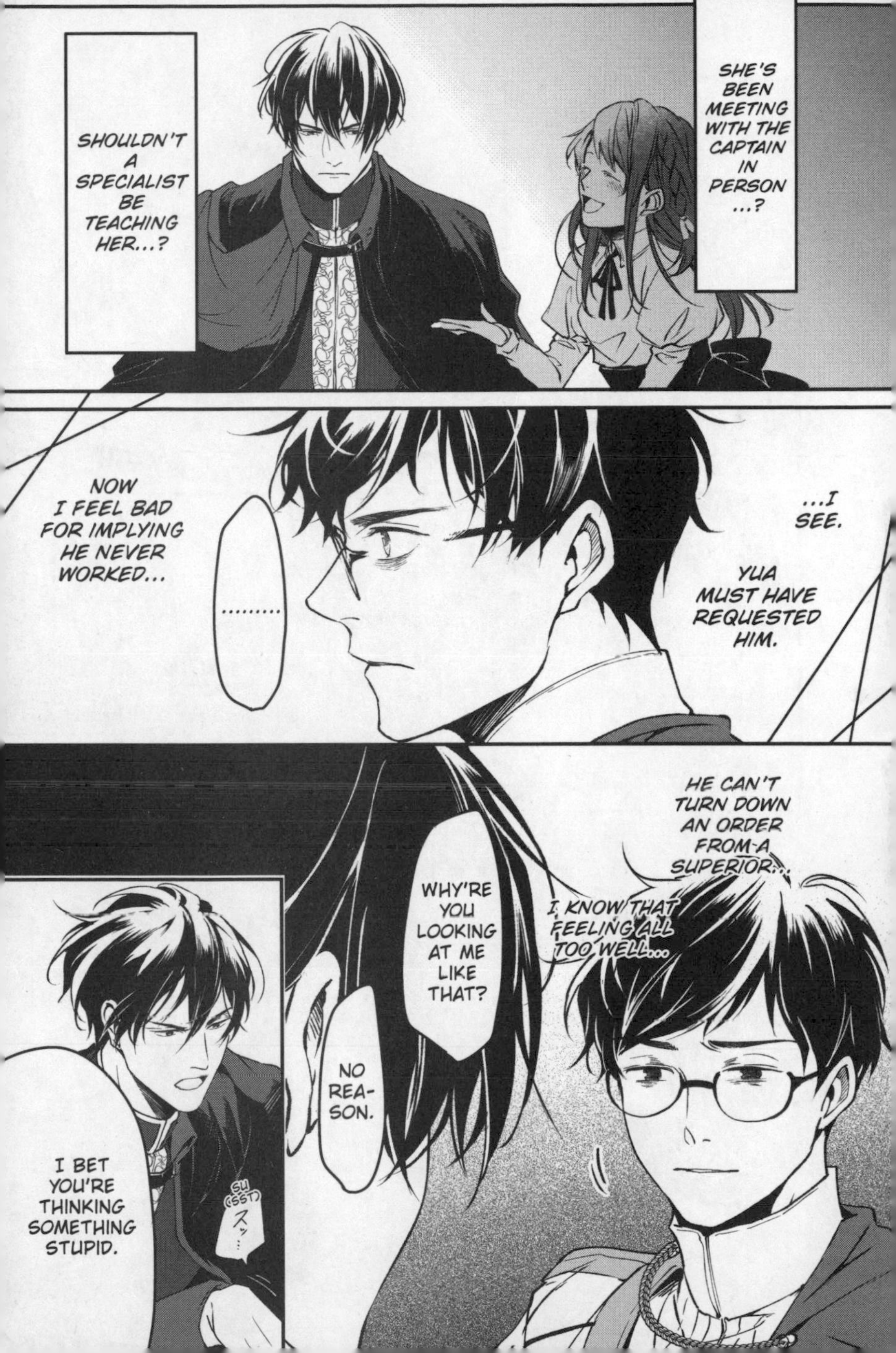
SHE'S BEEN MEETING WITH THE CAPTAIN IN PERSON ...?
SHOULDN'T A SPECIALIST BE TEACHING HER...?
...I SEE.
YUA MUST HAVE REQUESTED HIM.
....
NOW I FEEL BAD FOR IMPLYING HE NEVER WORKED...
HE CAN'T TURN DOWN AN ORDER FROM A SUPERIOR...
I KNOW THAT FEELING ALL TOO WELL...
WHY'RE YOU LOOKING AT ME LIKE THAT?
NO REA-SON.
SU (SST) スッ…
I BET YOU'RE THINKING SOMETHING STUPID.

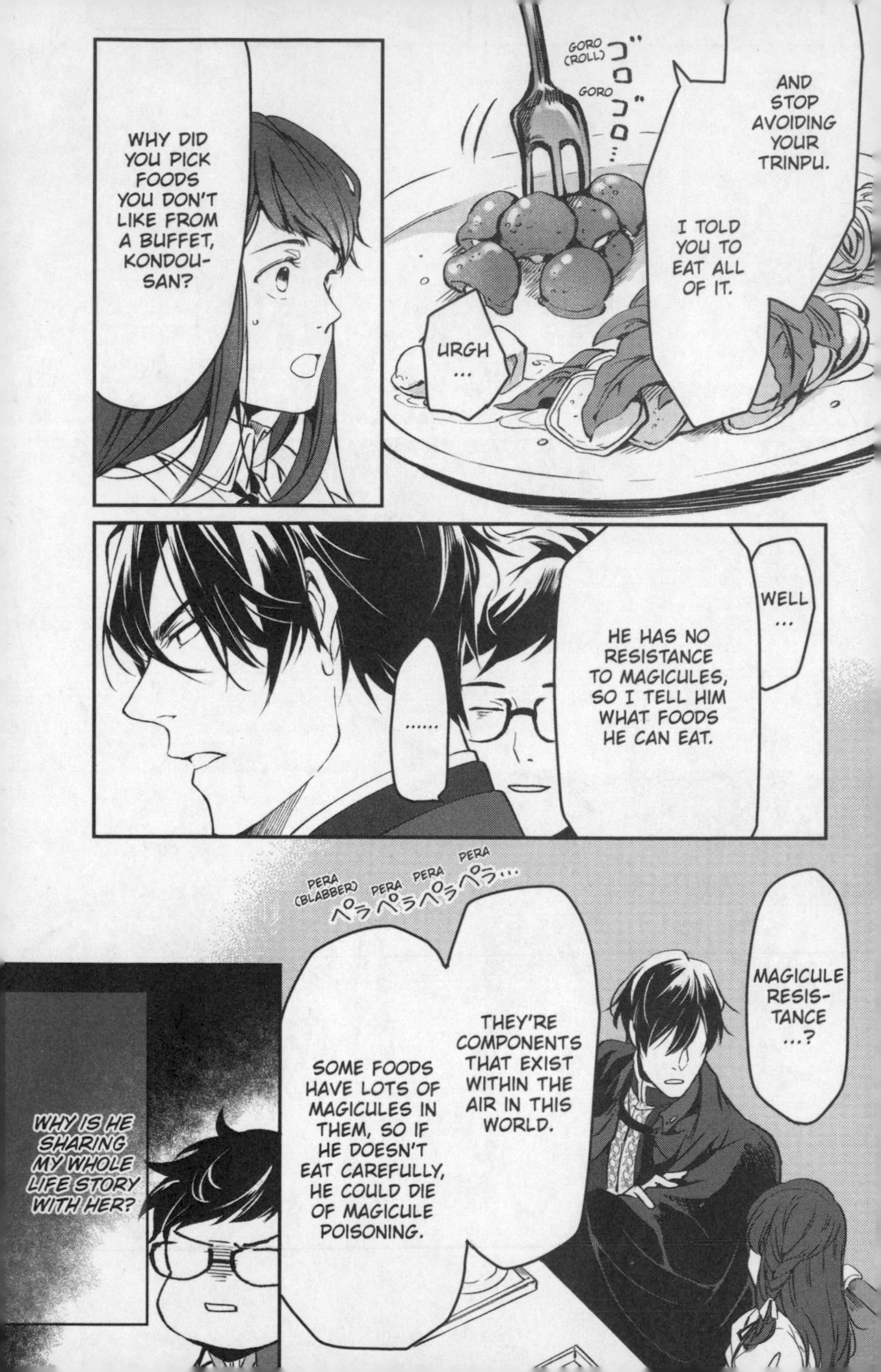
GORO (ROLL) ゴロ
GORO ゴロ…
I TOLD YOU TO EAT ALL OF IT.
AND STOP AVOIDING YOUR TRINPU.
URGH …
WHY DID YOU PICK FOODS YOU DON'T LIKE FROM A BUFFET, KONDOU-SAN?
WELL …
HE HAS NO RESISTANCE TO MAGICULES, SO I TELL HIM WHAT FOODS HE CAN EAT.
……
PERA (BLABBER) PERA PERA PERA ペラペラペラペラ…
MAGICULE RESIS-TANCE …?
THEY'RE COMPONENTS THAT EXIST WITHIN THE AIR IN THIS WORLD.
SOME FOODS HAVE LOTS OF MAGICULES IN THEM, SO IF HE DOESN'T EAT CAREFULLY, HE COULD DIE OF MAGICULE POISONING.
WHY IS HE SHARING MY WHOLE LIFE STORY WITH HER?

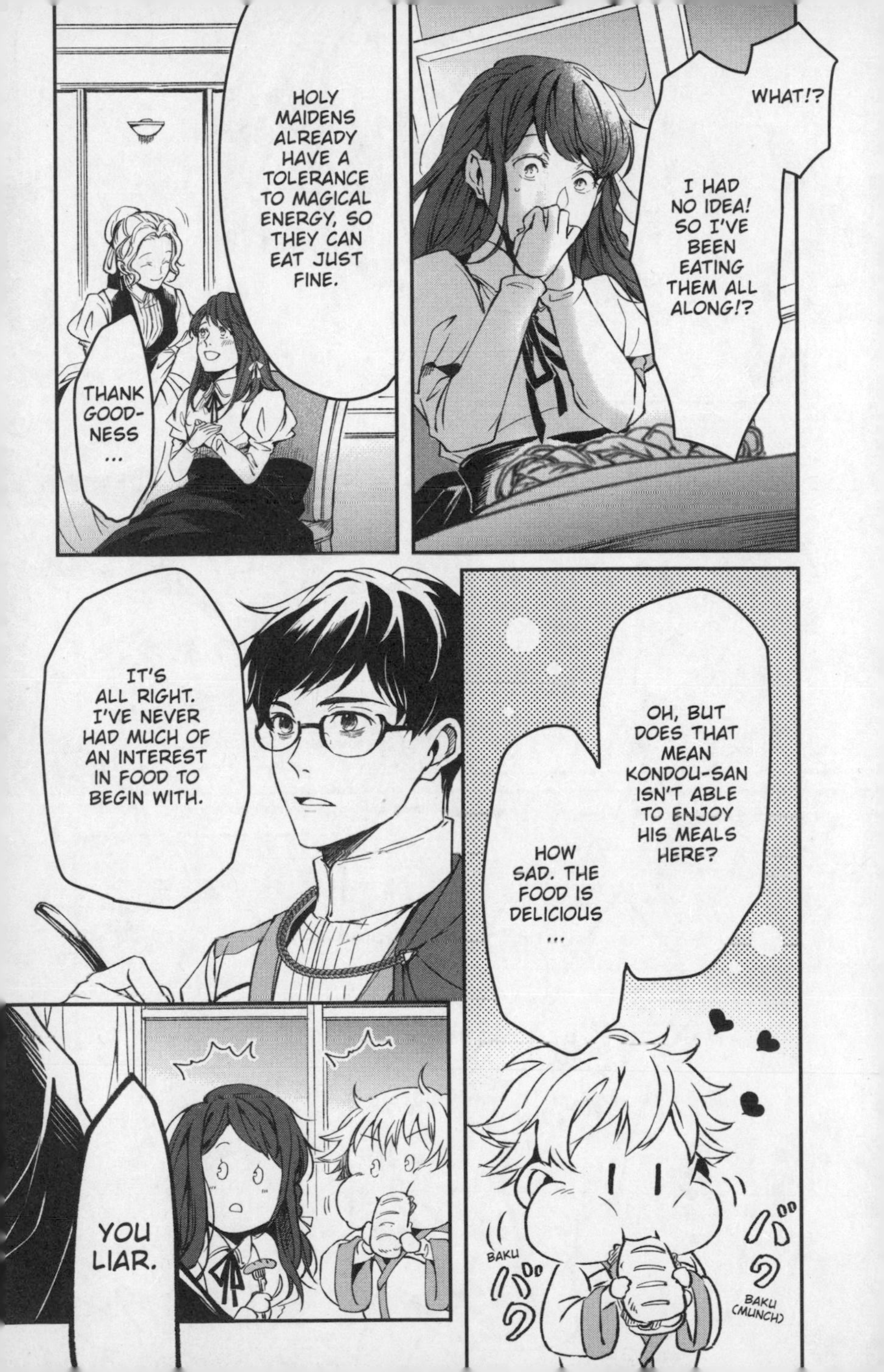
WHAT!?
I HAD NO IDEA! SO I'VE BEEN EATING THEM ALL ALONG!?
HOLY MAIDENS ALREADY HAVE A TOLERANCE TO MAGICAL ENERGY, SO THEY CAN EAT JUST FINE.
THANK GOOD-NESS ...
OH, BUT DOES THAT MEAN KONDOU-SAN ISN'T ABLE TO ENJOY HIS MEALS HERE?
HOW SAD. THE FOOD IS DELICIOUS ...
BAKU
BAKU (MUNCH)
IT'S ALL RIGHT. I'VE NEVER HAD MUCH OF AN INTEREST IN FOOD TO BEGIN WITH.
YOU LIAR.

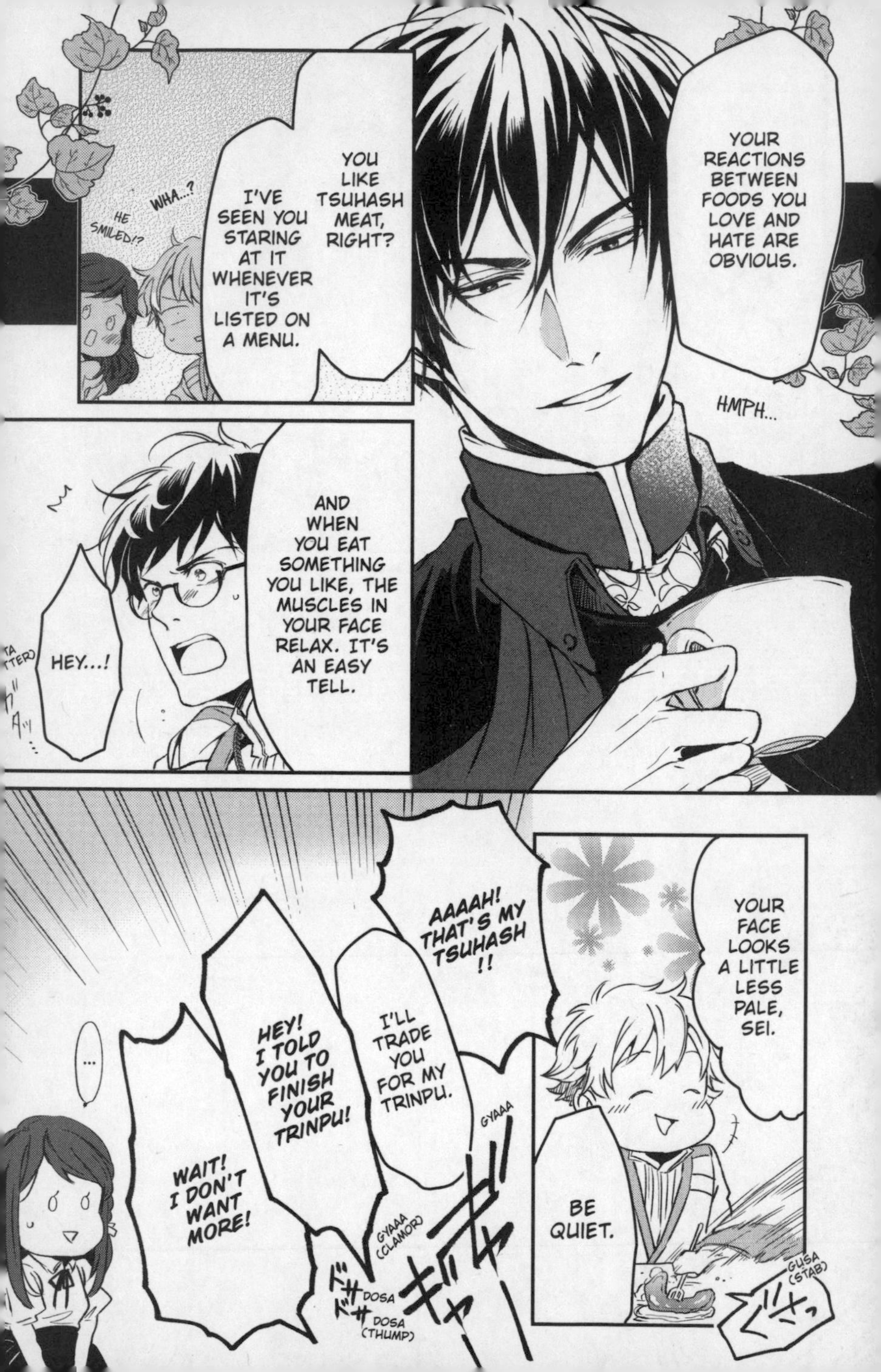
YOUR REACTIONS BETWEEN FOODS YOU LOVE AND HATE ARE OBVIOUS.
HMPH...
YOU LIKE TSUHASH MEAT, RIGHT?
I'VE SEEN YOU STARING AT IT WHENEVER IT'S LISTED ON A MENU.
WHA...?
HE SMILED!?
AND WHEN YOU EAT SOMETHING YOU LIKE, THE MUSCLES IN YOUR FACE RELAX. IT'S AN EASY TELL.
HEY...!
YOUR FACE LOOKS A LITTLE LESS PALE, SEI.
BE QUIET.
GUSA (STAB)
AAAAH! THAT'S MY TSUHASH!!
I'LL TRADE YOU FOR MY TRINPU.
HEY! I TOLD YOU TO FINISH YOUR TRINPU!
GYAAA
WAIT! I DON'T WANT MORE!
GYAAA (CLAMOR)
DOSA DOSA (THUMP)
...

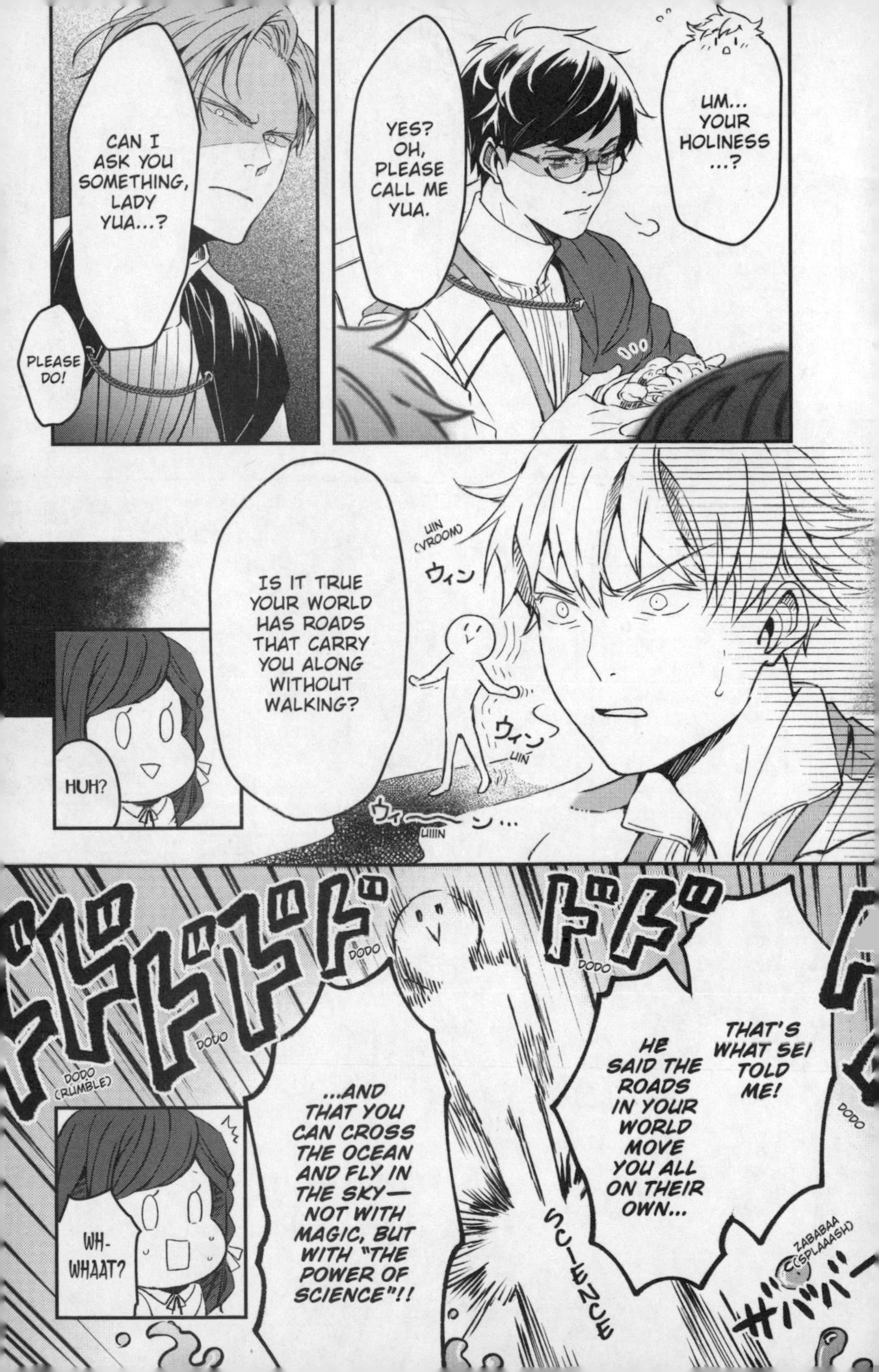
UM... YOUR HOLINESS ...?
YES? OH, PLEASE CALL ME YUA.
CAN I ASK YOU SOMETHING, LADY YUA...?
PLEASE DO!
IS IT TRUE YOUR WORLD HAS ROADS THAT CARRY YOU ALONG WITHOUT WALKING?
ウィン
UIN (VROOM)
ウィン
UIN
ウィーーン...
UIIIN
HUH?
DODO
DODO
DODO
THAT'S WHAT SEI TOLD ME!
HE SAID THE ROADS IN YOUR WORLD MOVE YOU ALL ON THEIR OWN...
...AND THAT YOU CAN CROSS THE OCEAN AND FLY IN THE SKY—NOT WITH MAGIC, BUT WITH "THE POWER OF SCIENCE"!!
SCIENCE
ZABABAA (SPLAAASH)
DODO (RUMBLE)
DODO
WH-WHAAT?

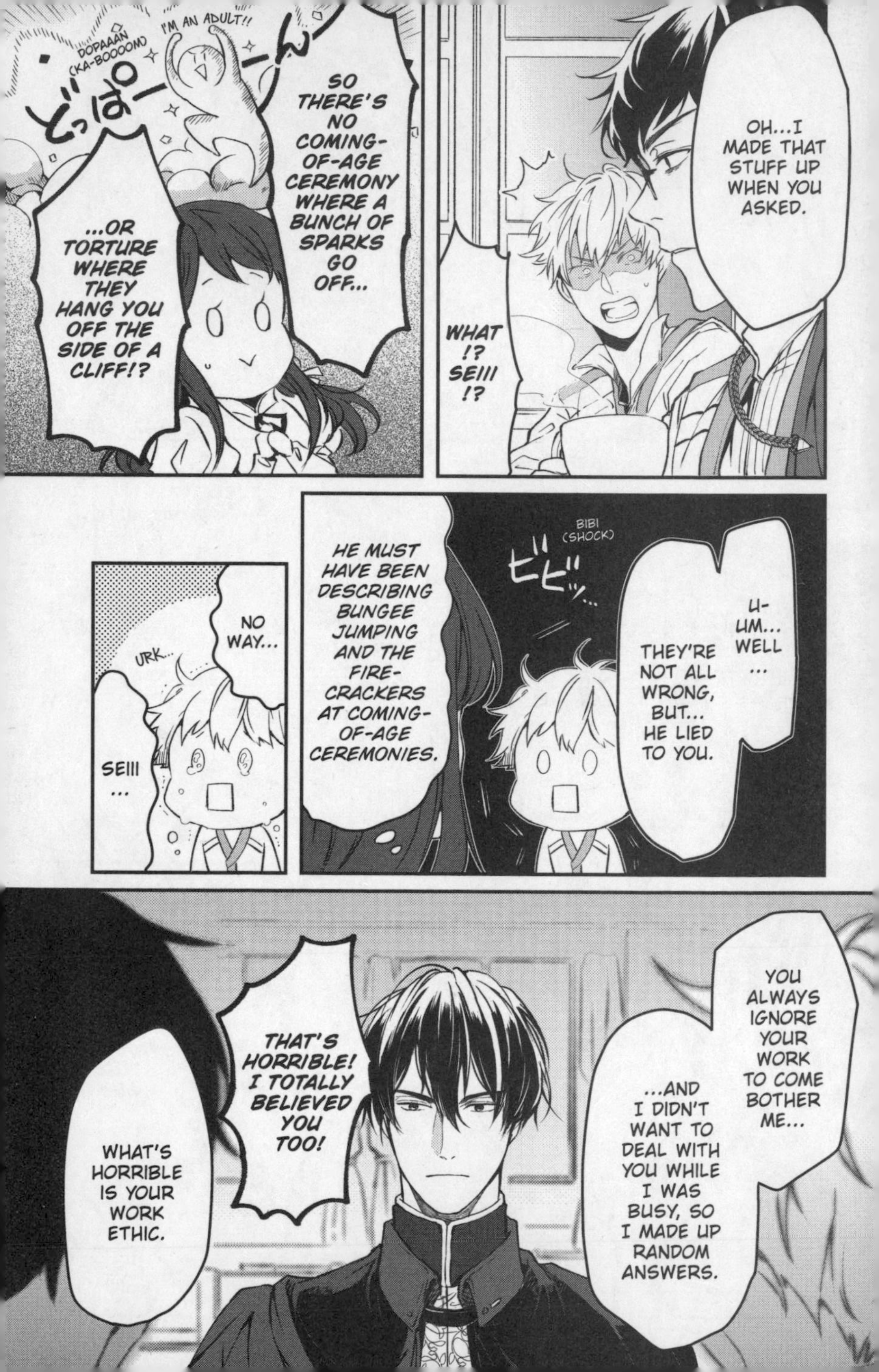
OH...I MADE THAT STUFF UP WHEN YOU ASKED.
WHAT!? SEIII!?
DOPAAAN (KA-BOOOOM)
I'M AN ADULT!!
SO THERE'S NO COMING-OF-AGE CEREMONY WHERE A BUNCH OF SPARKS GO OFF...
...OR TORTURE WHERE THEY HANG YOU OFF THE SIDE OF A CLIFF!?
BIBI (SHOCK)
U-UM... WELL...
THEY'RE NOT ALL WRONG, BUT... HE LIED TO YOU.
HE MUST HAVE BEEN DESCRIBING BUNGEE JUMPING AND THE FIRE-CRACKERS AT COMING-OF-AGE CEREMONIES.
NO WAY...
URK...
SEIII...
YOU ALWAYS IGNORE YOUR WORK TO COME BOTHER ME...
...AND I DIDN'T WANT TO DEAL WITH YOU WHILE I WAS BUSY, SO I MADE UP RANDOM ANSWERS.
THAT'S HORRIBLE! I TOTALLY BELIEVED YOU TOO!
WHAT'S HORRIBLE IS YOUR WORK ETHIC.

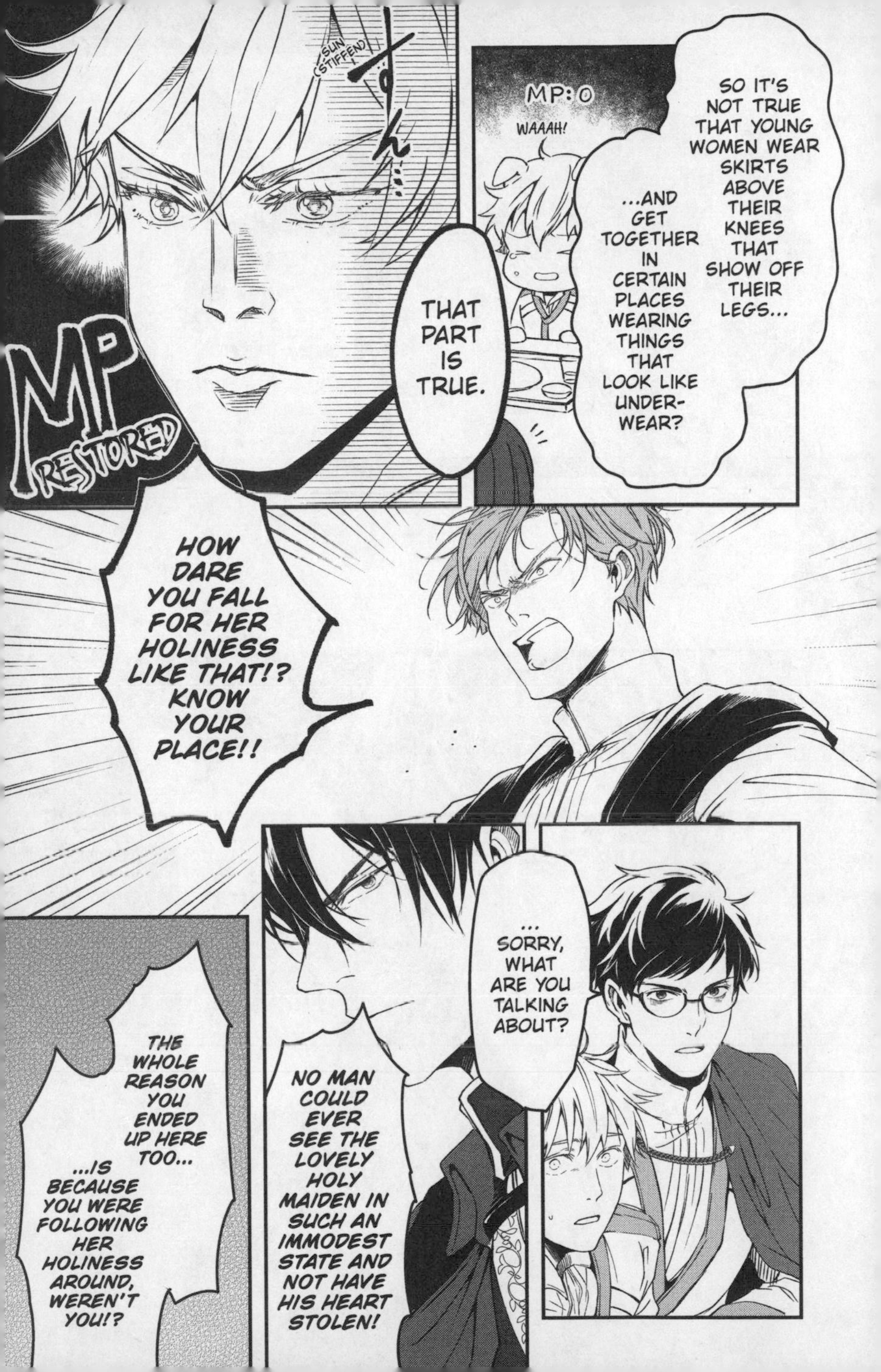
MP: 0
WAAAH!
SO IT'S NOT TRUE THAT YOUNG WOMEN WEAR SKIRTS ABOVE THEIR KNEES THAT SHOW OFF THEIR LEGS...
...AND GET TOGETHER IN CERTAIN PLACES WEARING THINGS THAT LOOK LIKE UNDER-WEAR?
THAT PART IS TRUE.
SUN (STIFFEN)
MP RESTORED
HOW DARE YOU FALL FOR HER HOLINESS LIKE THAT!? KNOW YOUR PLACE!!
... SORRY, WHAT ARE YOU TALKING ABOUT?
NO MAN COULD EVER SEE THE LOVELY HOLY MAIDEN IN SUCH AN IMMODEST STATE AND NOT HAVE HIS HEART STOLEN!
THE WHOLE REASON YOU ENDED UP HERE TOO...
...IS BECAUSE YOU WERE FOLLOWING HER HOLINESS AROUND, WEREN'T YOU!?

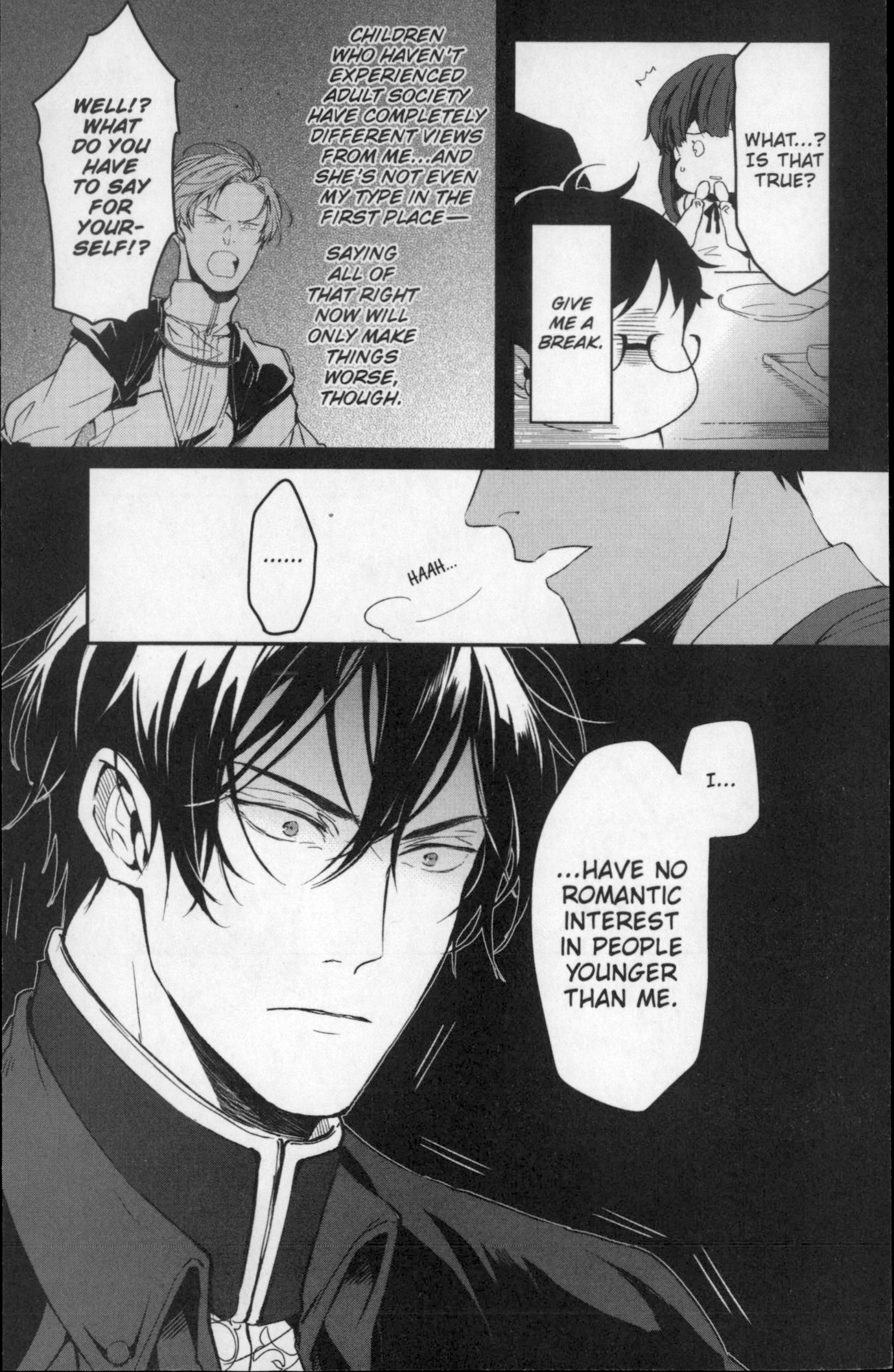
WHAT...? IS THAT TRUE?
GIVE ME A BREAK.
WELL!? WHAT DO YOU HAVE TO SAY FOR YOURSELF!?
CHILDREN WHO HAVEN'T EXPERIENCED ADULT SOCIETY HAVE COMPLETELY DIFFERENT VIEWS FROM ME...AND SHE'S NOT EVEN MY TYPE IN THE FIRST PLACE—
SAYING ALL OF THAT RIGHT NOW WILL ONLY MAKE THINGS WORSE, THOUGH.
HAAAH...
......
I...
...HAVE NO ROMANTIC INTEREST IN PEOPLE YOUNGER THAN ME.

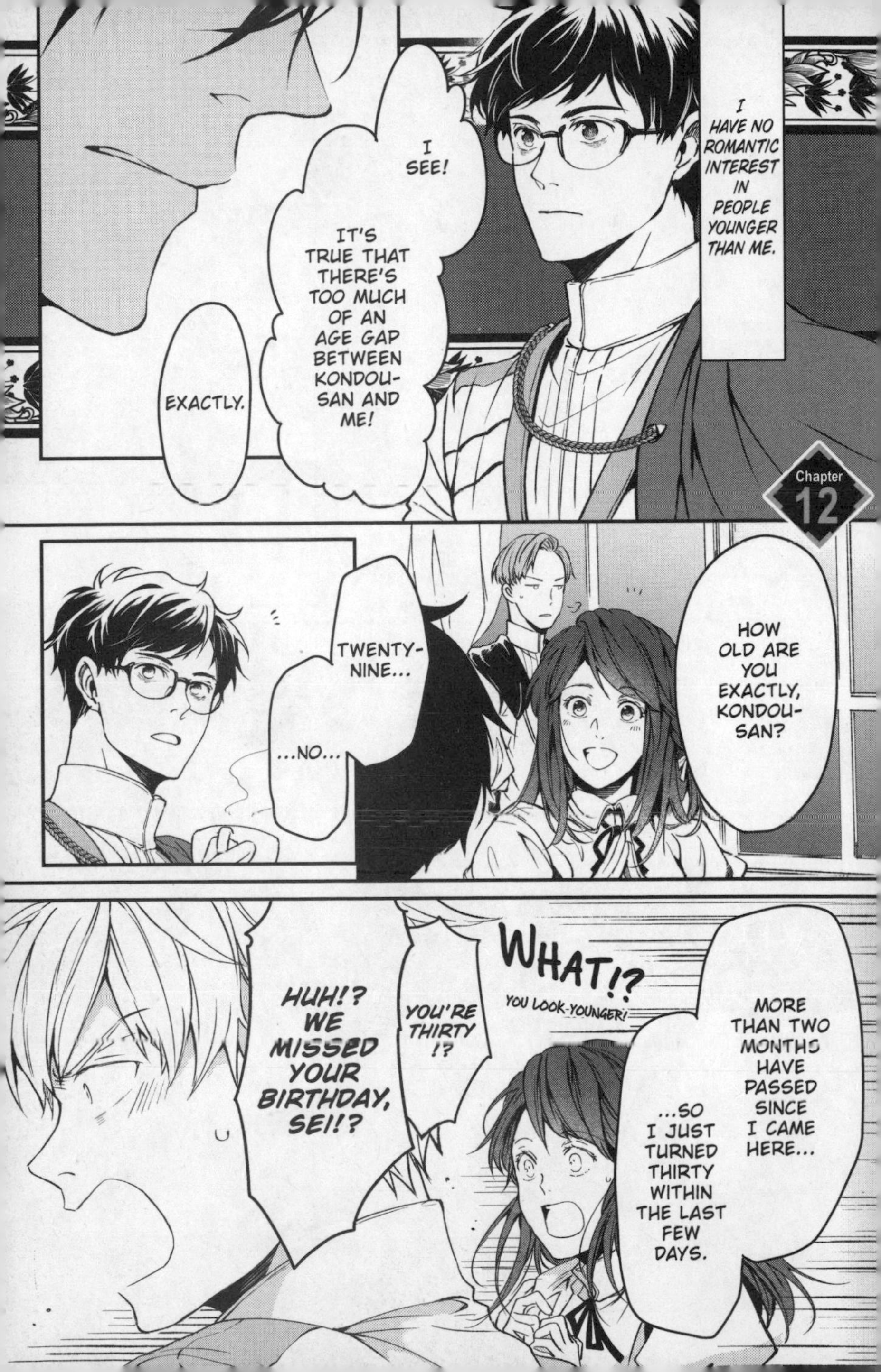
I HAVE NO ROMANTIC INTEREST IN PEOPLE YOUNGER THAN ME.
I SEE!
IT'S TRUE THAT THERE'S TOO MUCH OF AN AGE GAP BETWEEN KONDOU-SAN AND ME!
EXACTLY.
Chapter 12
HOW OLD ARE YOU EXACTLY, KONDOU-SAN?
TWENTY-NINE...
...NO...
MORE THAN TWO MONTHS HAVE PASSED SINCE I CAME HERE...
...SO I JUST TURNED THIRTY WITHIN THE LAST FEW DAYS.
WHAT!?
YOU LOOK YOUNGER!
YOU'RE THIRTY!?
HUH!? WE MISSED YOUR BIRTHDAY, SEI!?

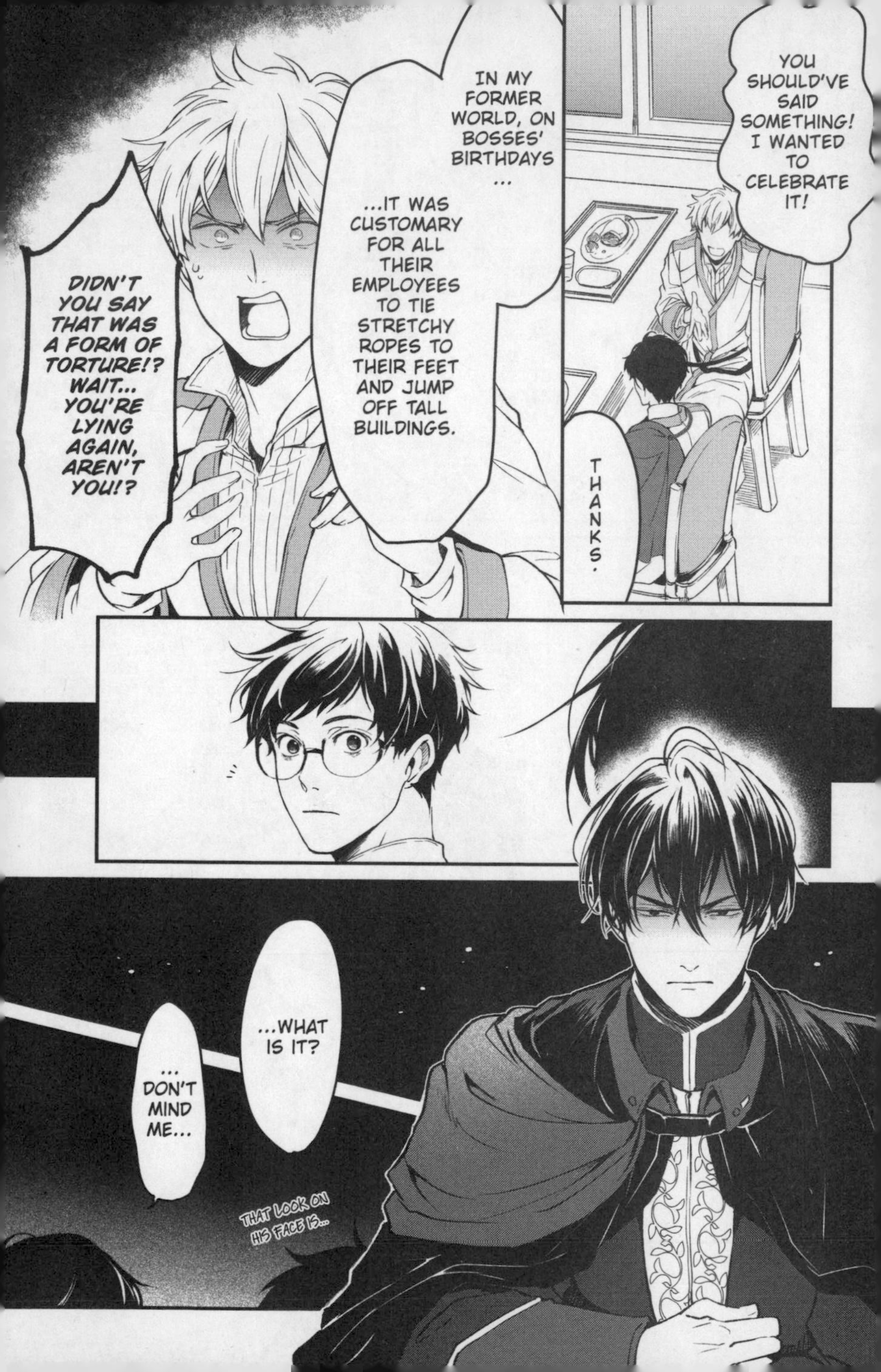
YOU SHOULD'VE SAID SOMETHING! I WANTED TO CELEBRATE IT!
THANKS.
IN MY FORMER WORLD, ON BOSSES' BIRTHDAYS...
...IT WAS CUSTOMARY FOR ALL THEIR EMPLOYEES TO TIE STRETCHY ROPES TO THEIR FEET AND JUMP OFF TALL BUILDINGS.
DIDN'T YOU SAY THAT WAS A FORM OF TORTURE!? WAIT... YOU'RE LYING AGAIN, AREN'T YOU!?
...WHAT IS IT?
...DON'T MIND ME...
THAT LOOK ON HIS FACE IS...

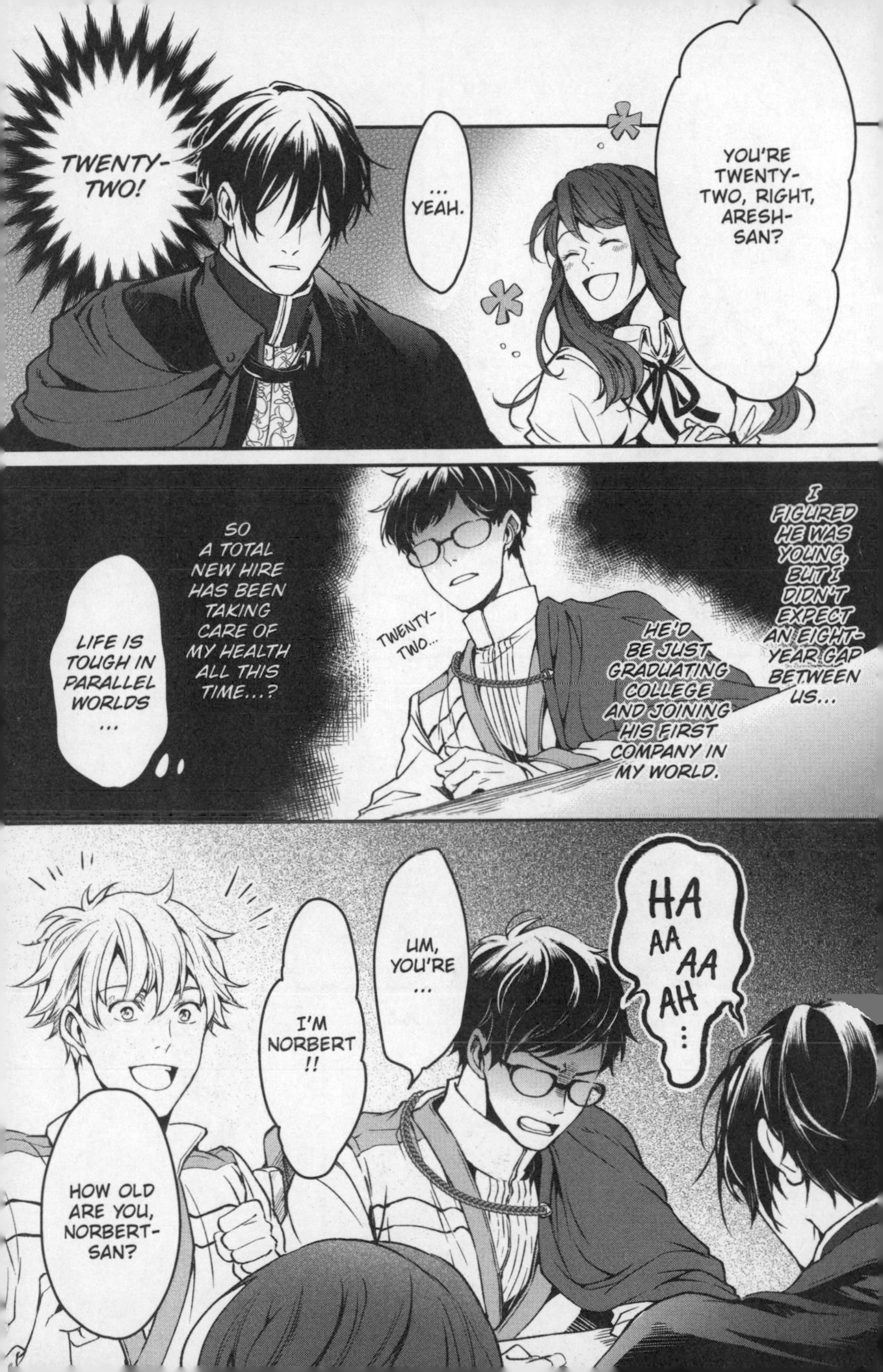
YOU'RE TWENTY-TWO, RIGHT, ARESH-SAN?
... YEAH.
TWENTY-TWO!
I FIGURED HE WAS YOUNG, BUT I DIDN'T EXPECT AN EIGHT-YEAR GAP BETWEEN US...
HE'D BE JUST GRADUATING COLLEGE AND JOINING HIS FIRST COMPANY IN MY WORLD.
TWENTY-TWO...
SO A TOTAL NEW HIRE HAS BEEN TAKING CARE OF MY HEALTH ALL THIS TIME...?
LIFE IS TOUGH IN PARALLEL WORLDS ...
HA AA AA AH ...
UM, YOU'RE ...
I'M NORBERT !!
HOW OLD ARE YOU, NORBERT-SAN?

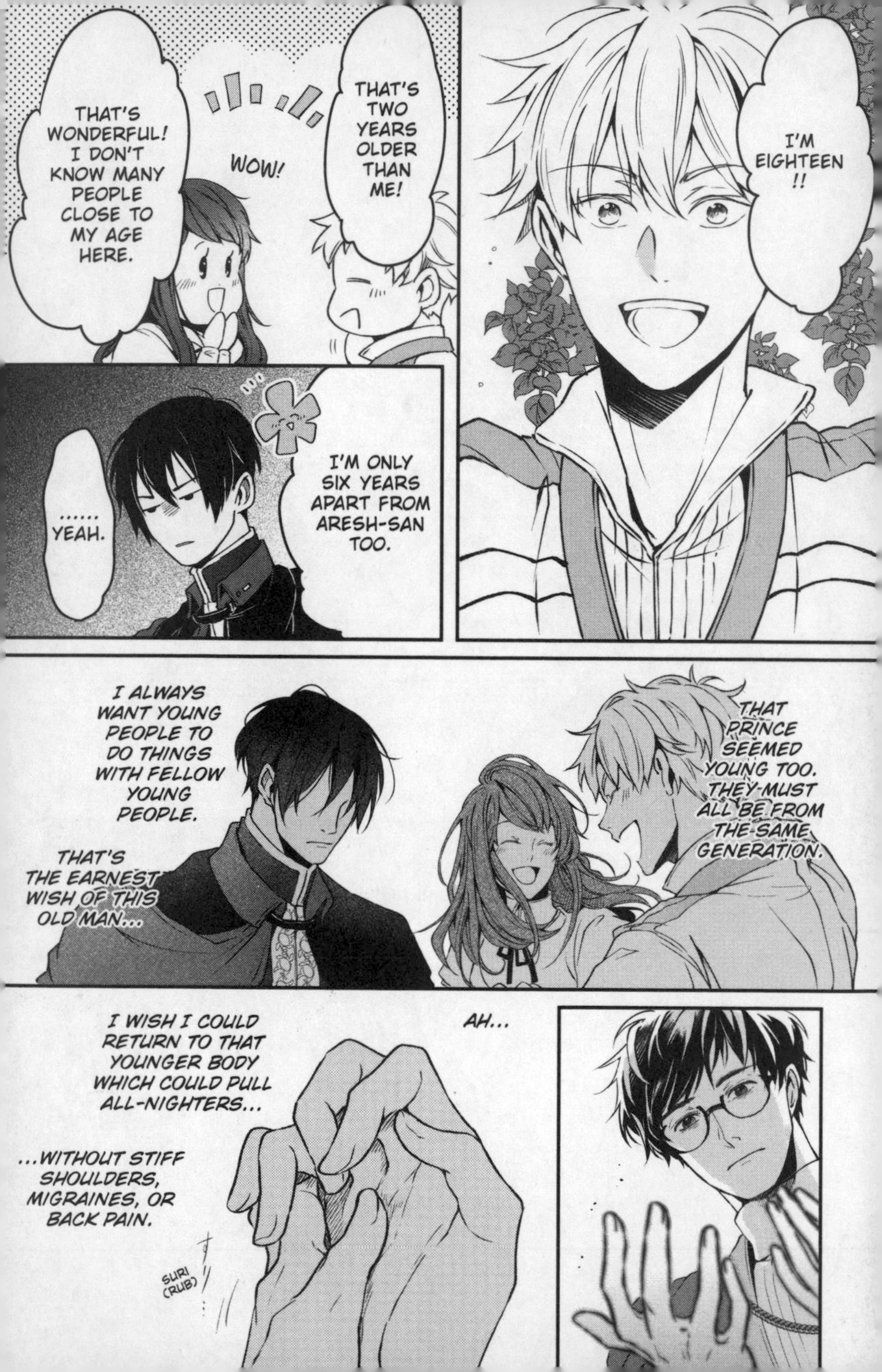

I'M EIGHTEEN !!
THAT'S TWO YEARS OLDER THAN ME!
WOW!
THAT'S WONDERFUL! I DON'T KNOW MANY PEOPLE CLOSE TO MY AGE HERE.
I'M ONLY SIX YEARS APART FROM ARESH-SAN TOO.
...... YEAH.
THAT PRINCE SEEMED YOUNG TOO. THEY MUST ALL BE FROM THE SAME GENERATION.
I ALWAYS WANT YOUNG PEOPLE TO DO THINGS WITH FELLOW YOUNG PEOPLE.
THAT'S THE EARNEST WISH OF THIS OLD MAN...
AH...
I WISH I COULD RETURN TO THAT YOUNGER BODY WHICH COULD PULL ALL-NIGHTERS...
...WITHOUT STIFF SHOULDERS, MIGRAINES, OR BACK PAIN.
SURI (RUB)

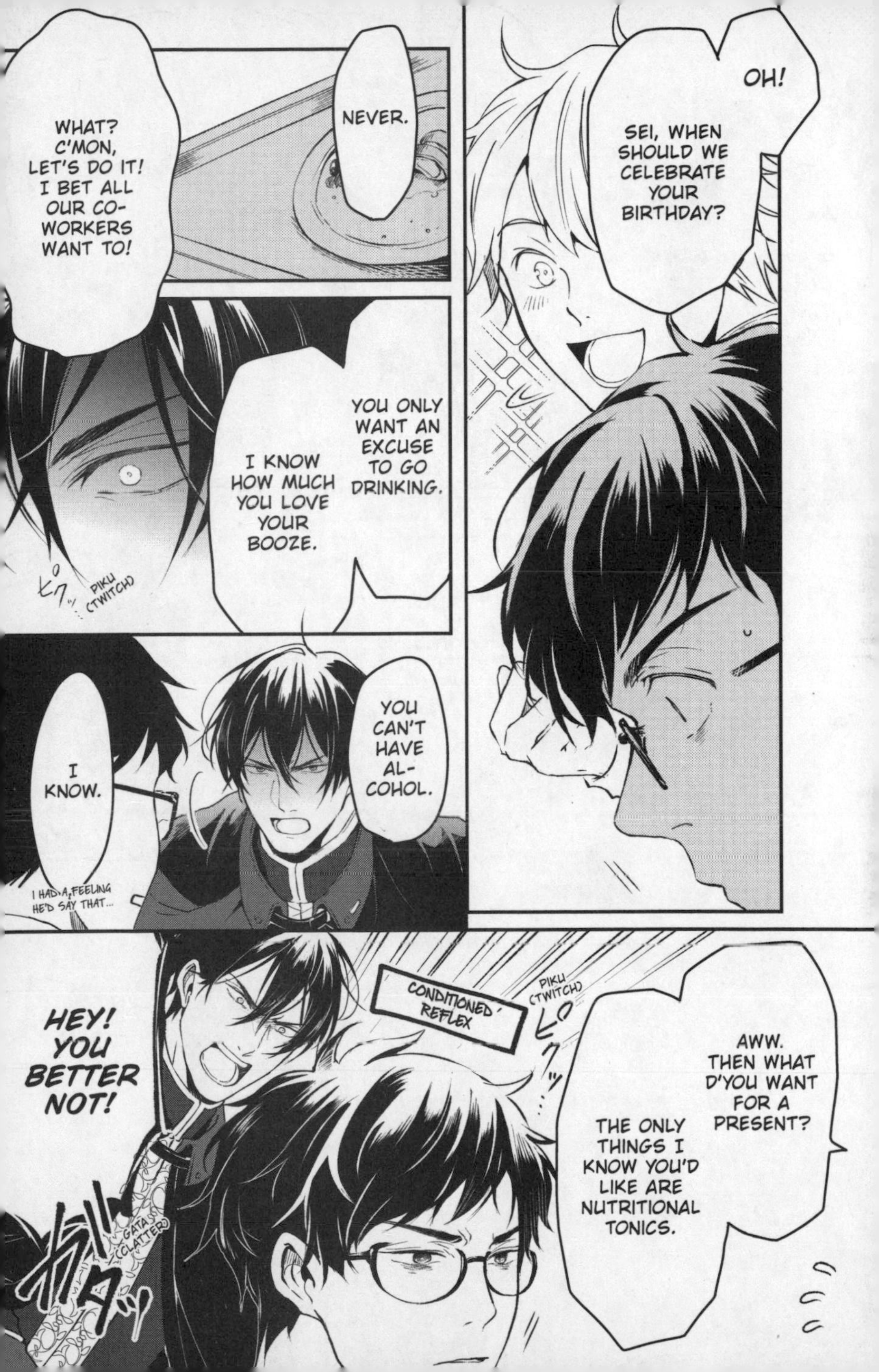
OH!
SEI, WHEN SHOULD WE CELEBRATE YOUR BIRTHDAY?
NEVER.
WHAT? C'MON, LET'S DO IT! I BET ALL OUR CO-WORKERS WANT TO!
YOU ONLY WANT AN EXCUSE TO GO DRINKING.
I KNOW HOW MUCH YOU LOVE YOUR BOOZE.
PIKU (TWITCH)
YOU CAN'T HAVE AL-COHOL.
I KNOW.
I HAD A FEELING HE'D SAY THAT...
AWW. THEN WHAT D'YOU WANT FOR A PRESENT?
THE ONLY THINGS I KNOW YOU'D LIKE ARE NUTRITIONAL TONICS.
PIKU (TWITCH)
CONDITIONED REFLEX
HEY! YOU BETTER NOT!
GATA (CLATTER)

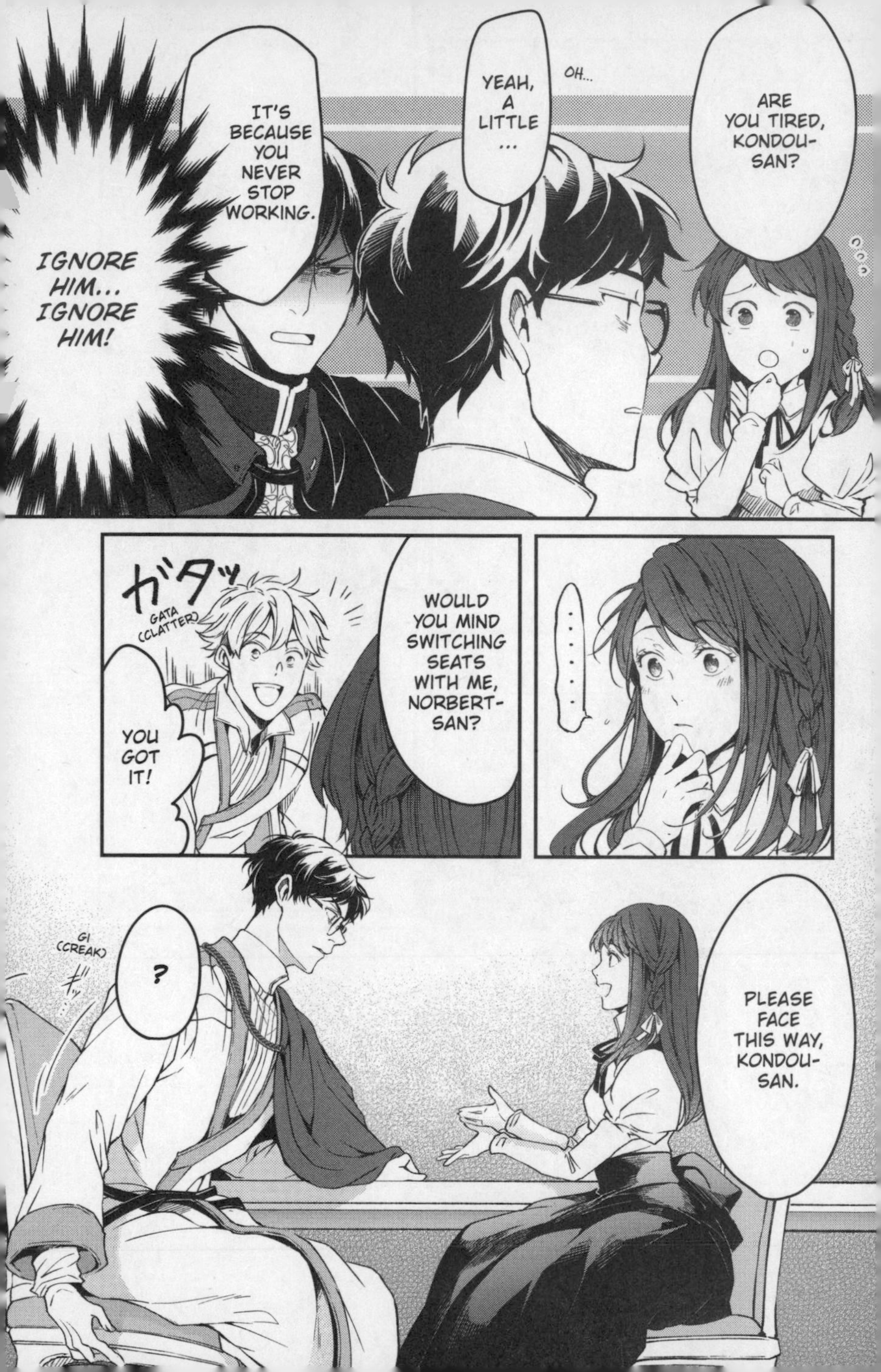
ARE YOU TIRED, KONDOU-SAN?
OH...
YEAH, A LITTLE ...
IT'S BECAUSE YOU NEVER STOP WORKING.
IGNORE HIM... IGNORE HIM!
......
WOULD YOU MIND SWITCHING SEATS WITH ME, NORBERT-SAN?
ガタッ
GATA (CLATTER)
YOU GOT IT!
PLEASE FACE THIS WAY, KONDOU-SAN.
?
ギッ
GI (CREAK)

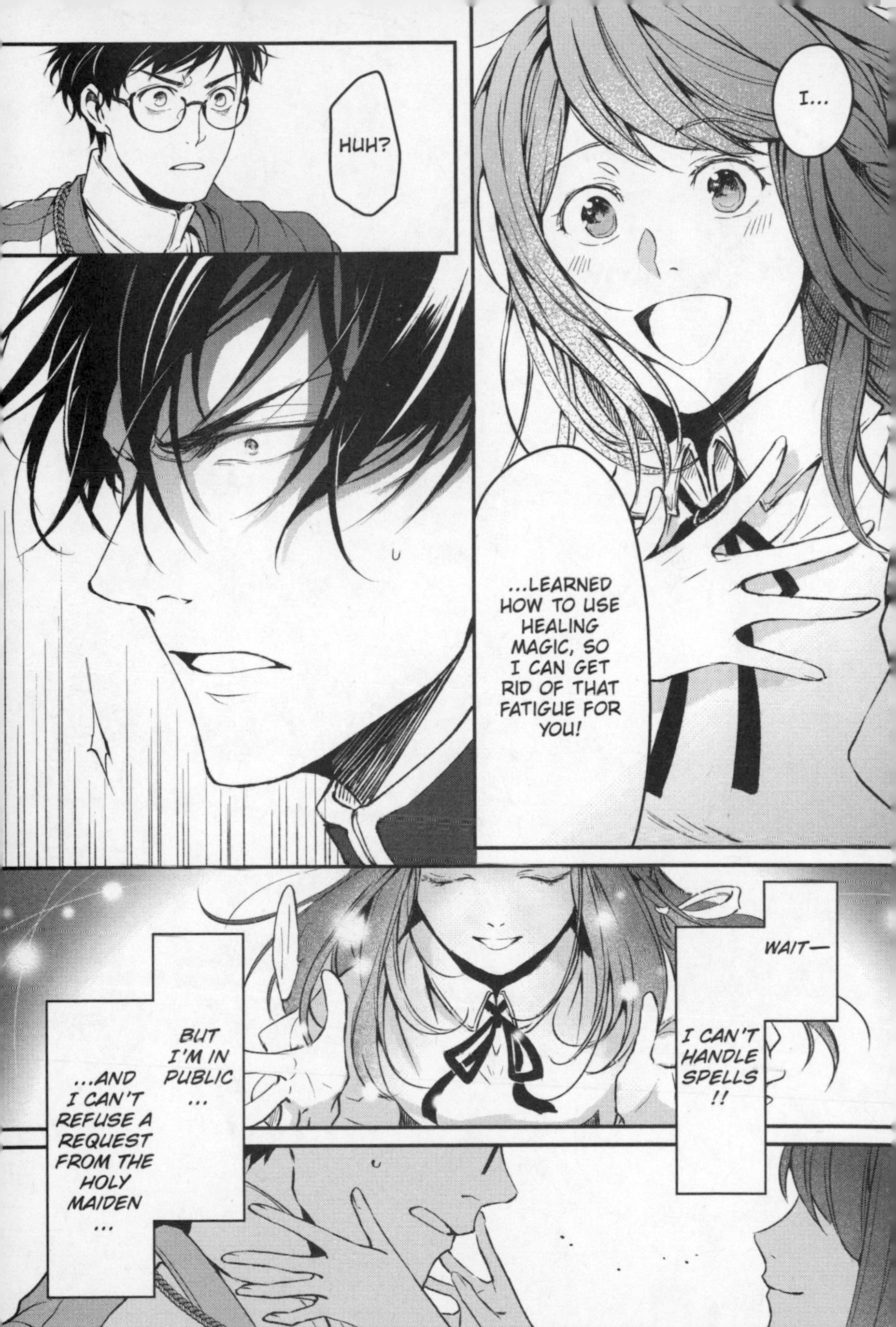
I...
...LEARNED HOW TO USE HEALING MAGIC, SO I CAN GET RID OF THAT FATIGUE FOR YOU!
HUH?
WAIT—
I CAN'T HANDLE SPELLS!!
BUT I'M IN PUBLIC...
...AND I CAN'T REFUSE A REQUEST FROM THE HOLY MAIDEN...

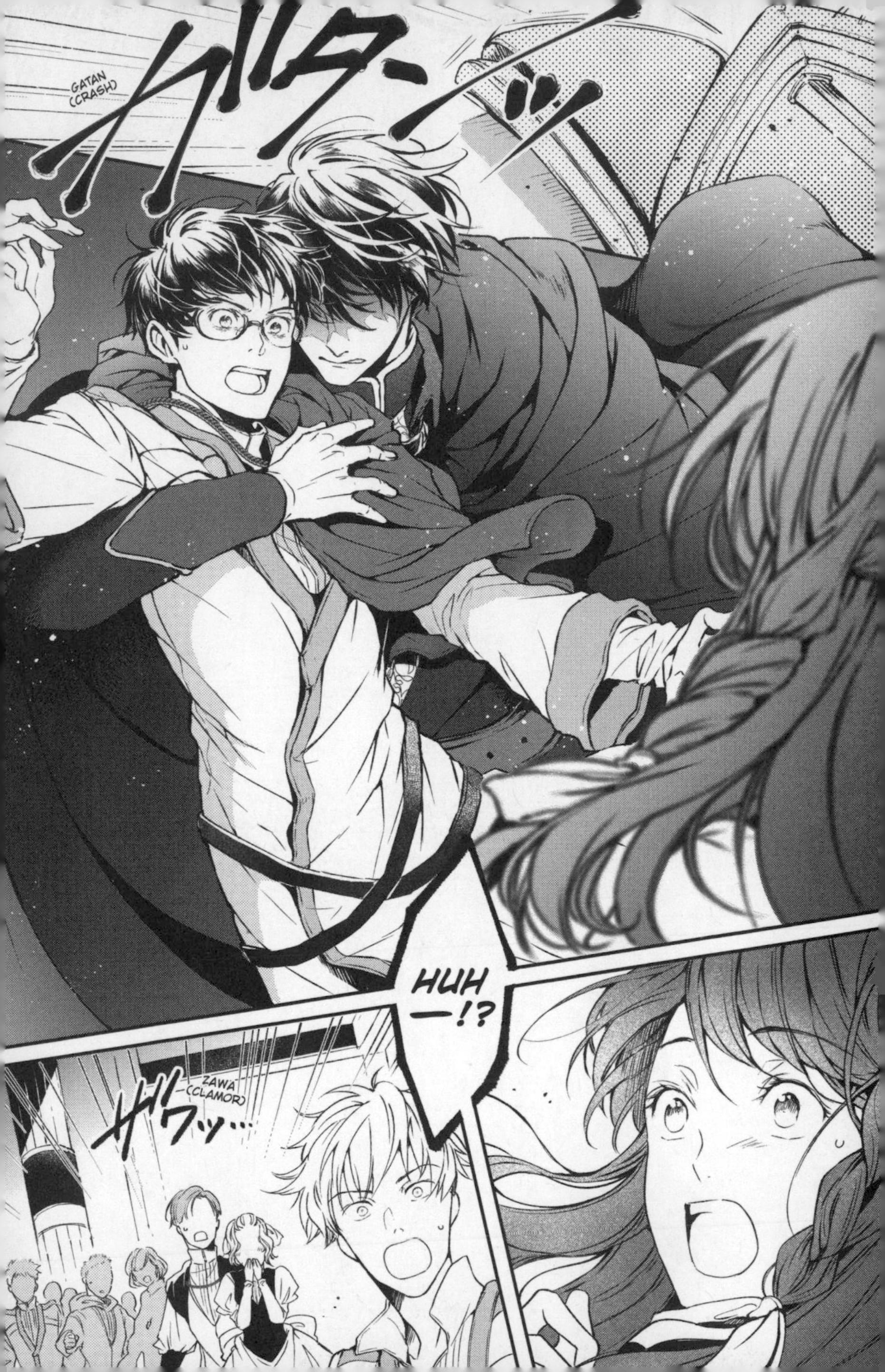
GATAN (CRASH)
HUH—!?
ZAWA (CLAMOR)

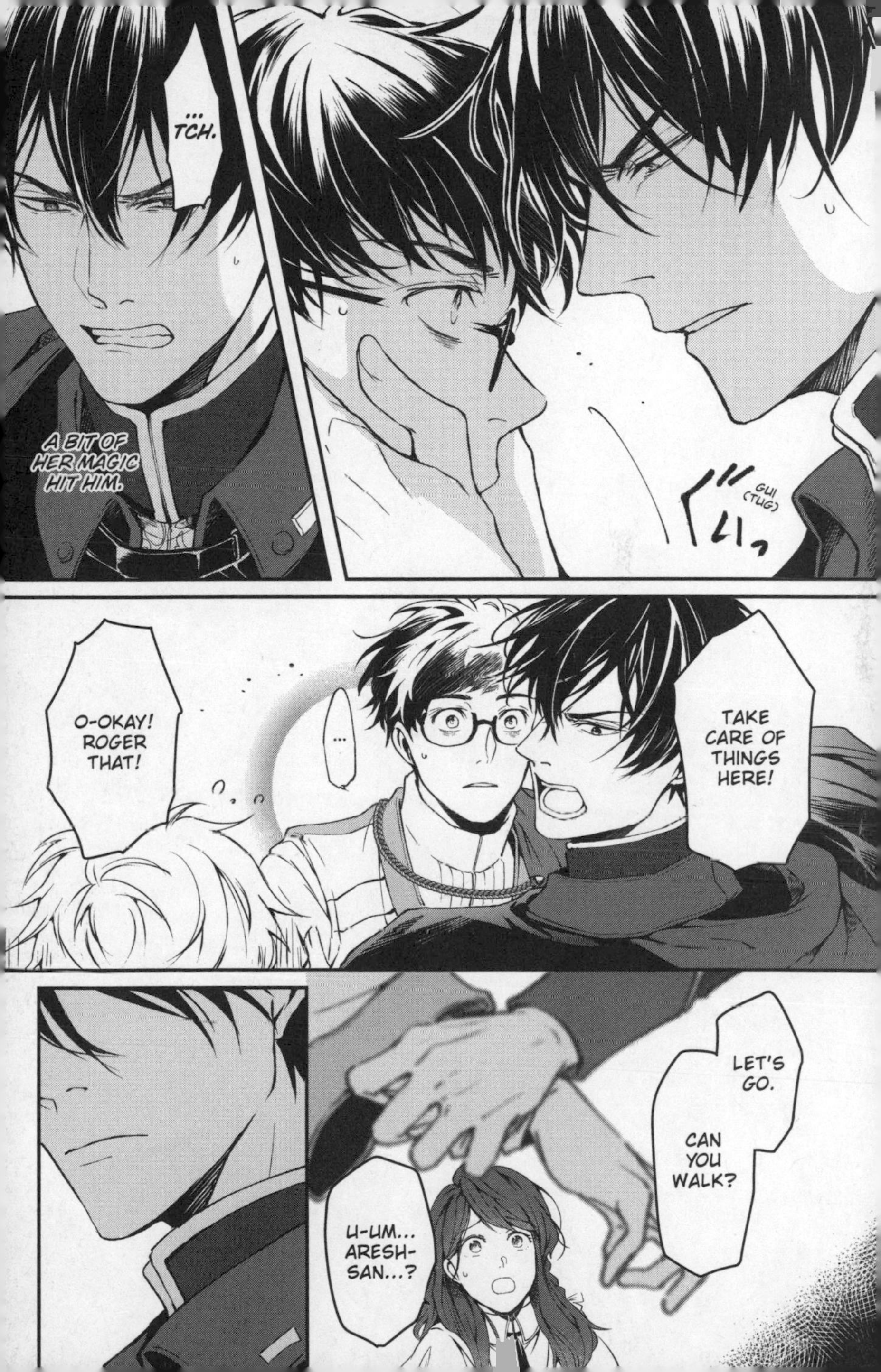
GUI (TUG)
...TCH.
A BIT OF HER MAGIC HIT HIM.
TAKE CARE OF THINGS HERE!
...
O-OKAY! ROGER THAT!
LET'S GO.
CAN YOU WALK?
U-UM... ARESH-SAN...?

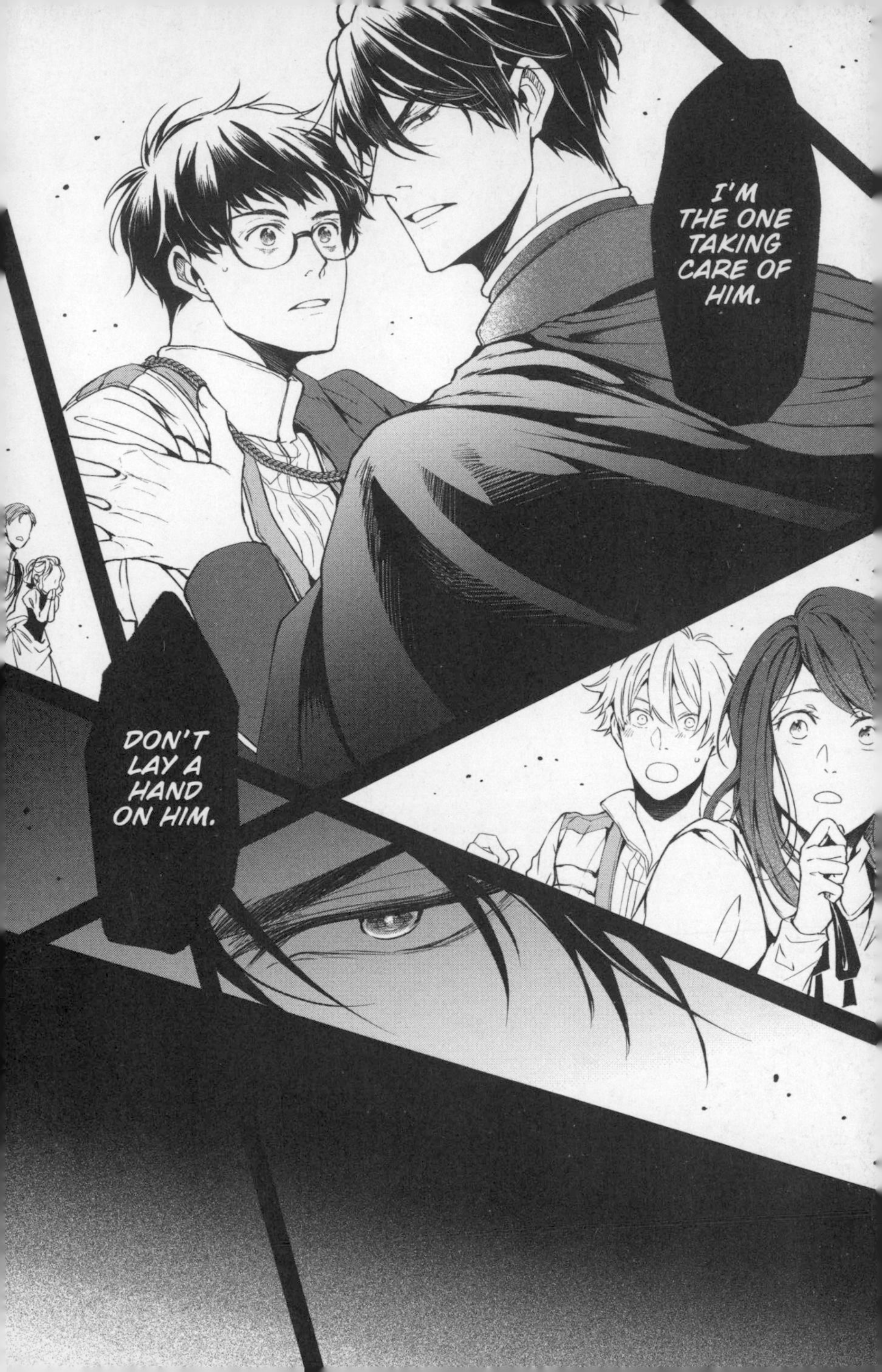
I'M THE ONE TAKING CARE OF HIM.
DON'T LAY A HAND ON HIM.

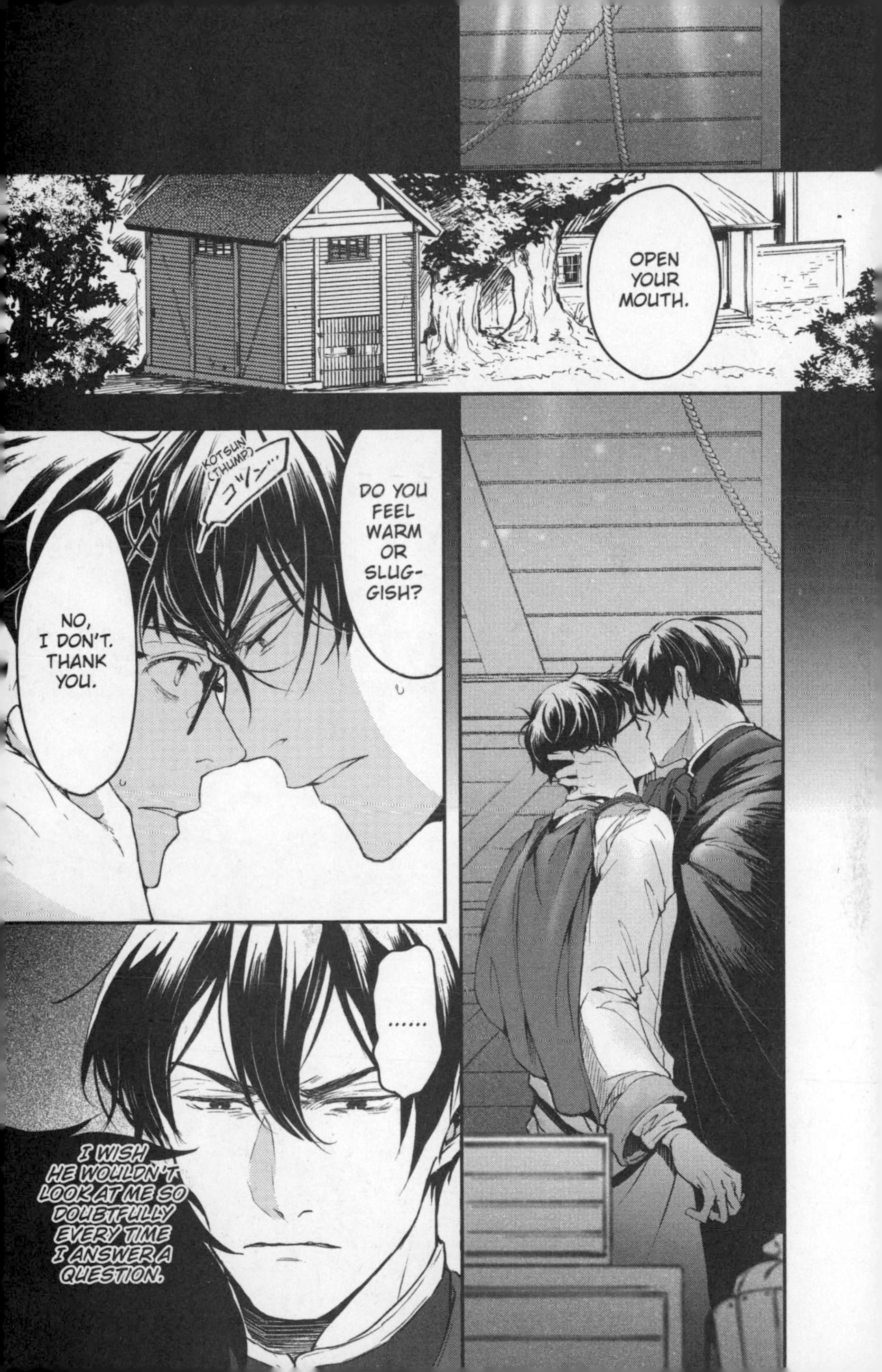
OPEN YOUR MOUTH.
DO YOU FEEL WARM OR SLUG-GISH?
KOTSUN (THUMP) コツン…
NO, I DON'T. THANK YOU.
......
I WISH HE WOULDN'T LOOK AT ME SO DOUBTFULLY EVERY TIME I ANSWER A QUESTION.

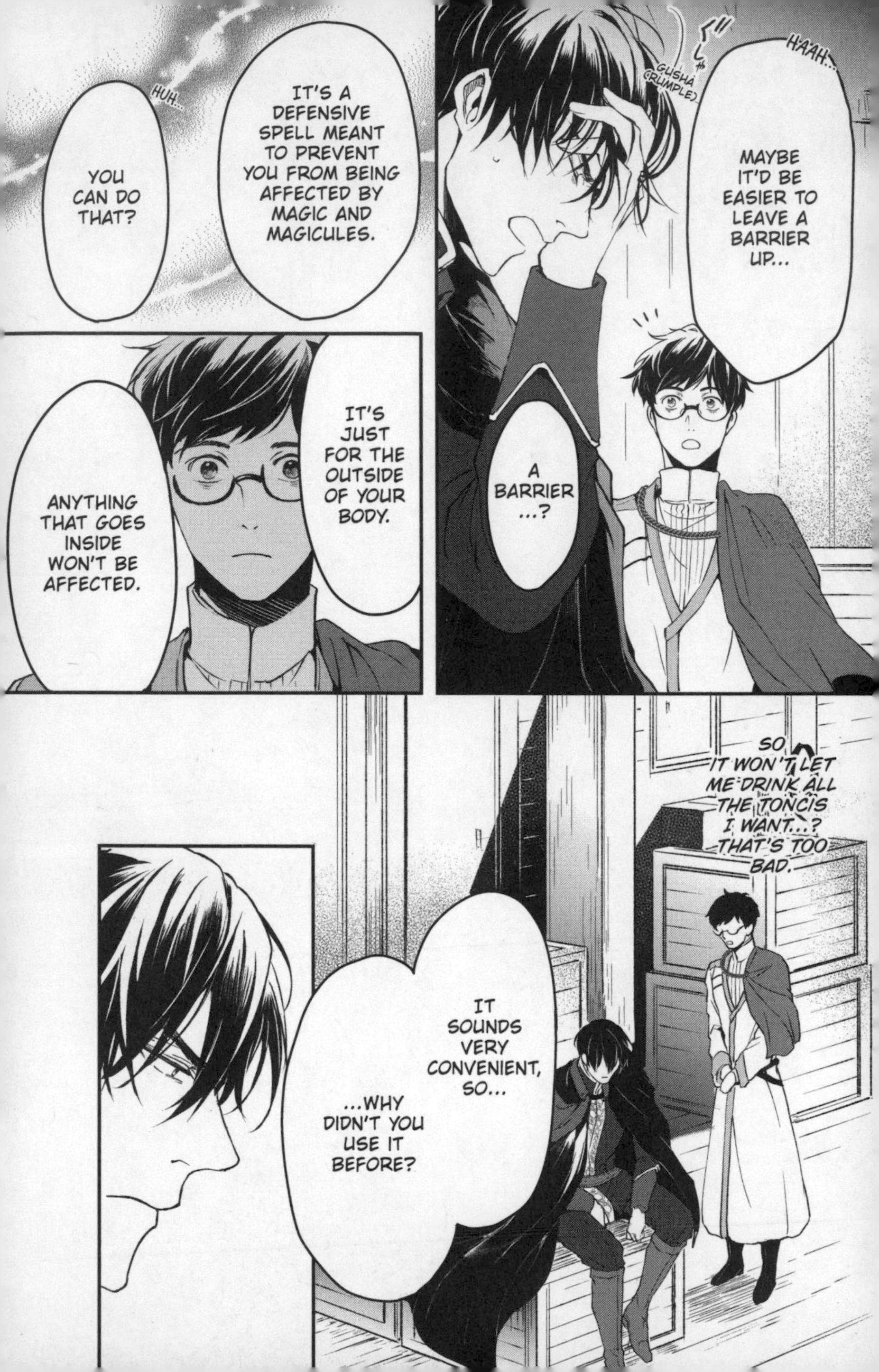
HAAAH...
GUSHA (RUMPLE)
MAYBE IT'D BE EASIER TO LEAVE A BARRIER UP...
A BARRIER ...?
IT'S A DEFENSIVE SPELL MEANT TO PREVENT YOU FROM BEING AFFECTED BY MAGIC AND MAGICULES.
HUH...
YOU CAN DO THAT?
IT'S JUST FOR THE OUTSIDE OF YOUR BODY.
ANYTHING THAT GOES INSIDE WON'T BE AFFECTED.
SO IT WON'T LET ME DRINK ALL THE TONCIS I WANT...? THAT'S TOO BAD.
IT SOUNDS VERY CONVENIENT, SO...
...WHY DIDN'T YOU USE IT BEFORE?

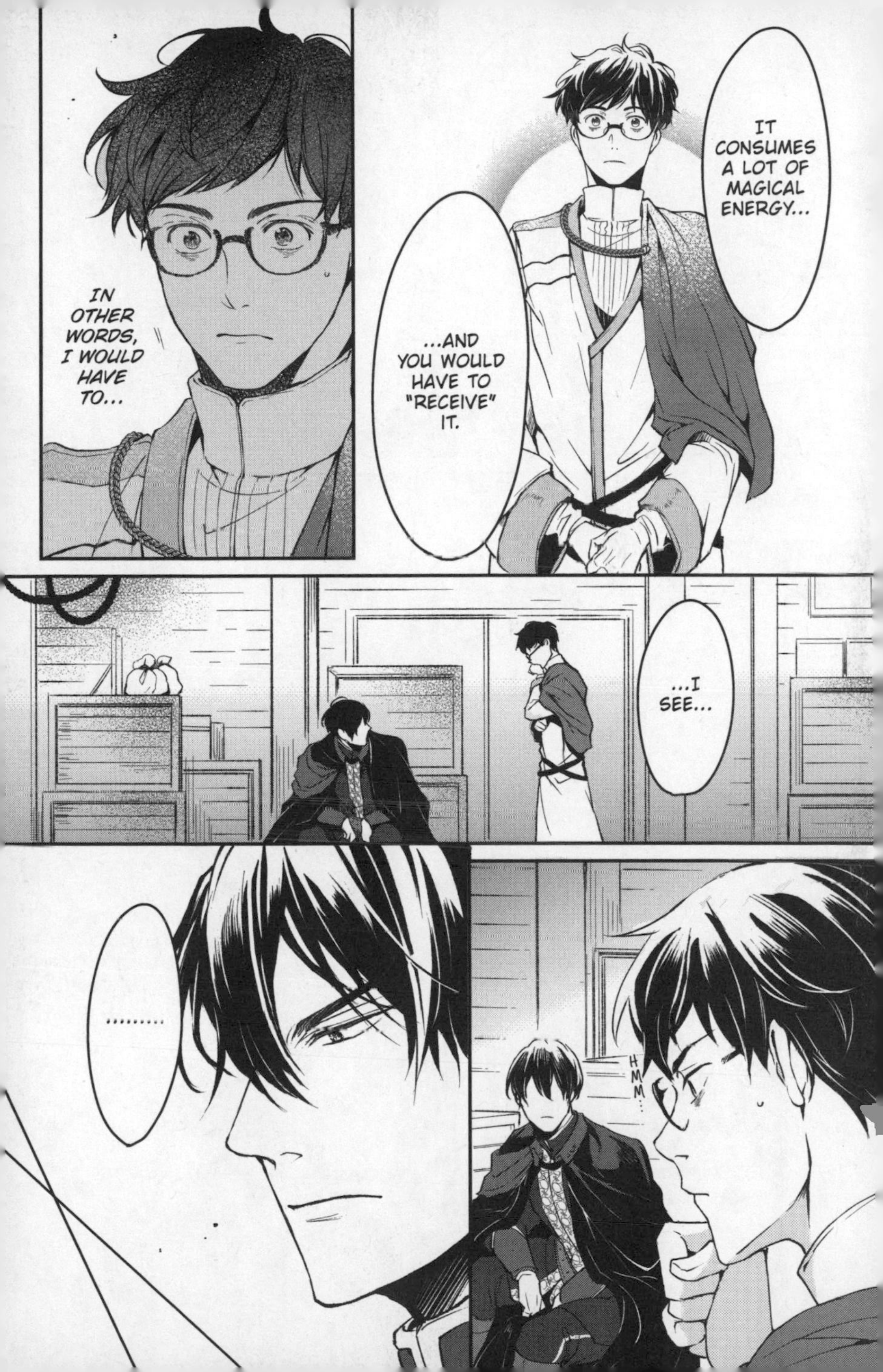
IT CONSUMES A LOT OF MAGICAL ENERGY...
...AND YOU WOULD HAVE TO "RECEIVE" IT.
IN OTHER WORDS, I WOULD HAVE TO...
...I SEE...
HMM...
....

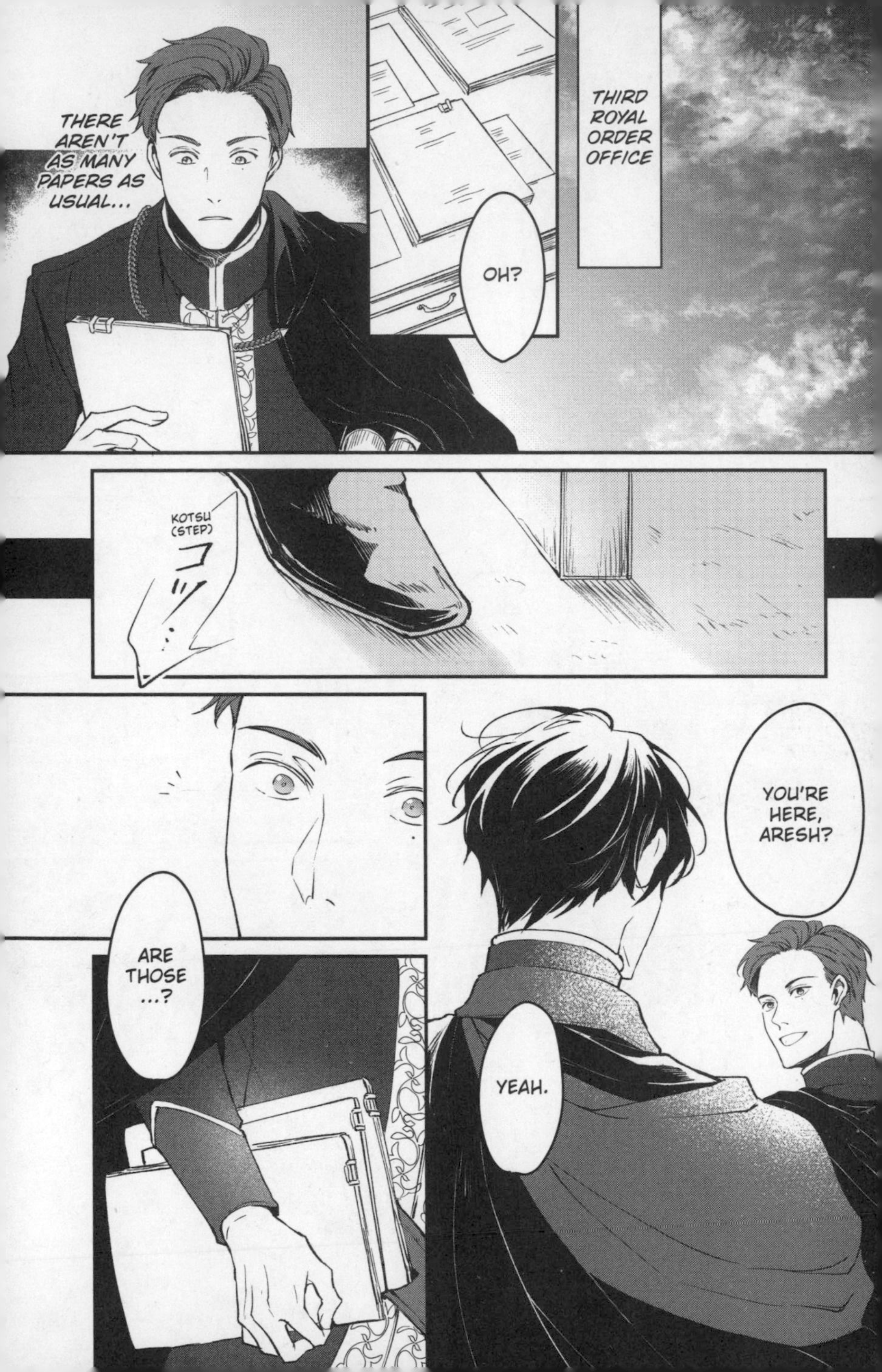
THIRD ROYAL ORDER OFFICE
OH?
THERE AREN'T AS MANY PAPERS AS USUAL...
KOTSU (STEP)
コツ
YOU'RE HERE, ARESH?
YEAH.
ARE THOSE ...?

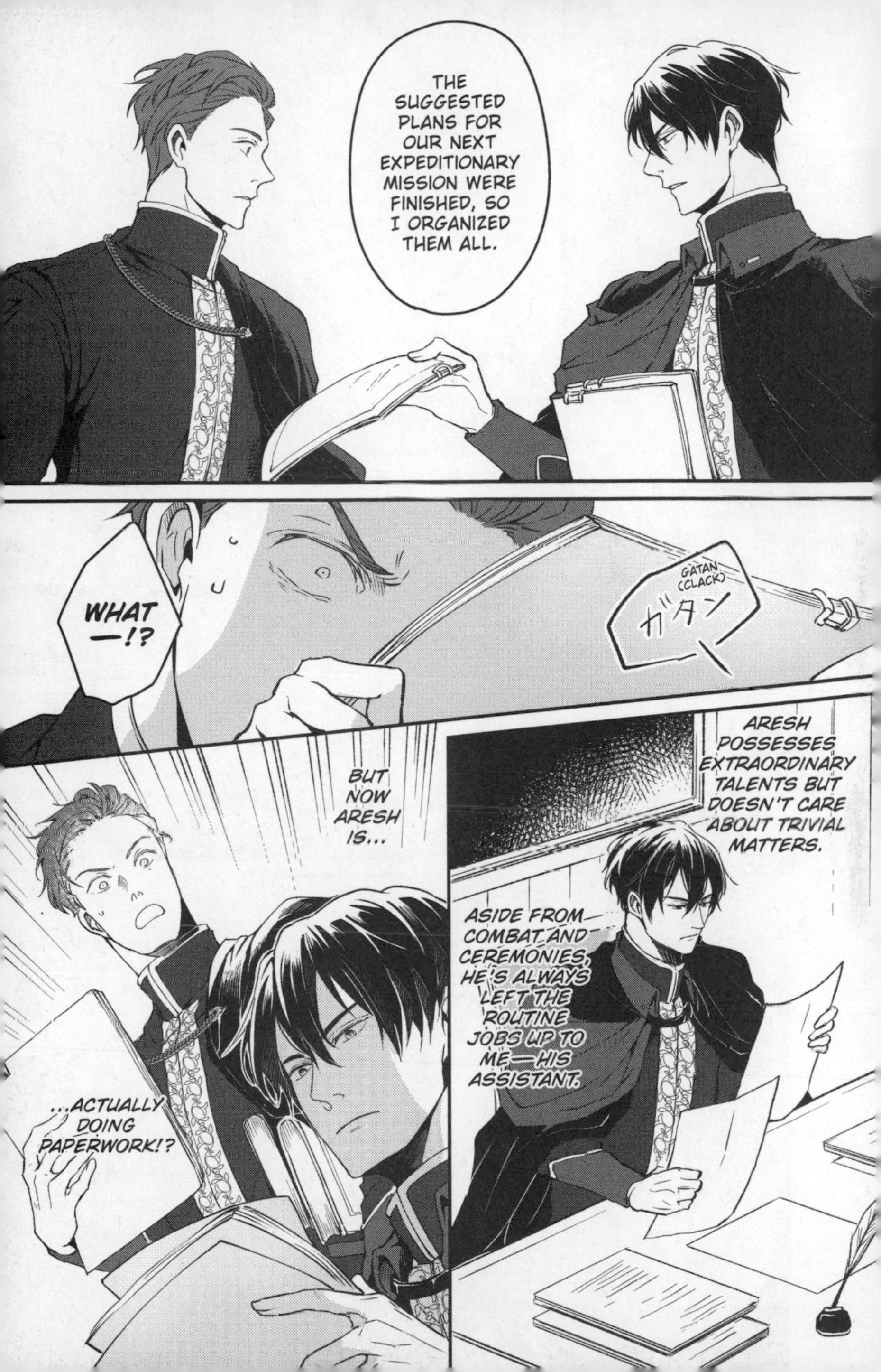
THE SUGGESTED PLANS FOR OUR NEXT EXPEDITIONARY MISSION WERE FINISHED, SO I ORGANIZED THEM ALL.
GATAN (CLACK)
ガタン
WHAT—!?
ARESH POSSESSES EXTRAORDINARY TALENTS BUT DOESN'T CARE ABOUT TRIVIAL MATTERS.
ASIDE FROM COMBAT AND CEREMONIES, HE'S ALWAYS LEFT THE ROUTINE JOBS UP TO ME—HIS ASSISTANT.
BUT NOW ARESH IS...
...ACTUALLY DOING PAPERWORK!?

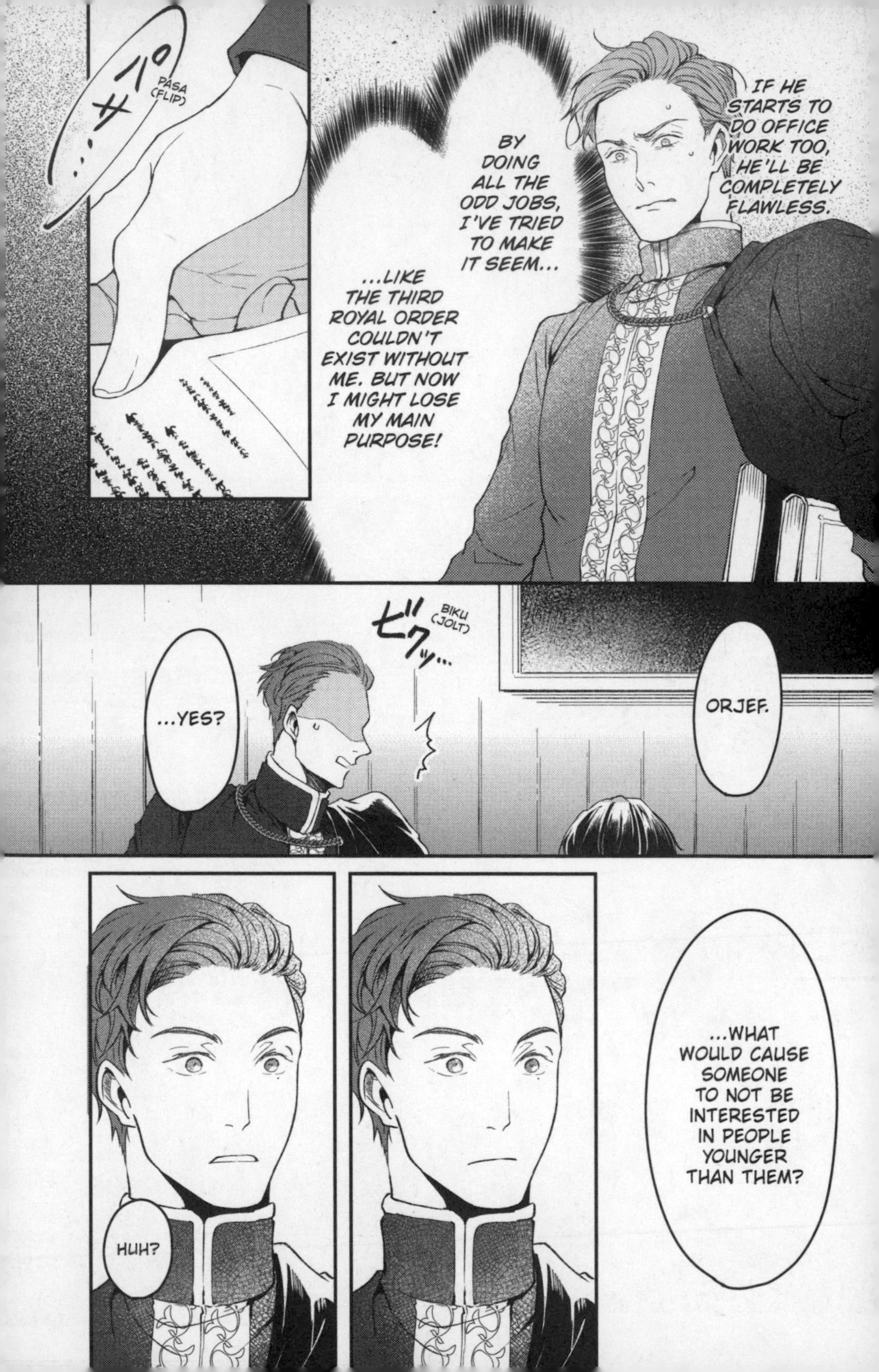
IF HE STARTS TO DO OFFICE WORK TOO, HE'LL BE COMPLETELY FLAWLESS.
BY DOING ALL THE ODD JOBS, I'VE TRIED TO MAKE IT SEEM...
...LIKE THE THIRD ROYAL ORDER COULDN'T EXIST WITHOUT ME. BUT NOW I MIGHT LOSE MY MAIN PURPOSE!
パサ…
PASA (FLIP)
ORJEF.
ビクッ…
BIKU (JOLT)
...YES?
...WHAT WOULD CAUSE SOMEONE TO NOT BE INTERESTED IN PEOPLE YOUNGER THAN THEM?
HUH?

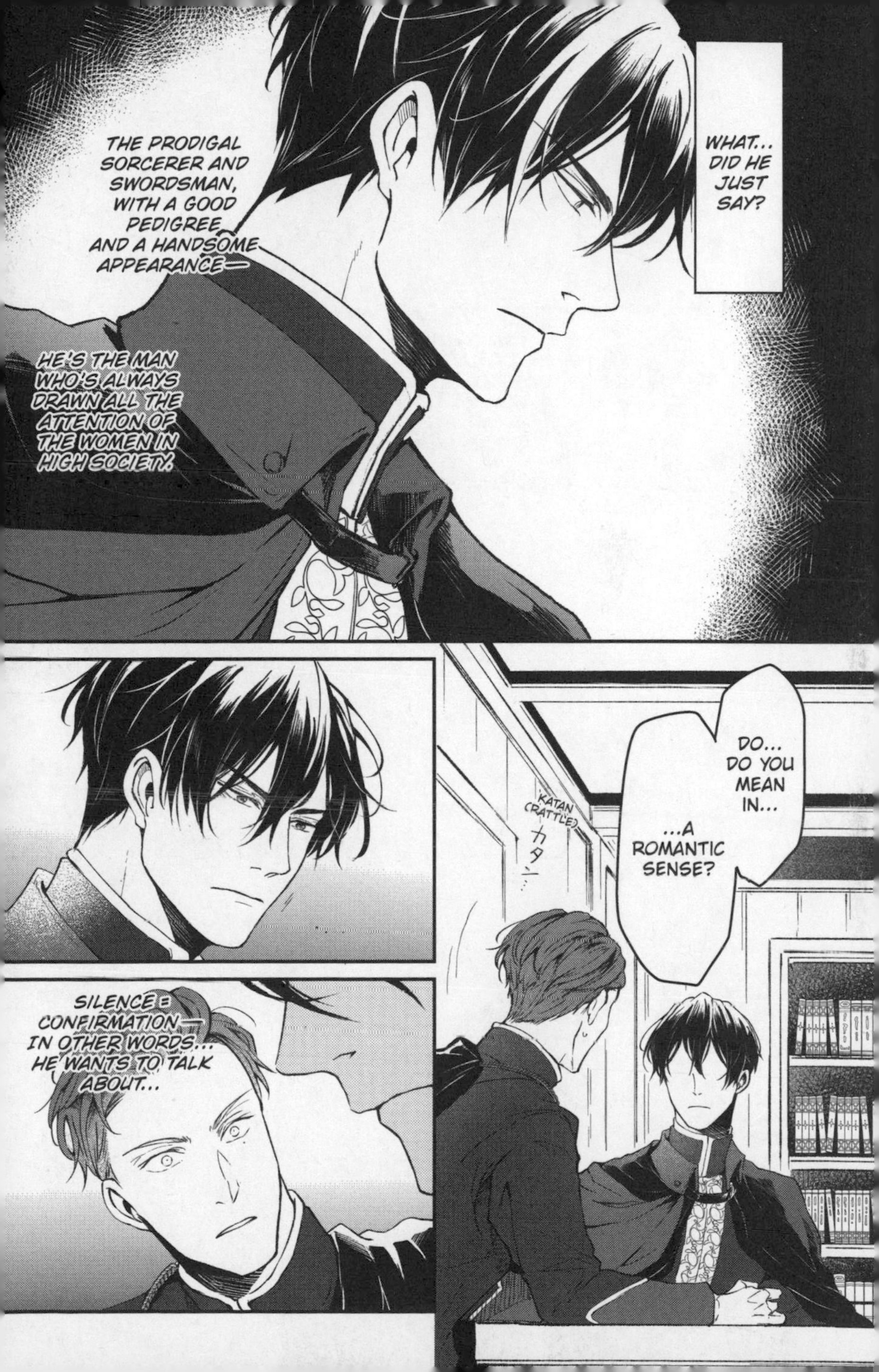
WHAT... DID HE JUST SAY?
THE PRODIGAL SORCERER AND SWORDSMAN, WITH A GOOD PEDIGREE AND A HANDSOME APPEARANCE—
HE'S THE MAN WHO'S ALWAYS DRAWN ALL THE ATTENTION OF THE WOMEN IN HIGH SOCIETY.
DO... DO YOU MEAN IN...
...A ROMANTIC SENSE?
KATAN (RATTLE)
カタ
SILENCE = CONFIRMATION— IN OTHER WORDS... HE WANTS TO TALK ABOUT...

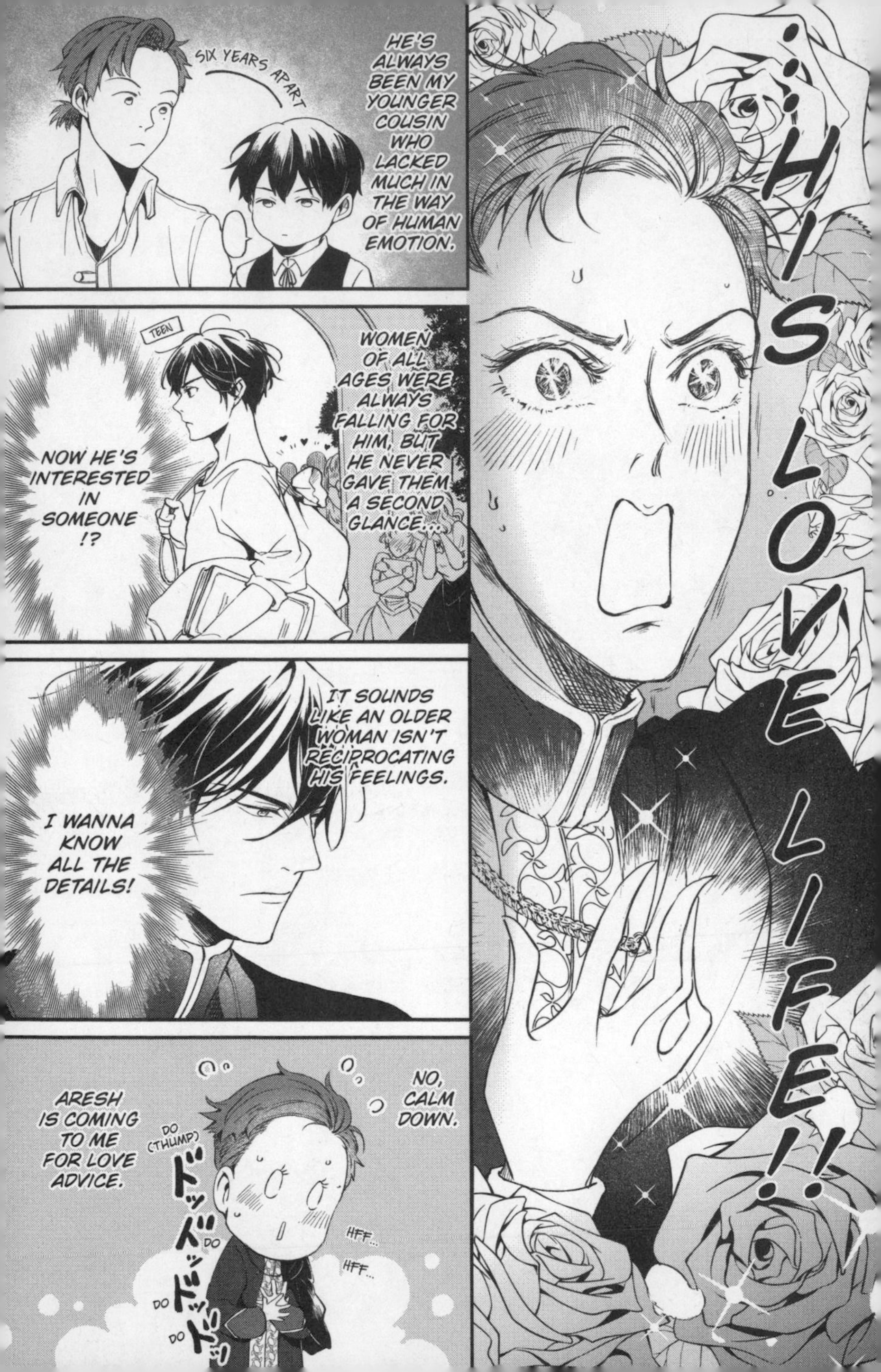
...HIS LOVE LIFE!!
HE'S ALWAYS BEEN MY YOUNGER COUSIN WHO LACKED MUCH IN THE WAY OF HUMAN EMOTION.
SIX YEARS APART
TEEN
WOMEN OF ALL AGES WERE ALWAYS FALLING FOR HIM, BUT HE NEVER GAVE THEM A SECOND GLANCE...
NOW HE'S INTERESTED IN SOMEONE !?
IT SOUNDS LIKE AN OLDER WOMAN ISN'T RECIPROCATING HIS FEELINGS.
I WANNA KNOW ALL THE DETAILS!
NO, CALM DOWN.
ARESH IS COMING TO ME FOR LOVE ADVICE.
DO (THUMP)
DO
DO
DO
HFF...
HFF...

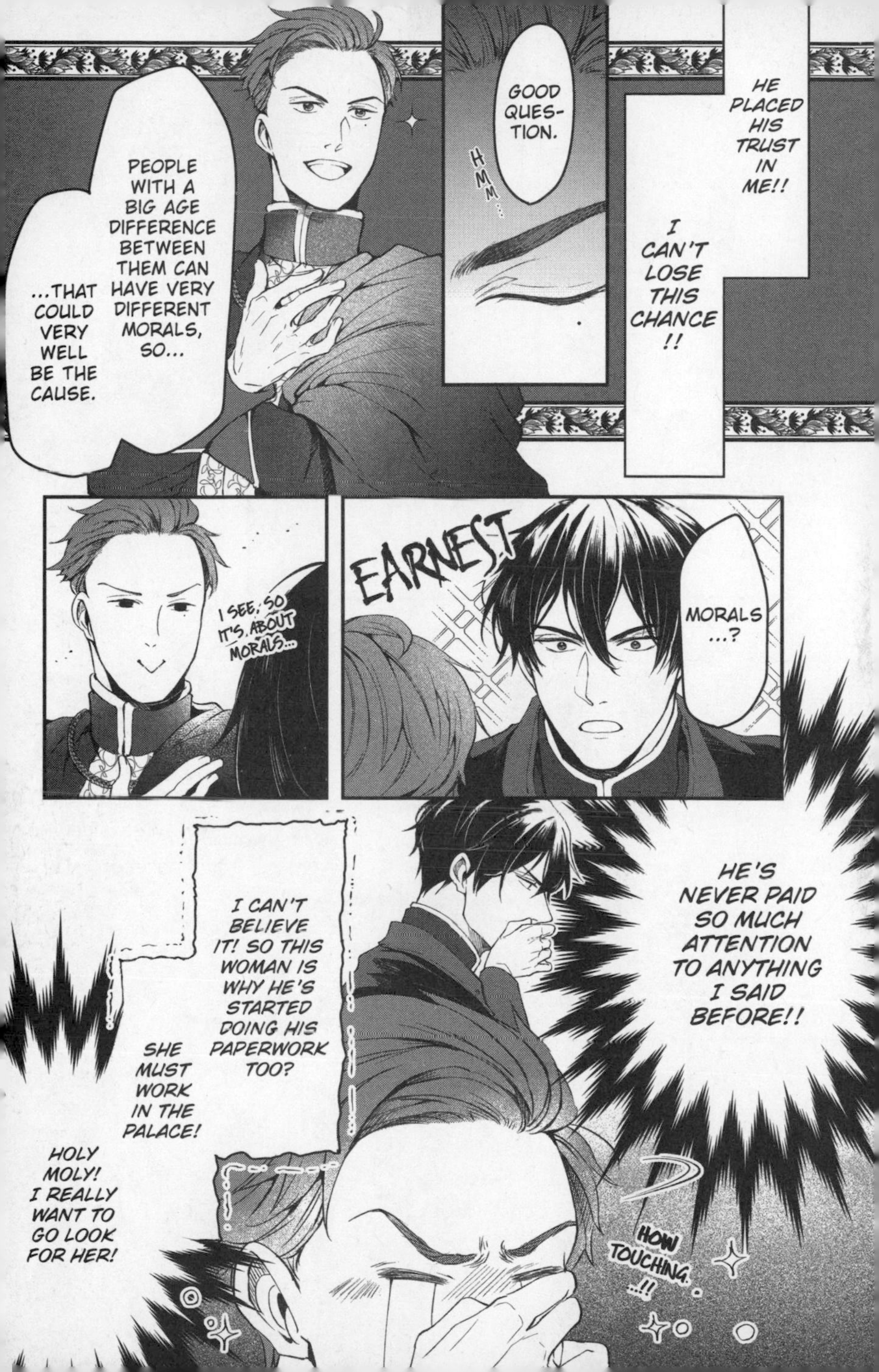

HE PLACED HIS TRUST IN ME!!
I CAN'T LOSE THIS CHANCE!!
GOOD QUES-TION.
HMM...
PEOPLE WITH A BIG AGE DIFFERENCE BETWEEN THEM CAN HAVE VERY DIFFERENT MORALS, SO...
...THAT COULD VERY WELL BE THE CAUSE.
EARNEST
MORALS ...?
I SEE, SO IT'S ABOUT MORALS...
HE'S NEVER PAID SO MUCH ATTENTION TO ANYTHING I SAID BEFORE!!
HOW TOUCHING..!!
I CAN'T BELIEVE IT! SO THIS WOMAN IS WHY HE'S STARTED DOING HIS PAPERWORK TOO?
SHE MUST WORK IN THE PALACE!
HOLY MOLY! I REALLY WANT TO GO LOOK FOR HER!

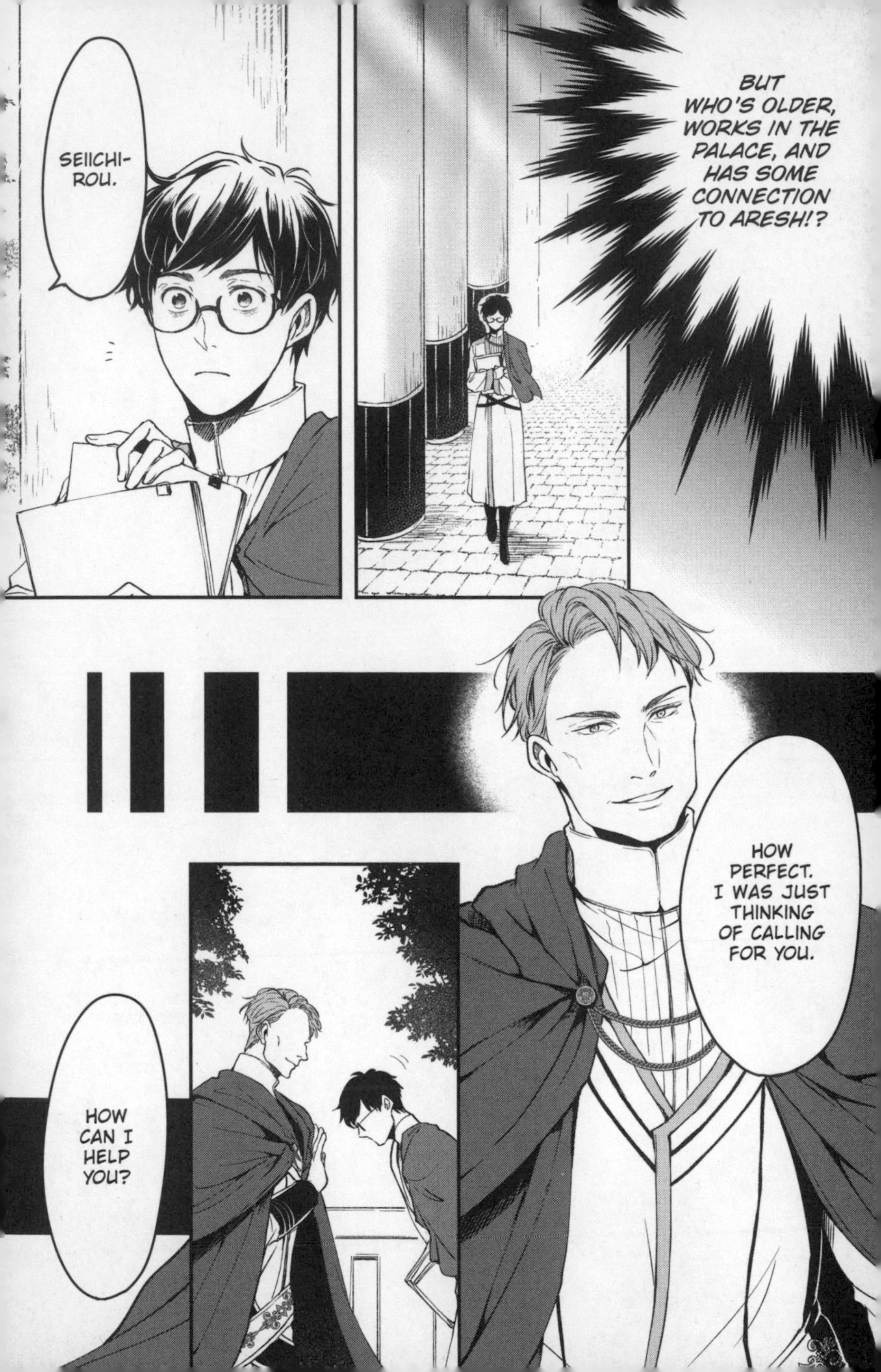
BUT WHO'S OLDER, WORKS IN THE PALACE, AND HAS SOME CONNECTION TO ARESH!?
SEIICHI-ROU.
HOW PERFECT. I WAS JUST THINKING OF CALLING FOR YOU.
HOW CAN I HELP YOU?

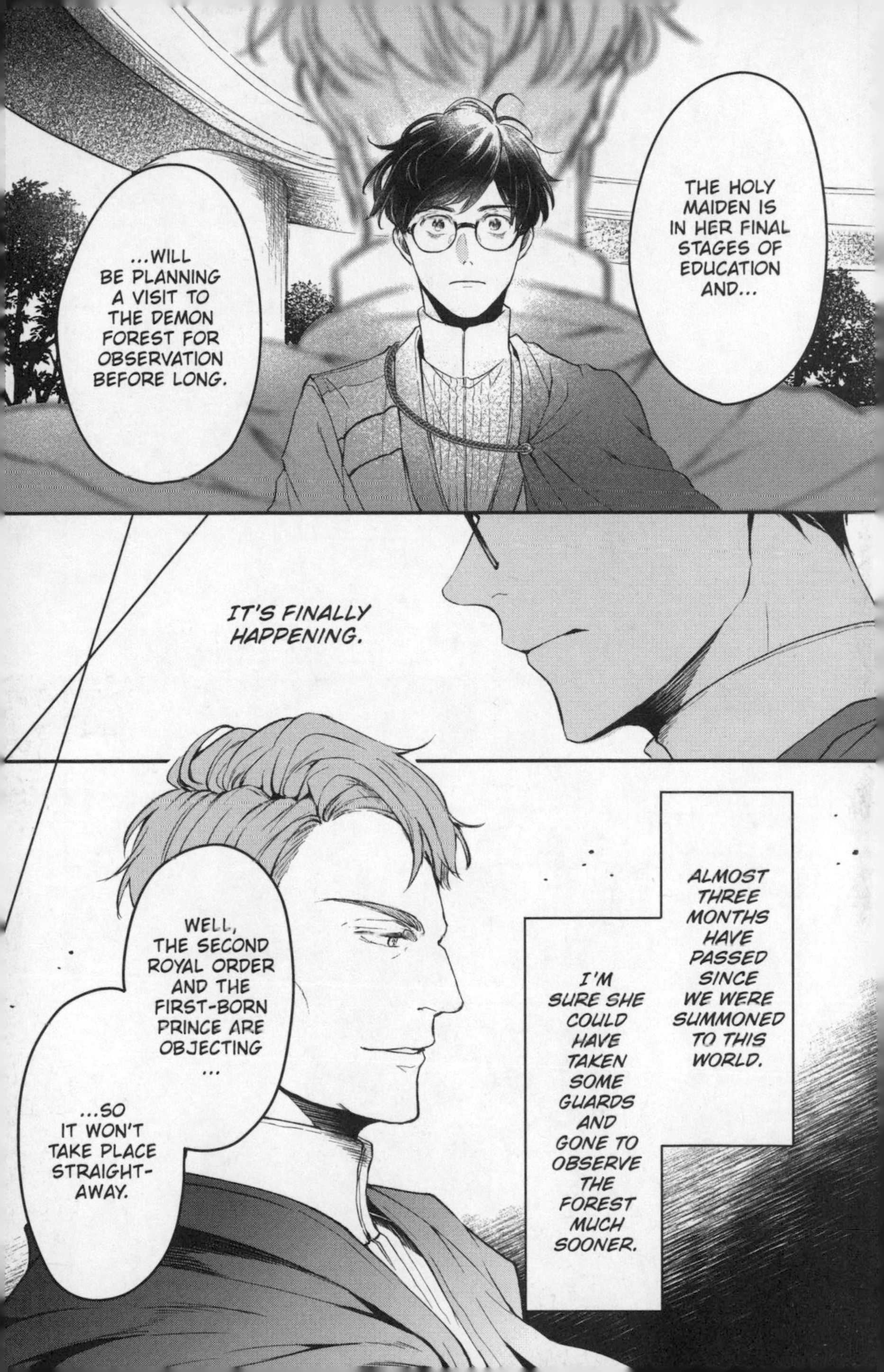
THE HOLY MAIDEN IS IN HER FINAL STAGES OF EDUCATION AND...
...WILL BE PLANNING A VISIT TO THE DEMON FOREST FOR OBSERVATION BEFORE LONG.
IT'S FINALLY HAPPENING.
ALMOST THREE MONTHS HAVE PASSED SINCE WE WERE SUMMONED TO THIS WORLD.
I'M SURE SHE COULD HAVE TAKEN SOME GUARDS AND GONE TO OBSERVE THE FOREST MUCH SOONER.
WELL, THE SECOND ROYAL ORDER AND THE FIRST-BORN PRINCE ARE OBJECTING...
...SO IT WON'T TAKE PLACE STRAIGHT-AWAY.

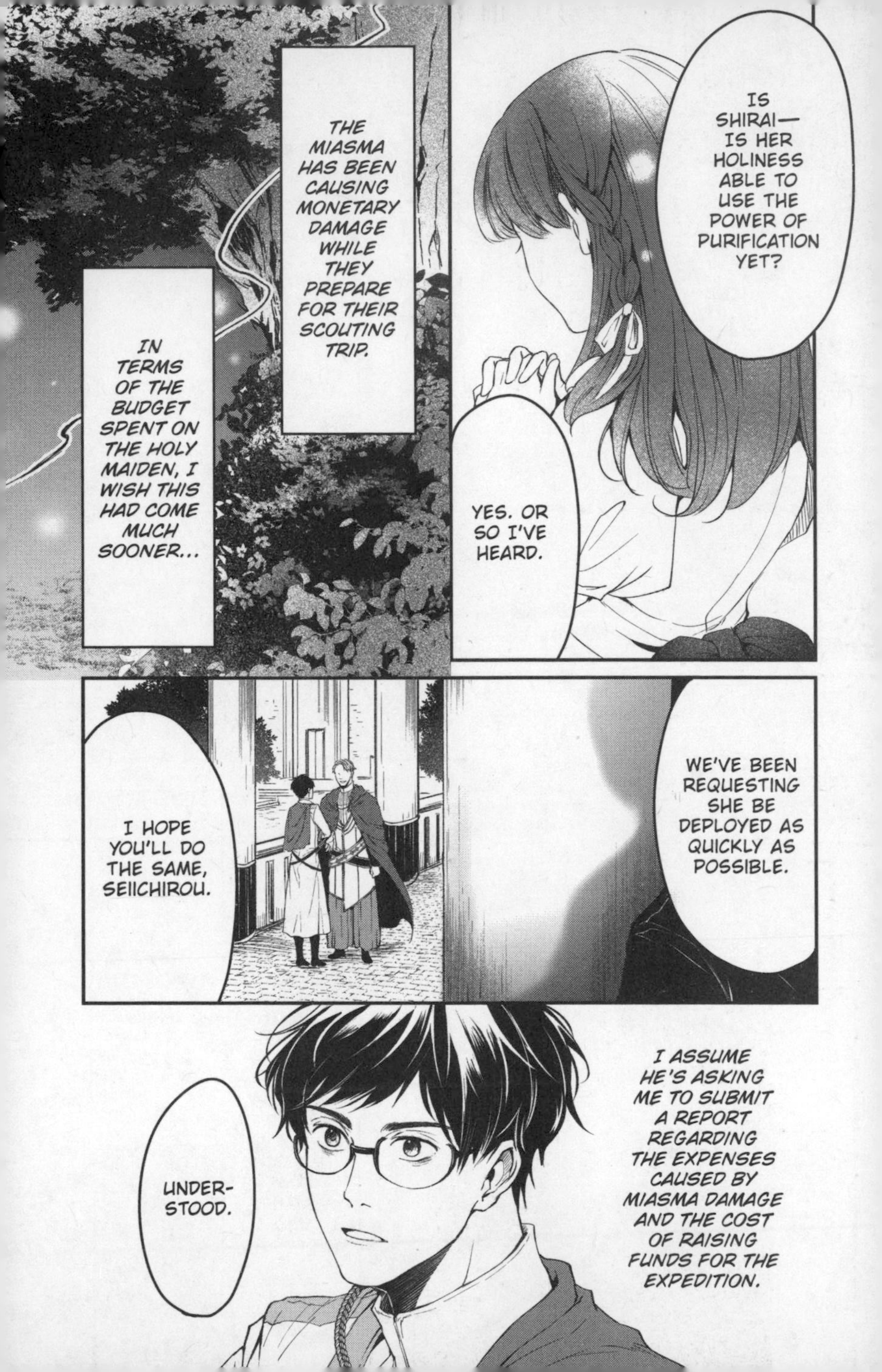
IS SHIRAI—IS HER HOLINESS ABLE TO USE THE POWER OF PURIFICATION YET?
YES. OR SO I'VE HEARD.
THE MIASMA HAS BEEN CAUSING MONETARY DAMAGE WHILE THEY PREPARE FOR THEIR SCOUTING TRIP.
IN TERMS OF THE BUDGET SPENT ON THE HOLY MAIDEN, I WISH THIS HAD COME MUCH SOONER...
WE'VE BEEN REQUESTING SHE BE DEPLOYED AS QUICKLY AS POSSIBLE.
I HOPE YOU'LL DO THE SAME, SEIICHIROU.
I ASSUME HE'S ASKING ME TO SUBMIT A REPORT REGARDING THE EXPENSES CAUSED BY MIASMA DAMAGE AND THE COST OF RAISING FUNDS FOR THE EXPEDITION.
UNDER-STOOD.

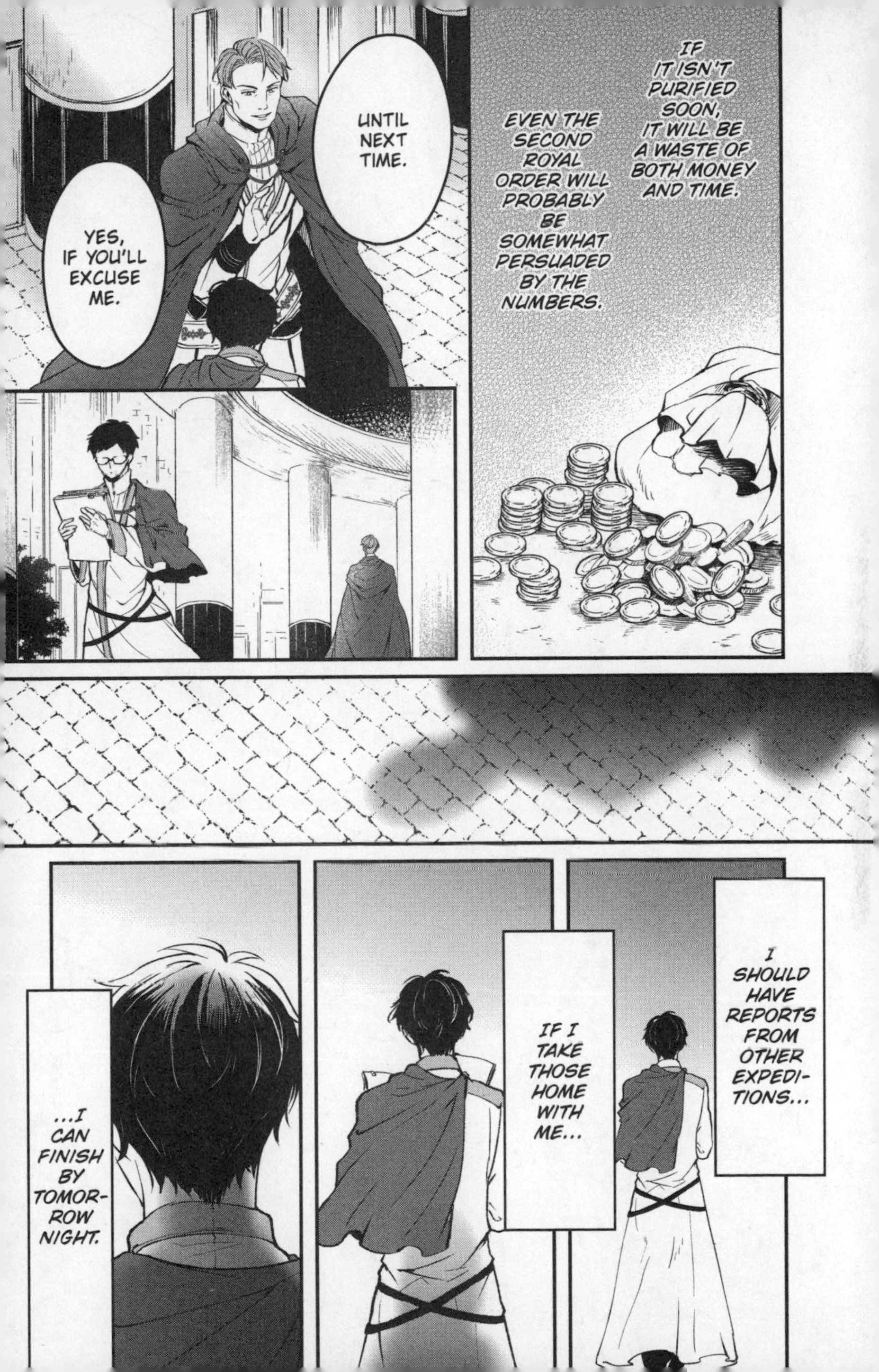
IF IT ISN'T PURIFIED SOON, IT WILL BE A WASTE OF BOTH MONEY AND TIME.
EVEN THE SECOND ROYAL ORDER WILL PROBABLY BE SOMEWHAT PERSUADED BY THE NUMBERS.
UNTIL NEXT TIME.
YES, IF YOU'LL EXCUSE ME.
I SHOULD HAVE REPORTS FROM OTHER EXPEDITIONS...
IF I TAKE THOSE HOME WITH ME...
...I CAN FINISH BY TOMORROW NIGHT.

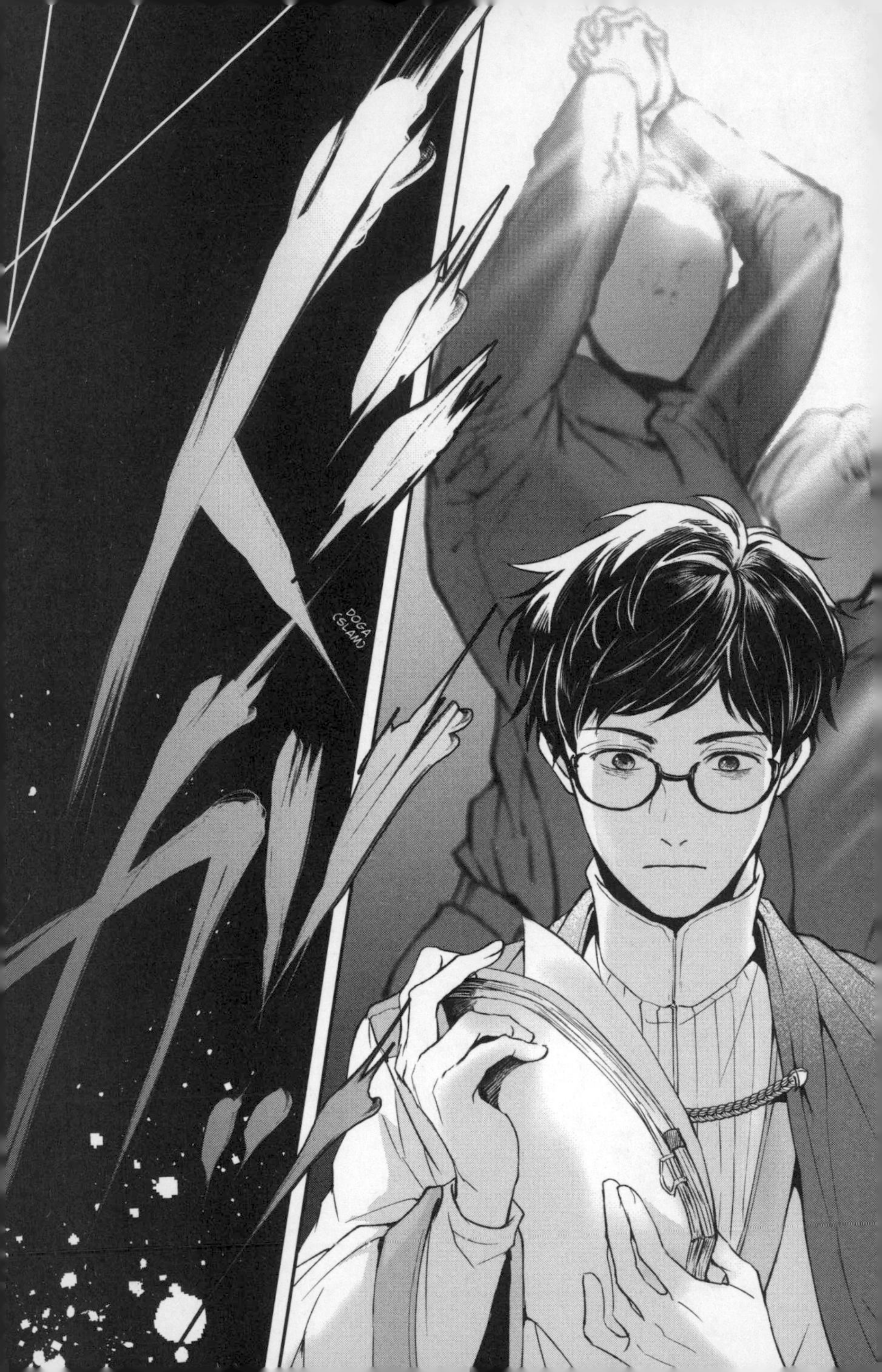
DOGA
(SLAM)

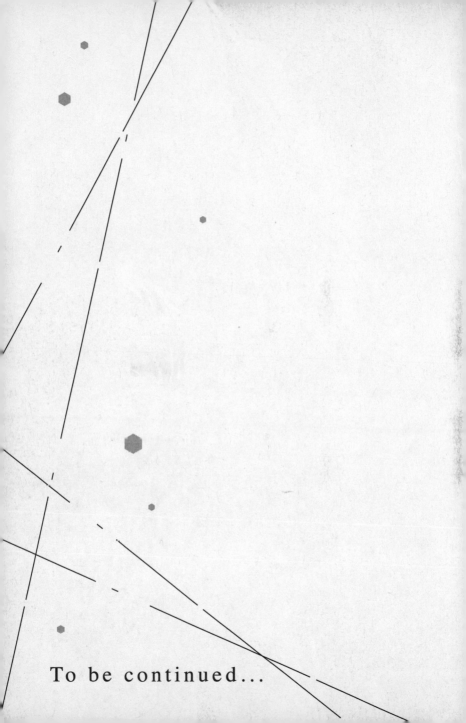

To be continued...

The Other World's Books Depend on the Bean Counter

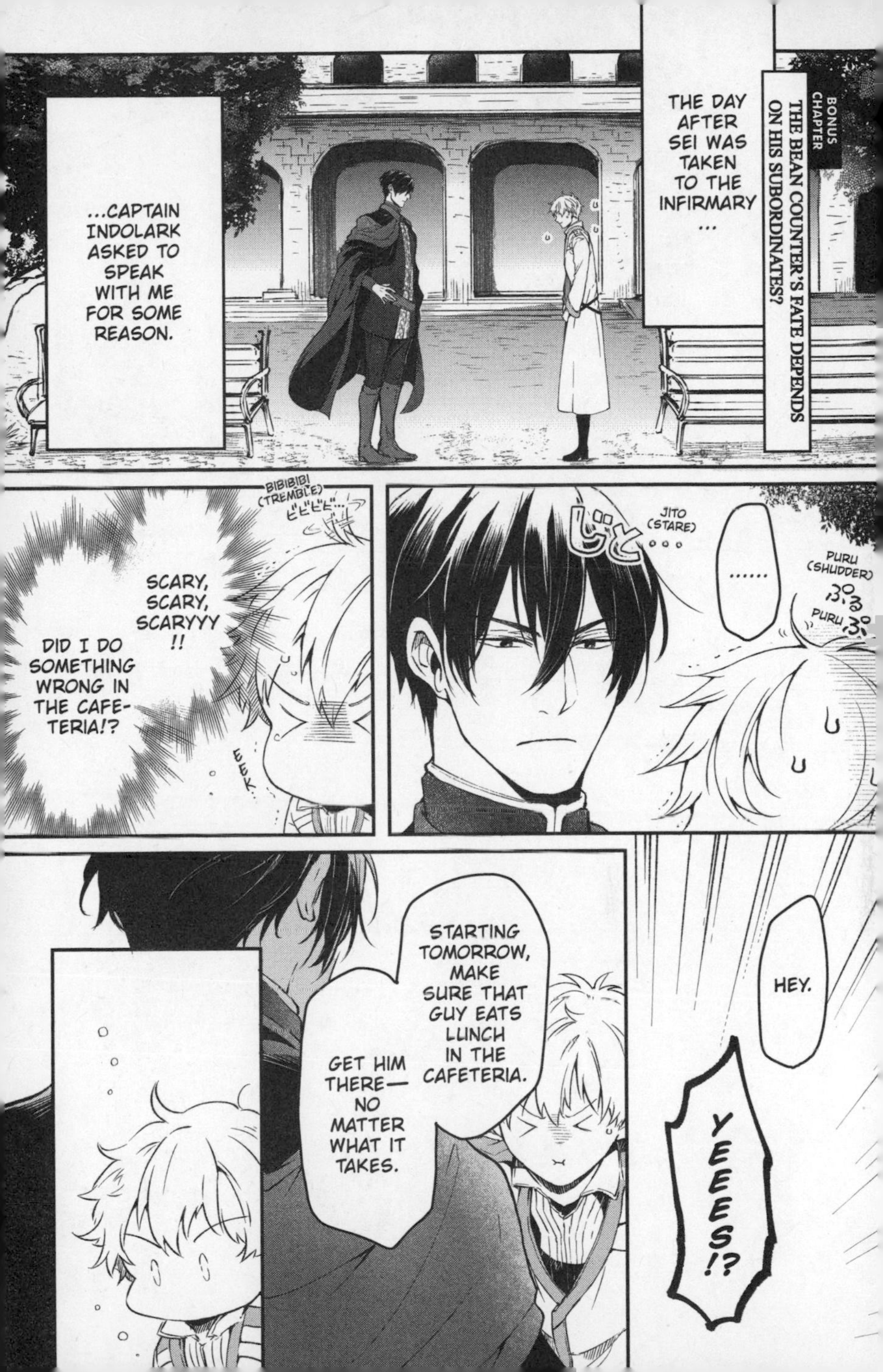
BONUS CHAPTER
THE BEAN COUNTER'S FATE DEPENDS ON HIS SUBORDINATES?
THE DAY AFTER SEI WAS TAKEN TO THE INFIRMARY...
...CAPTAIN INDOLARK ASKED TO SPEAK WITH ME FOR SOME REASON.
PURU (SHUDDER) ぷる
PURU ぷ
......
JITO (STARE) じと...
BIBIBIBI (TREMBLE) ビビビビ...
SCARY, SCARY, SCARYYY!!
DID I DO SOMETHING WRONG IN THE CAFETERIA!?
EEK...
HEY.
STARTING TOMORROW, MAKE SURE THAT GUY EATS LUNCH IN THE CAFETERIA.
GET HIM THERE— NO MATTER WHAT IT TAKES.
YEEES!?

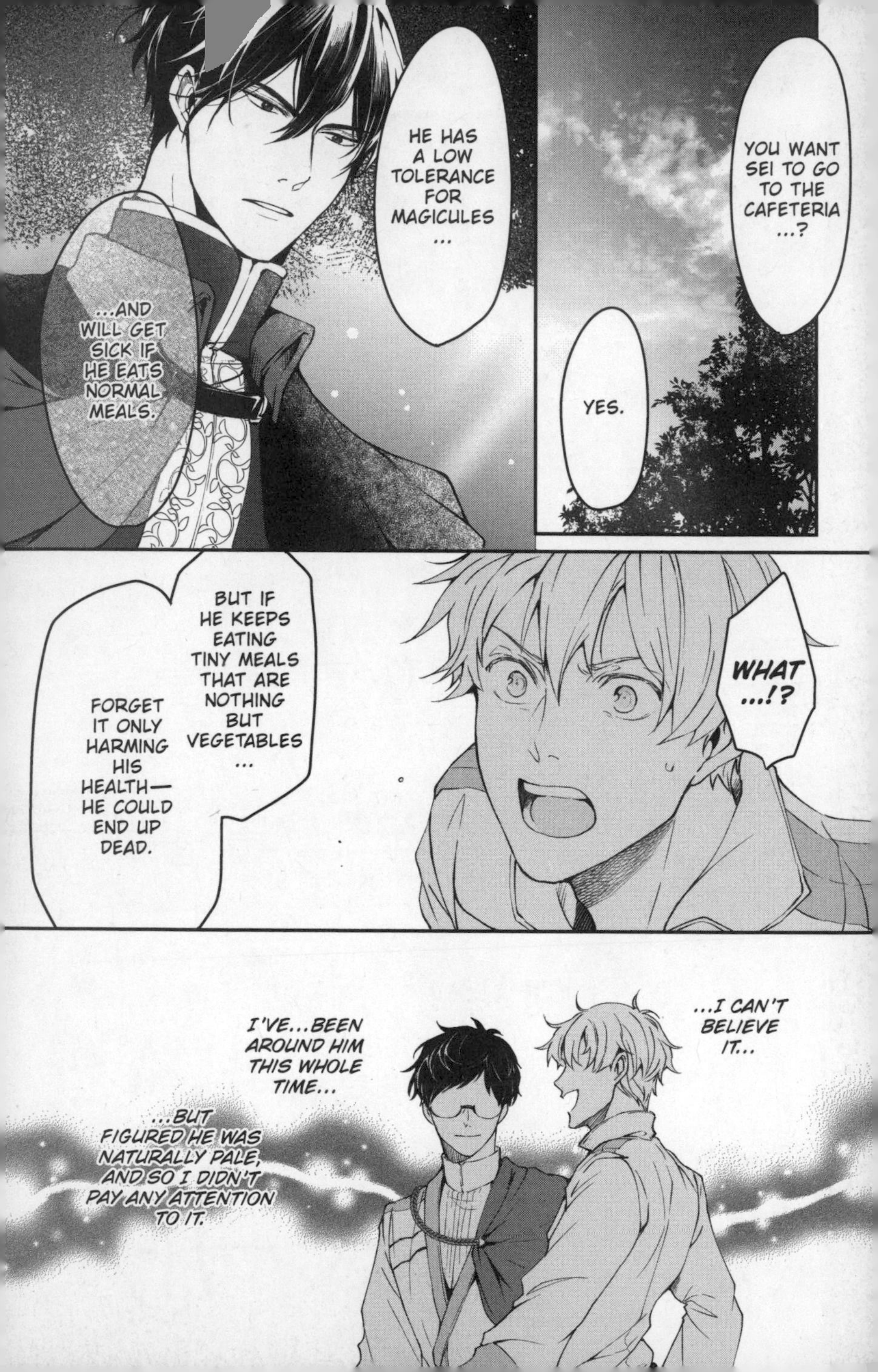
YOU WANT SEI TO GO TO THE CAFETERIA ...?
YES.
HE HAS A LOW TOLERANCE FOR MAGICULES ...
...AND WILL GET SICK IF HE EATS NORMAL MEALS.
WHAT ...!?
BUT IF HE KEEPS EATING TINY MEALS THAT ARE NOTHING BUT VEGETABLES ...
FORGET IT ONLY HARMING HIS HEALTH— HE COULD END UP DEAD.
...I CAN'T BELIEVE IT...
I'VE...BEEN AROUND HIM THIS WHOLE TIME...
...BUT FIGURED HE WAS NATURALLY PALE, AND SO I DIDN'T PAY ANY ATTENTION TO IT.

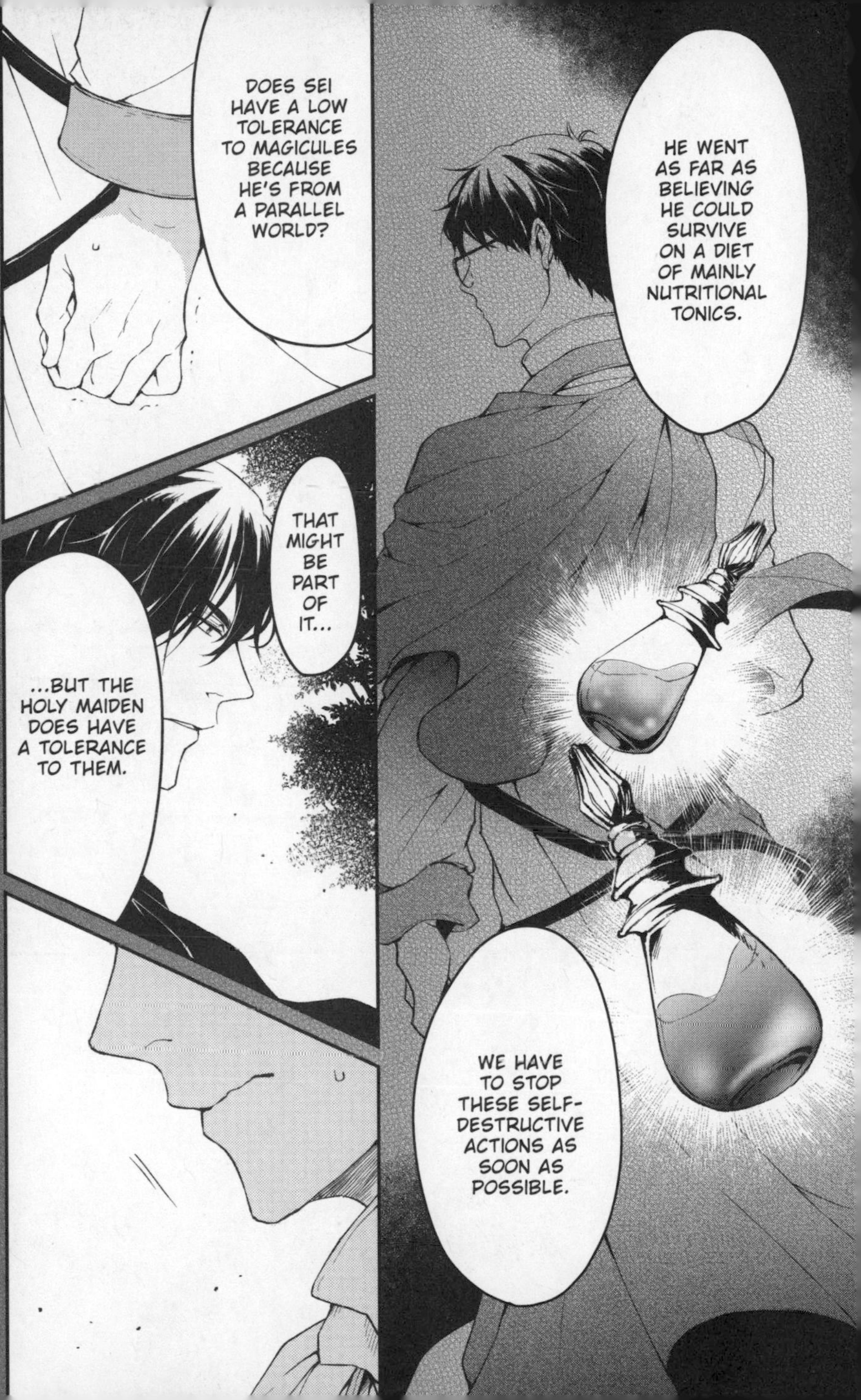
HE WENT AS FAR AS BELIEVING HE COULD SURVIVE ON A DIET OF MAINLY NUTRITIONAL TONICS.
WE HAVE TO STOP THESE SELF-DESTRUCTIVE ACTIONS AS SOON AS POSSIBLE.
DOES SEI HAVE A LOW TOLERANCE TO MAGICULES BECAUSE HE'S FROM A PARALLEL WORLD?
THAT MIGHT BE PART OF IT...
...BUT THE HOLY MAIDEN DOES HAVE A TOLERANCE TO THEM.

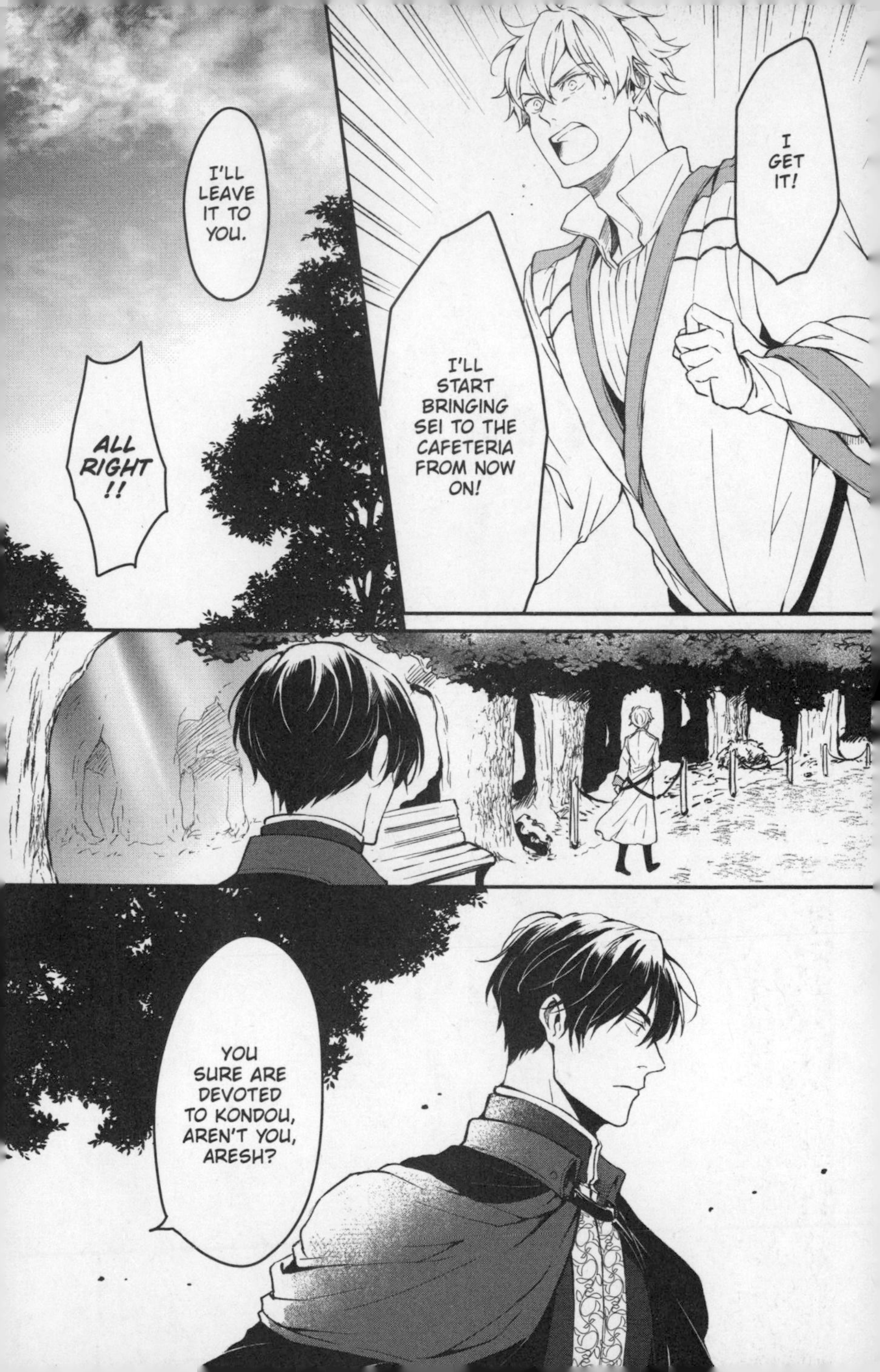
I GET IT!
I'LL START BRINGING SEI TO THE CAFETERIA FROM NOW ON!
I'LL LEAVE IT TO YOU.
ALL RIGHT!!
YOU SURE ARE DEVOTED TO KONDOU, AREN'T YOU, ARESH?

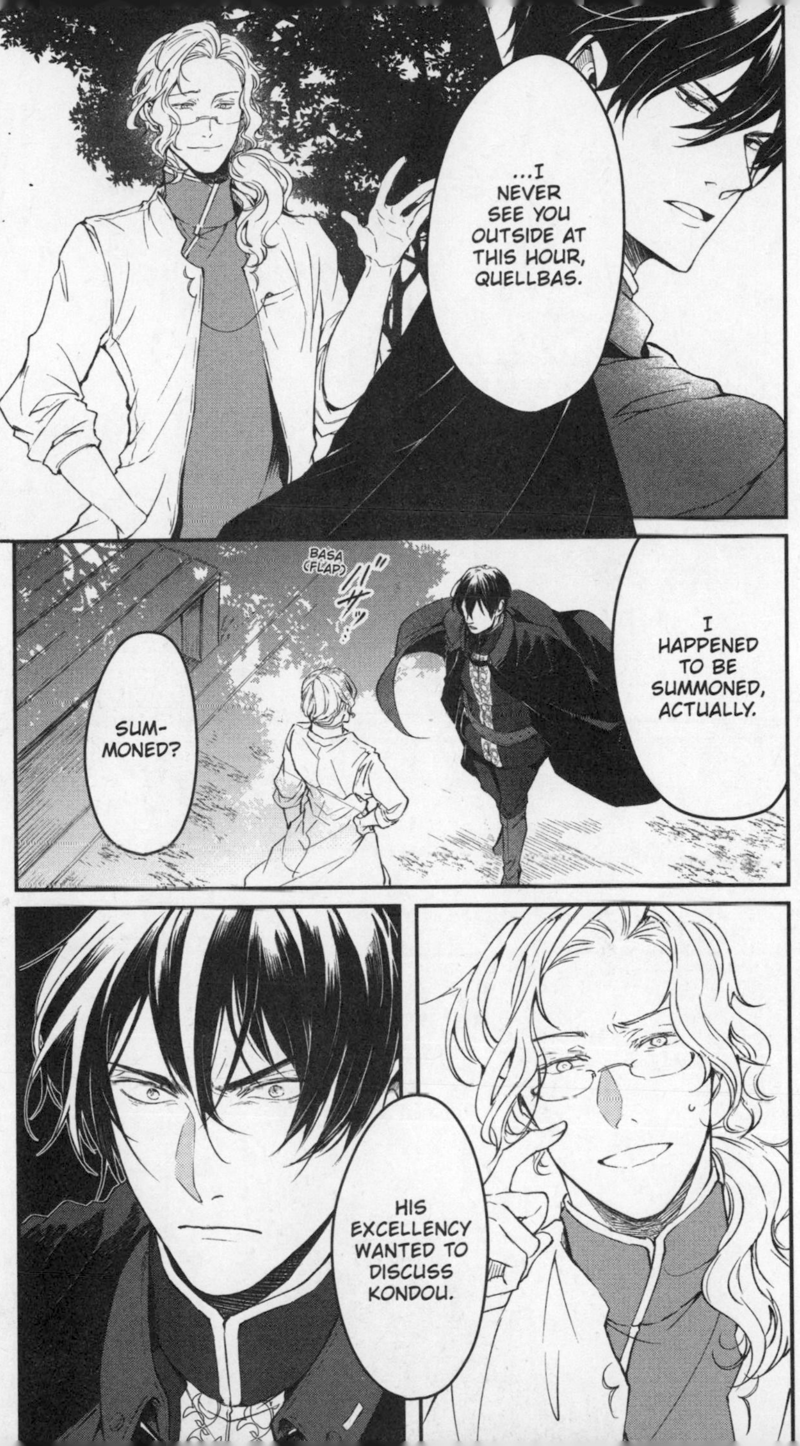
...I NEVER SEE YOU OUTSIDE AT THIS HOUR, QUELLBAS.
I HAPPENED TO BE SUMMONED, ACTUALLY.
BASA (FLAP)
SUM-MONED?
HIS EXCELLENCY WANTED TO DISCUSS KONDOU.

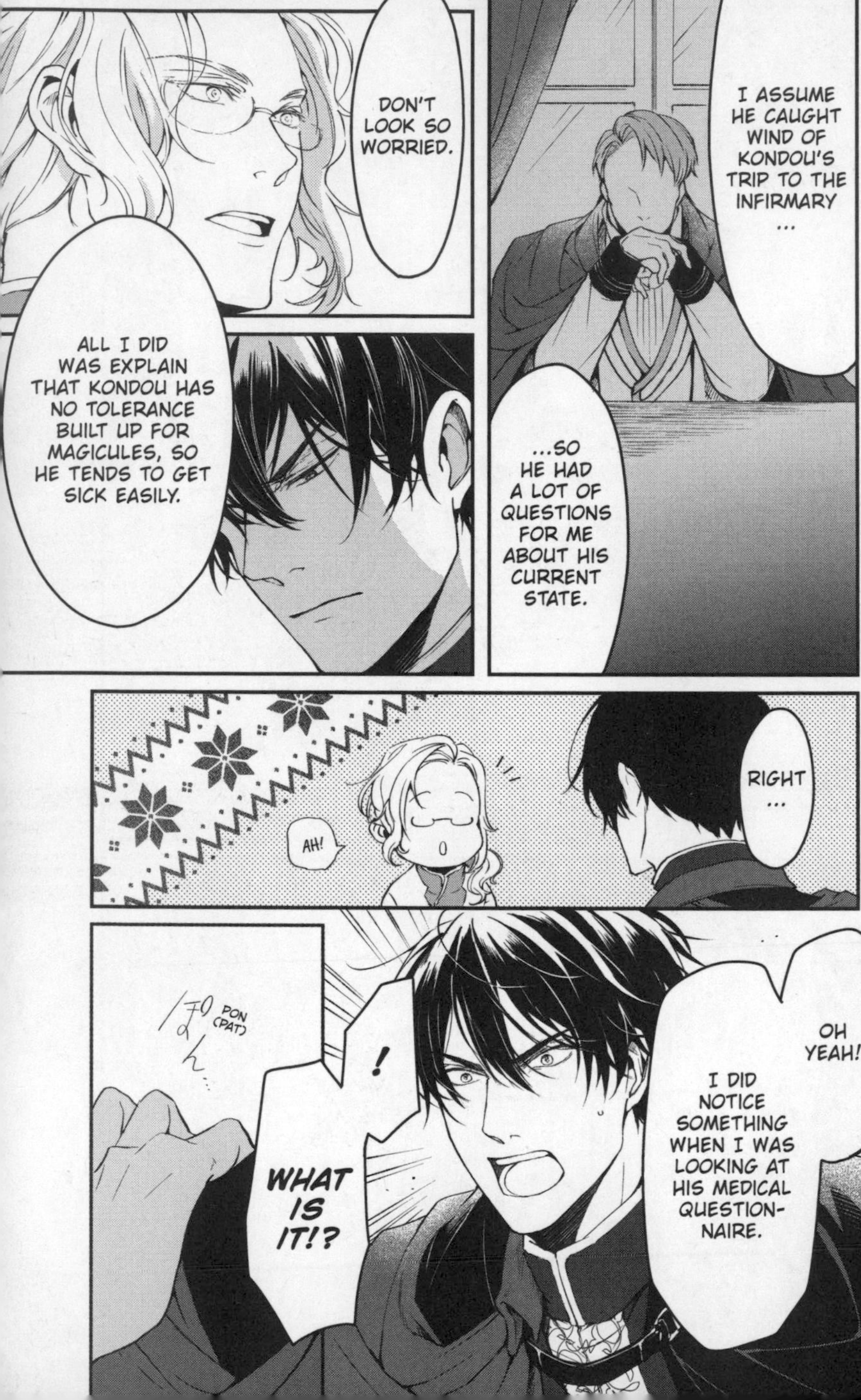
I ASSUME HE CAUGHT WIND OF KONDOU'S TRIP TO THE INFIRMARY ...
...SO HE HAD A LOT OF QUESTIONS FOR ME ABOUT HIS CURRENT STATE.
DON'T LOOK SO WORRIED.
ALL I DID WAS EXPLAIN THAT KONDOU HAS NO TOLERANCE BUILT UP FOR MAGICULES, SO HE TENDS TO GET SICK EASILY.
RIGHT ...
AH!
OH YEAH!
I DID NOTICE SOMETHING WHEN I WAS LOOKING AT HIS MEDICAL QUESTION-NAIRE.
!
WHAT IS IT!?
ぽん
PON (PAT)

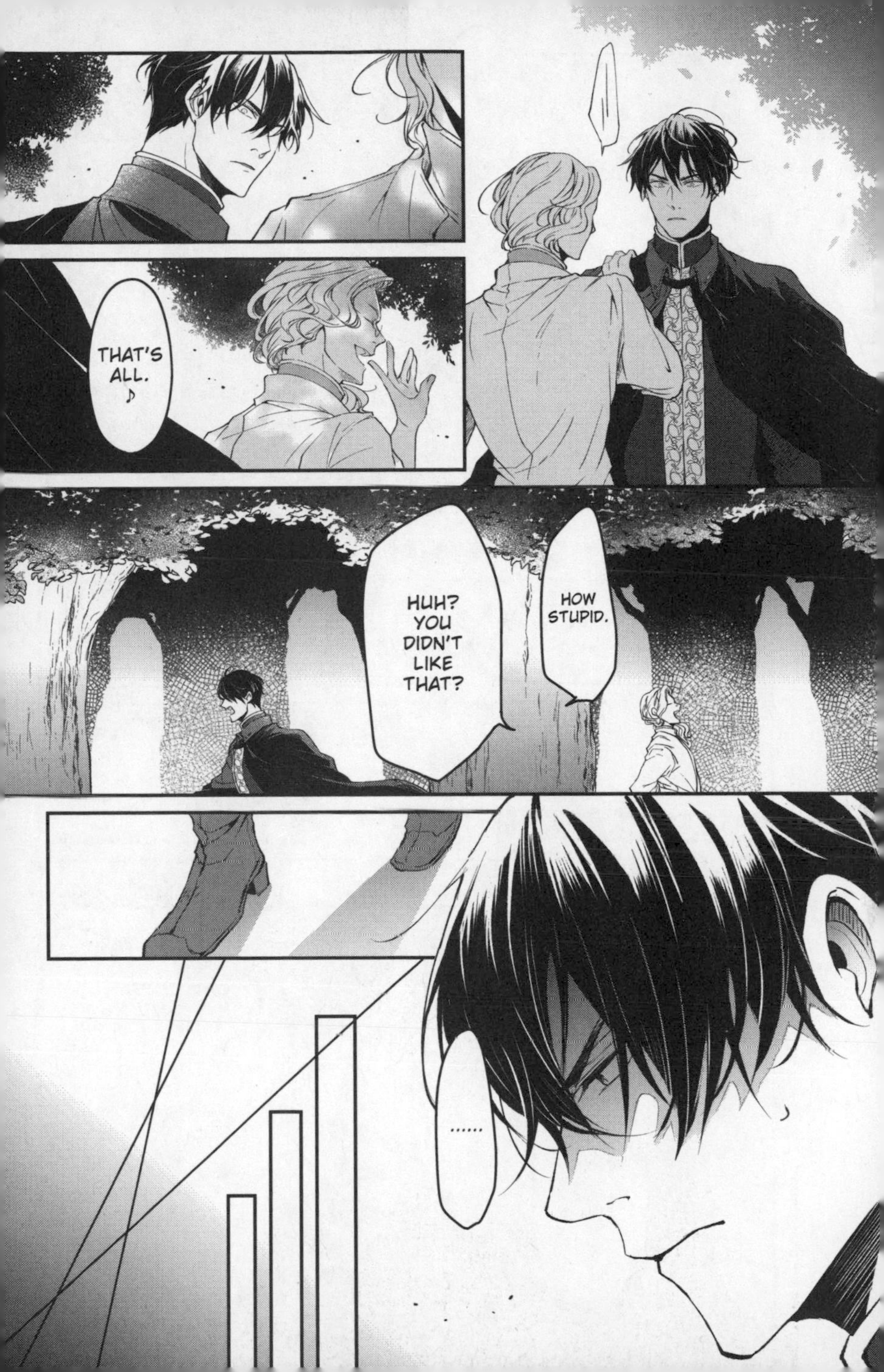
THAT'S ALL. ♪
HOW STUPID.
HUH? YOU DIDN'T LIKE THAT?
......

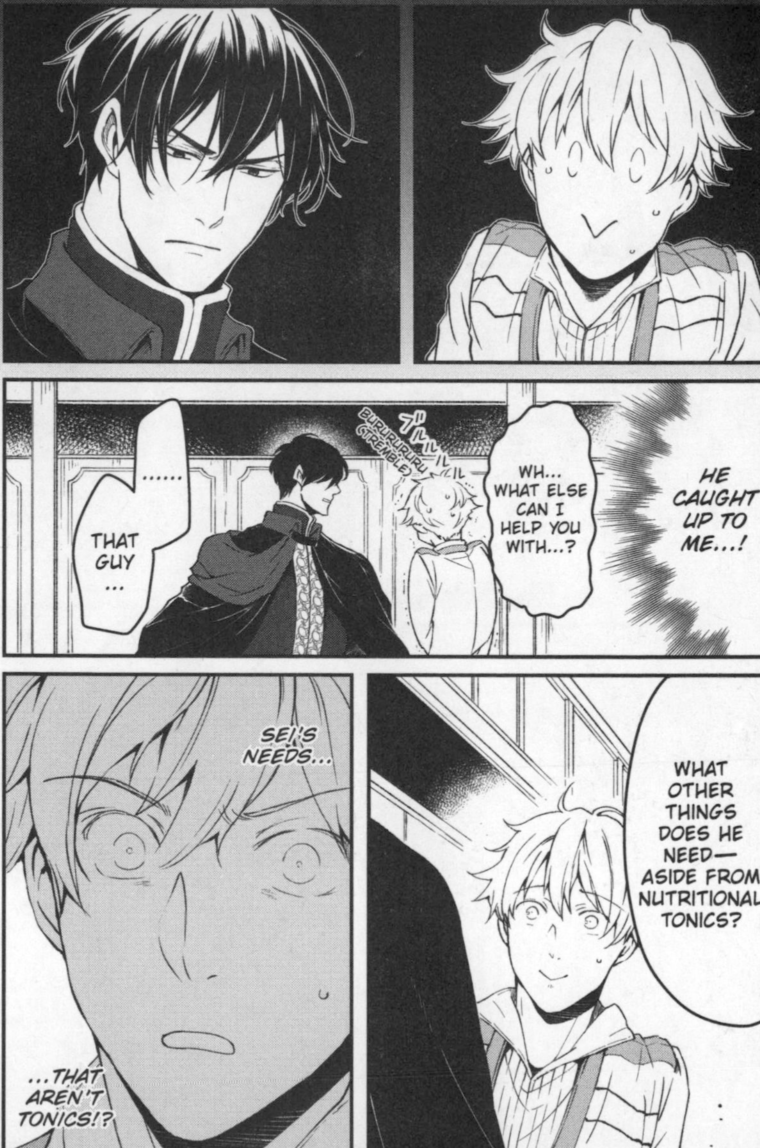
HE CAUGHT UP TO ME...!
WH... WHAT ELSE CAN I HELP YOU WITH...?
BURURURURU (TREMBLE)
......
THAT GUY ...
WHAT OTHER THINGS DOES HE NEED— ASIDE FROM NUTRITIONAL TONICS?
SEI'S NEEDS...
...THAT AREN'T TONICS!?

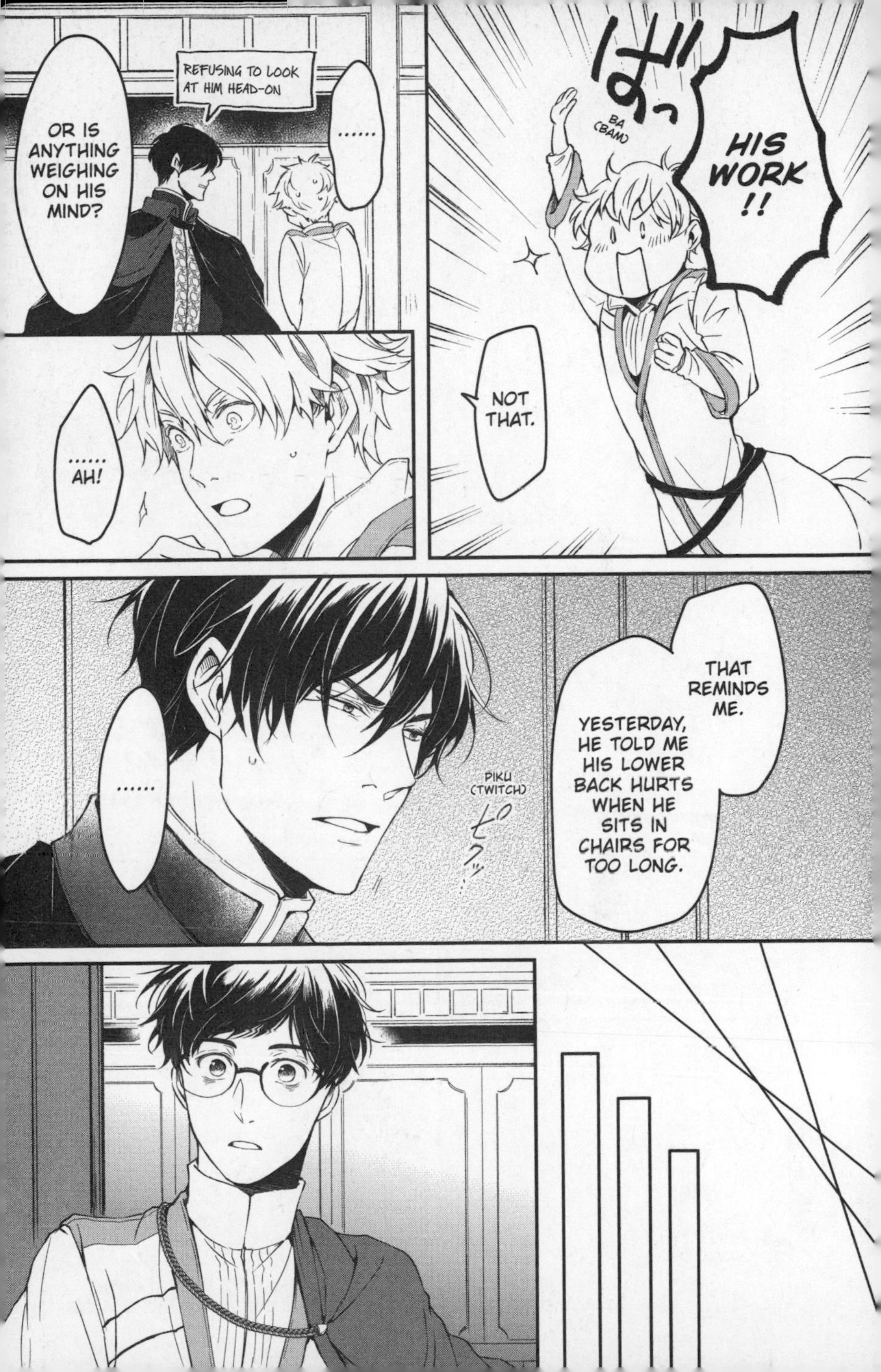
HIS WORK!!
ばっ
BA (BAM)
NOT THAT.
......
REFUSING TO LOOK AT HIM HEAD-ON
OR IS ANYTHING WEIGHING ON HIS MIND?
......AH!
THAT REMINDS ME.
YESTERDAY, HE TOLD ME HIS LOWER BACK HURTS WHEN HE SITS IN CHAIRS FOR TOO LONG.
PIKU (TWITCH)
ピクッ
......

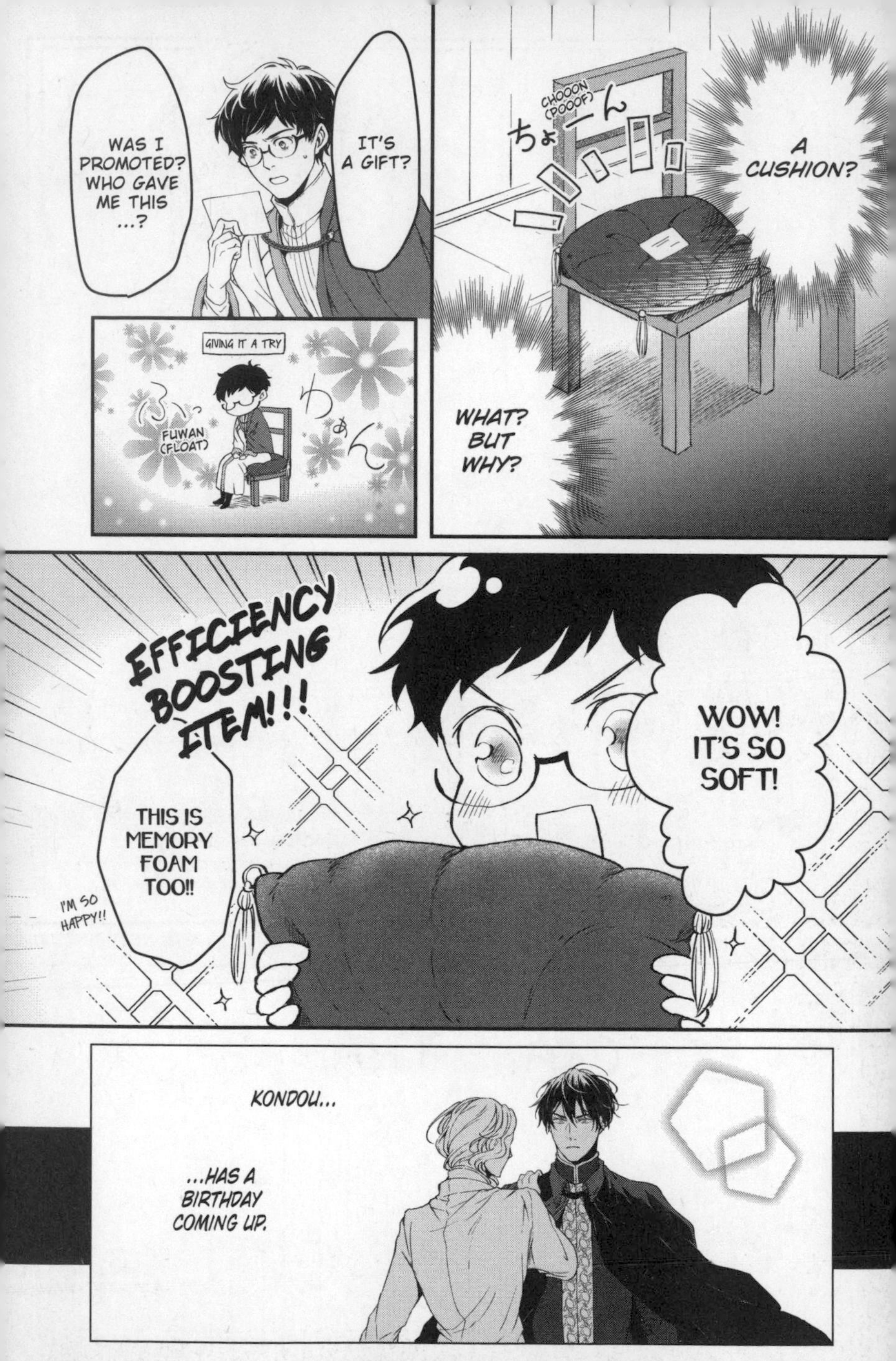
A CUSHION?
CHOOON (POOOF)
ちょーん
WHAT? BUT WHY?
IT'S A GIFT?
WAS I PROMOTED? WHO GAVE ME THIS ...?
GIVING IT A TRY
ふわん
FUWAN (FLOAT)
WOW! IT'S SO SOFT!
EFFICIENCY BOOSTING ITEM!!!
THIS IS MEMORY FOAM TOO!!
I'M SO HAPPY!!
KONDOU...
...HAS A BIRTHDAY COMING UP.

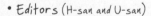

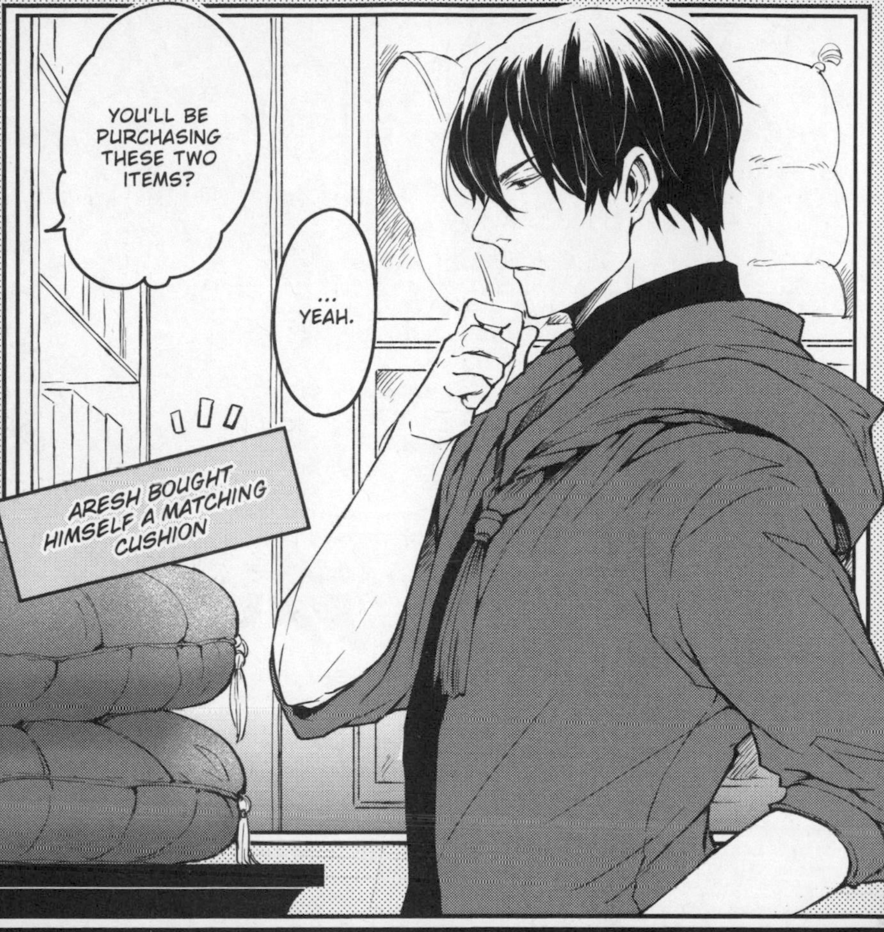
YOU'LL BE PURCHASING THESE TWO ITEMS?
...YEAH.
ARESH BOUGHT HIMSELF A MATCHING CUSHION

SPECIAL THANKS!!

- Editors (H-san and U-san)
- Cover designer (Sava Design-san)
- All my readers

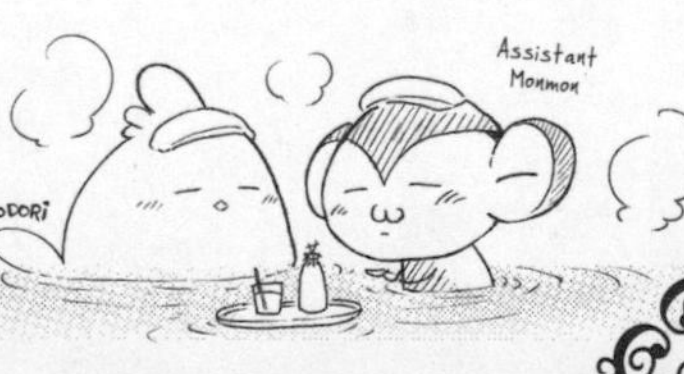
Assistant Monmon
IRODORI

2

Kazuki Irodori

ORIGINAL STORY
Yatsuki Wakatsu

CHARACTER DESIGN
Kikka Ohashi

TRANSLATION
Emma Schumacker

LETTERING
DK

ISEKAI NO SATA WA SHACHIKU SHIDAI Vol. 2
©Kazuki Irodori 2021
©Yatsuki Wakatsu 2021
©Kikka Ohashi 2021
First published in Japan in 2021 by KADOKAWA CORPORATION, Tokyo.
English translation rights arranged with KADOKAWA CORPORATION, Tokyo, through Tuttle-Mori Agency, Inc., Tokyo.

English translation © 2022 by Yen Press, LLC

Yen Press
150 West 30th Street, 19th Floor
New York, NY 10001

Visit us at yenpress.com
facebook.com/yenpress twitter.com/yenpress
yenpress.tumblr.com instagram.com/yenpress

First Yen Press Edition: August 2022
Edited by Yen Press Editorial: Danielle Niederkorn, JuYoun Lee
Designed by Yen Press Design: Liz Parlett

Yen Press is an imprint of Yen Press, LLC.
The Yen Press name and logo are trademarks of Yen Press, LLC.

Library of Congress Control Number: 2022935364

ISBNs: 978-1-9753-4514-3 (paperback)
        978-1-9753-4515-0 (ebook)

10 9 8 7 6 5 4 3 2 1

WOR

Printed in the United States of America